THE RISING SIGN

THE RISING SIGN

Your Astrological Mask

JEANNE AVERY

MAIN STREET BOOKS

DOUBLEDAY
NEW YORK LONDON TORONTO SYDNEY AUCKLAND

A MAIN STREET BOOK
PUBLISHED BY DOUBLEDAY
a division of Bantam Doubleday Dell Publishing Group, Inc.
1540 Broadway, New York, New York 10036

MAIN STREET BOOKS, DOUBLEDAY, and the portrayal of a
building with a tree are trademarks of Doubleday, a
division of Bantam Doubleday Dell Publishing Group, Inc.

Library of Congress Cataloging in Publication Data
Avery, Jeanne.
  The rising sign.
  "A Doubleday/Dolphin book."
  1. Astrology. 2. Zodiac. I. Title.
BF1708.1.A92   133.5'2   77-16894
AACR2
ISBN 0-385-13278-6

20   19   18   17   16

In loving memory
Claude Philippe
Elizabeth Hughes Gossett
Granny, Papa, and Sada, my Mother and Father

and for Sharon, Diane and David,
Berith, Lee, Tony, and Francesca,
and the newest light of my life, Charles

Without the help of my friends, I would not have been able to complete this book, let alone get through most of my life. I am also extremely grateful to any of my clients who waited so patiently for their charts at deadline times, but there are certain people I want to thank, who went above and beyond the call of duty in patience, loyalty, and support for my project.

It was due to Jess Stearn that I found Doubleday, but to the magic of the universe and one chance phone call that I found Jean Bennett Cumming, my first editor friend. With expert use of her Aries energy, she quietly and consistently continued to promote my book until we obtained a contract. Jean then left Doubleday to have an adorable daughter, and I was awarded a prize in Nan Grubbs, a wonderful friend and editor. Nan, a Gemini with Virgo rising, never criticized, diplomatically set me straight, got tough when necessary, and gave me her special brand of enthusiasm when she liked something. She never stepped on my sensitive Scorpio with Cancer rising toes. But it was Ferris Mack, my special astrological angel who, in spite of unmerciful teasing, introduced me to Field's Syndication, who publish my daily and weekly newspaper column. If not for Ferris, and many lunches, I would not have a chance to write about my favorite subject.

My research dates back to the five wonderful years of week-ends spent on "the farm" with Claude and Helga Philippe, my first surrogate family, and their fascinating guests. It was there that I met Elizabeth Karaman, who insisted that I turn professional and who became my first "real" client. Patty McLain predicted that I would give up acting for a life of astrology and a *lot* of travel. Patty McLeod, Jess Stearn, Nancy and Michele Hively, Lynne Forbes, Jack and Sally Nevius, and Aude Howard housed me, or my furniture, between my moves from East to West Coast and back again. Lynne Palmer, an excellent teacher, persisted and taught me astrological math. Nancy Hughes, my childhood friend, Fran Hartman, Patty McLain, Carl Sadler, and Greg Sierra aided me in my early days as an astrologer, as did Harvey Rosenberg, Gayle Gleckler, Marion Weisberg, Johannes Michael, Angela DiPene, Larry Keith, Luther Henderson, and Olga Stevens later on.

But without David Cogan, my business manager, Susan Horton, and Adrienne Landau, the actual writing process would have been impossible. My darling Dorothy, with her constant loving energy, healed me long distance, and it is finally, with deep love for Susan and Jennifer Strasberg, who shared their home with me and are indeed family, that I complete the dedication of this book.

CONTENTS

THE RISING SIGN

Having your astrological chart read is like getting an I.D. card from the Universe.

—TRISSIE CALLAN

INTRODUCTION

When I first began to study astrology, I had no idea that I would someday become a professional astrologer. The theater and music have always been my first loves. (My singing and acting debut came at the age of four when I played the lead role in a kindergarten production. It seemed perfectly natural to be on stage, front and center.) If I had known anything about astrology then, I might have saved myself a lot of time by looking at my own chart and realizing that I was destined to find my way to this precise moment in time, writing, lecturing, and practicing astrology practically around the clock. But self-discovery can take a good many years, and life has a way of presenting opportunity in its own good, sweet time. All of the impatience of youth would not bring things around any faster.

It was precisely the frustration—and the thrill—of not knowing just when I'd work again as an actress (a common syndrome among those in the profession) that led me to study astrology, in an attempt to decipher the rhythm of work and life in the theater. I had the additional excitement of living life as a single parent, long before it was fashionable, with three wonderful and uniquely talented children. Each child, in his and her own special way, responded to the circumstances of our life together in quite a different manner. It was like having three "only" children. The stimulation and companionship they provided made life especially exciting and challenging for me, and the fact that we were all involved in the theater kept things moving at a very fast pace. What started as a sharing of my life and interests, like Topsy, just kept growing. The juggling of schedules and experiences kept things from ever being boring or static, but sometimes presented me with challenges that were quite hair-raising. I was finally forced to take a look at the perils-of-Pauline type of life I was living, in New York City instead of some greener jungle, so that I might try to give up some of my "cheap thrills" for more productive kinds of excitement. Since I have a deadly fear of living an "ordinary" or boring existence, it finally dawned on me that I might be creating the circumstances of my life in order to avoid that possibility.

I began to experiment by deliberately, consciously manifesting different outer circumstances, such as more interesting roles, better salary and lifestyle. Sometimes I was quite good at it, but other times outer events took longer to become reality than I would have liked. Carl Jung said that if you are not aware of an energy on a conscious level, it manifests on the exterior as fate. Fate, in the guise of some very heavy externals, forced me to take a more serious look at the astrological research I had been conducting while sitting around on sets, waiting for lights to be adjusted and cameras to roll. (My curiosity about what makes people tick could be satisfied through astrology, whereas direct questions would have been considered quite rude.) My rebellious nature began to emerge fully, to be transformed into an activity ruled by that rebellious, or unusual, planet Uranus. But it was only after a few years of practicing astrology that my second love finally came into view.

I was always intrigued by underlying motivations, environmental conditioning, and manifest behavior characteristics. In the process of developing and learning acting technique, one learns how to diagram structures of plays, scenes, and characters. In order to portray a role successfully, with depth, one must delve into the innermost core of the character to understand his or her emotional response, why it is activated, and what led to that particular manner of reaction. One must also be able to get to the same emotional response in oneself, to know how it is triggered, and to be able to re-create that "sense memory" on cue. My own chart indicated which emotional responses were easy and natural for me, and also described the ones that were not, and why. The astrological chart became my therapist.

It was when I was reading a chart for someone else, however, that I made the most important breakthrough, psychologically, for both the other person and myself. Harvey Rosenberg, an extremely talented man, denied the existence of yet another talent that I described in the reading of his chart. Yet, scarcely one month later, in a therapy session, Harvey regressed to a childhood experience at a very young age when that talent was clearly marked. It was a trauma that made him repress a strong musical talent and send it underground. Less than two months after the reading of his chart, Harvey had his first job as an audio consultant for an advertising agency and began recommending a chart reading to the therapists he knew. It became truly apparent to me then that the astrological chart could act as a healing agent, pointing the way to the core of blocked energy, talent, and expression. The awareness of that potential seemed to enable the person to begin a process of making healthier decisions, which in turn could lead to a fuller, more productive life. The chart seemed to give permission to explore new possibilities.

It is due to the pioneering spirit of Marion Weisberg, a practicing therapist, that I had an opportunity to research the marriage of astrology and psychotherapy on a deeper level. We began conducting group workshops in which an astrological chart was set up for each participant in the group. Among other things, using the chart as a therapeutic tool enabled us to accomplish twice as much work in the same amount of time. Marion, well trained in many therapeutic disciplines, encouraged me, introduced me to other therapists who formed a wonderful support system, and enabled me to develop new meanings, in therapeutic language, for planets and houses. Our workshops provided a proving ground for the effectiveness of astrology in conjunction with modern therapy practices.

In this book, I have described many of the theories I have developed in conjunction with the study of Transactional Analysis, yet because of the nature of the rising sign, I have only been able to scratch the surface of the information revealed through our workshops. A great deal of information must necessarily await another book. Astrology, for instance, can point the way and describe particular life crises and situations that will enable an individual to grow, or decide to remain static. It can describe, in particular, the choices we may have to make at any given time. It describes outer conditions that we unconsciously set up in order to be forced to grow and learn and become more aware. For, indeed, life is a series of choices made on a yearly, daily, and hourly basis. The chart will only describe the *probability* of the choices we make. The final decisions naturally rest with the individual. The astrological chart can indicate, through the natural progression of the planets, the change of consciousness that comes at a particular time and which naturally, then, changes the world around us. Astrology only points the way, but any extra knowledge or tool for awakening or awareness can enable us to make healthier choices. Astrology describes human nature, the things we all share in common, and the ways in which we are uniquely different. It can describe the ultimate transmutation in life which sets our feet firmly on the path toward a goal or service or fulfillment that is uniquely our own. It can act as the "umbrella" through which we can achieve a healing on all levels, body, mind, and soul.

I chose to write about the ascendant because it is the starting point in life. The word "horoscope" literally means "search for the hour." It is the hour of birth that pinpoints the rising sign or ascendant. It describes the very beginning or initiation into the earth plane. Astrology and therapy ask the question "Who am I?" If through the understanding of your individual rising sign, you gain one tiny glimmer into the answer, and thought is stimulated, I've accomplished what I set out to do. The possibility of each person raising his or her consciousness one tiny bit gives hope to the possibility of raised consciousness on a broader level. It is there, to that end, that the Aquarian age is leading us. Here's to greater understanding of each other, greater love for humanity, and a better world as a result.

WHAT IS
THE RISING SIGN?

ASTROLOGY HAS BECOME SUCH A popular subject in the last few years that almost everyone knows his or her "sign." Not everyone knows that the astrological sign is in reality the zodiac sign in which the sun resides at the time of birth. In other words, the zodiac sign is the same as the "Sun" sign Aries, Taurus, Gemini, etc. Individuals may also have some knowledge of the characteristics attributed to each zodiac sign, but beyond that, unless a person has taken time to study the subject more thoroughly, very little is commonly known. Although in this book I plan to confine my attention to the study of the rising sign, it seems important to explain certain basic principles. The study of astrology can become extremely complex, with myriad possibilities for application of the knowledge gained. I will not attempt to defend or teach astrology, but merely present some ideas for consideration.

Throughout the ages, astrology has been misunderstood, associated with superstition, star worship, and fortune-telling. Yet the list of highly intelligent, rational people who have been interested in the subject is staggering. Among those who have considered the subject worthy of their attention are Sir Francis Bacon, the Reverend John Butler, rector of Litchborough (who began to read up on the subject in order to exterminate astrology in England. Instead, he concluded, "I find that next to Theology, nothing leads me more near unto the sight of God than this sacred astrological study of the great works of Nature,") Dante, Ralph Waldo Emerson, Tycho Brahe, Johannes Kepler, Sir Isaac Newton, Goethe, Dryden, Scott, St. Thomas Aquinas, John Milton, Hippocrates, Benjamin Franklin, Sir Philip Sidney, Shakespeare, Theodore Roosevelt, Mark Twain, and John Napier, who invented logarithms while seeking new methods of astrological research.

Astrology is truly an international language, but as with everything else, it can be badly misused. In 1939, during World War II, Hitler began to use astrologers. The SS captured astrologer

Wilhelm Wulff and coerced him into working for the Third Reich, casting horoscopes for individuals, nations, groups, and movements. Yet Hitler *publicly* decreed that the practice of astrology be banned in Germany. Wulff, in his book *Zodiac and the Swastika,* quotes Heinrich Himmler as saying, "In the Third Reich we have forbid astrology. We cannot permit any astrologer to follow their calling except those who are working for us. In the National Socialist state, astrology must remain a *privilegium singulorum.* It is not for the broad masses."

An astrologer tempted fate if he dared cast Hitler's horoscope without official approval. However, a Swiss astrologer, Karl Ernst Krafft, having used his knowledge to predict trends in the commodities market, said that Hitler's life would hang in the balance between November 7 and 10, 1939. When a bomb went off on November 7 just a few moments after Hitler had left an anniversary celebration, Krafft wired Herman Hess of the SS to warn him that Hitler would still not be safe for a few more days. He was promptly arrested. Later, however, he was released to work for the German cause.

Information came to the British about Krafft's astrological service to Hitler, and the British decided to hire the best astrologer they could find to second-guess Krafft. In this way, the British might not only know what Hitler was thinking, but might also slip pro-Allies propaganda, through forecasts similar to Krafft's, into Hitler's hands. Churchill said, "After all, why should Hitler have a monopoly on astrologers?" and he promptly hired Louis de Wohl. (De Wohl had accurately predicted the breakout of the war and the invasion of Poland in 1931 at a dinner party attended by Lord Halifax. De Wohl knew all five astrologers presumed to be working for Hitler, and had worked at some point with Krafft and was familiar with his methods.) In his first memo to the British War Office in 1940, he advised that the Germans would not invade England because he was sure Hitler's astrologers would counsel Hitler against it.

After the war, Ellic Howe, a friend of Wilhelm Wulff's working in the British Secret Service, discovered a great deal of information in Gestapo files about the Third Reich's use of astrology. Based on this information, he wrote a book entitled *As-*

trology: A Recent History, Including the Untold Story of Its Role in World War II.

Evangeline Adams won a giant step forward in the field when she presented evidence for astrology by reading a test chart in court for an individual she did not know. In 1914, an anonymous client brought suit against her. New York State had an archaic law against "fortune-tellers," and Evangeline was determined to legalize astrology by insisting on a public trial. She offered, as a test case, to read the chart of a person entirely unknown to her, with only the information of the date, place, and time of birth. Unbeknownst to her, the test case was the chart of the judge's own son. The judge admitted that her analysis gave him new insight into his son's character. The favorable decision elevated astrology out of the ranks of mere fortune-telling. The judge said, "The defendant raises astrology to the dignity of an exact science. She violated no law." One of Miss Adams' clients was J. P. Morgan, who consulted her regularly concerning his investments. Morgan said, "Astrology is for billionaires, not millionaires."

The person who influenced me a great deal in the development of my own theories was Carl Jung, who not only did research into the field of astrology but consulted the *I Ching*, read tarot cards, and conducted ESP experiments as well. Jung coined the term "synchronicity," which can describe the coincidence between the movement of the planets in the heavens and patterns in an individual's life. Jung said, "We are in a somewhat more favorable situation when we turn to the astrological method, as it presupposes a meaningful coincidence of planetary aspects and positions with the character or the existing psychic state of the questioner. Although the psychological interpretation of horoscopes is still a very uncertain matter . . . astrology is in the process of becoming a science. But as there are still large areas of uncertainty, I decided some time ago to make a test and find out how far an accepted astrological tradition would stand up to statistical investigation."

After the examination of 483 marriage charts—that is, 966 individual horoscopes—he concluded, "That the classical moon conjunctions (interpreted by astrologers as the ideal marriage relationship) should occur at all, however, can only be explained as the result of an intentional or unintentional fraud, or else as precisely such a meaningful coincidence, that is, synchronicity." The success of his experiment led him to say, "Although I was obliged to express doubt earlier about the mantic character of astrology, I am now forced, as a result of my astrological experiment, to recognize it again. The chance arrangement of the marriage horoscopes, which were simply piled on top of one another as they came in from diverse sources, suited the sanguine expectations of the research workers and produced an overall picture which could hardly have been improved upon from the standpoint of astrological hypothesis." (*The Portable Jung*, edited by Joseph Campbell.)

Michel Gauquelin continued the kind of astrological research that interested Jung. Gauquelin, whose work at the Sorbonne was in psychology and statistics, has written a book entitled, *Cosmic Influences on Human Behavior* in order to present some of the results of the statistical correlations he has discovered in thousands of case histories using the astrological chart. The book is a condensation of the actual research contained in thirteen volumes. He devoted more than twenty years' research to the subject of astrology. His book is an attempt to prove the validity of astrology from a strictly scientific point of view.

At the moment, there are fascinating new research projects being undertaken all over the world, yet astrologers have not convinced most scientists, stockbrokers, or personnel heads of major corporations of the value of using this study in practical ways. Untold amounts of time and money could be saved by using astrology to cut down the margin of error in hiring people for the right jobs, starting projects and companies at the right time, interpreting the trends of specific stocks. However, as time goes on and more is understood about the subject, the "mystery" will be eliminated.

Jung was concerned with symbology, and astrology is *primarily* a study of symbols. Astrologers may never be able to prove to the satisfaction of all scientists that planets have an effect on the activities of an individual. We are aware of the effect of the Moon on the tides. One could stretch the theory to suggest that the Moon could affect the water element in a human body. We can certainly observe the effect on our emotions at the time of the full moon. In hospitals for the mentally disturbed, it is not necessary to look at the Moon to know when it is full. Patients there behave in a very different manner at that time of the month. Someday, perhaps, research will be able to give scientific reasons and explanations for that phenomenon.

In the meantime, I prefer to go along with Jung's theory of synchronicity and ignore, for the moment, the notion that there may be rays emanating from planets that influence man. *It is man's free will that determines his destiny.* What is astounding about an astrological chart is that it can *indicate* how a man is liable to think and react to a particular set of circumstances. If an individual can understand his natural reactions, he is better able to make healthy decisions about his life. If astrology can help a person understand those underlying patterns and help him to make decisions, that is reason enough for its study. That is why astrology is a natural partner to psychology. Many astrologers are now practicing the humanistic approach to the subject. Many psychologists and psychiatrists are using an astrological chart as a guideline to help focus on specific problems of an individual.

Since an astrological chart can only pinpoint patterns, it can be likened to a road map. A road map cannot drive a car, it can only indicate the road conditions. After studying that road map, an individual may decide to take a shortcut, the scenic route, or the superhighway. When a person consults an astrological chart, he may become aware of his natural trends, natural energy cycles, and natural reactions. It is up to him to make choices, find mental antidotes, and learn to work with his natural timing and energy. Man's thoughts and desires lead to the manifestation of events in his life, but a chart can give him permission to follow his inclinations and natural impulses. It can stimulate thought and help him uncover his perhaps unrealized potential. It can pinpoint in a most profound manner the reasons for the blocking of energy and abilities—the fears and insecurities that prevent him from taking the chances necessary for his success. It can clearly show whether he reacts energetically to life's challenges or needs peace and harmony, whether he is agreeable or rebellious, static or dynamic. It indicates how he has photographed the circumstances of his environment and his life.

A professional astrologer is able to set up a chart by using an ephemeris, a table giving the precise placement of the stars in the heavens for each day of the year. With the date of birth, the time and place, a wheel is erected showing where the planets fall according to the precise moment of one's first breath. A complicated mathematical procedure is used to erect the chart, with calculations to determine the degree of those planets, and the Sun and Moon at the moment of birth. It is the *date* of birth that shows where the Sun, Moon, and planets are located on that wheel, but it is the *time* of birth that indicates the position of that wheel. The sign of the zodiac that appears on the eastern horizon the moment an individual is born is called the ascendant or rising sign. It is a person's own particular "horizon" or point of view. It is indicative of the personality of the individual.

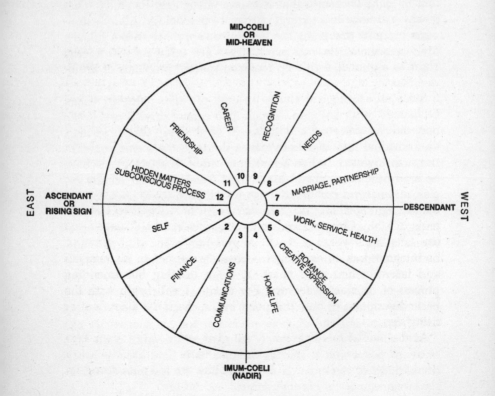

A chart looks like the wheel of a wagon laid flat on its side. The chart is divided into twelve sections, or "houses." If an astrologer used an equal-house system, those sections would be equally divided. More complex methods of interpreting a chart require using a more complex division, so with other mathematical systems, there may be intercepted signs, or two signs ruling one house. When I read a chart for a client, I prefer using the Placidus house system, a more complex method, for it has proven most accurate. For the sake of simplicity and clarity, however, for this book I will use the equal-house system and will discuss what it means to have each sign on the ascendant, following in natural progression all the signs around the wheel. In learning astrology, it seems necessary to first simplify everything, and then begin to integrate the information at hand, taking all factors into consideration. It is a process of learning general rules that may have to be modified later on.

Early in the study of the subject, we learn the meanings of individual planets, then the meanings of the houses. After a time, we take into consideration the characteristics of a planet found in a specific sign and house, and begin to gradually integrate all the simplified rules in order to see the whole instead of the parts. After those original steps, a student learns the meanings of "aspects," or the relationship of one planet to another. He can then see how planets "dialogue" with each other in the horoscope, indicating the harmonious or conflicting energy systems an individual has within himself. Finally, the mathematical process can be assimilated so that one learns how to erect an individual astrological chart, and can truly begin to understand the patterns described by an individual astrological chart. This process can take many years of study. More complicated processes can be integrated as an astrologer becomes proficient in his analysis and interpretation of a chart. It is an exciting but unending process of constant discovery. For clarity, I will begin with the basic description of only one point in the chart, the ascendant or rising sign.

At the end of this chapter, I will give some rules for arriving at the ascendant for a specific time of birth. The place of birth need not be considered in this book, since we are not setting up a chart for a specific degree of the zodiac found to be rising. Generally speaking, the Sun rises at approximately 6 a.m. (Some adjustment will have to be considered for certain latitudes, naturally.) The ascendant is the relationship of the Sun to the horizon. If a person is born at noontime, the Sun will be directly overhead in the chart as well. (The point at the top of the chart is another significant area in interpretation. It is called the mid-heaven or MC, standing for mid-coeli. Since the ascendant and the mid-coeli are not planets or stars, Jung's theory of synchronicity assumes even more importance. There cannot be rays emanating from a nebulous point in the sky. This zenith of a chart is related to the career and public life. It is indicative of how one reacts to public life and the kind of career one is attracted to or is best suited for.)

Since our focus is on the rising sign, we are not considering the planets and how they fall in an individual chart, except for those affecting the ascendant. Naturally, the way they fall into the various houses will modify and augment the interpretation. We are concerned with the rulership of each house cusp, or division of the chart. Since each house, or section, describes a specific "department" of life, we can derive much information by considering only these cusp rulerships. (Cusp is the imaginary dividing line between each house and between each sign.) The way the planets "aspect" each other will further modify the interpretation. (An aspect is the degree of relationship of one planet to another. Some aspects are positive and some are negative. This is not a judgment, as no chart is either good or bad. It only signifies whether an energy is easy to release or difficult to deal with. Some aspects indicate conflict and some indicate ease. Conflict is not necessarily bad nor is ease necessarily good.)

Many times, several planets will fall into the first house, indicating additional influences that describe the personality. For further insight, read the beginning of the chapter connected with each planet that falls in the first house (or first sector) of your chart. For instance, if Mars is in your first house, no matter what your rising sign read the initial section of the Aries chapter *in addition* to your rising sign chapter.

Aries is ruled by Mars.
Taurus is ruled by Venus.
Gemini is ruled by Mercury.
Cancer is ruled by the Moon.
Leo is ruled by the Sun.
Virgo is ruled by Mercury.
Libra is ruled by Venus.
Scorpio is ruled by Pluto.
Sagittarius is ruled by Jupiter.
Capricorn is ruled by Saturn.
Aquarius is ruled by Uranus.
Pisces is ruled by Neptune.

To find out which, if any, planets fall into the first house of your chart, consult an ephemeris or an astrological computer service (see page 22).

It is also possible, when we use more complex house systems, that an "intercepted" sign will fall into the first house. This can happen when one sign rules two houses. (The leftover sign is completely enclosed in one house. It is called an intercepted sign.) This intercepted sign can fall into the first house—or the house of the ascendant—and in this case, it is indicative that there are two "colors" affecting the personality. This additional color or hue will also be indicated when the ruler of the ascendant is conjunct (or sitting next to) another planet. The individual with these multiple influences will exhibit a multifaceted personality. He will tend to show different facets of himself at different times. (This is easy for the individual, as he may be unaware of the transition, yet it can be difficult for those around him, as he tends to switch gears unexpectedly.) All of these factors must be taken into consideration, as this is a discussion of general rules and observations.

Another factor to be considered is whether the ruler of the ascendant is cardinal, fixed, or mutable, and whether it is fire, earth, air, or water. Each planet not only has a characteristic ascribed to it, but also a quality. Cardinal quality is primarily sensitive and receptive. It is energy that wishes to set things in motion and create, but it is energy that is easily influenced. It is impressionable, but has initiative. Fixed energy is powerful, consistent, persistent, determined. It is strong and unchanging energy. It is not easily moved or swayed. Mutable energy is adaptable, changeable, agreeable. It adjusts in order to harmonize.

The four elements represent other qualities. Fire element indicates enthusiasm. Earth element equates to practicality. Air element is connected to intellect, and water element shows sensitivity. A well-integrated personality has a balance of the four elements, but if there is a preponderance of one element in the chart, an individual may have to learn how to balance a particular quality of energy. Aries, Leo, and Sagittarius are the fire signs. Taurus, Virgo, and Capricorn are earth signs. Gemini, Libra, and Aquarius are the air signs, whereas Cancer, Scorpio, and Pisces are water signs. If many planets fall into fire signs, an individual is especially enthusiastic, energetic, excited, generous, and vibrant. They can also be hasty, impetuous, hot-tempered, and always chasing rainbows. A preponderance of earth indicates a capable, practical person applying common sense to problems. He can be overly materialistic, "stuck," hard to excite. An overbalance of air brings about a love of the world of ideas. This individual is at home with theories and intellectual concepts of social justice, yet he may be the absentminded professor, living in an ivory tower. He may not know how to make his concepts practical. Too much water indicates a very sensitive person. He is receptive to other people, sympathetic and understanding, but he may be overly sensitive, inclined to indulge in his moods, feelings, and emotions. The consideration of these additional qualities, in relationship to the ascendant or rising sign, gives more information about the behavioral patterns of an individual.

If we realize that the rising sign is equivalent to the horizon, we can see that it is also the individual's own particular horizon, or viewpoint. It is the starting point in the chart and the starting point in a person's life. It is the initiation into the earth plane. The ascendant is interpreted as indicative of the individual's personality as well as his appearance. It also indicates the circumstances of childhood. The rising sign is one of the most important parts of a chart because it describes the influences that become a part of a person's being the very moment he takes his first breath. It describes, most of all, the vehicle chosen by the soul to carry us through life and the earth plane experience.

The Sun indicates the inner personality (something we don't always allow others to see), the vitality, the ego quality and the animus or male dominant. The Moon relates to the emotional quality or the anima or feminine sensitive. It is the rising sign that indicates an individual's particular outlook on life. Twelve people can stand around an object, each one of them seeing a different facet of that object. Each one has a different perspective. The object remains what it is, yet twelve people might describe it in different ways, depending on where they stand. We see life in different ways, with different perspectives, depending on where we stand. The circumstances of birth, the environment, and the conditions of childhood determine our particular point of view. We are the sum total of all those conditions. The ascendant indicates those conditions, but it also indicates *the decisions a person makes about those conditions* early on in life. More importantly, it indicates the decisions he makes about survival, perhaps at the moment of birth.

The ascendant can act like a wall or a façade that an individual erects around himself. It is often like a mask that he hides behind, simply because it is concerned with survival issues. It describes the part of the personality that is most easily expressed. It is also how a person *allows* others to see him. It sometimes protects the real identity (described by the Sun sign). It tells us how a person has "photographed" the circumstances around him and what he has decided will work best for him. It tells us about the techniques a person has developed to enable him to handle the conditions he has to cope with.

The physical body acts like a vehicle to carry us through life. The ascendant describes the kind of vehicle we have chosen, or built. But this physical body also acts like a barrier or division to keep us safe and apart from the rest of mankind. The ascendant also describes the *psychological* devices we use to keep us safe. Nature has symbolic ways of showing us patterns. Think of a chick breaking through its shell, a butterfly in its cocoon. When that creature can deal with life on its own, it is able to dispense

with that protective vehicle. It emerges, and reveals inner life
and beauty. It needs that shell and cocoon until it comes into its
own. Many times an individual's innermost self is quite different
from the picture he presents. If an individual can grow past his
façade and his barriers, he may find untold riches. As long as
he needs those safety devices, he may "hide" behind the outer
personality. Whenever a person feels less than safe, whether in
his personal or business life, he is liable to automatically assume
the behavior characteristics the ascendant describes.

There are many ways to break down attitudes and mannerisms that are no longer viable. Therapy is one way. Growth
comes when we are willing to surrender attitudes and explore
the interior. Those thick walls of protective behavior can hide a
pot of gold within. Whatever man can do to understand his no
longer effective or less than effective ways of dealing with life is
a step in breaking down all barriers.

If an individual has the same rising sign as his Sun sign (being
born around 6:00 a.m. to 8:00 a.m.) he may have a more integrated personality than if he has a vastly different rising sign
than Sun sign. He will *be* exactly what he *shows* on the surface.
His inner dialogue will not be in conflict with the way he reveals
himself to others. However, the Sun may be posited in either
the twelfth or the first house, depending on the exact time and
place of birth. If his Sun is in the first house, he will have a
strong, dominant, executive, leadership quality. He may have
almost a Leo cast to his personality. If, however, the Sun is in
the twelfth house, he shows only the tip of the iceberg of his
personality. He needs time alone to reflect, re-center, and re-
energize himself. Even though his inner and outer dialogue is
the same, he will be more thoughtful, occult oriented, and may
feel caged or boxed in, unable to really express the full force
of his inner dynamics.

In theatrical terms, the rising sign is the mask one puts up automatically, especially when in a scared or uncertain situation.
Actors must learn to break through this mask in order to tap the
rich resource of experience hiding behind that façade. Naturally
in an audition or class situation there is fear involved, or at least
uncertainty, so the actor whips into his "personality," thinking

this will bring the results he wants. If he can be courageous enough to let the façade drop down, the true self can emerge. The inner self is infinitely more rich in source material for the actor than his outer personality. In training talented actors, acting teachers Lee Strasberg and Sanford Meisner, among others, have devised various exercises to help the actor break down his outer walls. Their high success in training people for the theater has much to do with fantastic instincts about the mask each new actor is wearing. With encouragement and lots of training, the actor begins to trust his inner instincts. Acting is closely related to therapy and life, in that the "personality" is closely related to early survival decisions that may be totally inappropriate or ineffective later in life.

Aries rising, for instance, adopts an "angry" attitude or an overly antagonistic personality when he is on the firing line. Taurus may become stubborn or overly charming, hiding a completely different self underneath. Gemini invariably talks a blue streak when he is in an unsafe situation. Verbal facility, wit, and conversation may conceal someone sensitive or deep. Cancer rising hides behind his emotions, talking too much on an emotional level, overreacting or showing great vulnerability. Inner strength may be the hidden gem, or more analytical awareness may emerge if that mask can be penetrated.

Leo has a natural ability to be dramatic. He may overdo the drama and fiery personality when he is not safe. Lee Strasberg commented about his daughter Susan, with Leo rising, that if she were a baseball player she could always be counted on to hit a home run, but bunting would be difficult for her. Susan learned to do less rather than more in her work. Virgo can be counted on to ask questions if he is less than secure. He can be critical or overly analytical as his way of staying safe. Too much objectivity may hide sweetness or sensitivity. The Libra rising has great difficulty in dropping the sweetness and charm. His survival has to do with being especially *nice* early in life. He may have much hidden anger submerged beneath that overtly "nice" manner.

Scorpio rising comes on as tremendously intense, forceful, and powerful. He may hide a sweetness or sense of humor that only emerges when he feels safe. He has to learn to pull back his tremendous energy rather than knock people over, perhaps unknowingly. Sagittarius is always sunny and laughing, even if things are very difficult. His mask has to do with a Pollyanna attitude, an "Oh well, everything will be okay" outlook. Behind his cheeriness, perhaps even lying close to the surface, can be great strength or perhaps some sadness. In acting or performance, whether on stage or in life, new dimensions can emerge with the willingness to drop the façade.

For one with Capricorn ascendant, the stern or shy façade hides a different character altogether. Judgmental personality most often denotes tremendous insecurity and self-imposed hardships or pressures. The more erratic Aquarian personality may hide a deeply sensitive person. He is safe if he is "different," or rebelling. That is the part of his mask that is easy to show. For Pisces, the façade is simply to tune out, blur the images, and go up to dreamland. He avoids confrontation. It is hard for a Pisces rising to allow himself the possibility of seeing ugliness or pain. He is heavily invested in being right simply because he is safe as long as everything and everyone lives up to his expectations. Behind his perceptions and instincts, he may reveal greater strength by transmuting that façade of idealism into a practical, but visionary, approach.

One learns as an actor to sometimes work against emotion, because in real life at times of crisis or importance, the mask is broken, the real self emerges. In a crisis situation or when the individual feels at home, the individual has no time (or need, in the latter case) to erect the carefully honed defenses—perhaps perfected since childhood or even birth—that protect his inner self or soul. It is my hope and my belief that the study of the rising sign can help each individual release more of the inner beauty and energy that goes along with the rich inner self.

Mankind has a need to expand beyond the limiting self to selflessness. If we look at all the "new" forms of awareness techniques available to the general public, it appears that over the past two decades this need has been intensified. Soul awakening can be an intense struggle. The victory of transformation is terribly difficult and quite simple at the same time. A first step seems to be in learning to "let go." We can find many ways to hang on to what we think will keep us safe. Integration is an ultimate goal. Astrology is one more way to encourage man to get in touch with his best energy and to discover his highest potential. Trissie Callan says that "having your astrological chart read is like getting an I.D. card from the Universe." Living up to potential is a high goal, but in the final analysis, it is up to the individual to make that decision, when, where, and how he can.

To understand the ascendant means we understand how we present ourselves. If we are also aware that the methods we use to keep people out may be in conflict with our inner desires and needs, we have taken a giant step toward the synthesis of the external personality with the inner self. The release of new energy can be a reward in itself. Here's to the increased ability to balance our forces for more successful living.

HOW TO DETERMINE YOUR ASCENDANT

There are twelve houses in the zodiac wheel, but twenty-four hours in a day. Generally speaking, then, the ascendant changes every two hours. If you were born between 6 a.m. and 8 a.m., your rising sign would be the same as your Sun sign, since the Sun comes up over the horizon at approximately 6 a.m. For instance, an Aries born at 6 a.m. would also have Aries on the ascendant or rising. If the Aries were born between 8 and 10 a.m., the second sign of the zodiac, Taurus, would be on the ascendant. If that Aries person were born between 10 a.m. and 12 p.m., he would have Gemini rising, the third sign of the zodiac. A Taurus born at approximately 6 a.m. would have Taurus on the rise. If a Taurus were born between 8 and 10 a.m., he would have Gemini (the next sign on the zodiac wheel) on the rise. Born between approximately 10 a.m. and 12 p.m., the Taurus' ascendant would be Cancer, the sign that follows Gemini. A Gemini born at 6 a.m. would have Gemini rising, and so forth.

To help clarify this principle I've prepared the following tables that give a *general* timing. If you are born between the first and the fifteenth of the month, look at the closest list, or interpolate between the two dates. If the birthplace is considered in the erection of a horoscope prepared especially for an individual, the exact degree of the ascendant may modify this general rule, simply because longitudes and latitudes will indicate the precise degree and minute of the sign on the ascendant. If the description of the rising sign indicated by the tables does not fit you, read the chapters preceding it and following it; one of them should fit. Many times, the ascendant can fall on the cusp between two signs and only the exact erection of a chart would clarify which sign fell on the ascendant. Naturally, latitudes far to the north or far to the south can change this rule considerably. If you have any doubts about the accuracy of your calculation of your rising sign, it might be worth your while to invest a few dollars (five to ten dollars is the going rate) in having your chart erected by one of the astrological computer services. The printout you receive will not provide an interpretation of the meaning of your personal chart, but it will tell you the positions of the planets at the time of your birth, and will tell you what your rising sign is. Neil Michelson's Astro-Computing Service, P.O. Box 16297, San Diego, California 92116 will provide an accurate and complete printout of your chart. Simply send birth date, time, and place and ask for a natal chart.

For simplicity's sake, however, you may be given a clue as to your own rising sign by reading the following tables.

January 1		January 15	
12:25 A.M.	Libra	2:00 A.M.	Scorpio
3:00 A.M.	Scorpio	4:30 A.M.	Sagittarius
5:30 A.M.	Sagittarius	6:45 A.M.	Capricorn
7:40 A.M.	Capricorn	8:15 A.M.	Aquarius
9:20 A.M.	Aquarius	9:40 A.M.	Pisces
10:40 A.M.	Pisces	10:35 A.M.	Aries
11:50 A.M.	Aries	12:05 P.M.	Taurus
1:05 P.M.	Taurus	1:45 P.M.	Gemini
2:40 P.M.	Gemini	3:55 P.M.	Cancer
5:00 P.M.	Cancer	6:25 P.M.	Leo
7:25 P.M.	Leo	9:00 P.M.	Virgo
10:00 P.M.	Virgo	11:25 P.M.	Libra

February 1

1:00 A.M.	Scorpio
3:30 A.M.	Sagittarius
5:45 A.M.	Capricorn
7:15 A.M.	Aquarius
8:40 A.M.	Pisces
9:50 A.M.	Aries
11:05 A.M.	Taurus
12:45 P.M.	Gemini
3:00 P.M.	Cancer
5:20 P.M.	Leo
8:00 P.M.	Virgo
10:25 P.M.	Libra

February 15

12:10 A.M.	Scorpio
2:30 A.M.	Sagittarius
4:45 A.M.	Capricorn
6:20 A.M.	Aquarius
7:40 A.M.	Pisces
8:50 A.M.	Aries
10:05 A.M.	Taurus
1:40 A.M.	Gemini
2:00 P.M.	Cancer
4:25 P.M.	Leo
7:00 P.M.	Virgo
9:45 P.M.	Libra

March 1

1:25 A.M.	Sagittarius
3:45 A.M.	Capricorn
5:20 A.M.	Aquarius
6:40 A.M.	Pisces
7:50 A.M.	Aries
9:25 A.M.	Taurus
10:45 A.M.	Gemini
12:55 P.M.	Cancer
3:25 P.M.	Leo
6:00 P.M.	Virgo
8:25 P.M.	Libra
10:55 P.M.	Scorpio

March 15

12:30 A.M.	Sagittarius
2:45 A.M.	Capricorn
4:20 A.M.	Aquarius
5:40 A.M.	Pisces
6:50 A.M.	Aries
8:05 A.M.	Taurus
9:35 A.M.	Gemini
11:55 A.M.	Cancer
2:55 P.M.	Leo
4:55 P.M.	Virgo
7:25 P.M.	Libra
9:55 P.M.	Scorpio

April 1

1:45 A.M.	Capricorn
3:20 A.M.	Aquarius
4:40 A.M.	Pisces
5:55 A.M.	Aries
7:10 A.M.	Taurus
8:50 A.M.	Gemini
10:55 A.M.	Cancer
1:20 P.M.	Leo
4:05 P.M.	Virgo
6:20 P.M.	Libra
9:05 P.M.	Scorpio
11:30 P.M.	Sagittarius

April 15

12:25 A.M.	Capricorn
2:55 A.M.	Aquarius
3:40 A.M.	Pisces
4:50 A.M.	Aries
6:05 A.M.	Taurus
7:50 A.M.	Gemini
10:00 A.M.	Cancer
12:25 P.M.	Leo
3:10 P.M.	Virgo
5:25 P.M.	Libra
8:05 P.M.	Scorpio
10:45 P.M.	Sagittarius

May 1

1:20 A.M.	Aquarius
2:40 A.M.	Pisces
3:55 A.M.	Aries
5:05 A.M.	Taurus
6:45 A.M.	Gemini
9:00 A.M.	Cancer
11:25 A.M.	Leo
2:00 P.M.	Virgo
4:25 P.M.	Libra
7:05 P.M.	Scorpio
9:30 P.M.	Sagittarius
11:45 P.M.	Capricorn

May 16

2:20 A.M.	Aquarius
1:40 A.M.	Pisces
2:45 A.M.	Aries
4:05 A.M.	Taurus
5:40 A.M.	Gemini
8:00 A.M.	Cancer
10:20 A.M.	Leo
1:00 P.M.	Virgo
3:25 P.M.	Libra
6:00 P.M.	Scorpio
8:25 P.M.	Sagittarius
10:45 P.M.	Capricorn

June 1

12:40 A.M.	Pisces
1:50 A.M.	Aries
3:05 A.M.	Taurus
4:50 A.M.	Gemini
7:00 A.M.	Cancer
9:25 A.M.	Leo
11:55 A.M.	Virgo
2:25 P.M.	Libra
4:55 P.M.	Scorpio
7:25 P.M.	Sagittarius
9:45 P.M.	Capricorn
11:20 P.M.	Aquarius

June 16

2:50 A.M.	Aries
2:05 A.M.	Taurus
3:50 A.M.	Gemini
6:00 A.M.	Cancer
8:25 A.M.	Leo
11:00 A.M.	Virgo
1:25 P.M.	Libra
4:00 P.M.	Scorpio
6:25 P.M.	Sagittarius
8:45 P.M.	Capricorn
10:15 P.M.	Aquarius
11:35 P.M.	Pisces

July 1

1:05 A.M.	Taurus
2:45 A.M.	Gemini
5:10 A.M.	Cancer
7:25 A.M.	Leo
10:00 A.M.	Virgo
12:25 P.M.	Libra
3:05 P.M.	Scorpio
5:30 P.M.	Sagittarius
7:45 P.M.	Capricorn
9:20 P.M.	Aquarius
10:40 P.M.	Pisces
11:50 P.M.	Aries

July 16

12:00 A.M.	Taurus
1:35 A.M.	Gemini
4:00 A.M.	Cancer
6:25 A.M.	Leo
9:00 A.M.	Virgo
11:25 A.M.	Libra
2:00 P.M.	Scorpio
4:25 P.M.	Sagittarius
6:45 P.M.	Capricorn
8:20 P.M.	Aquarius
9:40 P.M.	Pisces
10:50 P.M.	Aries

August 1

12:45	A.M.	Gemini
3:00	A.M.	Cancer
5:25	A.M.	Leo
8:00	A.M.	Virgo
10:25	A.M.	Libra
12:55	P.M.	Scorpio
3:40	P.M.	Sagittarius
5:45	P.M.	Capricorn
7:20	P.M.	Aquarius
8:40	P.M.	Pisces
9:55	P.M.	Aries
11:05	P.M.	Taurus

August 16

2:00	A.M.	Cancer
4:25	A.M.	Leo
7:00	A.M.	Virgo
9:25	A.M.	Libra
12:00	P.M.	Scorpio
2:30	P.M.	Sagittarius
4:45	P.M.	Capricorn
6:15	P.M.	Aquarius
7:40	P.M.	Pisces
8:50	P.M.	Aries
10:05	P.M.	Taurus
11:40	P.M.	Gemini

September 1

1:10	A.M.	Cancer
3:25	A.M.	Leo
5:55	A.M.	Virgo
8:25	A.M.	Libra
11:05	A.M.	Scorpio
1:30	P.M.	Sagittarius
3:45	P.M.	Capricorn
5:15	P.M.	Aquarius
6:40	P.M.	Pisces
7:50	P.M.	Aries
9:00	P.M.	Taurus
10:55	P.M.	Gemini

September 16

12:00	A.M.	Cancer
2:30	A.M.	Leo
4:55	A.M.	Virgo
7:20	A.M.	Libra
10:00	A.M.	Scorpio
12:25	P.M.	Sagittarius
2:45	P.M.	Capricorn
4:20	P.M.	Aquarius
5:40	P.M.	Pisces
6:50	P.M.	Aries
8:05	P.M.	Taurus
9:55	P.M.	Gemini

October 1

1:20	A.M.	Leo
4:10	A.M.	Virgo
6:25	A.M.	Libra
8:55	A.M.	Scorpio
11:30	A.M.	Sagittarius
1:45	P.M.	Capricorn
3:20	P.M.	Aquarius
4:40	P.M.	Pisces
5:50	P.M.	Aries
7:05	P.M.	Taurus
8:55	P.M.	Gemini
10:55	P.M.	Cancer

October 16

12:25	A.M.	Leo
2:55	A.M.	Virgo
5:20	A.M.	Libra
7:55	A.M.	Scorpio
10:30	A.M.	Sagittarius
12:35	P.M.	Capricorn
2:15	P.M.	Aquarius
3:40	P.M.	Pisces
4:55	P.M.	Aries
6:05	P.M.	Taurus
7:40	P.M.	Gemini
10:15	P.M.	Cancer

November 1

1:55	A.M.	Virgo
4:20	A.M.	Libra
6:55	A.M.	Scorpio
9:35	A.M.	Sagittarius
11:40	A.M.	Capricorn
1:20	P.M.	Aquarius
2:35	P.M.	Pisces
3:40	P.M.	Aries
5:15	P.M.	Taurus
6:45	P.M.	Gemini
9:10	P.M.	Cancer
11:25	P.M.	Leo

November 16

12:55	A.M.	Virgo
3:25	A.M.	Libra
5:55	A.M.	Scorpio
8:25	A.M.	Sagittarius
10:45	A.M.	Capricorn
12:15	P.M.	Aquarius
1:40	P.M.	Pisces
12:50	P.M.	Aries
4:05	P.M.	Taurus
5:40	P.M.	Gemini
8:10	P.M.	Cancer
10:25	P.M.	Leo

December 1

12:00	A.M.	Virgo
2:25	A.M.	Libra
4:55	A.M.	Scorpio
7:30	A.M.	Sagittarius
9:45	A.M.	Capricorn
11:20	A.M.	Aquarius
12:35	P.M.	Pisces
1:45	P.M.	Aries
3:00	P.M.	Taurus
4:40	P.M.	Gemini
6:55	P.M.	Cancer
9:35	P.M.	Leo

December 16

1:25	A.M.	Libra
3:55	A.M.	Scorpio
6:25	A.M.	Sagittarius
8:45	A.M.	Capricorn
10:15	A.M.	Aquarius
11:40	A.M.	Pisces
12:45	P.M.	Aries
2:05	P.M.	Taurus
3:55	P.M.	Gemini
5:55	P.M.	Cancer
8:35	P.M.	Leo
11:10	P.M.	Virgo

ARIES
RISING

As THE FIRST THRUST OF SPRING brings life in the form of flowers bursting through the hard, cold crust of earth, so does the first sign of the zodiac bring vibrancy to the material world around him. His bursting forth may not be as gentle as that of the plants, yet the general impression he creates is that of breaking up old patterns in order to produce rebirth and new beauty. The ruler of Aries is Mars. The person with this ascendant expresses himself with the forcefulness of that aggressive, warlike planet, yet he also shows a romantic side that belies the fighting side of his personality.

Mars is the planet of action. It betokens activity, ambition, determination, and antagonism. It is sexual energy and high creative energy at the same time. It indicates impatience and frustration, competitive spirit and temper, yet without Mars energy, new fields would never be conquered. It is symbolic of creation itself. Aries is a fire sign, denoting high enthusiasm and vitality. It is also a cardinal sign, showing sensitivity and an open quality. Mars wants to go forward without thought of the risks involved. It is the planet of impetuosity and impulse. It is volatile and stimulating.

If we consider that Aries is the first sign of the zodiac, we see the similarity in the Aries personality, who always wants to be first. The individual with this ascendant is therefore a natural pioneer, as his daring and courage easily take him into uncharted territory. He is like the penetrating wedge, paving the way for the rest of the human race. He fights the battles, breaks the ice, and makes life easier for others who come behind. He is the explorer.

Since Mars is the planet of action, the most obvious form of self-expression for one with this ascendant is through physical activity. In fact, unless one with Aries rising gets enough physical exercise, the energy backs up and becomes temper and frustration. It has been proven through research that Mars is the strongest planet in the charts of athletes and dancers. The perfection of the physical instrument coupled with the competitive spirit makes sport a natural outlet for one with this ascendant. The discipline necessary to perfect dance techniques provides a perfect focus for the outlet of Mars energy.

In Mayan civilization, games were used to settle differences that might arise between people. Sports played a most important role in releasing anger and conflict, as well as indicating a winner. In our present times, the Olympic games provide a healthy outlet for competition between nations. The whole spirit of the Olympics is Martian in its nature. The directed energy, concentrated in its focus, enables athletic champion after champion to dare to set new world records. No one doubts the courage it requires to strive for new speed, new technique, more perfection. Athletic prowess is combined with the spirit of sportsmanship and fair play in healthy competitive activity. The drive and discipline necessary to overcome obstacles in the way of success is a perfect example of the way Mars energy works. Along with physical prowess, and need for competition, justice over evil, truth over falsehood is symbolic of sportsmanship. When the person with this fiery ascendant finds a cause and taps his natural aggressive energy, he becomes a champion in his own way, striving to pave the way for new achievement. He is also able to work through his inner frustrations and impatience.

St. George, the patron saint of England, is an example of the kind of "fight for right" that challenges the Mars-ruled person. (Remember the knights of the holy grail, who set out to conquer the unknown territory that would lead them to their victory and destiny?) Yet with all types of Mars energy, the fight for right may be combined with a goal that is unrealistic, even wrong in its concepts. Periods of war and military conquest are always rationalized by the vision of what is right. The Aries person, too, may see only his own point of view, his own vision and goals. But where his zest is unquestioned, his propriety may sometimes leave room for doubt.

Aries governed the period of civilization after Egypt's highly developed phase and before the Christian era. It covered the span of history that included the conquests of Alexander the Great and the military power of the Romans. The period of wars and military strength presaged the breaking of old conditions, stagnant civilizations, and brought forth the colonization of new lands. Migrations occurred as a result of the devastation. The times produced spiritual leaders to spearhead the change to come. Moses, with his fiery personality, courage, and daring battled the elements and the people to make his way across the desert. His anger was displayed in the breaking of the Tablets of the Law. His drive and determination brought his charges into line and pioneered a whole new civilization.

The ram was the symbol of religion at that time. Blood sacrifices were required by the faithful. The ram is the astrological symbol assigned to Aries, and Mars rules blood as well as war and conflict. The ram pushes through obstacles by butting his head against that barrier and forcing the wall to give way. One with an Aries ascendant can do the same thing. He may not use good judgment about his head-on collisions, but he will hammer away until he breaks through any impasse. Aries rules the head. It may be well for one with this ascendant to use his head for something other than a battering-ram. The clue comes from discovering the brains that lie inside.

The natural characteristics exhibited by one with this ascendant are manifold. Beyond that dynamic energy and aggression lies a real need for conquest and challenge. The fighting spirit is so strong that unless the individual with this rising sign learns to channel his energy constructively, he may find he antagonizes everyone around him. He is not usually a naturally tactful person and he may not care who he upsets in the process of fulfilling his ambition. And, ambitious and competitive he certainly is. The answer lies in the way he directs that ambitious, competitive force. He is either a fighter, or a fighter for people or causes. One way or another, he will fight. He has extraordinary drive and determination, as well as courage. He can initiate new cycles of activity that would overwhelm a more timid soul. He is forceful, self-assertive, and sometimes willful. That dynamic willpower is perhaps the most important asset he possesses if he learns how to use it wisely.

The individual with Aries rising will venture, sometimes unwisely, where angels fear to tread. He loves the thrill of daily combat. He thrives on hairbreadth escapes and danger. Crisis motivates him to excel. If there is no combat in his life, he may have to invent some. Without action, he becomes bored, impatient, frustrated, and tactless. His anger turned inward may cause him to seek release in less than fruitful experiences. He can be willful and may not listen to reason. He may become tricky and jealous. He is sometimes frank to the point of bluntness, wounding those around him with his cutting words. His hostility and aggression can produce dreadful wounds that he doesn't mean to inflict.

Mars governs the sexual energy and activity. Just as sexual energy can be compelling and sometimes non-discriminating, the person with this ascendant can use his energy in a non-discriminating manner. He needs to channel and discipline his exuberance to prevent excessive and possibly damaging expression. It is his fine power of reason that enables him to direct his abundant sexual drive into constructive areas. Mars also rules metals. A person with Aries on the ascendant can rechannel much of his impatience by working with metals in some way or another. He also releases energy through physical exercise. Whether he runs, dances, builds things with a metal hammer and nails, produces metal sculpture, or works with needles or knives, he must find a way to be "combative." Metals provide the resistance he needs for his energy release. It simply won't work to sit on all that dynamic energy or try to repress it. To ignore the frustrations would simply delay the reaction. Eventually, the lid will blow at the most inopportune time. The Aries temper, once vented, is quickly forgotten, however. He never intends to hurt anyone with his sudden outbursts.

Lucy Guercio, with Aries ascending, says this about the release of energy: "I never have any physical problems because I release the tension or energy. I never have headaches or stomachaches because sometimes I get in my car and just scream. As long as I scream and yell and get it out, I feel much better." One of the Reichian techniques for the release and rechanneling of tension is to scream and yell into a pillow if necessary. After such a session, almost anyone feels infinitely better physically.

Johnny Cash, with Aries ascending, sings songs about the painful experiences of his youthful foray on the wrong side of the law. Perhaps without knowing it, those metal strings on his guitar can keep him cool, calm, and reasonable. Barbra Streisand, accused of being difficult and temperamental, is also able to release a great deal of high creativity through the physical challenge of singing. David Cogan, with Mars affecting his personality, was on stage at Carnegie Hall as a child prodigy, playing violin as his mode of self-expression, releasing much physical energy through performance. Isadora Duncan chose dance as her creative mode of expression. Joan Baez and Louis Armstrong share this ascendant, as does Ringo Starr. John Philip Sousa released much of that frustrated, inventive energy in a creative way through Martian type of music. El Cordobes, the famous bullfighter, could have no other ascending sign in order to face the challenge in the bullring time after time. Susan Horton rides a motorcycle as one active way to express her Mars energy.

Since individuals with Aries rising are the most romantic people in the zodiac, it is interesting to note that Rudolph Valentino had Aries rising. Many of the screen's great lovers share this ascendant. The sexual image they project captivates women all over the world. Not only Valentino, but Paul Newman, Steve McQueen, and Warren Beatty share this rising sign. All of them come across as hard-driving, hard-loving men of action. Paul Newman races automobiles, Steve McQueen seemed born on a motorcycle. Susan Strasberg, in her book *Bittersweet*, describes Warren Beatty as a tremendously sexually motivated man, desiring to express the romantic nature as well as the need for conquest. She says that he had "a tremendous need to please women as well as conquer them."

The person with an Aries ascendant has a very strong constitution and terrific sense of direction. His physical movements are quick and impulsive. Former President Gerald Ford, with Mars affecting the personality, was accused of clumsiness. Actually, his tendency to trip over things is characteristic of the Martian impulse to go right through anything in his way. The ram will spend time battering down a wall rather than walking around it. The Martian personality runs the race at breakneck speed.

The person with this ascendant is a terrific starter, but not such a good finisher. He is daring and animated, but impatient with those who can't keep up with him. He wants everything yesterday, wants to see immediate results, and has no tolerance for limitation and restriction. The Aries personality can cut through extraneous matters and get right to the heart of a situation, but he can be lacking in self-control and patience. If a pet project or a situation doesn't work out the way he wants, he will simply walk away rather than take the time to discover what went wrong. His need to conquer new territory may not keep him around a project or relationship that is ailing, so he can appear rather unsympathetic and unfeeling at times.

After one with Aries ascending has run the gamut of experiences and discovers that there is still an unsatisfied longing, he may pause long enough to engage his fine mind and figure things out. Mercury is the esoteric, or higher-octave, ruler of Aries. Mercury is the planet of intellect and reason. Aries corresponds to the head and to the motor impulses that arise in the brain. If he refuses to pay attention to his intellect, he can develop headaches as a result of that backed-up energy. Yet, with analysis of a particular situation, he can focus his energy, direct his actions more carefully, and lead a more fulfilling life. The Aries personality is capable of doing almost anything he really wants to do, simply because he has no fear. If he becomes aware of his fascination for the new and untried, his need for exploration, he will find a constructive way to utilize that talent instead of simply scattering his energy.

Many individuals with this ascendant discover a talent for big business, where drive, ambition, and cunning enable them to employ innovative ideas that put them ahead of competitors. John D. Rockefeller, financial wizard, Henry Kaiser, industrialist, and Alexander Graham Bell, inventor, all chose interesting ways to harness their future to metals. Their Aries ascendant gives credence to the ability to forge new direction in business and in history, to find new and original solutions. One with this ascendant will always need to be in the race for progress. He enjoys the possibility of overcoming difficulties. He will not hesitate to challenge someone who opposes his ideas.

General George Marshall and General Douglas MacArthur chose the military life as vehicles to express this Martian energy. Rash courage and bold self-confidence made them natural leaders. The willingness to fight in the realm of ideas motivated Theosophist Annie Besant to devote her life to pioneering an organization for the betterment of humanity. Presidents Andrew

Jackson, Franklin Pierce, and John Tyler were willing to battle all opposition in order to rise to the highest position in the land. Alexander the Great, Leopold III, Savonarola, Oliver Cromwell, Cicero, Peter the Great of Russia, George V of England, and Rasputin share this ascendant.

Surgery and medicine provide a natural outlet for this quality of energy, as is evidenced in the case of Clara Barton. The success in animating and stimulating originality in others impels many natives with this ascendant to become theatrical directors. Jack Goodford, a TV director, has Mars posited in the first house, giving him an Aries "quality." A feisty disposition enables him to handle strong-willed personalities and temperamental talent. A Martian quality enables him to cut through to the heart of the message. A director can be most challenged in the field of thought and succeed due to his fine powers of discrimination. André Malraux was also born with this ascendant, as was Marcel Proust and Nostradamus.

The need for action and activity is directly connected to early survival decisions. The ascendant in a chart indicates the particular quality of energy we are most comfortable in expressing. It appears that the choice of ascendant is related to the conditions surrounding our arrival on the earth plane. During regression sessions, most individuals "remember" their birth. Many people are aware of a conscious decision about how they will handle their particular set of circumstances. Those decisions seem to precondition behavior throughout life, unless the individual becomes cognizant of their counterproductivity. When Aries is on the rise, it appears that the individual is born with a certain amount of anger or frustration. It may be that the birth process is difficult and he has to fight his way out, or the conditions awaiting him appear to be less than harmonious. Nevertheless, he seems to decide that he will make it as long as he can fight, take action, and explore. Many times, this decision is connected to a memory of a military past life. In that case, the aggressive tendency is the most familiar one.

Since survival depends on fight, it is important that the person find real situations to combat. Otherwise he is simply angry for the sake of anger, active to prevent boredom, and frustrated over limiting situations and restrictions. The ascendant also

describes how we behave when we are not on safe turf. For one
with Aries rising, scared behavior can manifest in overly violent
reactions, temper, and a caustic manner. If this person can decide why he is feeling threatened and unsure, he may lose the
need to be overbearing. He feels safe when he is leading the attack. His motto could very well be: "A good offense is the best
defense." This is the façade, of which he may be unaware on a
conscious level, that he develops early on in his life. If he discovers that this tendency to battle and rush headlong into the
fray becomes counterproductive and prevents his accomplishing
what he wants, he can learn to show his true resolution and
directed energy. He will always be a person of action, but with
more thought and decision he will outdistance others in his attempt to conquer new worlds.

Children with this ascendant can be very difficult to discipline. Discipline is essential, as they love to get into mischief,
but they are particularly resistant to the word "no." The impetuous, rebellious nature is so strong that the only way of reaching
children with this ascendant is through reason and appeal to
their sense of justice. If they learn for themselves that temper
tantrums and disobedience will only make life more difficult,
they will learn to be more rational. A quiet, calm presentation of
facts is the only way to reach them at times.

Even more important is to find a physical outlet for all the
abundant vitality. It is essential that the child be given an opportunity to explore and investigate life to prevent an overly rebellious attitude. Since he is intrigued by a challenge, perfection
of a talent will help him deal with his sexual, creative energy in
a healthy way. Music, dance, art, and athletics are important for
this child. Kristina Nevius, a Scorpio with Aries rising, is an extremely active young lady. Dancing and skating enable her to
channel some of that abundant energy. Since the sexual energy
is so strong in one with an Aries ascendant, there may be a tendency to experiment very early in life. Sound moral values, in-
stilled as early as possible, can help to prevent negative experiences in puberty.

This child is given to hero worship as well. Realistic presentation of facts about situations and people are also important.
Blind devotion can lead him into more trouble than almost any-

thing else. He rushes into a situation or involvement without really understanding the issues at hand. Once he is committed, it is difficult to dissuade him. Since he can't easily be persuaded to control his impulse, he may have to learn by trial and error. Being burned in a small way can prevent later, larger wounds. If he becomes aware of the boomerang effect of his actions and is allowed to take the consequences, he will develop more cautious behavior. Because of his wish to have immediate gratification, life can be difficult for a child with this ascendant. He will develop a strong love for truth, justice, and loyalty if he is given a chance.

The placement of Mars in an individual chart will indicate the ideal area for the release of this incredible drive. The *aspects* to Mars indicate how easy it is for the individual to realize his need for action. When Mars is posited in the first house, it intensifies the vivacious, extroverted personality but can also intensify the frustration and impatience. Mars in the second house indicates a resourceful quality in financial areas. The individual earns money through his dynamic personality, but may spend it in anger and on impulse. With a third house placement, impatience characterizes his relationships with relatives, neighbors, and traffic. He may have accidents while driving, simply because he is in too much of a hurry. He can be impatient on the telephone and be especially competitive with siblings. He can also be innovative and pioneering in the communications field. He can be an excellent director, for instance.

Since the fourth house in a chart describes the relationship with the parent of the opposite sex, if Mars is well aspected, that parent has been a good role model in showing daring and courage, ambition and resourcefulness. A positive identification with that parent enables the individual to easily follow the example set forth. If Mars is not well aspected, competition and jealousy characterize the relationship. The person may photograph that parent with tremendous frustrations and unresolved anger.

With a fifth house Mars, creative ability is high. The person with this ascendant is even more romantic, sexy, and inventive. If Mars is badly aspected, frustration with romance, sexuality, children, and creative expression is possible. There could be difficulty in pregnancy for a woman with this ascendant, with

some danger of hemorrhaging or miscarriage. Extra precaution
may be advisable. With a well-aspected Mars, the children will
be especially creative, brave, innovative, and ambitious, as well
as pioneering. A sixth house placement indicates a special need
to channel energy into physically exhausting work, such as
sports, dance, reforming, or competitive areas. Since Mars also
rules blood, if that planet is badly aspected, health problems
may be connected to blood disorders such as high blood pressure. Alcohol can be particularly injurious to one with this placement, although that is detrimental to one with Aries rising in
general, since it is hard enough to control the passions and anger
without any stimulant. Alcoholism could be a severe problem
with a badly aspected Mars connected to health matters. A tendency to drink or take drugs seems to be connected to frustration
and unreleased anger.

If the ruling planet, Mars, is placed in the seventh house of
partnership, the Aries rising looks for someone just like himself.
This can indicate a preference and attraction to someone dynam-
ically sexy and innovative and lead to a stimulating marriage
or partnership. If Mars is badly aspected, the relationship can be
full of conflict. Marriage will never be dull with this placement.
The eighth house in a chart indicates how one gets what he
needs from life, so if Mars is placed there, with Aries on the ascendant, he will direct his aggressive energy into getting what
he wants from life and people. He will either show tremendous
resourcefulness and initiative or have much anger and frustration in those areas. A ninth house placement indicates a need for
self-expression in areas of advertising, law, promotion, importing
and exporting. He can be involved with travel or international
affairs.

Career matters will command most of the attention in the life
of an Aries rising if Mars is posited in the tenth house of public
life. He will be a champion in leading the way for others,
fighting for what he feels is right and proper, and must be involved in areas where his competitive spirit can have full sway.
This is the house that indicates the relationship with the parent
of the same sex. If that relationship is a healthy, competitive
one, the career will bring much satisfaction. If there is unresolved and unexpressed anger toward that parent, the career is

liable to bring the same kinds of frustrations and aggravations. Friendship is the area that comes under fire with an eleventh house position for Mars. The individual will either attract healthy, active people to associate with, or find much competition among his associates. Group activity will be an area for the release of his Martian energy. If Mars is placed in the twelfth house, there will be difficulty in expressing all that his dynamic ascendant implies. He may work behind the scenes, have guilt about his sexuality and drive, and find much frustration that he has a hard time in expressing.

The individual with Aries ascending can learn much from examination of the qualities of his opposite sign, Libra. Each sign has a polarity with the opposite one in the chart. Health is in finding balance, and balance in this instance comes from adopting some of the diplomatic qualities of the Libran personality. He can also learn some lessons of graciousness and charm. (The Libran personality in turn can learn something from the aggressive energy of the Mars-ruled person.) The United Nations gives a perfect example of the integration of these qualities. With Aries ruling the ascendant of this world court, the pioneering quality is obvious. Issues that are brought to the attention of this body are certainly ones that could lead to conflict if unresolved. But with calm deliberation, diplomacy, and tact—while never losing sight of the fight involved—issues can be resolved peacefully. With a rational approach and examining all sides of the issue, reason solves potentially explosive situations. Aries rising can learn much from the way the UN operates. Since the Aries personality is the most romantic in the zodiac, if he learns to make love, not war, he is a winner beyond compare.

FINANCE

It is no accident that some of the most powerful financial tycoons were born with Aries rising. Ambition is part of the nature of the Aries personality, but with Venus ruling the second house of finance, there can also be a marked love of money, both the earning of it and the spending of it. Since Taurus is on the cusp of the house of finance with this house placement, and Venus is the ruler, the person with Aries rising earns money through "Venusian" means. He will also spend money on pleasurable things.

Venus governs a myriad of things, such as art, beauty, diplomacy, and social graces. It rules theater, music, sculpture, fabric, color, design, perfume, flowers, gourmet food, and almost anything that gives pleasure. The placement of Venus in a chart indicates what the individual loves most in his life. The *aspects* of Venus tell how easy it is for the person to allow that pleasure to be expressed. Since Venus is so connected with money in this instance, the aspects are most important. If, for instance, Venus is well placed in an individual chart, the person will be involved in artistic pursuits that are lucrative, bringing greater financial ease. Venus is one of the "benefics" in the zodiac, so this person is blessed with luxury in his life. He will spend money in social situations as well as to create greater social justice.

If Venus is not well aspected, the person can have some hesitations about expressing his artistry. He may take the easy way out with financial matters, and, in the extreme, be quite lazy about earning it; he resists making waves in the financial area of his life. Even the desire for a sensually comfortable life may not motivate him, or he finds non-productive ways of earning money. He can still be very self-indulgent about expenditures, however, as he will be tempted to part with whatever he has for the sake of pleasure. He may not be able to resist flowers and bubble baths, whereas more practical expenditures don't tempt him.

Artists with this ascendant have a natural outlet for financial increase, whether through theater, dance, or painting. Since Venus also rules fashion, many designers are born with this ascendant. Basia Poindexter, an exceptionally talented artist, developed her own unique style by hand-painting on silk fabric. Her talent was quickly noticed by designers such as Mary McFadden, and Basia's beautiful artwork now adorns many gorgeous gowns created for women who appreciate her talent. Her sociability and charm have attracted many celebrities to her side for custom-made gowns and wall hangings. Her scarves grace many a beautiful throat. Princess Margaret of England, with Aries rising, obviously loves to spend money on clothing, social events, and pleasure, as does Barbra Streisand. Grigori Rasputin was no doubt motivated by his love of money to influence the Russian Empress Alexandra to do his bidding. Rudolph Valentino was reputed to spend much money on expensive and beautiful enticements for the women in his life. Norbert Weisberg travels to exotic places to purchase interesting art for his beautiful home in fashionable East Hampton on Long Island. Lucy Angle Guercio earned money as a top model. Her beautiful face graced the cover of *Harper's Bazaar* when she was only sixteen.

If one with an Aries ascendant goes against his grain and attempts to earn money in areas that he dislikes, he will be unsuccessful. He must enjoy his financial activity or he will adopt the negative side of Venus and become lazy and unmotivated. Carroll West-Jones found a unique and inventive service for people who need food ordered, houses readied, and decorations for parties or as a welcome for their impending arrival. Rarely will someone with this ascendant be without some kind of beauty in their own lives, so they know how to provide it for others as well.

COMMUNICATIONS

Gemini rules the third house of communications with Aries rising. Gemini is the third sign of the zodiac and is ruled by Mercury. Since Mercury is the planet of intellect, thought, speech, and wit, the person with this ascendant is a naturally good conversationalist, a fact collector, and mentally stimulating. He is up on the latest information about what's happening in the world or at least in his own environment. He enjoys exchanges of ideas with his neighbors, and relates to his brothers and sisters on a mental level.

Mercury is the planet that rules writing and the mental process in general. The Gemini Mercury is airy, quick, and facile. The duality implied by Gemini indicates an ability to get close to a situation to investigate it well and then a need to pull away to retain some objectivity. It can appear that one with this ascendant can see both sides of a question and may be arbitrary at times. His active mind is never still and he may not stop long

enough to form conclusions. But if you want to know about ob-
scure facts, check it out with an Aries rising. He will be well informed about almost anything. Gossip is attributed to strong
Gemini characteristics, as the mental curiosity is insatiable. He is
a master at discussion, as his fascinating ideas cover such a
range of topics. It may be hard to pin him down to agreements
and contracts, for his restlessness keeps him on the move, finding
new and unparalleled ways of expressing thought. He can appear to flit from one subject to another, yet he will never be
bored or boring.

Susan Horton, a Sagittarian with Aries rising, chose to express
her vast knowledge and concepts of astrology by first writing a
column for her local Dallas society paper. She chose interesting
people in her community and wrote a character analysis based
on their birth information. Her biographies hit the target every
time. Because her quest for new information and discovery in
the field of astrology keeps her so stimulated toward new
research programs, she was elected to the board of directors of
the American Federation of Astrologers, a most prestigious astrological society, with over 4,000 members to choose from. Her
fiery Martian personality keeps her exploring and pioneering new
ideas and concepts, while a fascinating ability to communicate
enables her to disseminate that information.

Mercury also is related to the adult ego state in terms of
Transactional Analysis. The adult part of ourselves is the com-
municator, fact collector. If Mercury is well aspected in an individual chart, the person with this ascendant is well able to perform on a mental level. His facility in school can make him a
forerunner in the realm of ideas, yet his restless mind may be
difficult to discipline.

If Mercury is badly aspected, that restlessness can keep him in
hot water. Impatience over any delays, added to the need for
stimulation, makes him investigate anything new that comes on
the horizon, and this can sometimes get him into mischief. He
can become quite bored with routine methods of learning. He
can sometimes be too quick to explore subjects in depth, preferring to skim the surface, yet his wide range of interests coupled
with the facility and speed of his thought make him a natural in
the field of communications and ideas. Basil Rathbone, Henry

Miller, and John Hancock all share this ascendant. Marcel
Proust, André Malraux, and Simon Bolivar also exhibited the
ability to communicate ideas in an exciting way.

HOME LIFE

The individual with Aries rising can have a deep emotional attachment to his home. Cancer is the sign that rules the fourth
house of home and the Moon is the ruler of that sign. Since the
Moon indicates feelings, sensitivity, and vulnerability, it is in
connection with land, home, and his environment that one with
this ascendant may be most affected. He may show vulnerability, even moodiness, when he is in the safety of his own
surroundings. He will be hardest hit when anything happens to
change his home or home life. He *needs* a home in order to feel
secure emotionally. He will reveal more of his nurturing instincts
when he is there, and may allow himself to express his sensitive
side within the confines of his own four walls.

The Moon describes the feelings, emotions, and needs mankind shares in common. It is related to Jung's collective unconscious. By working through one's own emotional needs, instincts
about the needs of mankind in common become clear. The
Moon also describes the mothering instincts. For Aries rising, instincts about others' needs in connection with nesting impulses
or home life are especially strong. He may nurture others in his
own home. Lucy Angle Guercio, an Aquarian with Aries rising,
does just that on a large scale. Caribou Ranch in Colorado, the
home of James and Lucy Guercio, becomes the temporary home
for large groups of musicians and their families when they arrive
to record albums in the highly sophisticated, lavishly equipped
recording studio on the ranch. Each house on the property is
furnished with beautiful antiques. Fur rugs and cozy quilts,
ample leather sofas and chairs create an atmosphere of comfort
to meet the most particular needs. The subtle touches of choco-
late-chip cookies, fresh every day, baskets of fruit, plenty of
snacks in the refrigerators and bottles of wine, soda, and coffee
in each kitchen "feed" the needs of her guests between the huge
meals served in the massive mess hall. No detail is overlooked

that can make her guests feel at home. Her own two children, Katy and Willy, complete the feeling of family life on a grand scale by bestowing their loving presence on the laps of the guests, making each one feel at home, a relative by osmosis.

The fourth house indicates the relationship with the parent of the opposite sex. If the Moon is well aspected in the chart, the relationship is one of deep understanding and sensitivity. If the Moon is not well aspected, there may be a possibility of hurt feelings and vulnerable reactions. There may be a little of each quality in the overall picture. The parent of the opposite sex may be especially vulnerable, sensitive, and emotional. Since the Moon rules the anima part of the personality, this parent can show more of the "feminine" characteristics, no matter what sex. In the chart of a female with Aries rising, there is a strong possibility of role reversal between the two parents.

In many instances, the native with Aries rising will feel especially protective of this parent, even to the point of feeling like mothering that parent. Many times, the emotional reaction of the Aries ascendant has to give way to the vulnerability and sensitivity of that parent, so the parent is the one to be protected and understood, not the child. If the Moon is well aspected in the chart, the Aries rising is sensitive to that exchange, but if the Moon is not well aspected, the individual may resent it. He may have felt abandoned by that parent. This is the parent that can upset him most easily, yet a deep rapport and strong emotional ties can be established if the individual with this ascendant can show some objectivity where this parent is concerned.

Since the fourth house indicates the conditions in the third portion of an individual's life, it appears that one with Aries rising becomes more sensitive as he grows older. This sensitivity can lead him to an activity where his sense of the trends of the times impels him to show greater concern for humanity in general, women in particular. He may express the unfulfilled potential of that parent of the opposite sex. If he is in touch with his own emotional pain, he is able to show a nurturing and sympathetic concern for others who may have experienced difficulty in their lives. This quality of feeling makes him a natural writer as he grows older because of his ability to be more in touch with his own intellect and emotional quality. Even if he is involved in communications or writing early on, he will discover new sensitivity expressed in later life. Feelings that emerge lead to compassion on a greater scale. Emotional fulfillment becomes even stronger through identification with all mankind.

ROMANCE • CREATIVE EXPRESSION

The fifth house in a chart indicates romantic inclinations, the gambling instinct, creativity, and children. It rules the stock market as well. It is interesting to note that when we meet a loved one, it is under a fifth house aspect and it is a gamble. When we have children, it is a gamble, and certainly taking the chance to express a creative energy can be a gamble. When Aries is rising, the fifth house is ruled by Leo. Leo is the dramatic sign. It is ruled by the Sun, which indicates ego, vitality, energy, and leadership. Fifth house activity is the area where one with Aries rising can express his true individuality. The aspects to the Sun in the natal chart indicate the energy and success of any creative ventures. If the Sun is well aspected in the chart, a good healthy ego and feelings of self-esteem are indicated. Therefore the individual has no problem investigating and releasing his creative ability. A sense of pride is connected to romance and gambling instincts, and he will receive the most recognition in connection with those matters. A need for self-expression through creative projects, even entertaining, is high, and he can look for drama in connection with romance and love. His children will do him proud and investments will pay off handsomely. His children will reflect his own sense of self-worth and develop healthy egos. Their accomplishments can become noteworthy.

If the Sun is not well aspected and there is a lack of ego and security, the individual may demonstrate creativity for the sake of ego recognition and applause, or ignore those urges altogether. His self-esteem may go up and down depending on the amount of "applause" he generates. He may expect his children to provide him with ego gratification through their accomplishments, but his children's sense of pride and self-worth may reflect his own. It is possible for him to neglect giving his chil-

dren well-deserved praise and pats on the back in the guise of
keeping them humble. He may unwittingly transfer his own inferiority to his offspring. His children may inadvertently hurt his
pride and he may resist having children at all, for fear they may
not live up to his expectations and do him proud. It can be very
important to develop a strong sense of self-worth, give himself
positive strokes, so that his children will learn to do the same.
The children will then more easily be able to express the leadership, dominance, and sense of pride for their own accomplishments.

Actor Paul Newman has transmitted his pride of accomplishment to his own children, who have ventured into the realm
of acting as well. John D. Rockefeller certainly passed on a
strong sense of family pride to his children. Barbra Streisand receives tremendous accolades for her creative ability and generally assumes the executive, leadership role with her own creative
expression. Warren Beatty has pride not only in his creative ability but in his romantic ability. Isadora Duncan was never accused of being a shy, wilting flower. The dramatic, creative
quality carried over into her personal life.

WORK • SERVICE • HEALTH

Virgo rules the house of service, health, and occupation. Since
Virgo is ruled by Mercury, the individual with Aries rising needs
tremendous mental stimulation in order to stay vital and
healthy. His service capacity has to do with ideas and words.
Annie Besant used her words and ideas in the Theosophical
movement. Her books reflect a sense of service to mankind.
Writers and actors use speech and mental activity in their occupations. Thought and strategy had a great deal to do with the
success of military leaders such as General Douglas MacArthur
and Alexander the Great.

If Mercury is well aspected in the chart, it is easy for one with
this ascendant to assume responsibility for expression through
words. He can be quite analytical in his work. His thought
processes can have much to do with health; his own and that of
others. Since Virgo is associated with purity and "virginity,"

health foods or natural products appeal to one with this ascendant. He can become quite aware of the desire for purity of body. Athletes, for instance, need this kind of analytical care and body awareness in order to perform at peak capacity.

Virgo is associated with thoroughness and precision. Nit-picking is sometimes part of that thoroughness. Barbra Streisand has a reputation for being very analytical, thorough, and critical of her work. She will not allow a recording to be released unless she is convinced it is the best she can do. That kind of analytical approach, even to the point of nit-picking, is what keeps her work at top quality. Her constant striving for vocal perfection keeps her at the head of the list in a competitive field.

Mercury is the ruler of both Gemini and Virgo, one an air sign and one an earth sign. The combination of intellect (air) and practicality (earth) gives one with Aries rising a natural head start in work combining a need for both brilliance and analysis. With application, he is a natural for the communication fields, whether writing, directing, or performing. This kind of mentally challenging work is the antidote for restlessness and impatience. As long as he has an outlet for his intellect and release for his thoughts, he will remain healthy. It is negativity coupled with inaction that brings about lowered vitality and lack of energy. Inertia and mental boredom spell doom for one with this ascendant. Since Virgo rules the intestinal tract, it is in this area of the body that one with Aries ascendant can be most affected. That can include the digestive tract in general. Pure food is essential to retain good assimilation, as well as enough exercise. These two factors keep one with this ascendant healthy, happy, and productive.

MARRIAGE • PARTNERSHIP

The seventh house in a chart not only describes the kind of partner the individual is attracted to, both in business and in marriage, but the quality of that relationship. Libra is the sign on the cusp of the seventh house when Aries is ascending. The ruler of Libra is Venus. What one with a Martian personality needs and looks for in a relationship is the calming, tranquil influence of someone dedicated to keeping peace. If Venus is well aspected in the individual chart, there is a good chance that one with Aries rising will find just that in a partnership.

A Venus-ruled person is one who is easygoing, diplomatic, charming, and pleasant to look at. Graciousness is a natural part of the personality. Venus rules artistry, sociability, and balance. The poise associated with a Venusian personality is essential for the completion of the aggressive spirit of the Aries personality. In order to keep peace and restore harmony and balance, a Venus-ruled person needs the dynamic, hasty, impulsive Martian person to stir things up. In that way, they complement each other. The danger comes when the Venus-ruled person tries to keep peace at any cost, while the Mars-ruled personality forges ahead with unchecked ambition and drive. Sometimes the Mars-ruled person may be frustrated by lack of drive or zest on the part of the mate, who will never challenge him.

The aspects of Venus in an individual chart give the clues about the nature of the relationship. If Venus is well aspected, the Aries rising is successful in attracting that beautiful person to share his life or his business. If marriage is the issue, the Aries personality will find his true love. He will marry for only one reason and that is for love and to find the happiness and harmony he is seeking. That love will be returned and a good relationship is assured. If business is involved, the Libran diplomacy will smooth over any feathers that the Mars-ruled person ruffles. The ambitious, daring, pioneering quality of the Aries person is enhanced and harmonized by the Libran ability to negotiate. Libra rules legal affairs as well. The legal balance of the scales is sometimes necessary to check the impulsive quality of the Aries personality.

If Venus is not well aspected in the chart, the easygoing nature of the partner may very well keep him from expressing *active* diplomacy. Laziness, an unwillingness to make waves, can stimulate him to do anything to keep peace. The negative aspects indicate the possibility of being devious, tricky, and self-indulgent. Social graces give way to flattery, indiscrimination, inaction. Love gives way to possessiveness and jealousy. The Mars personality may not get the support and active harmony he needs. The relationship will not be stormy, but just the opposite.

It may lack the energy and magnetic attraction essential for true happiness. Aries rising can feel guilty if he is allowed to ride roughshod over someone too gentle to fight back, or to stand up for himself. The Mars personality may need to examine motives for the partnership or relationship. If the raison d'être is for public approval or for social contacts, the relationship will not provide what is truly essential for one with Aries rising. If opposites can learn from each other rather than forming a competitive relationship, their complementary qualities can bring greater enrichment. One with Aries rising can learn a great deal about tact from the Venusian personality.

NEEDS

When one with this ascendant is truly in touch with his ability, he has great power in transforming the lives of the people with whom he comes in contact. With a focusing of motivation, the innovation of one with Aries rising brings him into powerful situations with almost universal impact. The biggest change in his life has to do with his influence on masses of people as well as a phenomenal ability to get his own needs met.

The eighth house in traditional astrological terms is interpreted as inheritance, death, and sometimes sexuality. Yet in psychological terms, it seems to indicate how a person gets what he needs and wants from life or from individuals around him. The quality of energy used to obtain material things seems to have direct relationship with the quality of energy one sends out to humanity. After an individual is convinced of an ability to wrest from life the things he desires, he turns attention beyond himself to first his immediate family, then to his universal family. His motivation changes and, like the tides, what has come to him then goes out, and inadvertently comes in again.

Pluto rules this house when Aries is rising. Pluto is the most important and powerful planet in the zodiac as it relates to universal consciousness, transformation, and transmutation. It is associated with the highest good or the lowest evil. It indicates the most important, and sometimes drastic, change in a particular area of life. In this case, it describes "income" from one extreme to another. Pluto is the ruler of Scorpio and is related to the child ego state in terms of Transactional Analysis. The child ego is the most powerful ego state, but can be the most destructive and manipulative as well.

If one considers that the child's strongest message is: "I want what I want and I'm going to get it no matter what," the relationship to Pluto is obvious. The Pluto energy, in a negative sense, is determined to get whatever is desired at that moment, no matter what the consequences. Pluto can indicate compulsive and manipulative behavior. It is like a powerful body of water that if left to flood the land, is destructive. Yet that same body of water, backed up and dammed up, produces enough electricity to light up cities. So it is with Plutonian energy. The most powerful world leaders have strong Pluto energy as well as the most destructive people in history. Motivation seems to be the key issues in one's own evolution. If the will is for the good of all, then the power is transforming, but if the desire is for personal power, the effect can backfire. Grigori Rasputin, with Aries rising, had tremendous power over Empress Alexandra. His kind of demonic, hypnotic ability to manipulate the Russian throne through her backfired in his own murder. Yet Alexander Graham Bell, in contrast, transformed the lives of millions in a positive way through his power and invention. Peter the Great of Russia, Savonarola, and John Hancock exerted tremendous influence of a powerful nature. The planet Pluto knows no halfhearted measures. The effort is all or nothing at all; there are no grays when it comes to this kind of energy.

If Pluto is well aspected in the chart, the individual is willing to "let go" of negative situations that appear destructive in nature. The knowledge that one rotten apple spoils the whole barrel will keep the individual away from potentially harmful situations. If Pluto is badly aspected, the childlike reaction can get the person into deep water if he tries to compromise on his principles or justify the end by the means. Therefore, if he evidences the slightest bit of manipulation and compulsion, the individual may get the rug pulled out from under him. Many times a rebellious spirit or a need for revenge will motivate the Aries rising to do something that will rebound destructively. He may run up large bills that eventually have to be paid off, perhaps the hard way. He can overextend, simply because he wants what he wants when he wants it. He may know better than to be involved in less than savory schemes, yet he may close his eyes to negative factors in spite of an inner warning voice.

With a positive Pluto, the Aries personality is able to raise large sums of money in order to mass-produce or manufacture products. Tycoons who wheel and deal with large companies have the ability to borrow millions of dollars and reap the benefit in eventual huge profits. If Pluto is well aspected in a particular chart, these pieces of puzzle fall into place easily and deals go through. If Pluto is not well aspected, there is a temptation to pound the pieces into place, manipulate, and take ridiculous gambles to the extent that the whole project eventually falls apart. If the person with this dynamic rising sign raises his motivation to the level of humanitarian needs, he has a fantastic and powerful ability to get what he needs from life and the people around him. His own profits can be considerable if profits are his *secondary* motivation and he works for the good of his group.

RECOGNITION

The Aries personality has a built-in sense of philosophy. He can be quite universally minded. His good fortune has to do with matters at a distance, travel, higher education, advertising, promotional efforts, and publication. The planet Jupiter rules this ninth house. Jupiter is the planet that is called the "great benefic." In simpler terms it means luck and optimism. Jupiter, the ruler of Sagittarius, is associated with religion, teaching, and sales. Wherever Jupiter is placed in a chart is indicative of a blessing in that area. It is the focus of his optimism and expectancy. It indicates where the individual wants a challenge and is willing to set goals.

Perhaps because of the optimism and willingness to reach out, good fortune and abundance are returned to this person. When the Aries ascendant travels, he restores his sense of humor and becomes quite expansive. He can be philosophically tuned in to other countries. Enthusiasm leads to involvement in advertising, promotion, legal affairs, and higher education. He can be a good "salesman" in these areas. Flying is associated with the ninth house as well. Pilots have to show a great deal of Martian energy, daring, and courage. Aries rising can be recharged by travel, which restores his natural philosophical turn of mind.

Nostradamus, the German occultist Granz Hartmann, Cicero, and Annie Besant chose to express this Jupiterian urge through metaphysics, philosophy, and theology. Henry Miller is tuned in to his good fortune through publishing. Singers Joan Baez, Barbra Streisand, and Johnny Cash sell records which enable them to reach the public and also reap financial benefits, as did John Lennon. Actors Paul Newman and Warren Beatty are constantly involved in personal publicity. Abundance of recognition easily comes their way. The ability to set goals and be challenged by things just out of reach keeps an Aries personality awake and stimulated. It enables him to deal with career matters that can otherwise become tedious and full of responsibility.

CAREER

The tenth house in a chart indicates the kind of career one chooses, as well as the quality of relationship with the parent of the same sex. Just as luck and optimism are associated with promotion and travel, the career represents responsibility and sometimes burden. Saturn is the ruler of this house with Capricorn on the mid-heaven or mid-coeli. The MC, as it is sometimes called, indicates the image before the public as well. With Saturn affecting this image, duty is a strong keyword. This is the area of life that requires the most focus and concentration. It can sometimes be limiting and restrictive, but in a positive sense represents security.

Saturn is one of the most important planets in a chart as it indicates the heaviest karmic lesson to be dealt with in life. The word "karma" means the law, but it is the universal law of cause and effect. Saturn is related to the parent ego state in Transactional Analysis terms. The parent part of ourselves is the most judgmental. It is that small voice of conscience that can also be overbearing and guilty. The placement of Saturn in a chart indicates the areas where we put ourselves under the most pressure, sometimes combined with a little hair-shirt wearing.

The Kabbalists liken Saturn to the playpen that Mother Nature puts around her children. We put our children in playpens to keep them safe, but eventually, that child must have freedom and more room to investigate. We give our offspring more territory and space when we're sure he can take care of himself. If he becomes responsible, we give him more privileges. Life seems to work the same way. The judgmental part of our personality, i.e., the parent ego state, will let up on us if convinced that we're ready to really take care of ourselves. We then give ourselves more elbow room.

At first, with career responsibilities, the individual keeps himself under enormous pressure, as that is an easy energy for him to deal with. He feels safe and secure in a little corner. He may work for someone else where his perfectionist qualities are never appreciated. He may be so careful to ensure everything is perfect that he will work harder and harder to please his boss. Since the boss would be lost without him, he may never get the recognition he deserves or the confirmation of his invaluable assistance. It is when one with this ascendant becomes aware of his own value and diligence that he allows himself to assume the higher responsibility of working for himself. He trades in a limited security for the assurance that he will make it on his own by hard work and attention to detail.

The relationship to the parent of the same sex has much to do with the conditioning about his public image and career decisions. His relationship can be a karmic one, full of duty and obligation. He can either feel tremendous security from that parent or feel rejected and under judgmental scrutiny. The aspects to Saturn in an individual chart tell the true story about the relationship. If Saturn is well aspected, the karmic bonds are strong. That parent, even though strict and conservative, assumes high responsibility for himself and represents safety and dedication. The parent may be a strict disciplinarian, yet that strictness is tempered with love and devotion. The parent of the same sex will never be a frivolous person. The individual with Aries rising develops his own sense of duty and responsibility from the behavior of that parent. He will then go on to assume devotion and duty in the choice of his career, but he will be good to himself along the way. Progress is gradual and consistent, but he knows he will get to the top of his career and build a strong and dutiful public image. He can be motivated by a sense of responsibility for that parent, as well. He may sense limitation in the life of that parent and want to provide more security or pleasure.

If Saturn is badly aspected, the parent may be overly strict, aloof, cool, and unreachable. He may not be there at all. Death or separation can sometimes be a part of the early conditioning. He will photograph that parent as having deep insecurities, never getting out of his own "playpen." He may inadvertently keep himself in limited circumstances to avoid ultimate responsibility for that parent. He can feel rejected by that parent, under constant supervision and criticism. He may feel ignored or feel he will never live up to the expectations of that parent. His subconscious guilt may keep him from reaching out, for possible rejection from that parent is too much to handle. He may subconsciously feel it is ultimately his fault: if only he were more clever, charming, talented, or handsome that parent would love him. He can be comfortable with the same kind of behavior from his public. Rejection is expected. The opposite side of the coin is never to put himself in a position where he will be rejected in career matters.

The antidote for Saturn is twofold. First, the individual will develop security and confidence by learning a technique connected to career responsibilities. With increased confidence, he begins to moderate his judgmental messages. If he realizes his potential to make valuable contribution through his endeavor, he is challenged beyond any insecurity. Secondly, if the limited circumstances are due to an inner resolve about heavy responsibility connected to that parent, he may inadvertently keep himself from success. If he can adopt a different attitude about the caretaking of that parent, helping him out of the "playpen," he will find that he too is "sprung." His attention to detail is profound, his ability to work hard unquestioned. He simply needs to find an area where the compensation is worth his superior focus.

FRIENDSHIP

A person with Aries rising is attracted to unusual people in the area of friendship. His own sense of adventure connects him to people who are freedom-loving, inventive, avant-garde. He forms friendships quickly, finding spontaneity essential in the relationship. He is attracted to people who take chances with their lives, have humanitarian instincts, and may be avant-garde. He releases much of his own inventiveness in the company of unusual people. In public he may be conservative, even shy, but friendships release him from any feelings of restriction.

The sign Aquarius is on the cusp of the eleventh house of friendship with the planet Uranus ruling that sign. If that planet is well aspected, he is most fortunate to find exceptional types of people in his sphere of associates. He can be attracted to people who have made a name for themselves, or are perhaps quite famous. He will certainly not be interested in ordinary, run-of-the-mill personalities. He will enjoy group participation with music, astrology, electronics, or inventions. Humanitarian pursuits are right up his alley.

If that planet is not well aspected in the individual chart, Aries rising can find rebellious personalities most enticing. He may be occasionally disappointed by unreliable friendships and may find an escape in bizarre group situations. To the extreme, his curiosity will be piqued by anarchistic types of people, rebels, and "genius" types who may not live up to their true potential. His own rebellious nature will find solace in the company of people who are bucking the system in some way or another.

It is in the area of group participation, friendships, and associations that this Martian person will be able to let off steam. It is up to him to find a healthy way to release his own rebellious instincts. Music provides a natural outlet, as does anything connected to healing and metaphysical information. Susan Horton, by participating on the board of the AFA, and by investigating metaphysical principles, is able to express her own inventiveness and genius by association with astrologers and humanitarian people in general. Louis Armstrong associated and worked with outstanding musicians in the country, thereby stimulating and augmenting his musical genius.

The planet Uranus also acts like a catalyst in many situations. One with Aries rising can particularly enjoy introducing his fascinating friends to each other. If that planet is well aspected, he is particularly happy when they form friendships or become involved in projects with each other. Basia Poindexter enjoys introducing her unusual and varied group of friends to each other. Friends who are traveling to other countries find Basia's international friends warm and welcoming. Barbra Streisand's song "People who like people are the luckiest people in the world" expresses this humanitarian sentiment precisely.

If, however, Uranus is badly aspected, the individual with Aries rising feels left out if two friends get together without him. His association with overly rebellious people can be particularly detrimental to him, as his choices of the usage of his own energy are particularly critical to his health. Janis Joplin's association with hard drugs and alcohol eventually led to her own death. The positive connotation of Uranus is healing and humanitarianism. The negative is alcohol, drugs, nervous energy, rebellion, and anarchism.

HIDDEN MATTERS • SUBCONSCIOUS PROCESS

The area represented by the twelfth house indicates what lies just beneath the surface for an individual. It is the energy that is less easy to express and reveal. It is sometimes subconscious activity. The more an individual becomes aware of what is going on in the deepest recesses of his mind, the more release of positive energy is assured. The twelfth house traditionally represents hospitals, jail, incarceration, yet psychologically, it represents energy or thought that may be imprisoned. It also describes the way we feel or behave when we are all by ourselves, unarmored and with dropped defenses.

When Aries is on the rise, the planet Neptune rules this house of hidden matters. Neptune is the planet of dreams and illusion,

high inspiration and idealism. Neptune, the ruler of Pisces, is the
planet of psychic awareness, high intuition, and vision. In its
negative sense, it is the planet of disillusion, deception. Behind
all that aggressive action that is so comfortable for one with this
ascendant lies a dreamer of dreams, a visionary, and an idealist.
It is not the quality of energy that is easy for one with the Martian personality to express overtly. But when he is all alone, you
can be sure he spins webs of glorious colors. If he is able to in-
corporate those dreams into realistic outward events, this person
is truly one step ahead of everyone else, just where he wants to
be.

In an individual chart, the aspects of Neptune indicate
whether he is simply a dreamer, weaving webs of self-deception,
or tuning in to highly inspired ideas that lead to better conditions in his own life and eventually in others' lives. The positive
interpretation of Neptune is the ability to create the conditions
in the everyday life by visualization. It is an important metaphysical principle that whatever we can conceive in our imagination becomes a reality, unless we destroy those images by negative thinking or changing direction. Janene Schneider calls this
ability "sending out purchase orders to the universe." It is somewhat like planting seeds in the ground. If we water those seeds
and read the directions on the envelope, we will more than
likely grow the kind of flower that comes from those seeds. The
person with this rising sign has a good ability to visualize what
he wants, send out those purchase orders, and plant healthy
seeds. The outer conditions in his life are very indicative of what
he thinks about when he is alone.

If Neptune is badly aspected, he is liable to kid himself, or
pour poison on his plants before they have a chance to grow. He
stops his purchase orders and negates what he wants. Or he is
too impatient to let his dreams become realities. He pulls his
plants up by the roots to see if they're growing. The negative of
Neptune is non-confrontation. It is impractical and unrealistic. It
is like eating cotton candy. That luscious pink goodness melts in
your mouth before you can get a good taste.

The planet Neptune rules dreams. One with Aries rising can
have a very active dream life and may receive much valuable information through his dreams. It is the key to his subconscious.

Proper interpretation of his dreams may reveal a gift of insight and give tremendous aid in the outer life. Aries rising can be particularly intuitive and psychic. If he ignores this insight or chooses to neglect its messages, he may be ignoring the most valuable tool he possesses. He may have to learn to trust his intuition and learn the key to his own particular interpretation. The aspects to Neptune in his chart will indicate how easy that is for him.

With the combination of interior inspiration, outer ambition, and ability, the individual with this energetic ascendant can pave the way for less courageous individuals by showing his true initiative and doing battle for the rest of humanity. Aries is the first mighty thrust of the wave breaking far up on the shoreline. After that the rest is easy.

TAURUS RISING

THE PERSON WITH TAURUS RISING IS really a country squire at heart. His deepest desire is to acquire his own piece of land, whether large or small, because he needs to feel that special connection to the earth. A pastoral scene can be as inspiring to him as a beautiful painting would be to someone else. He is very loving, affectionate, steadfast, and loyal. His needs are basic: he wants good food, good sex, and a nice place to live.

The symbol of Taurus is the bull. More specifically, he is Ferdinand the bull. If you remember, Ferdinand was very happy to sit in the meadow, smelling the flowers and enjoying a cool summer breeze. But along came a bee to sting Ferdinand out of his reverie. It was then that he showed his bull-like nature and let out a mighty roar. Pawing the ground, with flames flaring from his nostrils, he reacted with a temper that is characteristic of one with this ascendant. Like Ferdinand, the person with Taurus rising is content and easygoing to a point, but when goaded beyond his point of endurance, he will let out the mightiest bellow in the zodiac. His temper can be so violent, unfurled in its fullest fury, that he scares even himself.

The ruler of Taurus is Venus. Venus is the planet that is associated with love, beauty, ease of living, graciousness, and charm. It is the planet that rules the arts. In its positive sense, Venus indicates tact, diplomacy, and sociability. In its negative interpretation, it indicates laziness and self-indulgence. Taurus is an earth sign, indicating practicality, and is fixed and determined.

The Taurean "earth" Venus is quite different in its manifestation than the "airy" Venus of Libra. The Libran Venus is more aesthetic and intellectual. The individual with Taurus rising is more inclined toward acquisition than self-expression in connection with the arts. There are exceptions, of course. Since Taurus rules the throat area and Venus rules beauty, this person is blessed with a naturally beautiful voice. He may express himself through singing, speaking, or acting. Another form of expression involves architecture. The Taurus rising is a builder at heart. His practical nature takes joy in erecting houses or monuments. But perhaps the greatest outlet he finds is in preparing food. Cooking becomes an art form when Taurus rising is concerned. He may never attend a school of Escoffier, but his natural ability leads him to gourmet excellence. His taste in anything can be superb, but he has a special sense about food, wine, and good living.

Vulcan is the esoteric ruler of Taurus. Vulcan is as yet an "undiscovered" planet. The twelve signs are presently associated with eight discovered planets and the Sun and the Moon. Two signs share Venus and two share Mercury. When two extra planets come into full view, Vulcan will no doubt be the ruler of Taurus. Its symbology fits the Taurean personality well, as Vulcan symbolizes the forge. The person with Taurus rising is a hard-working individual, carving his life out of the earth in a special way. He has great strength, is steadfast and loyal. His endurance is unsurpassed. He has a strong attachment to the earth plane and all its abundance, and will work very hard to secure that abundance. He wants to stay connected to the ground in a strong way; it's his way of being safe. His reward is the pleasure of good companionship over good food with a roaring fire in the background. He wants to celebrate his victory and success with those he loves, sharing the fruits of the earth with them. He loves the good life and wants pleasure and graciousness of living above almost anything else.

Taurus is the second sign of the zodiac. The second house in a chart is the house of finance. Taurus is one of the "money" signs. He can be a financial wizard. His desire to excel in financial matters has to do with his need for building security. He is never impressed by wealth, either his own or that of others; material success, being able to wrest a living out of the ground, is simply his way of staying attached to the earth. His acquisition of money is connected to his desire to build a foundation from which he can continue to fortify his position and grow. The world provides a feast for one with a Taurus ascendant. He wants to be able to enjoy his share of all the bounty.

The culture of the Egyptian age flourished under the sign of

Taurus. The symbol of the bull is featured in many artifacts and artworks from that time. The building of the great pyramids is tremendously symbolic of the steadfastness and determination of one with Taurus on the rise. The building instincts are strong and sure. This native may appear to be plodding and obstinate to the casual observer, yet as with the tortoise and the hare, the slow and steady progress of the Taurus rising will outlast swifter-footed signs, who burn themselves out along the way. Step by step, with an endurance that puts a weaker soul to shame, he gathers his strength to forge his monument. It will last, and weather the storms of centuries. Like the Egyptians, he prepares well for his eventual departure from the earth. In those days, the tombs were complete when there was sufficient wealth to ensure the departed one material comfort in the other life. The person with this ascendant wants to line his "temples" with his earthly acquisitions as well. He is a collector of things that represent security to him, whether it be stamps and records or objets d'art. He always has an insurance policy in his collections. It is hard for him to break his attachment to things. He wants them, just to have them.

The manifestation of Venus concerns the desire and love nature. When a person has Taurus rising, this desire nature is well developed. In fact, his decisions about survival have to do with his desires. Desire is the thing that helps him out of any tendency to inertia. He craves physical touch and is safe when he has it. He is tremendously sensual, earthy, and demonstrative. It is perhaps his well-developed love nature that inclines him to love and marriage early on. He will work hard, motivated by his love for his family.

Sometimes the Taurus rising's strong desire nature can bind him *too* tightly to the earth. He can become engrossed in his material existence, which obscures an overall perspective about a deeper meaning of life. If Venus is well aspected in his chart, he eventually uses that desire nature as a first step toward true illumination. That desire can be transmuted into universal love by first realizing the higher meaning of aspiration. It is then a short step toward spiritual love. Any selfishness is transmuted into selflessness. George Washington was born with a Taurus ascendant. Mount Vernon is the epitome of the kind of gracious living and lifestyle one with this ascendant wants to enjoy. But his duty to his country went far beyond any attachment to materialistic instincts. His fight for his land extended to the fight for the country. General Moshe Dayan and President Gamal Abdel Nasser of Egypt showed the same tenacity when it came to their country. Martin Luther King and Robert Kennedy also were born with Taurus on the horizon. The transmutation of the love for family extended to the human family in their cases as well.

If Venus is not well aspected in the chart, there is a strong likelihood that one with this ascendant can be mired in materialism on a completely negative level. He will be pigheaded and obstinate without any reason. His obsession with physical needs and the functions of the sexual energy can include low forms of humor, jokes about the love nature, and bawdy comedy. His bullheaded tendencies lead him to experiences that fulfill his sexual needs but not his spiritual ones. Charles Manson has Taurus rising. His self-indulgence went into the depths of depravity, taking so many innocent victims along with him. Adolf Eichmann shared this ascendant.

A Taurus ascendant is easily spotted by checking out the appearance. The eyes can be "cow-like," round and rimmed. The hairline, too, can be easily recognized. As it recedes, it forms a peak in the front, almost like allowing room for the horns to grow. The Taurean beauty is of an earthy nature—a lustiness coupled with a certain kind of sensual charm. Sometimes the neck tends to be quite thick, but broad shoulders balance the thickness nicely. The personality of one with this rising sign is pleasant and sociable, but the dead giveaway is his stubborn quality. Once he plants his feet, that will be that. Reason will not convince him to change his mind, and he cannot be swayed. He may not even know why he has suddenly called a halt to any further progress. There is simply no budging him when he has had enough.

Children with this ascendant require lots of affection. They exhibit a sensual quality even as little ones. The social nature seems well developed and their charm can melt even the coldest hearts. They are beautiful in appearance, with a sweetness that belies the temper lurking just beneath the surface. They are collectors early in life. Their survival decisions have much to do with the affection they require, and with the desire to please. If they are cuddled and loved, they fulfill their potential beyond all expectations. They are hard workers, perhaps even enjoying household duties *if* the jobs can be made appealing and special. They need to be encouraged to express their artistic tendencies. If their sociable, outgoing personality can find a creative outlet, either through art or through theater, they receive the love and attention they crave from many people and in a healthy way. They can be urged out of any lethargy by expressing an artistic talent. They need to associate with people, perhaps of all ages. A certain amount of freedom of the right kind, early in life, will channel their social needs in the right direction. They are fun to be around, pure delight and pleasure, as long as they are given free rein. If they are coerced, the stubborn, bull-like quality will emerge in full force. This child will show true loyalty as long as he is well loved and well treated. He responds to love with a full heart, spurred on to greater achievement by appreciation. He needs to spend time in the country, close to the earth that gives him such a sense of security.

Claude Philippe was born with Taurus on the rise. As a young man, he went to work in the kitchen of the Hotel Crillon in Paris. He rose to the status of room waiter very quickly because of his hard work and charming ways. Eventually, he worked his way up the ladder, becoming the banquet manager of the Waldorf-Astoria. He was well known as Philippe of the Waldorf. He was the creator of the famous April in Paris Ball, associating with the rich and famous in all walks of life, whether theatrical, political, or social. He was truly famous in his own right. He was a good friend to many, but never impressed with anyone. He took over the famous restaurant Pavillon after the death of Henri Soulé, and eventually built a fabulous resort hotel, expressing that natural architectural, building instinct that is so closely a part of the inherent talent of one with Taurus rising. His down-to-earth personality was really fully revealed when he was at home on his beloved "farm," a paradise of luxury. Yet everyone who visited the spectacular estate pitched in to work at whatever task was necessary, from the preparation of meals to the raking of leaves or weeding of the garden, depending on the

season. Even with full-time caretakers, there was always plenty
to do. After a rewarding period of work and play during the
day, fantastic food and wine were served in a beautifully elegant
but homey manner, usually in the huge wood-lined kitchen,
complete with restaurant stove and equipment.

Many times, the attire was casual, perhaps blue jeans. On
other occasions, elegance of clothing was instinctual. In either
case, the table was always spectacular with fabulous food, beautiful crystal, silver and flowers, and the finest wines available. If
you became a "regular," you were also a part of the family.
Claude's generosity and graciousness were unsurpassed. He continued to work hard all his life, keeping up with a schedule that
was beyond most people's capacity. The collection of beautiful
furniture, rare books, and art objects made his home a special
place to visit, yet Claude never lost his totally earthy quality.
Occasionally, the Taurean stubborn streak would emerge unexpectedly. He was nobody's pushover. As one sat around the
table, gazing into the distance toward the meadow, often the
cows would wander into view. At their side, quite naturally, was
the bull. Claude's greatest joy was to gaze over his beautiful
land with his friends around him, a fire roaring in the background, good food and wine shared with those he loved.

The picture of the bull surrounded by cows can give you some
indication of the attractiveness one with this ascendant has for
the opposite sex. Claude was often teased about having a harem,
as many ladies graced the table at the "farm." Sarah Bernhardt
was born with Taurus on the rise. She was famous not only for
her tremendous charisma on stage and her profound talent but
also for her backstage activities. She evidently had lovers waiting
in the wings wherever she went.

Taurus rules the throat and the voice. Not only is this person
blessed with a pleasant speaking voice, but if Venus is well
aspected in the chart, he has a way with words, can express himself easily, and may be fluent in vocabulary and languages. The
throat chakra is the power center, so if one with this rising sign
is in touch with his power on an esoteric level, he influences people far and wide, perhaps without knowing exactly how. He can
develop a singing voice if he so chooses, but even without for-
mal training, his vocal ability is more comprehensive than even

he is aware of. Singer Jenny Lind obviously reached people on levels beyond the mere sound of her voice, healing them as well as pleasing them, as did Mary Garden. Martin Luther King and Robert Kennedy, with Taurus on the ascendant, were the spokesmen of an era, reaching out to millions with their words. Carlos Castaneda has put metaphysical concepts into a practical form that many can accept and understand. The power of his words is beyond measure. Angela Davis was also born with this ascendant. Singer Liza Minnelli and actress Mia Farrow share a Taurus ascendant with Jackie Gleason, Orson Welles, and William Saroyan. Composer Giacomo Puccini affects people through his music, Percy Bysshe Shelley through poetry.

The greatest temptation for one with this rising sign is pleasure. That can include pleasure of the sight, taste, touch, and feelings. With Venus ruling the sensual nature, it is almost impossible for him to resist anything that promises delight. It is up to the individual to find healthy, productive ways to enjoy himself and feed his pleasure needs. Sylviane Sans, a beautiful, young architect-astrologer, had some interesting things to say about this desire for pleasure. "The problem and the lure of this aspect is that it seems anything is fine if it is fun, and that is not always true. Pleasure plays tricks." She felt she discovered an answer for herself when she realized that she could make anything fun and do it with pleasure, even routine tasks and drudgery. Actually, one with this ascendant needs routine, for routine is a way of establishing more security. Self-discipline convinces him that he can do what he sets out to do. He has great respect for discipline, perhaps because it is his antidote for lethargy and self-indulgence. Interestingly enough, the astrological antidote for Venus is Saturn. When too much "Venusian" temptation comes into view, a "Saturnian" discipline is essential. The converse is also true. When things are too heavy and routine, boring and detailed, a little pampering will go a long way toward making things easier. The end result is balance. The old saw "All work and no play . . ." could not be more fitting for one with Taurus on the rise—although the translation "All play and no work . . ." is just as apt at times.

Children with this ascendant thrive on the combination of cuddling and hugging coupled with strong discipline. A structured time provides the security that roots and grounds him. Almost as if proof of the pudding, I overheard a conversation my son, with Taurus on the ascendant, was having with a parent of a young child who was momentarily misbehaving. As the child's screams got louder, the lack of action impelled David to talk about how he would handle the situation. He began to talk about his childhood. He started: "My mother was so tough, if she said no, she meant no and there was no getting around her." I thought: "Uh-oh, here it comes." To my great surprise, I heard a note of pride creep into his voice as he continued discussing his theories about child raising. Since he had plenty of hugging and affection, evidently the discipline was something he respected and enjoyed. Enforced time structure enables a child with this ascendant to find a median between duty and desire. If he is reassured that he is responsible and reliable as well, he will be free to indulge himself in healthy ways, and to allow himself reward for his diligence. After the Taurus rising works hard to till the soil, he will be able to enjoy the fruits of his harvest.

In an individual chart, difficult aspects to Venus from other planets can modify the personality traits to a degree. Usually, those conflicting energies can impel the individual with this ascendant to want peace at any price, avoid making waves, and tend to take the easy way out. He can appear to be lazy, self-indulgent, and determined to go with sensuality to the exclusion of all else. Aspects to the planet Pluto can make him compulsively pleasure-seeking. With negative aspects to Neptune, the individual is naïve, somewhat unrealistically on cloud nine. He may look through rose-colored glasses and be unwilling to confront anything. With difficult aspects to Uranus, this native will be more impulsive, rebellious, and unpredictable than usual. He may have difficulty staying closely connected to the earth he needs so much. Saturn aspects form a natural antidote, enabling the Taurus rising to handle great responsibility and be more able to conform to routine and pressure. If Saturn is really heavy in the chart, the individual can be too hard on himself. He may have guilt about expressing his pleasure-loving nature to the fullest extent.

Since there is a tendency to overindulge in gourmet foods and fine wines, the one with Taurus ascendant needs exercise.

He can be somewhat lackadaisical in taking care of his body, unless his working routine compels him to exercise as a matter of course. Again the discipline of pleasurable physical activity can counteract the effect his overindulgence has on his overall appearance. With such a strong tendency to enjoyment of food, he can gain a great deal of weight without realizing it. Fatty Arbuckle and Orson Welles share a Taurus ascendant. Although this is not one of the signs that is thought of as overweight, any tendency to laziness will only make it harder to maintain the ideal weight.

One of the ways the overindulgence can work to his benefit is in his attire. The person with Taurus rising is always beautifully groomed. His clothes are especially tasteful and beautiful, his appearance neat to the extreme. Even after hard physical work, he rarely looks disheveled or dirty. Sloppiness of dress is not one of his problems. Venus rules scents, color, and elegance. When Taurus is on the rise, the person seems to exude an essence of tastefulness and refinement that is hard to beat.

FINANCE

The planet Mercury rules the second house when Taurus is on the ascendant. The position of Mercury in a chart is indicative of what the individual thinks about. The person with this ascendant may have his mind on financial matters most of the time, for this is the area where he is most challenged intellectually. He needs stimulating financial opportunity that will keep him on his toes. He becomes bored with ordinary methods of earning his daily bread.

This individual not only thinks about money, he earns it through his mental ability. He is never at a loss for fascinating ideas that will increase his ability to function in the material world. He is not as concerned with acquisition as he is with the stimulation of prospects when it comes to money. The thought of financial increase becomes a mental challenge, a form of expression. Since he is so agile in the conception of ideas, he needs to pin some of them down. Sometimes he can outsmart himself by taking on too much or by being too facile. He is never at a loss for get-rich-quick schemes and if he does his homework, can become very successful in the financial arena through his brilliant ideas.

Since Gemini is the sign ruling this house of money, and Gemini is a dual sign, the restlessness and need for variety in financial areas is apparent. This person can easily do more than one thing. He frequently needs two major occupations in order to function most efficiently. His rapidity of thought and speech play a major role in his success. He deals with the public in a special way. His "voice" is the instrument of his financial well-being, and speech has much to do with his earning capacity. Many politicians are born with this ascendant. Golden-tongued narrative is essential when one seeks a political career, but the ability to keep abreast of financial trends and juggle personal finance is imperative as well. Thomas E. Dewey, Senator Charles E. Percy, and Presidents William Henry Harrison and Herbert Hoover share this ascendant. Robert Kennedy was born with Taurus rising. Money can be earned through the written word also. Poet Percy Bysshe Shelley, French philosopher Auguste Comte, and Carlos Castaneda were born with this ascendant. Perhaps the best example of the kind of earning ability that goes hand in hand with this personality is that of William Randolph Hearst. Words became the tool for building his empire. His tireless, restless need to spread the news created tremendous success. The reporting of daily events started the financial empire that spread to other areas. It is the written word that is most often associated with his financial power.

Even though one with Taurus rising is a worker, he prefers to earn money through mental activity rather than through purely physical labor. After he has conceived a plan, he will then put in the physical effort and energy that is needed to ensure its success. His ideas come first, then the directed execution of the project. His mind is never still when it comes to new ideas. He can have a problem concerning priorities. He may tend to scatter his energies by juggling too many things at once. As long as he is mentally stimulated, his projects will be a success. If he is bored, he will neglect to feed his ventures with positive intellectual energy.

The placement of Mercury in the chart will indicate the direction of the Taurus rising's financial focus. If Mercury is placed in the first house, the native earns money through his personality. Liza Minnelli has a Mercurial caste to her ascendant, since that planet is a co-ruler of her ascendant. She is a "personality," which enables her to earn money, especially through her voice. With Mercury placed in the second house, there is further emphasis on the earning capacity through mental means. Communications is the strongest motivating factor with a third house Mercury, whether writing, speaking, or singing. Ideas for negotiations can be a vehicle for financial success. When Mercury is posited in the fourth house, land and real estate, as well as mining, occupy the interests of the individual. Matters connected with "home base," such as restaurants and production of food, are important in this individual's interests and financial success.

When Mercury is in the fifth house, the individual is especially creative when it comes to financial matters. The stock market can also capture his attention. A gambling instinct is pronounced in his earning capacity and he may be attracted by anything that is risky, whether that pertains to investment or his own creative expression. With a sixth house placement, the focus is on service. Intellectually oriented work is essential to prevent boredom and poor health. Financial success can come through foods, health, medicine, or those services related to care of the sick. When Mercury is posited in the seventh house, partnership projects compel the native to look for someone to share his ideas, support his ventures, and join him in financial matters.

Money can be earned through inheritance, residuals, or dividends when Mercury is in the eighth house. With this position, the individual may earn his own funds through raising money. He can obtain venture capital for important financial projects. He is particularly able to convince others of the soundness of his plans and projects, if Mercury is well aspected in his chart. Advertising, promotional matters, and legal affairs are connected to finance with Mercury in the ninth house. Ideas concerning travel, lectures, and higher education can become lucrative. In many instances, ventures connected to countries other than that of birth are important to money matters. Publishing can be part of the overall financial success with this placement. He may be on his soapbox over important financial issues. Anything that is able to bring recognition or increased publicity to the individual will also bring financial reward. Importing and exporting, methods of travel, or distributing can capture his attention.

Career activity that is connected to mental activity is connected with financial matters when Mercury is placed in the tenth house of public life and career. Actors, speakers, and statesmen can succeed in the financial world as well as in their public world when Mercury is in this house. The speech, thoughts, and ideas of this individual project him into the public eye and increase his pocketbook at the same time. With an eleventh house position, there is an indication of strong group activity connected to the financial focus. Projects requiring the cooperation of working associates stimulate financial interests. Group effort is more enticing than single-minded activity for one with this placement. When Mercury is posited in the twelfth house, financial matters are connected to anything that remains behind the scenes. Writers earn money by working quietly out of the public eye. Singers who are involved in recordings rather than public performance fit this category. Actors working on closed sets are earning money "behind the scenes." Many times, this can be an indication of an unwillingness to tap the true financial potential. Since the second house is a clue to the spending habits, this person will be attracted to expenditures on intellectual pursuits, whether literature, theater, or thought-provoking events. He can also spend money whenever he is particularly mentally restive.

If the Taurus rising is not utilizing his ideas, thoughts, or speech in a financial way, it can bring about much frustration. The aspects to Mercury in an individual chart will indicate why the individual neglects to channel his ideas into positive, productive, and rewarding areas. If Mercury is in difficult aspect to Saturn, for instance, the individual thinks negatively, has a "poor" complex, and stops himself before he begins. A defeatist outlook can be due to early conditioning. If Mercury and Pluto are afflicting each other, the individual can be tempted to play games, manipulate funds, and generally pull the rug out from under himself by bad judgment. Mercury-Neptune aspects can keep the individual from seeing the overall picture. His analytical mind may get in the way of his vision. Mercury-Jupiter combinations may keep the native in hock due to extravagance, overexpectation, and overextension with funds. Mercury combined with Mars brings about an impatience and frustration which prevents clear thinking about financial matters. Since sound financial judgment depends on clear adult decisions when this sign is on the ascendant, it is essential for the individual to collect facts about his ventures and to analyze matters carefully before he leaps in. The most important consideration in his ultimate financial success is the prevention of boredom. A stimulating challenge is half the battle for one with Taurus on the rise.

COMMUNICATIONS

Along with the Taurus rising's special quality of charm and sociability goes a very sensitive manner of communication. This individual can be quite tuned in to public trends and people's needs. He expresses himself in a very perceptive manner. The Moon is the ruler of the third house of communications when Taurus is on the rise. The Moon is the planet that rules emotions, vulnerability, and feeling. If the Moon is well aspected in an individual chart, the person with this rising sign is particularly receptive to the people around him. If the Moon is not well aspected, he will overreact, get his feelings hurt, and take things too personally. His ability to discuss matters rationally may be low, no matter what the aspects in an individual chart. He reacts to others in accordance with his own emotional yardstick. This can work on his behalf if he has worked through his own emotional pain. He can then adopt a very protective, nurturing, mothering feeling toward people around him.

The Moon is the planet that relates to mankind in general and the "collective unconscious." Whatever one with this ascendant does to relate to his fellow man will bring emotional fulfillment. As long as he remains in the understanding, nurturing role, his own life is enriched. Martin Luther King became the spokesman for his people, and with great feeling discussed the needs of blacks everywhere. He became the "mother" of his people, in a sense. His own needs were the commodity in common with suppressed people of all races, so his pain became the barometer for all those in need of his protection and nurturing assistance. Carlos Castaneda touches people with stories of his own experiences. He reveals his own soul for others to see. Sarah Bernhardt, Saroyan, and Puccini, have one thing in common—their appeal to people through touching of others' feelings. The Moon is related to magnetism and public appeal. It is the planet of the subconscious mind, the anima part of the personality. As the Moon's rays pull on the tides, Taurus rising can pull on people's emotions. It is the planet that indicates special receptivity and rapport.

In early life, the person with this ascendant may be too vulnerable, moody, and emotional to do especially well in school. The Moon is the fastest-moving body in the heavens, so the moods can change drastically, every few hours. This child may relate to his siblings on an emotional level. In the positive sense, he develops protective feelings toward brothers and sisters. In a negative sense, he can be too easily hurt by them. His relationship with his family on an emotional level will indicate his development along lines of interpersonal relationships all through his life. If those early relationships are emotionally satisfying, he will easily assume the protective role in later life. He will love to take people under his wing and give comfort, but he can just as easily be hurt by lack of appreciation. He may sometimes appear quite chilly or short on sympathy, yet his attitude really depends on his ability to do something about the situation. If someone presents a problem to him that he can solve, he will be enormously receptive. On the other hand, a helplessness sets in if he is unable to help, and his defense mechanism is to appear unfeeling, uncaring. If the Moon is badly aspected in an individual chart, the person may turn inward, ignoring the plight of others as a self-protective device.

A child with this ascendant should be encouraged to let out his feelings in the family environment as well as in a creative way. If he learns early on to express his hurt and upsets, whether through talking it out, writing about it, or acting it out, he will learn to handle this vulnerable part of himself. Later on in life, he will turn this to his advantage, as it is this very sensitivity that enables him to reach the public in his own unusual way. A child with this ascendant needs ample opportunity to express himself artistically, for artistic expression can be a channel to release unresolved emotions. Otherwise, these feelings remain buried to haunt him throughout life. The Taurus rising is able to be in touch with the trends of the times, whether through artistry, words, politics, writing, speaking, or singing. He touches the emotions he shares with mankind and establishes sensitive bonds. Mia Farrow typifies this kind of vulnerable appeal through acting roles, as did Sarah Bernhardt. Liza Minnelli and Jenny Lind have revealed this quality through the voice. Kennedy and Martin Luther King showed the protective quality through politics and humanitarian concerns.

HOME LIFE

It is in the area of home life that the Taurus rising expresses his true pride and ego. It is especially important that he have the kind of home that reflects his true personality. Land and real estate mean more to him than to almost anyone else. Having his own piece of land gives him his greatest sense of self-worth. It roots and grounds him, and makes him secure. Even if he only works with products from the earth, he can express that need for grounding.

The Sun rules the fourth house of home with a Taurus ascendant. The Sun is the planet that indicates ego, vitality, pride, leadership, dominance. It is connected to the animus part of the personality and can give clues about the executive ability. No matter what sex, one with Taurus rising is the boss in his own home. He or she is the one who calls the shots, makes the decisions, and leads the parade. If the individual with this ascendant has a good sense of self-worth, he will naturally assume his right to have a magnificent home. If he does not think much of himself, he may not allow himself the kind of home situation he'd really like. His sense of self-worth, and therefore the kind of lifestyle he chooses, is very much related to his relationship with the parent of the opposite sex.

The fourth house in a chart shows how an individual has photographed the parent of the opposite sex. His clear identification depends on good strong pictures of that parent early on. The aspects to the Sun in an individual chart tell just how he sees that parent and precisely the facet he identifies with most readily. If the Sun has primarily good aspects, he has great pride in that parent. He naturally sees that parent as the dominant one, no matter what sex, and feels that parent has lived up to his potential and shown leadership or executive ability. However, if the Sun is not well aspected, he may photograph that parent with a lack of ego that affects his feelings about himself. Consequently, he chooses a lifestyle that does not truly reflect his inner sense of self-worth. Since there is such strong inner identification with that parent, he may subconsciously be unwilling to surpass that parent. If the Sun is well aspected, pride in his parent translates into healthy pride in himself, and he will be able to choose a home or lifestyle that reflects a good sense of self-worth.

The fourth house also indicates the conditions in the third portion of an individual's earth existence. In many instances, an individual has the potential not only to live up to the image of that parent, but to accomplish things the parent was unable to fulfill in his own life. The parental role model will indicate how easy it is for him to assume his own executive, leadership potential later on. If the individual has taken up the gauntlet and set greatness as his goal, he clearly can achieve success and recognition as he grows older. The aspects to the Sun in his chart will give clues as to his willingness to do just that.

If the Sun and Saturn are badly aspected in his chart, the person with the Taurus ascendant sees the parent of the opposite sex as having a deep insecurity. The strong judgmental, severe, "be safe" messages he receives from that parent, either overtly or subconsciously, will prevent him from feeling truly good about himself. He may not be sure about his leadership quality, or be unwilling to assume that kind of responsibility. If the Sun is in difficult aspect to Neptune, that parent may have set himself up for disillusion by setting unrealistic goals. The Taurus rising may not set high standards for himself for fear that he will fail and become disillusioned, as the parent was. Sun-Mars aspects indicate frustration on the part of the parent, as well as impatience and anger. Sun-Uranus aspects can be a clue to the rebellious nature or "inverted" genius he inherited. With the Sun in difficult aspect to Pluto, the parent may have been compulsive, overly forceful, or game-playing. The individual is then inclined to put too much pressure on others, play some games—and he eventually will pull the rug out from under himself. With bad aspects to Venus, the individual sees the parent as being lazy or taking the easy way out. Jupiterian aspects, if difficult, can indicate overexpectation, overextension. The native may have been disappointed in the life of that parent.

Observation of the kind of home one with this rising sign lives in can give strong clues as to the overall sense of pride. It is up to the individual to reward himself for a job well done, if there was a lack of ego recognition coming from the parent of the opposite sex. He must learn to evaluate himself in a healthier way. With proper attention, he is able to release more energy by feeling good about himself and allowing his lifestyle to truly reflect the inner values.

ROMANCE • CREATIVE EXPRESSION

Virgo is the sign that lies on the cusp of the fifth house when Taurus is ascending. The ruler of Virgo is Mercury, the mental planet. Since Mercury rules the second house of money as well, it is clear that there is a natural tie-in between money and fifth house activities. The fifth house in a chart shows creative tendencies, the kind of self-expression that comes most naturally, the quality of the gambling instincts, if any, and how one feels about romance and children. In some instances, the ability to express oneself through words, ideas, thoughts, and speech can be a part of the overall financial success. Projects connected to children's interests can be tied in to financial activity, or the stock market can bring success. This house also describes the quality of entertainment, and the kind of personality and experience one looks for in a romantic situation.

The Virgo Mercury is more practical than the airy Gemini Mercury. It is in the areas ruled by the Virgo Mercury that one with a Taurus ascendant will be most analytical and adult. He will spend time researching a creative project. He will feel it necessary to collect all the data he can concerning any invest-

ment or situation requiring creative ability. His gambling instincts are more calculated than impulsive. Inadvertently, he
produces children who are mentally polarized, and are quite
adult. He will relate to them on an intellectual level rather than
a feeling level, and must take care not to criticize unnecessarily.
He will certainly be aware of all the faults with a romantic interest and will be attracted to someone with an analytical approach to life, or someone who is at least highly intelligent, data
collecting, and research-oriented.

Mercury's placement in a chart also describes what the person
thinks about. This individual thinks about romance, his children,
his ability to entertain, and his investments. Claude Philippe was
a master at organizing massive entertainment projects, first as
the banquet manager of the Waldorf-Astoria, then with the
April in Paris Ball. No detail was overlooked. Sylviane Sans in
creating a theater in Caracas had, of necessity, to be aware of all
the nit-picky problems connected with the design. Her creative
self-expression with architecture is clearly connected to a thorough analysis of a situation at hand. David Henesy must be
aware of current prices in the commodities market in order to
complete transactions he makes with large quantities of food.
Technique is essential for an actor with this ascendant. He will
be gifted in analyzing roles. Writers with this rising sign must
spend their creative hours carving form out of their imagination,
researching an idea.

Again, it is the aspects to Mercury in an individual chart that
will indicate how easy it is for this individual to get in touch
with his natural creative instincts. His biggest danger can come
from too much analysis in the area of self-expression. If, for instance, Mercury in an individual chart is in difficult aspect to Saturn, this person takes a defeatist, negative attitude before he
begins. If Mercury and Pluto are in bad combination, the individual may be less cautious and more compulsive with the stock
market. Mercury-Neptune aspects indicate an unwillingness to
see the overall picture and be inspired. (Again, too much attention to detail.) Mercury-Mars brings impatience. Mercury-
Jupiter, overexpectancy; Mercury-Uranus too much rebellious,
high-strung energy. Whatever one with Taurus ascendant wishes
to accomplish in his own creative expression, you can be sure it

will be as perfect as is possible. Attention to detail is a natural talent no matter what the vehicle or direction.

WORK • SERVICE • HEALTH

It is important for one with Taurus rising to enjoy his work or he will simply not perform to the best of his ability. The other side of the coin is that he will love to work if it is work he loves. If he puts himself in a less than harmonious work environment, he will find that his energy is low and he is unable to accomplish what he must. Beauty and harmony are essential to his soul. If he is surrounded by strife and discord, he may get sick. However, if small problems arise, he will jump to the occasion and be the perfect arbitrator and negotiator. As a natural diplomat, it is really his job to keep everyone and everything on an even keel.

Venus is the planet that rules the sixth house of work, service, and health. Venus is the planet of beauty, sociability, charm, culture, graciousness, and the arts. Since Venus is also the ruler of Taurus, it is clear that when Taurus is on the ascendant this individual needs to find work that not only is harmonious but is an outlet for his true Taurus personality. His service capacity is connected to bringing beauty to people. His natural sense of artistry impels him to be involved in projects connected to design, food, clothing, art, pleasure. Since the pleasure principle is so strong in his personality, anything that is pleasurable is also successful. He is a natural artist and artisan. If Venus is well aspected in his chart, he has no problems in selecting pleasurable, artistic projects for his occupation. If Venus is badly aspected, however, there is a tendency to take the easy way out for the sake of peace, or even be lazy with work and artistic occupation.

The sixth house also indicates the health of an individual. Venus indicates a natural sweet tooth, so if Venus is not well aspected in the chart, there is a possibility of hypoglycemia or diabetes. No matter what the aspects to Venus, the biggest detriment to good health is indulgence in rich, luscious foods and drink that can be hard to assimilate in the system. Laziness can lead to lack of exercise and lack of proper body tone as a result.

Beautiful food can be especially enticing to one with this ascendant. With a tendency to self-indulgence, the person with this ascendant can discover that a surfeit of pleasure can lead to no energy and may contribute to a possibly already lazy tendency.

One of the positive ways of utilizing this need to indulge is through cooking. The person with this ascendant has a natural ability with the preparation of food, making it beautiful to look at as well as to taste. Many people with Taurus on the rise spend time learning gourmet cooking to augment a natural talent. The Taurus rising's artistry will shine forth in table arrangements, flowers, crystal, and silver that complete the painting he creates with edibles.

MARRIAGE • PARTNERSHIP

Early marriage is a strong possibility for one with this ascendant. With Pluto ruling the seventh house of marriage and partnership, there is almost a compulsion for partnership of some kind, whether in business or in personal life. Venus-ruled people crave companionship more than most. The sensual nature of one with Taurus on the ascendant makes it natural for him to seek someone who typifies the response he craves from a mate. It is in this area that he may be more adventurous than practical, however. He can rush into a partnership situation with all the blinders intact. Even if he senses a mistake, he may go forth so compulsively and forcefully that no one could stop him.

The planet Pluto is associated with power, magnetism, compulsion. In terms of Transactional Analysis, it relates to the child ego state. A child's strongest message is: "I want what I want when I want it, even if it hurts me, and nobody's going to stop me." Wherever Pluto is located in an individual chart is the area where those compulsions are most likely to be directed. More than likely, the person with a Taurus ascendant is attracted by a childlike quality in a partner, even if it is carefully hidden. A child symbolizes fun and games. The magnetic personality of a Plutonian type of person appeals to the pleasure-loving Taurean. He releases his own child ego in selecting a partner. If he is not naturally able to get in touch with his need to be powerful and potent, he may look for a mate to express it for him. He can be attracted to someone who appears exotic, magnetic, but is perhaps manipulative. Since he makes his partnership selection based on his child ego's need to play, he may not make particularly adult decisions. He can be drawn to one who is inwardly powerful or rebellious. He may be expressing his own inner rebellion by picking someone his family or friends will not approve of, or he can be attracted to someone who wields tremendous influence and tremendous charismatic appeal.

The aspects to the planet Pluto will indicate how fortunate the individual is in the healthy choice of mate or business partner. It will also describe the person who is the partner. If Pluto is well aspected in a particular chart, the Taurus rising will find himself associated with someone who is dynamic, potent, and powerful. That power will take the form of a relaxed, easy quality, rather than an overly forceful one. That partner is able to accomplish things with little effort, and has the kind of magnetic personality that draws people to his side instantly. The personality is especially dynamic and intense, but has a peculiar wash of innocence, in spite of an exotic quality as well. Life will never be dull with this type of partner by the side of Taurus ascendant.

If Pluto is badly aspected in the chart, the individual with this ascendant will find he has jumped from the frying pan into the fire. His compulsion and rebellion will lead him to someone who is manipulative, game-playing, a gambler at heart. The Taurus rising may discover he has put himself in a situation where the rug will inevitably be pulled out from under him. In order to upgrade the quality of marriage and partnership it is essential for one with this ascendant to avoid setting up the circumstances where the partner feels it necessary to manipulate him. In the worst sense, this aspect has been described by someone as "putting on a blindfold, walking to the edge of a diving board, and jumping into a bottomless pit." Since the individual has been compulsive about the union, he will rarely admit he has made a mistake. His true test will come in the willingness to let go of a person or partnership situation if it doesn't fall into place easily. If he has to play games to obtain the relationship or feels he must manipulate to attract that individual, it is probably

the wrong person. If he has an ulterior motive, the partnership
will blow up in his face.

Wherever Pluto is posited in a chart can indicate the most dynamic change in a person's life. If Pluto is well aspected for one
with Taurus ascendant, he will find his life changed for the best
by a fantastic marriage or business partnership. Taurus rising
is energized by the Scorpio-type partner, whereas the Plutonian
partner is "sweetened" by Taurus. Both will obtain unforeseen
benefits through the essence of the partner's personality. It is
the area in his life where Taurus rising must "let go" and trust
his instincts. The joy of the compelling relationship will keep
him happy and stimulated on a very powerful level. An ability to
"play" together will create a dynamic bond. Partnership will be
either the best thing that ever happened to him or the very
worst.

NEEDS

The eighth house in a chart is the house of "other people's
money" in terms of "traditional" astrology. In more psychological
terms, it is the way we get our needs met and therefore the quality of energy we have to send out to humanity. When Taurus is
on the rise, the planet Jupiter rules this house. Jupiter is the
planet of luck and abundance. It indicates wealth, optimism,
and wealth of spirit. The natural expectancy and enthusiasm
connected to the Taurus ascendant brings wonderful good fortune to him all his life. If he needs something from someone, his
contagious good humor enables him to get what he needs and
wants most easily. He will be most fortunate in establishing his
goals and selling others on his ideas. Consequently, he is generous to a fault, outgoing, and encouraging to others. His greatest
gift to humanity is his good-humored philosophical nature and
his ability to "give permission" to those around him. He needs
financial challenge, being bored with routine, and therefore en-
courages others to take chances with their lives and financial
well-being. His willingness to give is the quality that enables
him to get.

The difficulty with this aspect is the tendency to overextend, run up bills due to optimism and high expectations, and set the stage for a big letdown. Jupiter and Venus are the two "benefics" in a chart. Things are never dark where these planets are concerned. The one with Taurus ascendant is more fortunate than he realizes in his ability to attract wonderful things in his life. It is "easy" in many respects. His greatest danger is in overdoing things. If he suffers too many disappointments, he paralyzes himself in the financial arena. This person wants, above all, to be challenged in financial areas. If he has a goal, he will set out after it with high hopes, enormous enthusiasm, great expectancy, and will more than likely accomplish what he started out to do. He will have especially high goals if humanitarian concerns are at the back of his projects. The knowledge that he is helping others will encourage him to "full speed ahead." He may have to avoid rescue missions, for this is where he can set himself up for big disappointments.

If Jupiter is well aspected in the chart, he will live up to his goals, react to challenges, and share his wealth, no matter what form that wealth takes. Abundance of help, money, and philosophy are his for the asking. If Jupiter is not well aspected in the chart, disappointment may prevent him from setting goals and letting himself be stimulated to take chances. The fear of disappointment can paralyze him. If he is able to reach high for his goals and then allow for discounts, he will discover he can prevent major discouragement. He may always need to ask for more than he needs and wants, and then settle for less. He can be stimulated by having many projects going on at once. In fact, it is probably wise for him to have many irons in the fire, for that increases the chances that some of his plans will work out some of the time.

RECOGNITION

With Saturn ruling the ninth house of recognition, the Taurus rising may have some fears about getting the kind of recognition which he is really capable of attracting. For one thing, Saturn implies routine and restriction which may keep him from enjoying the ease of living and sense of expansion he so desperately wants. In a sort of perverse way, he may inadvertently trap himself in lesser forms of routine which keep him tied down and away from recognition. On a subconscious level, there can be a "deep down" fear of attracting any extra kind of limelight. Not only does Saturn ruling the ninth house imply responsibility on a high level but perhaps also a sense of burden in connection with publicity or recognition.

Saturn is the planet that indicates the heaviest karmic situation to be dealt with in this lifetime. It is the planet that relates to restriction, fear, guilt, insecurity, duty. In a negative sense it means limitation, but the positive interpretation is responsibility. The ninth house is the house of promotional effort, publicity, travel, higher education, publishing, legal affairs, philosophy, and the higher mind. These are the areas that require focus when Taurus is on the rise, but often they are the very areas the native tends to avoid.

The Kabbalists call Saturn the "playpen" that Mother Nature puts her children into. A playpen represents safety and security, yet it is restrictive. When a child is ready to take care of himself, he is released from its boundaries. We are placed in a kind of playpen that keeps us safe until we are ready to assume higher responsibility for ourselves. Many times that playpen is a psychological one. Saturn is also related to the parent ego state, that is, the judgmental part of ourselves. In a positive sense, the parent also takes care of us. When we are really ready to assume the level of duty Saturn implies, we also begin taking care of ourselves on a new plateau. We may never walk away from the inner pressures, yet we can upgrade them considerably.

The individual with this ascendant will be exceedingly responsible and reliable with any task he assumes in connection with travel, diplomacy, dealings with other countries. He is good at research and detail. He may keep himself under his own thumb to prevent attracting too much attention, for attention carries its own penalties. For Martin Luther King and Bobby Kennedy, the call of duty and responsibility was so overwhelming it had to be heeded, yet the penalty was indeed high. Amelia Earhart, with Taurus rising, made a profound contribution to aviation through her willingness to take the lonely, pioneering road. For all these heroes, honor and acclaim are heaped upon them forever for their willingness to take up the sword of truth and duty. It is possible that this impelling kind of duty is carried over from a previous time in memory. These courageous people with Taurus rising may have had little choice in their own minds but to do what they had to do.

That kind of penalty is certainly not preordained for everyone with this ascendant, but on some level this kind of fear is probable for anyone with this ascendant. The call to duty implies hardship of some kind, even if that hardship is simply loss of privacy. The Taurus rising cares too much about his public image and what people may think. He would suffer tremendously with bad press or publicity. He cares about his reputation. It is easier to stay out of the prying eye of the public rather than chance disaster. If Saturn is badly aspected in the chart, the avoidance will be extreme. If it is well aspected, the call to duty will be easier to assume. Until that ultimate responsibility is really clear, the person with Taurus rising can put himself under interesting pressures. Bill Danoff chose to study Chinese in college, a ninth house activity. The kind of hard work and diligence required to learn such a language is obvious. Later on, however, he gained recognition for himself by writing hit songs and being published. His composition "Country Roads," written with and sung by John Denver, was a step in the right direction. Later on, with his beautiful wife, Taffy, he formed a group and had his own television show. The song "Afternoon Delight" was but one more in a string of hit songs and records.

In the most negative sense, the person with this ascendant can receive a recognition that is coupled with horror. Both Charles Manson and mass murderer Adolf Eichmann were born with this ascendant. It is interesting to observe that there seem to be fewer well-known people with Taurus rising than with other rising signs. The unwillingness to work through fears or give up the good life may be one explanation. It is certainly not for the lack of capability. Exploration of karmic fears can release much energy in these directions. The awareness of what fears those memories hold can set the individual on a whole new path.

CAREER

The planet Uranus rules the house of career with this house placement. Uranus is the planet of "genius," freedom, humanity, or rebellion. The Taurus rising is capable of doing tremendously humanitarian things in his public life if he is in touch with that part of his nature, or he can refuse to let himself take the chances necessary to achieve greatness. He is capable of attracting great fame through his public life if he is able to work through the "scare" connected with that kind of recognition.

The tenth house in a chart is also indicative of the relationship with the parent of the same sex. The photographs the individual took of his same-sex parent early in life are most important in the development of his potential. He seems to tune in to one facet of the personality of this parent, which points the way for his future career interests. It appears that the parent has "genius" qualities and a humanitarian and avant-garde approach to life. Uranus in a negative sense can indicate a high-strung nervous disposition or, in a positive interpretation, a musical or inventive ability. If Uranus is well aspected in the chart, the parent has allowed himself to live up to his potential and is therefore a good role model for the native with Taurus rising. If that parent has achieved some degree of greatness or fame or has taken healthy, positive chances with his own career, the Taurus personality is better able to take those chances connected to his own career. If that planet is not well aspected, the parent may resist the unique part of himself, and try to go against the extra "electrical" energy penetrating his system. Taurus rising becomes rebellious in his own career, or perhaps resists healthy risks necessary for his true success.

In many cases, this sign can represent an "alcoholic" personality on the part of the parent, whether that parent indulged in excess drinking or not. A general tendency toward impulse, spontaneity, or nervousness is possible as well. Uranus can describe a hysterical quality. It is as if that parent has an extra amount of electricity racing through his system. Sometimes there is a combination of both positive and negative manifestations of

Uranus, but if the parent has been able to utilize his unique qualities constructively, the nervous predisposition is greatly lessened. Therefore the photographs are more in focus. Liza Minnelli photographed her mother's high-strung energy, her fame, and her erratic behavior, as well as a tendency to drink too much. Yet the overwhelming odds stacked on the side of talent enabled her to successfully realize her own fame. Her brother and sister may have photographed a different facet of their mother's personality. Bobby Kennedy evidently related to the avant-garde part of his father's personality. His father, incidentally, participated in the distribution of alcohol.

When Uranus is badly aspected in the chart of one with a Taurus ascendant, there is also the possibility of an abrupt departure by that parent. This individual could see that parent as being unpredictable, unable to bear much pressure, and somewhat unreliable. In his own career, he may blow things up prematurely by taking off at just the wrong moment. It may be that just as matters appear most uncertain with his own career situation, he can be blasted into high recognition. This aspect can also indicate strong seven-year cycles. He may never be able to work for anyone else, as his own need for freedom is so great that he will have to do some sort of work that allows for his own time schedule.

The planet Uranus ruling the tenth house of career also indicates a strong messianic complex. He can wish to be the torch bearer to humanity by acting as a catalyst for others. He will have to learn to let go of the people he puts together, or he may feel left out at times. He needs to ensure his own freedom of action in order to combine new groups, new people. An ever progressing need for new experiences will keep this person stimulated in his public life. Uranus rules awakening on a spiritual level. The lesson the Taurus rising may have to learn is somewhat like learning to let plaster fall, in order to create new walls. The change can be nerve-racking, the results splendid.

Matters connected to healing, metaphysics, astrology, music, recordings, and electronics are connected to the planet Uranus. Uranus also rules inventions. The planet Uranus was discovered simultaneously with electricity. Any of these areas are perfect for the release of this unusual kind of eccentric, electrical energy. No matter what occupation one with this ascendant chooses, it is obvious that his own special inventive quality will be stamped on the end product. He must be willing to take many chances, work through his own fear in order to achieve his potential in the public arena. Fame, on some level, is very possible for one with this ascendant.

FRIENDSHIP

With Pisces ruling the house of group associations, friendships, and interrelationships, the individual with this ascendant may put his loved ones on a pedestal. The planet Neptune is the planet of vision or myopia. If this planet is well aspected in the chart, the individual is attracted to people of great vision. Yet he may still expect them to be perfect in all respects. If that planet is not well aspected, he can put his friends on a pedestal, never seeing their faults and setting himself up for a major disillusionment if he is ever let down by them.

If one with this particular need for artistic and loving expression is involved in group activity with high goals and high purpose, he is able to handle this quality of energy well. He may have to read the fine print, in many instances, to avoid deception. He may expect all those participating in a project to have the same high ideals as himself and find himself surprised when they do not. He can deal with the glamour world easily if this aspect is strong in his chart. If not, he may be unrealistic about how glamorous the glamour world really is. Wherever Neptune is placed in a chart is indicative of the area where an individual tends to be naïve. He loves the rose-colored glasses he wears and he may be unable to confront situations easily. He fears never having a dream again if he sees the cold harsh truth of a situation or about a person. If he can look at the truth and retain his sense of idealism within group situations or with friendships, this person with a Venus outlook on life is ahead of the game.

There have been too many sad stories of misunderstandings between friends in business where deals were based on their supposed mutual trust. Somehow it seems unsociable to ask for agreements in writing between friends, yet in the case of one with Taurus rising, especially if Neptune is not well situated in his chart, it is imperative to have firm, concrete agreements about any visionary projects. If this person is able to get commitments in writing or clarity about goals he can count on the conditions agreed upon. If not, it is better to disregard idealistic concepts and dreams that can't be pinned down.

One gentleman with this ascendant found a large portion of land for future investment and development. He wanted to share this with his good friend, so he loaned him the money to join him in the purchase. Years later, when the value of that land had skyrocketed, the friend asked to be bought out. The gentleman with Taurus rising then paid him the going rate for the same land he could have bought by himself. His disillusion with that particular friendship was most upsetting. Clarification of intent, with legally binding agreements, will actually protect a treasured friendship from any future difficulties. If Neptune is well aspected in the individual chart, the probability is that the group projects he participates in are not only far-reaching but practical and legal at the very outset.

HIDDEN MATTERS • SUBCONSCIOUS PROCESS

Aries is on the cusp of the twelfth house when Taurus is ascending. The ruler of Aries is Mars, the planet of aggression, activity, ambition, and drive. It is also the ruler of sex and warfare. Twelfth house matters are less easy to express overtly than what is indicated by the first house, or ascendant. It is easy for the Taurus rising to show his sensuality and love nature, but less easy to show aggression, frustration, temper, and ambition. As a child, the person with this ascendant is so sweet, easygoing, and loving that one would never suspect the temper lurking behind that charming facade. Because that energy is difficult for him to express, when it emerges it is overwhelming.

In a safe situation, the person is able to release his true aggressive energies. He will be most ambitious in the deepest recesses of his mind, yet only shows his easygoing sociability. It may be difficult, early on, to be easily in touch with his sexuality, preferring to keep that part of his nature in the dark. Since

Mars also rules physical activity, the Taurus on the rise may not be inclined to competitive physical exercise or sports. He prefers more sociable activity. His competitive nature may not be well developed or easily expressed. His sexual experiences may be well hidden—part of a guilt complex. He may also hide the fighting, truly innovative, creative, and pioneering part of his nature.

The more the Taurus rising is able to release his pent-up creative, sexual energy in healthy ways, the less frustration he has to bear privately. Since the sexual energy is coupled with creative energy, the release can come on many levels, but without any release, it builds to become temper, frustration, impatience, and overwhelming aggravation. Things may never happen fast enough for one with this ascendant, so he appears to be rather deliberate in his haste to get ahead. He may have difficulty in allowing himself to be truly pioneering enough to express the innovative part of his creative energy. Laziness and too much ease of living can weaken his resolve to get going on some of his projects.

This native may have hidden rage, while only showing his diplomatic side. Since Mars rules physical exercise and metals, if he releases some of that rage and frustration with activity using metals, he will find himself free of unusual aggravations and temper. A writer can use a metal typewriter to release pent-up frustrations; a painter using a palette knife or doing metal sculpture finds his outlet. Actors working on closed sets use up much of their creative energy, and singers in recording sessions release their frustrations through a great deal of physical activity. One with this ascendant will discover that working with metal tools, building things, and getting exercise, when alone, are marvelous ways to rechannel some of his creative energy onto a new level. The fine contribution made to the reformation of the human condition by one with this ascendant is worth the effort of breaking through the barriers, working through the scare, and letting out the unique part of the creative energy.

GEMINI RISING

LIFE IS NEVER DULL AROUND A Gemini rising. One with this personable rising sign can keep you entertained for hours on end because he can't stand to be bored himself. He needs constant mental stimulation because his active mind simply will not rest. Therefore, you'll find him surrounded by people, activity, and exciting situations. His keynote may well be: "Life is just a bowl of cherries." He is witty, amusing, and lots of fun.

The ruler of Gemini is the planet Mercury. This is the planet that indicates mentality, thought, speech. Since Gemini is an air sign, the swiftness of the intellect is even more pronounced. The person with this ascendant is a fascinating conversationalist, as words and ideas are his specialty. The word "mercurial" fits his facile mentality to a tee.

In mythology, Mercury was the messenger of the gods. Mercury was the servant and beloved of Jupiter. Even though he frequently chose to use situations to his own end, he remained the interpreter to whom many secrets were entrusted. He could move with the speed of lightning and excelled in mental agility. It was very difficult, if not impossible, to pin him down and capture him. This analogy can help one understand the individual with Gemini ascending, as the personality can be puckish, mischievous, and tricky. Yet he bears no malice and holds no grudges. Like Mercury, he is hard to pin down, as his safety depends on quick flight. He can switch gears so quickly that you'll be unaware of what's happened. You're still pondering one situation while he has ascended to another plane and is off on another tack. You'll have to be on your toes at all times just to keep up with him. You may be in big trouble if you try to outsmart him, or enter into a contest of wit or will. Just occasionally, however, he goes one step too far and outsmarts himself.

The symbol of Gemini is the twins. A Gemini is accused of having a dual personality; indeed, he may actually be fickle. He probably feels safer if he has two situations in his life at once, whether in his personal life or in his business life. He can certainly switch gears and do two jobs more easily than someone less agile. However, the true duality has to do with his need to be close and his need to be objective at the same time. He is a walking example of the closeness-freedom syndrome. On the one hand, he needs love almost more than most people, but the minute he allows himself to become truly close to someone, his freedom is endangered. He then must pull away to become more objective.

Venus is the esoteric ruler of this sign. The person with Gemini rising is really looking for his true love. He searches endlessly, perhaps without really knowing why. He may not consciously feel he is lacking in any way. But in an intimate situation, he keeps one eye on the horizon, just in case his true, *true* love should appear. It may be difficult for him to express this need for love, so his safety depends on his lack of total commitment. He is poised for flight at all times. He may be fickle only on a mental level, but you can be sure he has explored many avenues of exciting fantasy in his mind. His standard of virtue may be slightly different than what is generally presumed. He can experiment in many ways without feeling the least bit disloyal. In fact, he would be astonished if you accused him of neglecting those close to him, even when his wandering eye takes him into deep water. He can be happily married and still need to have a tiny corner of his mind open to new possibilities. If the Gemini rising is truly in love, however, it is forever. If he feels safety in that love, he will devote himself unstintingly to its cause. His whole life will respond to the excitement of that attachment. He will be totally and wholly committed. He won't have to resort to words to express his feelings, for there is no one so obviously ardent in love as the one with Gemini rising. It shines through his whole being when it's real. That may be the one time when words desert him altogether, for he'll have no need of their protection.

All signs have a negative and a positive expression, but perhaps none is more extreme and varied than with Gemini rising. Since it is a dual sign to begin with, its duality takes on interesting colors. The level of evolution seems to manifest itself in the

kind of mental activity he indulges in. The evolved type is
dedicated to the uplifting of humanity. His keen insight and
brilliance of achievement can produce great literature, drama,
and poetry. His dynamic personality can vitalize words that
remain meaningless otherwise. Some of the greatest contributions to literature, politics, music, and theater have come from
those with Gemini rising. When one with this ascendant is given
a mission of the noblest nature, he is activated to use his brilliant mind to reach humanity on a profound level, but he must
use his mental energy in constructive ways or his restlessness
can get him into trouble.

The negative expression of the personality reveals a gossip, an
instigator, and a game player. He can enjoy attracting people for
the sake of the attention and to see what he can get from them.
He is good at keeping others on a string, just for the fun of seeing how much he can rope them in and out. He may have the
unfortunate tendency to run away from the very people who
care the most. He can be a will-o'-the-wisp. The grass may always look greener on the other side of the fence. In his quest for
exciting adventure, he may not care who gets hurt in the bargain. He is less concerned with others' feelings than with his
own need for activity and variety. He can use people to his own
ends. Actually, he is only concerned with his own life, his own
observations, and his needs. He talks only about himself and his
interests—and that barrage of words and frantic need for activity
may well prevent him from standing still long enough to really
face himself.

If he understands his true nature, it can be through this very
restlessness that the Gemini rising learns and grows. In esoteric
terms, the symbol of the twins is truly the duality of the human
condition. Each man is both body and soul. When the inner adventure begins, and true integration occurs, the Gemini rising
becomes one. The pull of the pair of polar opposites can be intense, causing the Gemini rising to swing rapidly like a pendulum, until he understands the necessity of bringing the spiritual
and the mundane together within himself. His spiritual needs
become as strong as his need to experience life. He finally learns
how to provide himself with what he truly requires to become
whole and fulfilled. He realizes that his true yearning and

searching is for union with his inner and higher self. His spiritual growth becomes profound. True integration means never being bored again.

Until that time, it may appear that the Gemini rising talks from both sides of his mouth. That may very well be true. He not only sees both sides of the coin, he lives them. The confusion inside this individual can be profound until he has found his way. At the extreme, schizophrenic personalities exhibit some of these tendencies. The duality with the Gemini rising may be so intense that he cannot face some of the things he is doing, so he blocks out the negative and hides behind the positive. Avoidance of the ultimate experience of integration compels him to keep things moving in a very fast way. When he has had enough of the less than savory experiences he finds himself attracted to, he can come full swing and express his need for adventure in a different way. His total devotion to family and friends is obvious. He delivers a high spiritual and moral message by his behavior. He shares his depth of understanding and his joy.

This person should be allowed to follow an apparently erratic course, as this eventually leads him to his highest expression. He can appear irresponsible at times, as he will not allow himself to be trapped under heavy and dampening pressures. Drudgery or routine can squelch his enthusiasm and spirit faster than anything else. He needs to be valued and appreciated, but can't handle obligation. He may not be much help when sickness or problems arise. If pressure is brought to bear, or life temporarily deals him a difficult hand, this person may disappear for a period of time in order to sort things out and solve his own problems by himself. He will use this quiet time to restore his perspective, gather his thoughts, recoup his boundless energy. He may look for greener pastures occasionally, just to test his theories, charm, and magnetism. He wants to be sure they still work so he can come back to you a more interesting personality. He may also pull away to remind you, in his own subtle way, that you really need him. Life can be a lot less colorful without him around.

When he is not on safe ground, or is in a less than safe situation, he can remove himself without ever leaving the scene. If this person decides to shut you out, his usual warmth disappears behind a cloud and the chill that is left is very penetrating. You may wonder what you've said to displease him, or you may suspect he is angry or upset. If you force the attention back to you, he can resent the intrusion. He may not really know he has left you so far out in the cold, and then again, he may want to see how much he can get away with before you protest. Or he may simply be scared and feel the need to take a brief vacation from the threat of the moment.

Part of his enormous appeal and magnetism is that you may never know quite where you stand with this individual. Just when you're about to take your relationship for granted, you'll find him behaving in his distant manner. When you decide he's bored and about to take flight, he'll come back in his most charming, gracious, and loving way to captivate you all over again. This kind of drama can prevent boredom in a most unusual—and exasperating—way. His attitude may appear to be "out of sight, out of mind," for he deals with matters at hand. His concentration is intense, but he can immediately focus in on another topic. When you come into view again, he tunes in to the "file" he has on you and for the moment, at least, you receive his undivided attention. Quick changes are part of his personality and only occasionally is he really scattered, although to others' eyes that's how he can appear. Darting from one topic to another to challenge the restlessness of his intellect is the way his mind works best. He is a collector of trivia and random information. He can be a walking encyclopedia. He is the one who remembers the lyrics to a song that everyone else has forgotten. The way to keep him intrigued is to be well informed about many subjects, but above all, be a good listener.

It can be a tricky matter dealing with a tricky Gemini rising. He can outtalk you, outthink you, and probably outsmart you. He can certainly outmaneuver you. He'll only respect you if you can keep up with him, yet he won't like it if you get ahead of him. You can't let him get away with too much or you're no challenge, but you can't call him on everything or you'll be putting him under too much pressure and he'll simply walk away. He is probably waiting for you to break through his quicksilver façade and discover the depth that is waiting there, like buried treasure. If you take him at face value, you'll miss much of his true worth. It can be a challenge to keep up with all that energy, that spirited front, that duality, yet life will be a rich experience if your patience holds out. A sense of humor can help a great deal. Expect the best of him, overlook his transgressions, and you'll find a pot of gold at the end of the rainbow.

In the language of Transactional Analysis, Mercury relates to the adult ego state. The adult part of ourselves is the part that can collect facts, clearly say what we mean, disseminate information, and communicate. The individual with Mercury ruling the ascendant expresses his adult ego most easily. It can be extremely important to relate to a child with this rising sign on an intellectual level. If he is given permission early in life to express himself and is encouraged to utilize his restless, inquisitive mentality in experimentation on a high level, he will learn how to channel his thoughts in the right direction. It is essential to deal with this child on a totally honest level and to explain things to him. He is aware early on that he is an adult at a very young age. His salvation comes with self-expression. If he can clearly state his needs, ask for what he wants, state opinions without fear of reprisal, he has a better chance of living up to his extraordinary potential. School will only be a problem for him if he finds it boring or slow. He is liable to skim the surface, however, leaving the drudgery and research to others. He wants to be on to more exciting territory. If he is not allowed to express his true curiosity or if life is fearful or tedious, his self-protection is to retreat into his fantasy life. He cannot take too much punishment or heavy judgment, for not only is he mercurial, but he is deeply sensitive.

Consider holding a ball of mercury in the palm of your hand. If you hold it gently, it nestles in one spot, but if you push your finger down, it simply slides away. This is what happens to a child with this ascendant when too much pressure is brought to bear. He slides into his rich imagination and retreats inside himself. Experimentation begins early on with one who has Gemini rising. This child needs to be surrounded by lofty but totally realistic values early in his life. He is more than desirous of pleasing his family and associates, but may show only what he thinks is acceptable. If his perceptions don't coincide with the family values, then he goes into hiding. He is a no-nonsense child and is very perceptive at an early age. He rarely becomes judgmental; he believes in "live and let live." You can appeal to him through logic and ideas, yet he arrives at his own truth through the process of epistemology. He wants to look at both sides of an issue and then make up his own mind.

Since the ascendant is the mask or façade and it indicates the way one keeps oneself safe, it is interesting to observe what happens when one with Gemini rising is confronted with a new or unsure situation, either socially or in business. He will engage in conversation, perhaps darting from one subject to another, or he'll ramble on, never seeming to come to the point. This gives him time to size up the occasion, get himself on safe ground, and decide how he wants to relate to a particular person or situation. Mental activity keeps him on familiar ground. Marion Weisberg, a successful and brilliant therapist with this ascendant, said she finally became aware of the fact that she hid behind her mind. Early decisions have to do with the safety of words. The Gemini rising will survive as long as he can use his brain, collect facts, and communicate. But all this left-brain mental activity may keep him from tuning in to his real love nature—intellectual stimulation is easier to handle than emotional involvement. It is important to encourage children with this ascendant to organize their thoughts, say what they mean and mean what they say, and look for intellectual challenges that lead toward a goal.

The placement of Mercury in the chart and its aspects to the other planets will indicate the focus of the mind and thoughts of a particular individual with this ascendant. It also indicates the quality of his expression and what he talks about. For instance, Mercury in the first house emphasizes the need for self-expression. In the second house, the focus is on financial matters. He earns money through mental activity and through the force of his personality. In the third house, communications are stressed even more—writing, speaking, the communications fields in general. A fourth house Mercury indicates a strong identification with the parent of the opposite sex. His life seems to come full cycle and he really hits his stride in the third portion of his life. Real estate, land, and home are focal points for him. When Mercury is posited in the fifth house, a "gambling" instinct may lead him to tremendous creative ideas, the stock market, romance, and involvement with children. Health matters and interesting work situations are especially important with a sixth house Mercury. He can be a workaholic with this placement.

Partnership matters hold his attention when Mercury is in the seventh house, as this house indicates both marriage and business partnership. This individual wants more than anything to relate to a mate on an equal intellectual level. His words, ideas, and thoughts go toward reaching humanity on a profound level when Mercury is in the eighth house. He also has a great ability to get his own needs met simply by asking for what he wants. He is good at fund raising as well. Ninth house placement inclines this individual to distances, travel, advertising, public relations. He is likely to win public recognition in some way. He can be a good teacher, lecturer, and may be published. Career matters are emphasized when Mercury is in the tenth house. Public life appeals to him and the identification is with the parent of the same sex. Group associations are most important to one with his Mercury in the eleventh house. He needs people and friends. He attracts intelligent people and thinks about his associates. When Mercury is in the twelfth house, the individual shows only the tip of the iceberg of his personality. He needs much time alone and can work well in isolation. He can be interested in "unseen" matters such as the occult and the esoteric. This person definitely does his best thinking when he is by himself.

The way Mercury relates to other planets gives a clue as to the quality of his thoughts and speech. If Mercury is in difficult aspect to Saturn, he may squelch much of his natural inclination for self-expression. He will be insecure about his mental ability or hesitant to display it. When Mercury and the Sun are conjunct (or together) in the chart, as is frequently the case, an added dramatic color affects his mental ability and personality. Mercury and Venus in good aspect give a beautiful quality to the speaking or singing voice. A Mars-Mercury combination inclines the individual to sarcasm and a caustic way of expressing himself. Aspects to Uranus indicate extra amounts of "electricity" coming into the mental body, which can be manifested as genius or eccentricity. He may be rebellious or ahead of his time. His speech can be particularly disjointed and erratic. He may never be able to finish a thought before his active mind is on to something else. When the planet Pluto is affecting Mercury, it can produce great ability to sway people with words. Magnetic ability to influence on a mass level is possible. If this planet is negatively affecting Mercury, you will find a compulsive talker. He may never let anyone get a word in edgewise. A Moon-Mercury combination indicates an even greater sensitivity on an intellectual level. He will either be very tuned in to trends and ideas, or he will tend to say things when he is emotionally upset that would be better left unsaid. This person may not be able to express himself clearly and concisely. Mercury and Neptune in good combination produce a wonderful ability to see matters with perspective and insight. He can see the overall concepts and also be aware of details. When these planets are in negative aspect, the individual may negate his vision by too much analysis. It is necessary to look at the chart as a whole in order to integrate these examples.

FINANCE

Cancer is the sign on the cusp of the second house of finance when Gemini is rising. The Moon is the ruler of Cancer, and indicates emotional quality; it is easy to see that one with this ascendant relates to money and financial matters on an emotional level. Dealing with money, either earning it or spending it, can be his way of getting in touch with his emotions and his nurturing instincts. When this individual is on a high emotional level, he is easy and comfortable making necessary expenditures, but if his emotions are upset, he is liable to relate to financial matters in a less than objective manner. He may spend money when he is upset, just as others eat when they are upset, or he may not be able to deal with financial matters at that time, as money pushes all his emotional buttons.

The second house describes not only how one spends money but how one earns it as well. The Moon is the planet that relates to the public. It describes the anima part of the personality, or the feminine, sensitive side. Gemini rising needs to earn money through his sensitivity toward the public's needs, and specifically through relating to the general public on a nurturing, protective level. He is financially successful when he puts his emotions and sympathetic nature to work for him instead of against him.

Marion Weisberg, successful in her therapy practice, earns money through her ability to nurture and show understanding in her work with her patients. Dick Bass, a Texas oil man with Gemini rising, owns and operates a fabulous ski resort in Utah named Snowbird, which caters to the public's needs with recreational facilities, restaurants, and shelter. Although this nurturing is done on a luxurious level, he must be in touch with the public's desires as well as show a protective concern for the welfare of his guests. Actors and comedians with this ascendant must be aware of trends in the public's taste. Writers must expose their feelings and emotions in order to communicate to the general public. They earn money through their sensitivity.

The Moon is a "cool" body. With the Moon ruling the financial house, there is a tendency to appear quite cool about money, although financial matters often hit this person on a very deeply sensitive level. This cool façade often hides deep feelings that may be difficult for the Gemini rising to handle openly.

If the Moon is well aspected in the chart, the individual has a healthy emotional reaction to financial matters and is a very successful earner. If the Moon is not well aspected, he may be concerned about not having money or fearful of losing it. This person is not the big spender of the zodiac. He may end up spending quite a bit of his funds, as he spends in accordance with his moods, but extravagance is not his problem. The Moon is the fastest-moving planet in the zodiac, and this person's feelings about financial matters can vary from hour to hour. He will be fluid one moment and extremely cautious and upset the next.

The sign of the Moon in an individual chart will indicate an additional quality connected to expenditures and earning capacity. With an Aries Moon, he will spend money impatiently and perhaps impulsively; he may spend it when he is angry or frustrated. With a Taurus or Libran Moon, money will be spent on

Venusian things such as art, pleasure, beauty, fashion, cosmetics, and sociable affairs. With a Gemini Moon, mental stimulation is the trigger for spending. A Cancer Moon is especially sensitive about his financial dealings. Spending for effect and to impress can be the quality of one with a Leo Moon. When the Moon is in Virgo, the individual looks for quality and serviceability in his purchases. He will analyze before he spends money. A Scorpio Moon may spend compulsively, perhaps in a rebellious manner or to get even. A Sagittarius Moon will tend to extravagance, whereas a Capricorn Moon is just the opposite. A conservative streak makes him extremely cautious, even penurious at times. He will certainly look for bargains. Impulse buying is characteristic of the Moon in Aquarius. Nervous energy and erratic expenditures keep money running through the fingers with this Moon sign. One with a Pisces Moon will be inclined to spend money on matters that are visionary, idealistic, or perhaps glamorous.

The placement of the Moon in the chart indicates what the individual will spend money on most easily. If the Moon is in the first house, he spends money on himself. If it's in the second house he spends money in order to earn money. Communications capture his financial attention with a third house Moon. Land, real estate, home, and matters connected with the earth—oil, mining, ecology—are the focus for one with the Moon in the fourth house. This can include an interest in architecture or decor as well. One with the Moon in the fifth house is much more of a gambler with his money. He spends on entertainment, romantic interests, the stock market. Since the sixth house indicates food, service, and health, these are the matters that on a financial level interest one with a sixth house Moon. Partnership is connected with the seventh house and is much related to financial matters when the Moon is posited there. With an eighth house placement, inheritance is more than likely, or at least money earned on a residual, dividend basis. This is the individual who is inclined to run up bills when he is emotionally upset. Higher education, travel, and promotional efforts entice one with the Moon in the ninth house. Social events and career matters help one with a tenth house Moon part with his money.

When the Moon is in the eleventh house, friendships and group situations trigger expenditures. A twelfth house placement inclines one to the occult. This is a person who earns money "behind the scenes." There may be an inability to really get in touch with financial needs. The aspects of other planets to the Moon naturally modify these general characteristics.

COMMUNICATIONS

Some of the outstanding writers and actors of our time were born with Gemini rising. The list is most impressive. Since the Sun is the ruler of the third house of communications when Gemini is rising, the individual's pride and vitality are connected to his ability to communicate and share ideas. This is the area where he is most likely to receive recognition, if the Sun is strongly aspected. He can also express himself in a rather dramatic manner. Sir Laurence Olivier, Humphrey Bogart, Gregory Peck, Gary Cooper, Henry Fonda, and Joseph Cotton are among the actors with this ascendant. Actresses Greta Garbo, Joan Bennett, Ginger Rogers, Loretta Young, and Audrey Hepburn also have Gemini rising. Comediennes Phyllis Diller and Carol Channing exhibit the kind of mercurial, witty quality which brings recognition to a Gemini rising. Perhaps the most expressive example of communicative brilliance is shown by the playwright George Bernard Shaw. Other writers with this ascendant are Arthur Conan Doyle, Jules Verne, Jean Jacques Rousseau, Dante Alighieri, Voltaire, T. E. Lawrence, John Steinbeck, and Jack London. Singer Harry Belafonte and poets John Keats and Alfred Tennyson have Gemini on the ascendant. Composers Rossini, Verdi, Wagner, and Gounod were born with Gemini rising. Statesmen, politicians, and diplomats Henry Kissinger, Hubert Humphrey, Alexander Hamilton, Jefferson Davis, and George McGovern were born with this sign coming over the horizon at the time of their birth. Presidents Theodore Roosevelt and James Knox Polk, columnist Walter Winchell, philosopher Baruch Spinoza, and General George Patton share this ascendant. Even though these outstanding people have different Sun signs, the rising sign indicates a common denominator in their ability to express themselves and attract recognition in the process.

HOME LIFE

Life seems to come full cycle for one with this ascendant. The intellectual potential that is indicated by this rising sign is sometimes not completely fulfilled until his latter days. That potential, indicated early on, may be put on hold during the middle years of exploration. It is stimulated again in a more concrete manner as he grows older. The middle years may be enormously idealistic, full of dreams and glamour. After that part of the cycle is completed it appears that one with this ascendant begins to settle down.

Virgo rules the fourth house when Gemini is rising. The fourth house is related to the home life, the kind of home environment one is attracted to, and the conditions at the "base" of one's life, as exemplified by the parent of the opposite sex. There is strong identification with the parent of the opposite sex with this rising sign. Many times this parent's latent talents seem to be passed on and later in life may become the focal point for the individual with Gemini rising. He begins to manifest the particular quality of that parent that he has photographed throughout his life. The whimsical quality of Gemini rising becomes more down-to-earth with maturity. In youth, it is hard for one with this ascendant to sit still long enough to fully explore his intellectual capacities, but later on as he slows down and has sorted out his ideas, he pins down his intellect in a different way. He becomes more analytical. He puts ideas through the fires of purification, sorts out extraneous distractions, and explores on more practical levels.

The parent of the opposite sex often is photographed by the individual as being analytical, even critical, but strong intellectual direction seems to come from this parent. If the relationship is a good one, the Gemini rising is encouraged to express his curiosity and need for exploration. If the relationship is difficult, he may be a target of criticism from this parent. The quality of the relationship is indicated by the aspects to the planet Mercury in the chart. Good rapport with this parent means good "adult" programming. If the adult input was negative, it may take a lifetime for this individual to work past those early criticisms to find his own way.

Gemini rising looks for a home base that will allow him to express ideas. He may think a great deal about his environment, home life, surroundings. He can be interested in land, real estate, ecology. He may use his home as a base of operations; writers and composers work at home and actors learn lines at home. The Gemini rising does his best thinking when he is surrounded by his own four walls. Libraries and books can be essential for one with this rising sign.

ROMANCE • CREATIVE EXPRESSION

One of the blessings in the life of one with this ascendant comes in the expression of artistic temperament and the natural creative ability. The fifth house in a chart not only indicates the quality of creativity, but also the gambling instincts, children, and romantic patterns. Venus is the ruler of the fifth house when Gemini is on the rise. Venus is one of the two "benefic" planets in the zodiac. (Jupiter is the other.) Venus relates to diplomacy, beauty, and the arts. With Venus ruling the house of romance and Jupiter ruling the seventh house of marriage, one with Gemini rising can be most fortunate in relationships.

If Venus is well aspected in the chart, there is a natural ease in the expression of his loving nature. If Venus is not well placed, a desperate need for love, affection, peace and harmony can keep the individual from showing the strength of the creative nature. He may hesitate to make waves, opting for peace at any price. In the extreme, a badly aspected Venus can indicate laziness and self-indulgence. He may take the easy way out in using his talents or in love relationships. He can spoil his offspring, give in to the demands of those he loves, or be afraid to express affection. He may also be attracted only to those individuals who will give in to him and keep peace at any price.

He is certainly attracted to beauty. Collecting art can be a good investment for him as well as being a pleasurable pursuit. He can explore the many facets of his artistry through a variety of means—painting, architecture, design, literature, theater, and music. His artistic and social inclinations make him a terrific host. He has a talent for combining people who are especially creative and interesting, thus maintaining the intellectual stimulation he needs in his home. His parties are often "beautiful," with profusions of color and flowers to create atmosphere. Em Leeds Green channels much of her artistic temperament into entertaining. She paints pictures with food, flowers and colorful, tasteful decor. She expresses much of her love nature in this way, combining people in such a sociable way that strong companionship bonds are created among strangers.

The individual with this ascendant will produce beautiful offspring, and may pass on his talents to his children. With a well aspected Venus, strong bonds of love exist between parent and child. They may show a flair for the arts, as in the case of Henry Fonda's children. Social causes hold tremendous interest for both Peter and Jane Fonda, as well as the theater, whereas Henry Fonda expresses artistic ability through his painting as well as through acting. Gary Cooper passed on an exceptional artistic talent to his beautiful daughter, Maria Cooper Janis, whose canvases show an exceptionally interesting combination of color, depth, and philosophy.

WORK • SERVICE • HEALTH

A person with this ascendant can be a compulsive worker. He has a profound ability to combine people for work projects. He is effective in any kind of work where he can be in touch with his child ego; he must "play" as well as work. The planet Pluto is the ruler of Scorpio, the sign on the cusp of the sixth house when Gemini is ascending. Pluto is the power planet. Pluto is like a powerful but turbulent body of water that must be dammed up in order to prevent flooding and consequent destruction. That same body of water, when channeled, can produce enough electricity to light up a city. The kind of energy one with this ascendant can generate with his work is similar to that body of water. In a negative sense, the Gemini rising can force others to work as hard as he does, come on too strong, and find that he pushes people away from him instead of bringing them together. When he works compulsively, he can undermine his health. Eventually, this exertion catches up with him. He must find work projects that use up an enormous store of vitality or he will redirect that energy into less than constructive areas. He is particularly effective when he reaches people on a mass level or through mass media, for his energy may be too strong for a one-to-one kind of cooperation; he can knock people over without knowing it. Greg Sierra, with Gemini rising, is an actor constantly in demand. He has worked in several television series, where his character protrayal is especially dynamic. On an ultimate level, he has the ability to transform lives through his work. Lieutenant Commander William Mulholland of the U. S. Navy performs a profound service to humanity through his work as a test pilot. Lieutenant Robin Read, by making decisions about which tests should be conducted with new equipment, exhibits this kind of power in his job with the Air Force. His decisions may well affect the lives of masses of people.

Pluto relates to the child ego state in Transactional Analysis terms. The native with Gemini rising must avoid any tyrannical manipulation, like that used by a child who wants what he wants when he wants it. When he gets in touch with a universal rhythm, he is more willing to let go when things don't fall into place easily. He will find he is more effective when he deals from a position of "laid-back" power. His tremendous magnetism enables him to combine people most effectively, sometimes acting almost in a producer's capacity for his particular group. He can work most effectively with major organizations without getting lost in the shuffle. His robust health will never fail him if he enjoys what he is doing on the job. Queen Victoria of England had Gemini rising, as does Prince Philip of England. Frederick the Great of Prussia and labor leader Walter Reuther share the ascendant. The effectiveness of their influence is apparent. On the negative side, John Wilkes Booth chose to use the revengeful side of Pluto in his life's "work." Pluto's power is either highly evolved and transforming or totally destructive. This kind of energy knows no middle ground. The native with Gemini rising must learn to handle this "all or nothing at all" approach in his business endeavors, and resist any temptation to get even or exhibit an "I'll show you" attitude on the job. Rebellion can be a strong motivation in his selection of an occupation. Surgeons Walter Reed and Christiaan Barnard are fine examples of the kind of transformation that can be accomplished when this energy is put in positive gear.

MARRIAGE • PARTNERSHIP

The seventh house in a chart indicates not only marriage but business partnership as well. It is in this area that Gemini rising can be most fortunate. The planet Jupiter rules this partnership house, and it is the "luckiest" planet in the zodiac. Jupiter is called the "great benefic." It describes a person who is philosophical, optimistic, happy-go-lucky, and nature-loving. The person with Gemini rising is naturally attracted to one with this kind of personality, as the humor and optimism prevent him from being bored. A Jupiterian personality is never content to remain in a rut, so the Gemini rising can feel assured of stimulation with this challenging and interesting personality.

Jupiter in the chart can indicate not only luck but wealth and humor. The Gemini personality can be attracted to someone who appears wealthy, whether materially or in spirit. The aspects to Jupiter in the chart indicate whether or not he finds what he is looking for. If Jupiter is well aspected and strong in the chart, the Gemini rising is most fortunate indeed. He finds a mate who is blessed with a sense of humor, a desire for stimulation, and a natural curiosity about the workings of the universe. This keeps the partnership challenging and exciting. A Jupiterian personality, whether in reality a Sagittarian or just one who exudes enthusiasm, is a natural complement to one with Gemini rising. There will be plenty of room for Gemini rising to find the freedom he needs to do his own thing since the Jupiterian partner also wants room to grow and expand. He finds safety in that freedom. The mate can be off chasing rainbows while the Gemini rising is dancing his own dance. The two feed each other's "script" of life. The Sagittarian personality needs constant challenge and loses interest in anyone who is within reach. The Gemini personality is always ready to do his disappearance act, which keeps the Sagittarian on his toes and happy. If Jupiter is well aspected in the chart, this works out harmoniously, but if Jupiter is not well aspected, there is consequent disappointment, perhaps for both parties.

A Jupiterian type of personality tends to promise a great deal, overschedule his time, and overextend in many ways. He or she may promise more than can be delivered. If Jupiter is not well aspected in the chart of one with Gemini rising he may be disappointed in his partner's lack of goals and enthusiasm, or may have to take his partner's promises with a grain of salt. The partner may promise the Moon and only be able to deliver a cardboard cutout. The partner probably means well, but simply overestimates his own time and abilities. Fear of disappointment may keep the partner from living up to potential. If the Gemini rising is willing to temper his expectations, he can prevent major disappointment, and can still find great happiness with one of this vibrant personality.

Perhaps what the Gemini rising needs most in a partnership or marriage is humor. He cannot feel safe with one who is rigid or unyielding. As long as most of his needs are fulfilled and the partners share common goals, a lot will be overlooked. Wealth of spirit is essential to keep things light and fun in this relationship. The Jupiterian personality is the outdoorsy type and is constantly goal-seeking. Some of the goals come into easy reach and some do not. The Gemini rising is willing to go along with the game if the odds are right. He is enticed by Jupiter's optimistic nature. He may actually look for someone who is materially successful, as that seems to take the financial pressure off of him. In his mind, wealth means freedom. If he looks for spiritual wealth, however, he finds he is much more satisfied, for it is this quality he is really looking for in a partner. Financial success can follow closely behind. He wants a mate who has a life and goals of his or her own. In this way, the relationship can be a celebration of joy and searching.

NEEDS

"Obligation" may well be the dirtiest word in the dictionary
for the one with a Gemini ascendant. This fun-loving individual
cannot stand to owe anyone anything. His freedom is assured as
long as he is not obligated, and so he will hesitate to ask anyone
for anything in case there are strings attached. Much of this
sense of independence comes from early childhood. It appears
that for one reason or another, this individual did not get a lot of
help from his family. He learned early on not to ask for things in
case the answer was no. As a child, he was unable to see the circumstances that brought about that negative response. Instead
he concluded that the reason had to do with his own un-
worthiness. As he grows older and understands the reality of the
situation, he is better able to deal with his fears. In traditional
astrology, the eighth house ruled the death of an individual.
That might easily describe the feelings one with this ascendant
has when he is under obligation. Those feelings can be above
and beyond whatever rational reactions are called for in a particular situation. If this person must borrow money from a bank,
he will procrastinate, finally presenting conservative figures that
corroborate the validity of his request. He will certainly never
ask for frivolous needs to be met. He may not know how to accept a gift or any "strokes" with grace. He may wonder what
strings are attached, what price he has to pay.

The eighth house is the house that indicates how one gets his
needs met, whether psychologically or materially. In the evolution of the person, it also is indicative of the quality of energy
one has to send out to humanity. With Saturn ruling this house
when Gemini is on the rise, it is obvious that there are heavy
judgmental messages about asking for anything. It can indicate a
"karmic" guilt about having help or money. There may have
been a death or imprisonment connected with debt. The leftover
fear may have little to do with the circumstances that really
exist, but the individual has concluded that it is not safe to ask
for aid; the rejection that is possible is simply not worth the
benefits that could result. If he does have to make a request, he

is so reluctant he is liable to appear quite cold about it. It is as if he asks through gritted teeth. The turning point can come when he is able to look beyond his own needs to see the desperate needs of others. He then assumes his karmic responsibility to mankind. He breaks through his early parent messages about being safe. He breaks down the walls he has erected between himself and the rest of humanity.

If he finds a project that is so important he can transcend his fears, he will then take a good, hard look at the sufferings of others and can be most effective in finding practical ways to assist them. He will do for others what he is unable to do for himself. Em Leeds Green, in her work with Odyssey House, was able to implement public service messages through her connections with people in the entertainment world. She could ask for things for Odyssey House that she would never ask for herself. After a childhood that was less than luxurious, Betty Barney has devoted her life work to bettering the condition of those chosen in her "family." She counsels those who come to her as well as teaching about her cultural heritage. Looking past the "No one helped me, why should I help" message has brought greater joy and richness to her life. Breaking through the negative parent messages, the fears and insecurities, enables one with this ascendant to work in his highest "parent" state to assume responsibility for others, and therefore himself, on a profound level. He breaks through insecurities about his abilities to help and does what he can.

RECOGNITION

The freedom that is so important to one with Gemini rising comes through travel, higher education, dealing with distances. The Gemini personality naturally lends itself to taking chances, going beyond the boundaries prescribed in his early life, and attracting some rather exciting and stimulating experiences. When he works through the "scare" he might have in breaking through the limitations of childhood, he finds the world an exciting place to be, full of adventure. Travel experiences can begin early on in many instances. Lieutenant Commander William Mulholland has taken this need for adventure to an extreme by flying planes over twice the speed of sound. Some of the equipment he tests may be ten years ahead of its time.

The ninth house in a chart describes many types of activities. It can mean the higher mind, and therefore higher education. It indicates the ability to attract publicity and be involved with promotion or advertising as an occupation. Legal affairs come under this heading as well as philosophical trends. The native with Gemini rising is not willing to deal with ordinary philosophical ideas. He is in the forefront of avant-garde thought. He is more willing than most to walk out to the edge of a limb, express his genius, and therefore attract an extra amount of attention in the bargain. He wants life to be beyond the ordinary, either on a conscious or subconscious level. He sets out to create the circumstances that will keep him from being bored.

For Em Leeds Green the adventurous life began before she could consciously choose it. Emigration from Hungary to Australia started her on a life full of travel, with London and the United States on the agenda later. She managed to go around the world before she was ready to settle down—for a while. Betty Barney began her commute to Africa from Brooklyn as soon as she could, taking her children with her. Marion Weisberg went on her first trip to Europe as a teenager. She eventually returned to share her knowledge of Transactional Analysis, conducting workshops and training programs all over Europe. She is responsible for the training of many TA therapists in other countries. No ordinary life will satisfy these restless individuals with Gemini rising.

Since the planet Uranus rules this ninth house when Gemini is on the ascendant, these people have a great possibility of attracting attention or fame by doing something that is uniquely their own. Marion Weisberg has been a pioneer in the use of astrology in conjunction with therapy workshops. When we look at the list of famous people with this ascendant we can see that they express a quality that is out of the ordinary. The desire to experience life on a high level of awareness compels them to take the chances that will catapult them into the public eye. Fame and recognition that come suddenly are possible at various periods in the life of one with this ascendant, usually as a result of developing something unusual and different. (Surgeon Christiaan Barnard was the pioneer in the area of organ transplants.) The risks one must take to express uniqueness on a grand scale are always great, but the rewards are well worth the chance taking. Limelight can come to Gemini rising almost inadvertently.

CAREER

The planet Neptune rules the tenth house of career with Gemini rising. Neptune is the planet of idealism and vision. It indicates a natural inclination toward therapy, film, and the glamour world in general. It is certainly the planet that indicates inspiration. An individual with this ascendant evidences his true visionary spirit through career and public life. His deepest desire is connected to "saving the world" in one way or another. He wants to uplift his fellow man and make life more ideal. He finds ways to inspire others through his career. If he succeeds in his dreams, he may end up on a public pedestal.

The tenth house is also the house that rules the parent of the same sex. The way this parent is photographed by the individual has much to do with whether he easily fulfills his dreams in regard to his career. With Neptune ruling this house, the Gemini rising can idolize this parent. If Neptune is well aspected in the chart, the parent may deserve it. That parent can be a true visionary, encouraging the child to follow his dreams and inspirations. If Neptune is badly aspected the parent may have been disillusioned in his life. The photographs are therefore out of focus, distorted, and do not give a clear image for the Gemini rising to follow. Instead of being the guiding light for others, he can be unrealistic about his public life. He may be unwilling to let himself follow his intuitions and go for broke, or he may have a Don Quixote complex, fighting windmills all the way. The Don Quixote soul may suddenly wake up to reality one day and be devastated, not knowing how to put his dreams back together again.

One young man was on cloud nine about running the offices of a large metaphysical organization. He had dreams of fulfilling his desires to be of service to humanity. With a badly aspected Neptune in his chart, he did not stop to look at reality or read the fine print. He expected perfection and a high level of devotion from all those around him. When he discovered that the organization was also a business, and that the motivation of everyone was not as high as his own, the disillusionment was hard to take. His dreams crashed into millions of pieces, impossible to put together again. He turned to the lower registers of Neptune; with drugs, he attempted to climb back to the heights where the colors were rosy and glowing at all times. His acting career fell to pieces, and life was less than beautiful for a long time.

With Neptune ruling the tenth house, the Gemini rising needs to be a *practical* idealist in the career arena. Neptune is the planet that indicates how well we visualize, thereby creating the circumstances around us. Metaphysically, we are taught that whatever we can conceive will become a reality. It is important to dream dreams and give them a chance to become manifest. Fantasy is essential as part of the creative process. If Neptune is well aspected, the fantasy life is clear, sharp, and in focus. The events in the life of the individual with Gemini rising are products of his intuitive mind. He goes past his adult ego façade and allows himself to see the broader scope. He deals on the higher octave of the intellect in his choice of career. If Neptune is not well aspected that fantasy can get him into trouble. This can often indicate a tendency toward the manic state. His need to be "high" can cause him to be unrealistic and less than practical. This desire for service may give one a Christ complex as well, as he may *really* want to save the world. It is important for the individual with Gemini rising to learn how to make his dreams a reality.

Planting a thought is like planting a seed in a flower pot. If we plant zinnia seeds, we get a zinnia plant. If we plant orchids, that is what grows. We get into trouble when we don't realize what "seeds" we're sending out to the universe. If Neptune is not well aspected, we can fool ourselves into thinking that our dreams are in sharp focus when they're not. When we don't get what we think we want, the resulting crash is hard to take. It is easy to blame circumstances, "life," or the breaks. It can be important for Gemini rising to find a practical way to bring vision and inspiration into the area of career by planting the right seeds. Learning to read the fine print is one way of confronting the reality of a situation. Building on vision and not on hope is another. A natural outlet for one with this ascendant is to channel those career energies where his conceptual ability is utilized. Therapy is ideal, as well as film, theater, music, and literature.

A look at an individual chart indicates whether one can easily bring his concepts into view or whether he finds a way to prevent himself from the possibility of being disillusioned. It can clearly indicate how the parent of the same sex influenced the child. With a difficult aspect to Mercury, the Gemini rising tends to overanalyze his concepts, blowing them to pieces before he can be let down. Saturn in difficult aspect indicates a cynical outlook—a wonderful self-protective device. Neptune and Mars in negative aspect indicate a "liar's aspect"; this person may have been told partial truths in order to protect him from possible disappointments. Neptune-Jupiter in difficult aspect is the "con man's aspect." It indicates a tendency to gild the lily. If the native is aware of his tendency to overlook the reality of certain situations because of the conditioning of childhood, he can work past those messages and learn to bring better conditions into his life.

FRIENDSHIP

The eleventh house in the chart indicates the type of friends to whom one is attracted. It can also give a clue as to the kind of group activity that will appeal to an individual, as well as the type of energy one will put into that group. Mars is the ruler of this house when Gemini is on the rise. Mars indicates activity, energy, and action. It is also the planet of ambition, drive, determination, and the pioneering instincts. It rules the sexual energy, and when directed, the highest creative energy. It can indicate resourcefulness or competition, and the fighting instinct.

When Mars is the ruler of the house of friendship or is placed in that house, the person is inclined to have one strong friendship at a time. He may have many friends and acquaintances, but seems to spend a lot of time with one person in particular and will put a great deal of energy into the friendship. He can focus on one activity as well as one person. He will enjoy spending active time with friends rather than sedentary time. He enjoys dancing or sports activities such as skiing, running, or swimming. In a sense, sharing and competition with a friend can spur him on to greater achievement of his own. He is stimulated by people who are energetic, dynamic, and who direct their drive easily. He will stop at nothing to help a friend, devoting time and physical energy where it is needed. Melinda Reed Love, an actress and writer, has gone to bat for her friends in situations where her initiative has made the difference in their success. Many times it has been above and beyond the call of duty, but she has been willing to stick her neck out for someone who is a friend.

If Mars is well aspected in the chart, the Gemini rising is most fortunate in finding exciting friendships, and the camaraderie is fantastic. But if that planet is not well aspected, the competitive spirit can turn sour and produce the wrong kind of competition and frustration. He will be attracted to people who keep him charged up negatively. He can get into upsetting situations with group activity. The negative energy of Mars can indicate impatience as well as frustration. Many times, undirected Mars energy can cause excessive drinking. If Mars is badly aspected in a chart, the individual may spend his time bar hopping, getting into situations that periodically produce fights and arguments. If occasionally the person with Gemini rising finds he is in sticky situations with friends, he can assume he needs more physical exercise. If he has worked off his own excess Mars energy, he is less likely to react to situations with anger or frustration.

Actors with this ascendant find a natural outlet for their need for group association. A rehearsal or a performance uses up a great deal of physical energy. Even then, the strife that can occur occasionally in that kind of situation can run like wildfire throughout the whole group. If the Gemini rising has released his ambitious, aggressive energy in a good way, he will be less likely to be caught up in a negative situation that will soon blow over. Courage and daring are positive traits of Mars. Actors need a certain amount of that energy to be willing to put themselves on the line in group participation. A healthy competitive spirit is essential as well.

Writers with this rising sign may have to search for some kind of energetic outlet for excess Mars energy. Many writers are known for drinking in their leisure hours away from the typewriter, instead of using up that excess energy with sports or physical exercise. Marion Weisberg has chosen not only health-associated activities but has resumed playing the piano with a chamber music group. (Mars is the planet that rules metals. A piano has metal strings.) Dick Bass skis with his friends. Betty Barney gives dance concerts with her group. Bob Nunez had the courage to do the lead in a summer stock production of a difficult play without ever having been on stage before.

HIDDEN MATTERS • SUBCONSCIOUS PROCESS

The twelfth house is the sector of a chart that rules the occult, behind-the-scenes action, the subconscious mind. It indicates the quality that is the most difficult to express overtly. With a Gemini ascendant, Venus rules the twelfth house. Venus is primarily associated with the love nature. Many times, one with this rising sign has a difficulty in expressing his love. He feels deeply, but may not be able to say "I love you" easily. He will show his love in many ways, but the words can be elusive. He will be able to get in touch with that affectionate nature when he is alone. He will only be "lazy" when he is comfortable with someone or when he is off by himself. He may have difficulty relaxing when people are around. This person is not usually demonstrative in public. He may also find difficulty in handling the social scene. He is comfortable with words, ideas, and his intellect, but not so comfortable with the sociable, charming, easygoing part of himself. Subconsciously, he craves love, ease of living, and beauty. He begins to express more of that part of his nature when he has broken through some protective walls. He feels great love and affection for those he loves, and may not know he has trouble expressing it overtly. When he gets in touch with his repressed love energy, it can be an antidote for the fears and insecurities he has about humanity in general. The turning point can come through his reaching out for the expression of his love nature on a psychic level, his willingness to take the chance to show it. It can truly transform his own life and that of people around him.

CANCER
RISING

THE MOON IS THE RULER OF CANCER. In a chart, the Moon indicates not only the emotional quality, the feelings, and sensitivity, but the mothering urges and protective instincts. When you spot someone who expresses that motherly concern for your welfare—picking lint off your jacket, asking if you've eaten lately, checking to see that you're all right—you can guess that you're in the company of someone who has Cancer rising. Another giveaway sign is talkativeness, with an emotional quality coming through loud and clear. The Cancer rising talks about feelings, rather than ideas, for the Moon works completely through the emotional nature. It is related to the anima part of the personality; therefore, the feminine, sensitive, vulnerable facet.

The Moon is the fastest-moving body in the heavens, waxing and waning, going through constant changes, often hiding behind the clouds. Yet when it emerges, it is there to act as a beacon in the dark. Since the person with Cancer rising is ruled by his emotions, the moody, changeable quality of this rising sign is apparent to everyone around. He can change moods drastically every few hours in a day. When he is in control of his emotions, this is the most understanding, sensitive person you could hope to find. He is nurturing, compassionate, and receptive. He is in touch with the emotional reactions of those around him and will always be ready to help. If he is not in control, he can be extremely miserable. When he allows a greater sense of reason to come into play, he begins to take charge of his emotions, rather than letting himself be a victim of those moods.

The mythological ruler of Cancer is the goddess Diana. She represents the bursting of life, the dawning of seasons, and ceremonies. Tradition, as related to harvest and hearth, are assigned to Diana. She represents cool, feminine beauty—aloof, yet concerned with germination and birth. She is representative of Mother Earth. Natives with this ascendant are tremendously connected to family and traditions, leaning toward a sense of heritage and warm, homey things. It makes no difference whether the native is male or female, the expression is that of the Mother. Cancer is the fourth sign of the zodiac, the home described by the fourth house. Cancer rising is particularly invested in his home and family.

The symbol of Cancer is the crab. The crab has two phases of his existence. One where he is vulnerable and naked without his shell, one where he is protected by the hard, rock-like covering he grows around his exposed, sensitive body. The crab's habits can shed particularly symbolic light on the personality of a person with Cancer rising. When the crab is frightened or exposed, he scuttles behind a rock or into the sea. When the Cancer rising is hurt or finds his moods too much to deal with, he goes into hiding. He only emerges into the light of day when he has worked out his hurt or disappointment to his own satisfaction. The crab moves sideways toward his prey. He sidles up to the object of his attention and firmly fixes a claw. He clings to his prey and holds on with a vise-like grip. The native with this ascendant can do the same thing. When he has focused on his objective, he approaches it indirectly and grabs hold. His tenacity is unparalleled. He can hold you in an emotional grip that is extremely difficult to get away from. He can become "crabby" and irritable at times, yet will be the personification of sensitivity and understanding at others. He can seem quite cool and aloof sometimes, yet when he is exposed and without his shell, he is the soul of warmth and protection. He can appear unfeeling and uncaring when he is in one of his moods, yet when he emerges from his hiding place, he basks in the sunlight of friendship and resumes his concern for your welfare.

This is the most sentimental sign of the zodiac. He can become attached to possessions that remind him of warm times and special people. Cancer is a water sign, again emphasizing the sensitivity and receptiveness. Emotion and intuitive qualities are assigned to water signs in general, but the Cancer rising shows these qualities most easily of all. He is nothing if not fluid in his emotional nature. Cancer rising is also a cardinal sign, therefore, even more receptive, sensitive, and vulnerable. These attributes can be both positive and negative. If there is a preponderance of these qualities, the native will be somewhat like a sponge. He picks up the feelings of those around him too easily. He can be swayed off his path and deterred from his goals by negative influences. He is especially receptive to upsetting conditions, as Cancer rules the stomach or solar plexus area, the point of attachment of the astral or emotional body. If the Cancer rising leaves his home in a happy mood and runs into someone angry or upset, he immediately takes on that emotional quality, unless he knows how to prevent that from happening. He is especially sensitive to jealousies from others and can be stopped from taking action in a rather subtle way. In a negative expression of his energy, he can become guilt-ridden, or can be envious of others' good fortune.

It is most important for this individual to pick associates carefully. The magnetic quality of his personality will attract all types of people to his side. Since he is so receptive and sensitive, and tends to pick up others' pain, he can find himself in an emotional whirlpool if he is around negative people. He must guard against those unhappy individuals who need the brightness of his light to see by. He can be susceptible to energy rip-off from others. If he has chosen to mother people unworthy of his attentions, it can be disastrous to his emotional balance. His very mothering instincts can turn against him and prevent him from achieving what he wants in his own life. He can be the biggest "rescuer" in the zodiac.

The process by which the Cancer rising comes to grips with his life can be very interesting. He may start with vision and a purpose. But with distractions, either from negative people or from life circumstances, he begins to look sideways. Whenever he compares his life with that of others, he starts on a nonproductive course of action. If he becomes aware of a situation in someone else's life that appears desirable, an emotional reaction can take hold and he can indulge in self-pity, blame circumstances or "life," and feel wounded. Then comes a period of hiding out. There may be a refusal to analyze a situation realistically, as this is not an easy thing for a Cancerian to do, since the immediate emotional reaction clouds the real issue. After a period of misery, he comes to the realization that circumstances are not to blame for his own shortcomings, but he, himself. Then the guilt takes hold and the process continues, until he is somehow able to get himself out of this emotional morass.

Until that time, no one can be more miserable than the person with Cancer rising. He is the only one who can solve his problem, but when he is drowning in self-pity, it is hard for him to look at the overall picture with perspective. His pride can be so easily hurt that family and friends may not even know he is wounded. He can be especially touchy, bitter, resentful. He puts up his prickly shell and keeps everyone away. In this emotional condition, he begins to overeat, overindulge in the very foods and drink that make his emotions harder to handle. His digestive system is his weak spot, anyway. He is not known for self-discipline and self-denial, so he feels justified in indulging himself, even if it is self-defeating. When he then begins to feel physically sluggish, he complains and is taken for a hypochondriac. With no pity from those around him, he feels even more wounded, morbid, and willful. He tries to satisfy his oral needs by putting food, drink, or cigarettes in his mouth. He may proceed to sleep too much, neglect exercise even more, fall further away from a healthy routine. It is almost impossible for anyone else to rouse him from this self-indulgent state, just as it may be impossible to rouse him from sleep. His depression deepens, and self-doubt hangs on. It appears there is no end to the round robin he finds himself in. Greater intellectual awareness of his patterns can be his saving grace. Concentrated effort toward self-discipline and healthy habits can make it easier to handle emotional reactions.

Actually, he may be very simple to understand if one watches the movement of the crab. When he is protected by his shell, he can be the aggressor. He moves toward his prey with decisive sideways motion. He seizes his prey, and he is in control. It is when he sheds his skin that he is naked and exposed like jelly. The important consideration is that this is the way the crab grows. It is a natural process. If the person with Cancer rising gets in touch with his own natural timing and avoids putting himself under undue pressure, he can analyze which state he is in, watch his movements, and understand why he is acting the way he is. He can then wait out his sensitive time with more

awareness. It is through his own emotional pain that he understands the needs of others and emerges once more to do battle
for the common man. The individual with Cancer rising who
refuses to relate to the pain and suffering of others cannot possibly find solutions to his own problems. The Moon relates to the
collective unconscious. The depth of feeling that he can eventually reach will lead him to the attunement necessary for his life's
work.

Once he begins to be aroused to action, with a fully developed
crusty armor, he can do battle on a very sensitive level. If he
outgrows his shell, he may have outgrown his usefulness in a
particular field. He must then go through that painful growth
process once again to find a new level of sensitivity. It is this
particular sensitivity and understanding that makes him a natural writer. If he uses intelligence and analysis, his mental antidotes, to put his own feelings in perspective, he is a beacon to
those around him. Protective instincts can emerge once more,
and he becomes a healer par excellence.

Most of the Cancer rising's guilt comes from blaming himself
for reacting to other people's moods, creating lack of action on
his part. This wasted energy can further paralyze him. Self-
doubt and guilt take hold and he's trapped once again. It is easy
to see how essential it is for one with this ascendant to get in
touch with his own natural, emotional timing. The symbology of
the Moon is appropriate. There are times when the Moon is full
and shining, and times when it goes behind a cloud. It moves
through a different sign of the zodiac every two days or so. It
can be eclipsed, it waxes and wanes, yet its effect on the tides is
unquestioned. The effect that one with this ascendant has on his
public is equally noticeable. He pulls and tugs on your emotional sleeve until you have to sit up and take notice.

One of the first things that one with this ascendant needs to
be aware of is the meaning of transference. Many times he will
get hurt feelings because of what someone says to him. Usually,
if that remark is accurate, the Cancer rising is able to slough it
off with a shrug. It is when something really inaccurate and un-
true is said that the Cancer rising overreacts. If he is able to
look past the remark and realize that much of what he takes personally is only what the other person is feeling about himself, he

can go into his mothering syndrome, decide what will make the
other person feel better, and be saved from a drastic emotional
overreaction. He picks up other people's pain and thinks it is his
own. This can be too much to bear at times, especially if he is in
pain himself. He feels for everyone. Fortunately, he can also
pick up others' high spirits, and this can be a lifesaver. If he surrounds himself with positive, happy people, he has gone a long
way toward his own happiness.

Invariably, there are great hunger needs in one with this ascendant. These can be manifested by oral activities. The Cancer
rising has a tendency to overeat, overtalk, overdrink. Smoking
can be another manifestation of his oral hungers. Many chroni-
cally overweight people have Cancer rising or the Moon in the
first house. This individual tends to gain weight easily, no doubt
due to the overeating that is directly related to his emotional
hunger and to his tendency to retain fluids, reflective of his tendency to hang on to hurt. Food seems to be the pacifier he needs
when he is upset. When he is in his thin phase, it is difficult to
detect the rising sign by his appearance only, for as with the
crab, his arms and legs can remain long and lean, perhaps even
spindly. His face will always be on the round side, though with
a strong jawline, retaining that "moon-like" look.

Childhood is a tremendously traumatic time for one with Cancer rising. This rising sign is related to the "orphan" complex.
Whether the individual was really orphaned or not is irrelevant;
he *feels* orphaned and abandoned early on, and his emotional
coloring starts right then. He feels a distinct lack of mothering
and tender loving care from childhood. My daughter, Diane
Henesy, recalled an incident during a regression session that
clarified many of her childhood reactions. In that session, she
went back to the age of five months, when she was sick and in
the hospital. She recalled seeing me standing above her, seeming
to ignore her fears by not picking her up and holding her close.
She said she was scared and needed to be held. When I kept
my distance, she decided right then I didn't love her. She
felt, and decided to act, like an outsider in our family for
much of her childhood. The recollection of this incident was a
revelation to both of us, and I was grateful for an opportunity to
present the "facts" of that moment. Her grandfather was the

Chief of Staff of the hospital and the fashion of his day was not to let mothers stay with their babies. His words were: "Hysterical mothers have no business being around sick children." That moment she recalled took place when she was in the nursery undergoing a blood transfusion. I was behind a plate-glass window, with my heart in my mouth, watching her, aching to take her in my arms to comfort her. There was no fighting the boss, however, and I was sent home, knowing it was the wrong thing to do. What Diane didn't photograph was my feelings. She only saw my actions. Her behavior during her childhood certainly reflected the decision she had made about my love. Fortunately she has no doubts about that love now, but her childhood was made more difficult because of this early reaction. I, in my state of unawareness, did not think to talk to her, at five months, to explain what was going on. She said that many times after that, when she felt particularly alone or abandoned, she would think of that incident and feel better almost immediately. The deprivation of touch at that critical and traumatic time has affected her whole life. It is interesting to note that the sensitive area for one with Cancer rising is the stomach and digestion. Diane was in the hospital because she was having trouble digesting food and was not receiving enough nourishment. The actual first memory of feeling abandoned could have come with my inability to nurse her for very long. Again, an example of oral needs connected with this rising sign.

It is almost impossible to know how to discipline a child with this ascendant. Too much severity and pressure will send him into hiding. He becomes more sensitive as pressure is brought to bear. Criticism won't work, as he becomes depressed if he feels he is a failure. Discipline must be sugar-coated. Otherwise, the child will only *appear* to obey. Eventually, he gathers his hurt feelings, gets in touch with his natural tendency to armor himself, and is more difficult to deal with in the long run. An injustice is not easily forgotten. A clue to understanding the child with Cancer rising comes with the understanding of Neptune, the esoteric ruler of Cancer. Neptune is the planet of vision, idealism, inspiration. This child can be inspired through his ideals to productive action. He is sympathetic, loyal and devoted to family, and will feel ennobled by working toward ideals in those areas. It is essential that his imagination be given an outlet, as it will provide a release for his feelings. Otherwise that imagination can run rampant, keeping him in dramatic and possibly morbid fantasies. The imagination must be fed with good food or else there is a tendency toward untruthfulness. Later on, he takes up the sword of truth and fights injustice with all his might.

If he has a vision to follow, he can make others feel through his imagination. Judy Garland was born with Cancer rising. She felt that her mother was unconcerned about her welfare as a working child. She resented the coercion used by Louis B. Mayer to keep her in line, yet she touched millions of people through her magical quality, reaching them through emotional response. One of her great problems had to do with the early hours required of her by film work. The Cancer rising is essentially a night person, wanting to sleep all day, if possible. Judy Garland was not able to get in touch with her natural rhythm in film work, and felt she never got enough sleep.

It is when Cancer rising works through his feelings and begins to express them overtly that he finds success in his life. He has a pipeline to masses of people through his own emotional reactions. Through his sensitivity he understands what mankind has in common, and he knows how to meet its needs. This is really the sign of the writer. It has been proven statistically that the Moon is most prominent in the charts of well-known writers. The quality of writing is less intellectual and more in tune with feelings we all share in common. When Cancer rising confronts his own feelings, he realizes that everyone suffers what he suffers to a greater or lesser degree. By bringing out his compassion, he saves his own life. He enriches his own experiences by assuming the natural role of the mother to mankind. Neil Simon writes about his own life experiences, touching on areas common to everyone. He writes about painful times in a humorous way to help everyone move beyond their own painful moments. It is interesting to note that he writes about his family. Again, Cancer rising is particularly concerned with the family, whether his own or the family of mankind.

This individual is not only able to pick up the feelings of others; people pick up his feelings, too. There is great identification by the public with one born with this ascendant. The response is a showering of public love and understanding. Judy Garland was beloved by her fans, as was Babe Ruth. Will Rogers was adored by all who knew him, or even knew of him. Marlon Brando and Shelley Winters have received great acclaim from the public by their portrayal of particularly sensitive and emotional screen roles. Ava Gardner and Edward G. Robinson are both household names. The public at large responds to one with Cancer rising in a special way. Jean Nidetsch touched a response that spread like wildfire when she began to play an understanding, mothering, nurturing role with her overweight friends. Her encouragement mushroomed into Weight Watchers. It brought more than emotional satisfaction into her life. Her book is an inspiration to everyone, overweight or thin. Jonathan Winters addresses the humor in situations we can all identify with, and Virginia Graham, again adored by her public, shares much of the humor of her family life on her talk shows. Since Cancer is the sign identified with the female sex in particular, Virginia reached many women through her appeal on "Girl Talk." People literally stop her on the street to tell her how much they love her. Hardly anyone reached a higher response from the public than Enrico Caruso. William Shakespeare has profoundly affected people's lives for centuries. The wave of sensitivity inherent in this personality can reach humanity on a healing, psychic level.

The person with Cancer on the ascendant will go out of his way to give aid and comfort. He will literally give you the shirt off his back if you need it. He cares not that he is cold, for your needs can seem more important than his own. He may sometimes overreact, yet his identification with others' problems is very real. If anything, he should show caution about overextending himself where he is not appreciated. He is a giver without thought of recompense, but if he feels unappreciated, it can be a devastating letdown. He gives what he can, and whatever he does or gives, is done or given with love. He may have to discover the meaning of discrimination by "casting his pearls before swine" and having his gifts thrown back in his face. If he "rescues" and then gets "persecuted," he begins to learn to value what he has to offer. He must guard against surrounding himself with people he feels sorry for in order to satisfy his mothering urges. He will reach a turning point in his own development and awareness when he begins to "feel" on a less personal basis. Since his decisions about survival have to do with assuming the protective role, universal mothering brings deeper satisfaction on a much higher level.

FINANCE

Financial matters are directly related to self-esteem, with Leo ruling the house of money. It may be a matter of pride for one with Cancer rising to earn his own money. His ego focus is largely on financial capabilities, therefore his earning capacity has much to do with his sense of self-worth. If he thinks well of himself, his income is high. If he is going through a phase of self-doubt, his income is liable to reflect insecurities of the moment. He is very capable of earning money through his own good name, and through building a strong reputation.

The Sun rules the second house when Cancer is on the rise. The Sun indicates vitality, energy, strength, pride, and ego. The aspects to the Sun in the natal chart will indicate how easy it is for this native to deal with financial matters. If the Sun is well aspected and strong in the chart, the individual has a natural desire to have a healthy income. His sense of self-worth makes it possible for him to put a good price tag on his time and energy. He knows what he is worth to his employer or public, and does not hesitate to assume that he will be well compensated. He often earns money through his executive ability. Leadership is easy for him in the financial arena and he can take charge when it comes to money. Eventually, he may earn income through building a "name" and being identified with a product or a creative venture. Gayle Gleckler worked for several advertising agencies, handling top-notch commercial products. She became the head of her creative group, but was still working for someone else. Finally, she got in touch with an executive ability as well as reaffirming her creative talent and opened her own agency. Her name is now on the door—Gleckler Associates.

Energy seems directly related to an earning capacity. When
the person with Cancer rising is on top of his financial world, his
energy is high. When his income drops, he experiences lowered
vitality. It can work in the reverse as well. If he has good energy, he is more capable of assuming top-dog position with management of funds. No matter how the Sun is aspected in the
chart, you can assume that this person will be stimulated by
financial matters. It may be difficult for him to work for someone
else, for he needs to be the boss. He must eventually assume
leadership in the way he earns his money. With his sensitive rising sign, he is already in touch with the trends of the times. It
may be a matter of simply taking charge in a stronger way. A
need to be generous can also stimulate him to earn money. He
taps the "masculine" or animus part of himself in financial areas,
whereas he exhibits the "feminine" or anima side in his personal
life.

If the Sun is not well aspected in the chart, problems can
occur in connection with income. His earning capacity may be a
substitute for a sense of self-worth, that sense of self-esteem
depending on the size of his income. These aspects can also indicate how he spends money. If, for instance, the Sun is badly
aspected to the planet Uranus, money can run through his
fingers. He may have erratic, unpredictable earning periods. He
may be rebellious about earning and spending money. With a
difficult aspect to Saturn, this person can have fears about his
earning capacity and worry about financial matters. He will be
inclined toward bargains, be cautious with expenditures, and
have a "poor" complex. No sum of money will resolve insecurity
about finance. If there is a difficult aspect to Pluto, he can be a
compulsive spender and a gambler. He will earn funds in big
chunks, and then perhaps none at all. He will tend to spend
money in the same way. If he has a bad aspect to Neptune, he
may be especially unrealistic about financial matters. Jupiter aspects indicate extravagance, whereas Mars aspects show frustrations and impatience with money matters. With a negative aspect to the Moon, emotional upsets can compel this person to
extra expenditures.

The placement of the Sun in the chart will indicate how the

person earns money. If the Sun is in the first house, he naturally earns money through his personality. With a second house Sun, there is a double indication of his emphasis on the financial arena. If the Sun is posited in the third house, his income is derived through contracts, communication, writing, the media industry. Real estate, home, land will be the source of income with a fourth house position. The fifth house indicates a creative or gambling ability. With this position the stock market can be a focal point for income. The sixth house indicates service, foods, work in general, and health matters. This individual may be a workaholic in areas related to food, health, and service capacity. Partnership is the prime source of income with a seventh house placement. An eighth house Sun indicates that money may come through residuals, dividends, commissions. Inheritance is a factor sometimes; this Cancer rising may earn money through using others' funds or through raising venture capital or getting grants. The ninth house indicates promotional areas, advertising, travel, higher education, legal matters, and there is an emphasis both on spending and on earning in those areas. With a tenth house placement, a career is a necessity for this individual, and public life is the area where he places emphasis and where he earns his income. It is emphasized very clearly that he needs to earn money through association with his name or executive ability. He must be in top-dog position. An eleventh house position indicates that group activity can be a source of income. If the Sun is placed in the twelfth house, the person may not be in touch with his earning capacity, or he may earn funds by working alone, on "closed sets," away from the public eye.

COMMUNICATIONS

With Mercury ruling the third house of communications when Cancer is on the ascendant, it would appear that writing or communications in general will be even more strongly emphasized. This individual has an analytical ability that can modify his emotional reactions when he allows it to come into play. It emphasizes his need to talk, discuss things, read and learn. If

Mercury is well aspected in the chart, it is easy for him to study and learn. School should never be a problem as long as he is stimulated intellectually, but discipline may be a problem in early school years.

The placement of Mercury in the chart is the indication of what the person will talk about and think about. With this ascendant, the native is particularly concerned with community and family. The third house also rules brothers and sisters. Virgo is the sign on the cusp of the third house when Cancer is rising, and Virgo is the sign of criticism and analysis. This native may tend to "analyze" his family, especially brothers and sisters. He can criticize them at times, but it can work the other way as well. If Mercury is not well aspected in the chart, his siblings can analyze or criticize him. If there are good aspects, however, there will be good communication between brothers, sisters, and neighbors. Since he thinks about his family, and in this instance brothers and sisters in particular, he can also write about them. Neil Simon has portrayed his brother Danny in almost all of his plays. Danny is the older brother in *Come Blow Your Horn*, Felix Unger in *The Odd Couple*, and Ralph in *Chapter Two*. The telephone will be an important instrument of communication for one with this ascendant. He will keep in touch with people easily and constantly if Mercury is well placed and aspected in his chart. The general need to communicate is stressed.

This person may do his best thinking when he is walking, commuting or running around town. His intellect seems to be stimulated by activity. He may get particularly sensational ideas when he is driving a car. The manner and style of communications can vary tremendously. The list of poets and artists with this ascendant is long. Composers include Tchaikovsky, Richard Strauss, Berlioz, Franz Schubert, and Rimski-Korsakov. Artists include Vincent van Gogh, Francisco Goya, and Salvador Dali. Poets Lord Byron, Walt Whitman, and Rod McKuen share this ascendant. Authors Pearl Buck, Tolstoy, Rudyard Kipling, and Truman Capote also have Cancer rising. William Blake—poet, artist, and mystic—was born with Cancer rising, as was TV personality David Frost.

HOME LIFE

The fourth house in a chart indicates not only the kind of home and lifestyle one is attracted to but the way in which the individual has photographed the parent of the opposite sex. It can give a clue as to the conditions at the latter part of one's life. It is clear that the trying time for one with Cancer rising is in childhood. Once the individual has worked past oversensitivity and overly emotional reactions to make contact with his particular abilities, it appears that he allows himself to have beauty and love in his life. Venus is one of the planets that is called a "benefic." Venus indicates love, beauty, art, ease of living, and social matters. The parent of the opposite sex is photographed as a loving person, perhaps artistic. This is the parent that the individual loves and adores. If Venus is well aspected in the chart, the love flows easily between the child and the parent, but if Venus is not well aspected, the child may have photographed that parent as copping out for the sake of peace and easy living, or one who avoids making waves in life, taking the easy way out, or being overly diplomatic.

The person with Cancer rising is so invested in his home that you can be assured it will be a place of beauty and color, as well as ease and comfort. He will certainly love his home and will surround himself with the kind of environment that will provide the right atmosphere for his nurturing instincts. Color is especially essential for the sensitive nature of one with Cancer rising. This emotional person must have peace and harmony, love and affection, at home to restore his emotional balance. Often the attunement to public tastes and sense of color and decor can lead this person to interior design. Jeffrey Chester, although not a professional interior designer, is especially talented in this area. A well developed sense of color, design, and taste make his home a wonderful place to visit. The atmosphere is beautiful but restful, with a wonderfully homey feeling. Everyone feels nurtured when they leave. Jeffrey has taken charge of the decor for the homes of many of his friends, always giving excellent advice.

If Venus is badly aspected, the individual with this ascendant may not put effort into beautifying his home. He may not realize how sensitive he is to environment and color. The very shades of the spectrum of color can affect his emotional state at any given time. If he is depressed, it can be important that he surround himself with bright colors—yellows, oranges, greens, and vivid shades. If he tends toward brown, gray, and black, he is only making it harder to pull himself out of his emotional rut. Examination of the relationship with the parent of the opposite sex can give him special clues as to the kind of environment he chooses, and why. He may tend to be easygoing and more peaceful when he is at home, even inclining toward laziness. This is where he wants to let down, desiring peace and harmony more than anything. He goes to his home when he is in a vulnerable state, to restore himself. Venusian activities occupy him there—cooking, painting, and social activities in general. He becomes more diplomatic as he grows older, being inclined toward peacemaking, social justice, and finding balance. Love and affection seem assured in later life. He may have problems and lessons to be learned in those areas early in his life, but as he works past emotions, he comes to the understanding of love in a different way.

ROMANCE • CREATIVE EXPRESSION

The person with Cancer rising is magnetized by a certain type of individual. A natural desire and need for emotional attachments and romantic encounters brings him into contact with very dynamic, charismatic people. He may also discover that he gets the rug pulled out from under him by those same magnetic, attractive people unless he makes wise choices. Pluto rules this house when Cancer is on the ascendant. Pluto is the planet that describes extremes in life. It indicates the greatest transmutation and change in life, as well as power, compulsion, and the child ego state. In the positive sense, Pluto indicates someone who is highly evolved, effective, and powerful. The evolved Pluto energy is like a dammed-up body of water, releasing enough electricity to light up cities. In its negative state, it describes someone conditioned to play games, manipulate, and live on a destructive level. The individual with Cancer rising, with his compulsion for romance, can be determined to get what or who he wants, regardless of the health of that situation. He is usually successful, but when he forces a situation or a person, he gets it back all too fast. He may discover too late that he would have been better off without that particular experience. It is most essential that he look for someone in touch with his or her own powerful nature, and who lives on the "positive" side of life, or the Cancer rising finds himself in deep water. Since this is such a strong mothering sign, he has a strong compulsion for children. In romantic situations he can often attract magnetic "children" who have little regard for his ultimate welfare.

The person with this sensitive ascendant has great difficulty in areas connected to his emotional and love life. This difficulty is more than likely due to his unwillingness to pick people who are good for him. It may be his unconscious way of rebelling or getting even. In some way it can be his expression of mischief. Until he realizes what he is really doing, he is completely drawn to the type of personality that does not ensure a stable relationship. He wants to "play" in the area of romance. He wants someone exciting and magnetic, but he often finds destruction instead. He can get hooked by a desire to transform the other person and release that person's potential. This is where he can kid himself and get into trouble, and so he needs to be especially careful about his selection. When he is willing to let go of any situation that he must manipulate to keep, he'll find himself attracting healthier people. If he has a well-aspected Pluto in his natal chart, he will only be attracted to the highly evolved people who match his own sense of morality and purpose.

The fifth house in a chart indicates many things. It shows not only the romantic inclination but the creative energy, children, and the gambling instincts. With Pluto, the power planet, ruling this house when Cancer is rising, there is even greater indication of the power this person has through his ability to reach masses of people with his creative energy. There is so much intensity and forcefulness connected with the creative energy that it must be released on a healthy level, or it can overwhelm the average person. It can literally knock people over. It is this energy that can get the Cancer rising into trouble. If the individual is motivated to release his creativity and gambling instincts on a high level where he can reach masses of people, the energy that is left will attract the right kind of romantic situation. Using that powerful energy where it can be diversified creates a "void" that brings in positive situations and people on a personal level. If he is not using it up, his need to "play" is too great and he can get into "mischief" or less than healthy situations. He can be attracted to the gambling type and to substitute children. The end result of these attractions can be very painful indeed.

Children of a person with Cancer rising will be especially magnetic and personable. The Cancer rising needs to teach them early on to be aware of an ability to charm and magnetize people. Those children need to be encouraged to use energy in an open way so as not to manipulate, to put their cards on the table and take their chances. They can learn all too easily how to play on this parent's emotions to get what they need and want. These children can grow up to be very powerful, with tremendous charisma and ability to wield influence. They will never be children to be ignored.

Actors with this ascendant find a natural outlet for their creative ability in reaching masses of people through film and television. Pluto rules the television industry, but also the underworld of the gambler or outlaw. Jesse James had Cancer rising. His concern for his family was well known. He went about taking care of them in a negative Plutonian manner, however.

One with Cancer on the rise will satisfy many of his playful urges through entertaining his friends. He can handle large groups of people quite easily. He may have a compulsion to give bigger and bigger parties. He has a knack for attracting fascinating people. Sarah Callandar, publicity director for Laura Ashley, may well be the Perle Mesta of her day. Her parties are a fascinating combination of young and old, with all types of interesting people from all walks of life thrown together. She loves to entertain people visiting from other countries in order to introduce them to her American friends. It seems as easy for her to entertain fifty as it is to entertain five.

WORK • SERVICE • HEALTH

With Jupiter ruling the sixth house of work, service, health, and foods, this person needs constant challenges when it comes to these areas. Jupiter indicates expansion and optimism. It is the "lucky" planet. The native with Cancer rising dives into new projects with tremendous enthusiasm and with high hopes for success. If boredom sets in, however, that project is a lost cause for him. He needs to be challenged, on his toes, and able to expand constantly in his work. If he is bored on the job, he may once again turn to food and drink to satisfy those urges for emotional satisfaction. In its negative sense, Jupiter indicates disappointment and overindulgence. Therefore, the Cancer rising needs to be sure he is in a working situation that will grow along with him so he'll avoid disappointment. Gayle Gleckler has found a perfect working situation in advertising. Each new campaign is a new challenge. Jean Nidetsch used her enthusiasm to sell her friends on losing weight. (Jupiter also rules selling.) Since the sixth house also rules foods, it is interesting to note that part of the Weight Watchers package involves selling calorie-counted foods. Jeffrey Chester channels his Jupiterian instincts into preparing fantastic gourmet meals, as beautiful to look at as to taste. With typical Jupiterian extravagance, there is always a great deal of food left over from his fabulous parties, to give away or to freeze for a contribution when a friend is in need of something interesting to serve. Gayle Gleckler remarked that one of the first things she did in her new office was to be sure the refrigerator was well stocked. She feeds her friends frequently, also with great panache. One with this ascendant has extravagant taste in food and drink. Alex Bespaloff uses his Jupiterian tastes to write about fine wines. His wine racks overflow with fabulous samples of his excellent taste.

Since Jupiter also indicates a tendency to overdo or overindulge, it is important for one with this ascendant to discover his patterns, especially when he is disappointed, let down, or hurt. He is inclined to feed his oral needs with food, trying to satisfy his emotional craving by stuffing himself. He can discover better substitutes for his cravings than rich food; his health depends on it. Jupiter rules the liver, so overindulgence will only aggravate digestive problems. Cooking for others is one way to release many of his creative, mothering urges.

Jupiter also indicates a desire to be close to nature. It is essential for one with this ascendant to find time for walks in the woods to keep in touch with the great outdoors. He may also have a natural green thumb. Working with plants can satisfy his nature-loving instincts.

MARRIAGE • PARTNERSHIP

This is the area that comes under "karmic" fire in the life of one with Cancer on the rise. Saturn is the ruler of partnership in this placement, whether business or marital. Since Saturn indicates the lessons we need to learn and the heaviest karmic situation from the past, one with this ascendant must be especially careful in his selection of a mate.

It appears that what one with this ascendant is looking for in a marriage is security. His own emotional swings keep him coming and going, so when he finds a person who appears to be stable, reliable, and responsible, that person represents the security he feels he needs. If Saturn is well aspected in the chart, it will be a serene and stable marriage, but if Saturn is badly aspected, the likelihood is that the marriage can be heavy, restricting, and limiting. Many times, a heavy Saturn in the chart can indicate an inherent fear of marriage. It is as if the individual senses the restrictions connected with partnership. It is especially important to examine the relationship to see where the limitation will end and the sense of stability will begin.

If it is well aspected, Saturn is the planet that indicates responsibility, practicality, and steadfastness. It can represent the parent type, who is there to give a solid base, be supportive and responsible. In its positive sense, the one with Cancer rising can act as the mother and the partner will assume the father role, the disciplinarian. If Saturn is not well aspected, however, it represents one who is insecure, overly cautious, and judgmental instead of supportive. The Cancer rising can find himself in a

limiting, restrictive partnership with someone cold and unresponsive, hardly what he needs to ensure security.

The Kabbalists liken Saturn to the "playpen" Mother Nature
puts her children in. That playpen can be important for the
safety of the child early on, but later it can be restrictive and
limiting. Safety can also be fun, so the person with a Cancer ascendant must be sure there are plenty of toys in his playpen to
keep him happy. He needs to look for someone who is responsible without being overly conservative. A "proper" person, but
fun-loving. He must be careful not to let the prospect of a sturdy
family tree keep him from looking at the realistic potential of the
individual. He wants a heavyweight, but one that will act as a
supportive agent, not a limiting one.

The most important facet of the partner to be aware of is a
strong sense of self-worth. If that person is sure of himself or
herself, the support in the marriage is fantastic. It will be long-
lasting and comfortable—a forever situation. But if the partner
has insecurities, he will tend to keep the one with Cancer rising
tied to the limitations he feels in himself. He will convince the
Cancer rising that he can't live without the partnership, whereas
in fact it is the partner that can't live without the energy of one
with Cancer rising. This person, the partner, will act like a rock,
stuck in the mud at the shoreline, keeping one with the Cancer
ascendant tied up, rather than acting as a stabilizing anchor. A
rock creates its own little whirlpool, pulling things to its own
stuck place. Unless he is very careful, the one with Cancer
rising is sometimes easily pulled in by negative strokes, negative
messages, and negative situations. Since he is so sensitive, he
needs to be aware of the first judgmental message he hears from
one he is interested in. He will never be able to do anything
about another person's feelings of self-worth; all he can do is
take care of his own. He needs to understand what he has to give
in a partnership situation and look for someone who truly
appreciates him. He must guard against a desire to rescue; a
rock will remain a rock as long as its behavior produces the
desired results. The Cancer rising will have to deal with his
mothering instincts most carefully in this instance. He may have
to consider that marriage may be his own way of keeping him-

self safe and in the playpen. If he is willing to assume responsibility for his own happiness and life, he ultimately attracts one to his side who is protective and who is desirous of fulfilling the same sense of destiny and duty on a humanitarian level as Cancer rising. Together they can act as "mother and father" on a profound level, being mutually supportive and nurturing to each other and to mankind.

NEEDS

The eighth house indicates how a person gets his needs met and the quality of energy he has to send out to humanity. With the planet Uranus ruling this house when Cancer is on the rise, many of his needs are filled at the last split second, or in an unpredictable manner. His nervous energy can be redirected, like electricity, to act like a healing agent. If he chooses, he can get in touch with truly unique qualities and act as a healer in his own way. The planet Uranus rules many things seemingly unrelated, yet it primarily indicates the unique, genius part of oneself. It rules music, electricity, inventions, recordings, electronics, and humanitarian concerns. It is interesting to note the kind of gifts that have been released through this interesting energy. Judy Garland sent out healing energy through her voice, perhaps without knowing it. Her gift was certainly her musical genius. Peter Hurkos uses his psychic energy to help people by solving crimes. (Psychic energy is also ruled by Uranus.) Clergymen James Pike and Pope Pius XII shared this ascendant. Their gift of healing through their religious works is well known. Uranus is the first of the higher-octave planets, describing instincts and spirituality. Dean Pike explored his interest in metaphysics, or that higher-octave realm, to peer beyond death. His encouragement to humanity to raise its consciousness is truly a gift.

Psychologist Richard Alpert got in touch with his humanitarian instincts to become Guru Baba Ram Dass, touching thousands of lives through his work. Astrologer Charles Jayne reaches many people through his writing. He sends out healing energy through his work. Theosophists Helena Blavatsky and Korla Pandit share this ascendant. Uranus describes unique discoveries; scientists Marie Curie, Thomas Huxley, and Albert Einstein were born with Cancer rising. The genius these brilliant people released with their discoveries is beyond compare. Explorer Amerigo Vespucci changed the course of history through his gift to the world, as did inventor Guglielmo Marconi. Whether through music, science, invention, religion, or astrology, these people have worked through emotional pain to release something unique to humanity. You can be sure it was not easy for any one of them. It appears that when this humanitarian instinct is released, the individual is taken care of in a special way. Last-minute nerves must give way to high-energy direction. If the "rebellious" nature is channeled into humanitarian concerns, the energy seems to smooth out, like electricity running through wires. A short circuit can produce a fire, however. It is important for an individual with the Cancer ascendant to take action to avoid blowing up his own system. High-tension wires can be dangerous. Since Uranus rules chance-taking and risks, it is possible that one of the ways this individual finds an outlet for a rebellious type energy is to run up bills without thinking. It may be the way of challenging himself to utmost productivity. He gives himself no choice but to walk out on the edge of a limb to take chances in order to rectify the damage he's done. He may be happier if he finds a better way to motivate himself to express that genius, inventive, unique energy.

RECOGNITION

Neptune rules the ninth house when Cancer is on the ascendant. Neptune is the planet of vision and inspiration. It is the altruistic planet. Since Neptune rules the ninth house of the "higher mind," the person with Cancer rising is very idealistic. He can be inspired by high purpose, vision, and ideals. His sense of the overall picture on a philosophical level can be a natural antidote for the emotional quality of his personality. It again emphasizes his ability to be in touch with the trends of the times and to inspire others.

The ninth house is the house that rules advertising, publishing, publicity, and promotional effort. It also rules legal affairs, distances, travel, and other countries. If Neptune is well aspected in the natal chart, this person has a natural desire to travel and explore other countries. His idealistic sense keeps him high on life and attracts publicity and public attention. Either he has a knack for publicizing someone or something else, or the public identifies with him and puts him on a pedestal of sorts. He can be easily recognized or published.

If Neptune is not well aspected, however, there is a tendency to overidealize, stay with naïveté instead of reality, and set himself up for disillusionment of some sort. His ability to confront will not be well developed. He will overglamorize ideals and be let down in some way. His own publicity will either be terrific or disillusioning. Marie Antoinette had Cancer rising. Her famous remark about cake was not said by, but about, her. Nevertheless, she was not loved or adored by her public. The Duchess of Windsor received notorious publicity all her life. She might have made headlines no matter what the circumstances of her life. Mary Todd Lincoln did not share in the public's admiration of her husband. Hetty Green was another target for the press, as was actress Hedy Lamarr. Only one part of the country admired General Sherman. His name is still anathema to children in the South. All of the actors with this ascendant have run the risk of bad publicity at one time or another. Yet many of the well-known people with this rising sign have been lionized by their fans. If Neptune is well aspected in the chart, it is clear that a person with this ascendant has a particular kind of vision. He is able to see the overall concept, get the overall picture. If Neptune is not well aspected, he can continue on his merry way, regardless of the truth of a particular situation. If this individual is able to take off the rose-colored glasses, work past his illusions, and still retain the dream, it seems he has it made. His instincts are fantastic, his vision incredible. Since he really wants to save the world on some level, he reaches philosophical heights that give perspective not only on his own life but on the lives of all those around him. He can be the visionary, leading others by his own example.

CAREER

The tenth house in a chart indicates career areas, social matters, and public life. It also indicates the way the individual has photographed the parent of the same sex. Mars rules this house when Cancer is on the ascendant. Mars is the planet of action, determination, drive, and ambition. Mars is indicative of the pioneering spirit. If Mars is well aspected in the natal chart, a sense of competition will spur him on to an innovative way of handling career activities. His natural energy will be directed toward a career situation which requires drive and determination to succeed. He will naturally be attracted to areas where competition is possible. He will enjoy a good fight with competitors equally talented or capable as he. A challenge will stimulate him to do bigger and better things with his energy. He will enjoy spending time discovering innovative ways to handle certain matters and will be quite resourceful when it comes to his public life and career. Nonnie Moore, an Aquarian with Cancer rising, is a top editor at *Harper's Bazaar*. Nonnie deals with the highly competitive fashion industry and must stay on her toes to be in the vanguard of forecasting new trends. Much of the ability to handle this kind of ambition comes from the relationship with the parent of the same sex. There can be a kind of healthy competition with this parent which programs him to be ready for the challenges ahead. He can photograph this parent as energetic, ambitious, determined, and a fighter. This will naturally make it "okay" for him to use the same kind of energy in his own career. If, however, he has photographed that parent as frustrated, angry, and impatient, he may have difficulty in releasing his own angry energy in a creative manner.

Mars is the planet that rules sex as well as highly creative energy. If that energy is turned inward it becomes frustration, impatience, and anger. Much of the ability to release the sexual, creative energy has to do with subliminal parent messages about that energy. If there was guilt on the part of the parent about his own drives and sexual energy, the child, too, will feel guilty. If that parent gave good encouraging messages to the child with Cancer rising about directing that creative energy, the individual will have no trouble finding a career that utilizes his ambitious, directed, sexual energy in a good way. No matter what kind of messages he received, there is a likelihood that frustration with the slow pace of career situations can sometimes occur. It is in this area that the native with this ascendant is most impatient.

It is toward career matters or public life that he will direct much of his sexual energy, however. If his career is not challenging enough, he will find that an active social life can keep him calm and more patient. He will probably enjoy dancing or some sort of physical activity in connection with his social life. If he is in a career situation that is especially frustrating, he is liable to use up some of that excess energy in less than healthy ways. Mars energy can indicate a tendency to fight, drink too much, rebel. Politician George Wallace was the target of a negative Mars attack in connection with his public life, as was Marie Antoinette. Mars indicates strife, wars, metals, the military. Emperor Maximilian of Mexico and Kaiser Wilhelm II of Germany share this ascendant.

In a positive sense, Mars indicates being "first" in career matters, a pioneer. Lucille Ball certainly utilized much of her energy in pioneering situation comedy on television. The person with Cancer rising needs to be free to show his resourcefulness in the career arena. If he is in business for himself, he will do away with many of the frustrations he would ordinarily have with employers and bosses. If he was frustrated in his relationship with the parent of the same sex, he will allow himself to stay in a frustrated career situation. Actors with this ascendant find a natural release just by being involved in a competitive business. Recognition comes through the willingness to take chances and pave the way for others. High creative ability is possible with a better direction of energy.

FRIENDSHIP

The sentimental nature of one with Cancer rising certainly extends to friendships as well. He loves his friends and that feeling

of affection is returned to him. His sociability extends to group
situations too. He will be most gracious in relating to any group
of people combined for work or play. His love nature seems to
have a natural release when it comes to attracting loving, beautiful, pleasure loving, easygoing people into his life. If he loves
someone, it would take a lot to destroy the feelings he has for
them. At times, he may avoid making waves in areas of friendship.

Venus rules this house when Cancer is ascending. Venus is the
planet of love and beauty, the arts. Venus badly aspected indicates laziness, too much desire for peace and harmony. If Venus
is not well aspected in the natal chart, one with this ascendant
may not make an effort to see his friends. He may hesitate to
confront any situation that might include a showdown. He'd
keep peace, hoping any difficult situation would blow over,
rather than chance losing someone dear to him. If Venus is well
aspected, he has a natural talent for combining interesting people who may never see each other away from his environment,
but who enjoy the companionship and warmth he extends. The
person with this ascendant will show tremendous diplomacy,
love, and graciousness when it comes to any group situation or
friendship.

At one of the parties given by Gayle Gleckler, everyone ended
up in a huge circle, hugging each other—an unplanned, spontaneous reaction to the warmth of her hospitality. No one could
forget the loving feelings in that group, mainly a demonstration
of the love felt for Gayle. One could hardly find a better friend
than Terry Schaeffer, who extended the hospitality of his Paris
and New York apartments to special friends who visited him
there. Both Jeffrey Chester and Sarah Callandar remain attached
to their friends, and enjoy extending the warmth of their personal lives to those they love. Allison Hayes stayed in touch with
school chums long after she went to Hollywood to work as an
actress. Years later, the door of friendship remained open in
spite of the passage of years and varying experiences.

The person with this ascendant may have a preference for
"beautiful" or artistic people. With Venus ruling this house,
there is a proclivity for graciousness, charm, and sociability. People with these attributes naturally gravitate to the side of one

with this rising sign. Time spent with friends is likely to be quiet but pleasurable time, visiting art galleries, museums, theaters, or talking over good food. Since he directs much of his dynamic, aggressive energy toward career, he will enjoy pastimes with friends that are easier, more relaxing. He may enjoy the companionship of a few people on an intimate level, even though he can entertain large groups quite easily. A quiet dinner with good food and a beautiful atmosphere is more to his liking than sports, games, or competitive activity.

HIDDEN MATTERS • SUBCONSCIOUS PROCESS

The twelfth house in a chart is indicative of the way one feels when alone, as well as the quality that is less easy to express overtly. When Cancer is on the rise, the planet Mercury rules this house of hidden matters. This individual does his best thinking when he is alone. His mind is never still and he is able to come up with all the clever things he may not be able to quickly think of when he is surrounded by too many people. When he is exposed or in his vulnerable state, the mind may take second place to emotional reactions. It is when he goes off by himself that he is able to think and analyze.

The natural antidote for the emotional reactions of this sign is the mental quality. Whatever he can do to learn how to express himself more easily is essential for his ultimate well-being. He may have to actually practice a technique for saying what he means and meaning what he says. Many of his comments are tinged with the feelings of the moment. He may have to pull away to get some perspective, to decide what he really thinks about a particular subject. His feelings change from hour to hour. Any kind of therapy which enables him to get in touch with his thoughts is especially helpful. Many people need therapy to get in touch with their feelings; the Cancer rising is all too much in touch with his feelings. He needs the mental overview.

In childhood this person with Cancer ascendant may not be able to take advantage of his intellect. He has a clever mind, but may not easily think on his feet. Under pressure, the pages blur,

the mind goes blank, and he appears less capable than he really
is. He can be easily distracted by other children in a classroom
or by any minor disturbances. When he is really off by himself,
he can begin to think more clearly. He can sharpen his perceptions and clarify his thoughts by writing. If a child is encouraged early on to put his feelings on paper, it can help
release him from the sometimes terrible emotional grip he is in.

It is this ability to be stimulated mentally when he is alone
that enhances his natural creative ability. He can spend hours
working on a canvas or at a typewriter. He will enjoy mentally
stimulating activities when he is all by himself. In fact, he needs
to be stimulated on an intellectual level when he is alone. He
can read, think, solve puzzles in order to keep himself from
boredom. If Mercury is well aspected in the chart, it is easy for
him to find that stimulation, but if Mercury is not well aspected,
he can at times be bombarded on a mental level, or find a substitute for thinking such as television. The clarity of his thoughts
will be indicated by the planets affecting Mercury. He may tend
to be depressed if Saturn is affecting Mercury or exaggerate
matters if Jupiter is the offending planet. With Pluto, his
thoughts carry great weight, but may be difficult to transmute.
With Neptune, an idealistic quality is superimposed. Mars
brings an angry touch and Venus makes for lazy thinking. If
Mercury and the Moon are badly aspected, it is difficult for him
to sort out his thoughts. If Uranus is affecting Mercury, it is almost impossible for him to turn off his mind. Meditation can
help him gain greater control of his mental processes.

The twelfth house also indicates any psychic inclinations. If
one with this ascendant is inclined toward the occult or unseen
matters, he can develop his psychic talent on a purely mental
level. He will not receive any flashes in the night, or experience
sensationalism to indicate his extrasensory perceptions. He will
simply begin to "know" things. His knowledge about people and
patterns will grow quietly but surely. If he is able to discipline
himself to sit at a typewriter or with pen in hand, he may be
surprised at the flow of ideas that come to him at that time. He
becomes especially sensitive to the thought patterns others have
when he finds time to be alone. Solitude may be difficult for him
early on, as he is given too much time to think. However, after a

period of adjustment, he may come to like his own company very much. Training himself to be disciplined mentally brings him full circle to face his true creative ability. When he is ready to assume the responsibility of his healing gifts to humanity, he will uncover the true intellectual genius stored in the hidden recesses of his mind.

LEO
RISING

LEO IS THE ROYAL SIGN. THE PERSON with this ascendant is dramatic, regal in his bearing, and certainly in control of any situation. Leo rising is the ascendant of "kingship"; the symbol is the lion, king of the beasts. (You can see the natural comparison.) Leadership and executive ability are easy for one with this ascendant. It seems that he came into this world to express individuality, dominance, and strength. When he walks into a room, he exudes a vibrancy that is not easily ignored. There is no doubt about his dramatic ability, as that seems to be a natural quality for him to express. He is the actor of the zodiac.

The ruler of Leo is the Sun. Since the Sun is the source of heat, energy, and light, the kind of dynamic personality that goes with this ascendant is especially sparkling. Leo rising is literally a ball of fire. His energy is almost always high. He is an extrovert and can be somewhat of an exhibitionist at heart. If he is the shy type of Leo, he still commands attention. He can be the life of any party and is never at a loss for social invitations and friendship. Everyone else may actually seem a little tame in comparison.

The lion may look ferocious, but the Leo rising is really a kitten at heart. If you stroke and pet him and tell him how wonderful he is, he can be easily tamed, for he is a pussycat underneath. He may growl loudly and go after big game, but after the conquest, he always wants his fur stroked. He is a lovable sort when you get past the roar. With a little understanding of how to tame him, you'll have him eating out of your hand.

His appearance is also characteristic of the lion. If you look carefully, you will see the similarity. He usually has a wonderful abundance of hair, growing in thick profusion, framing his face like a mane, and he has a "lion-like" face. He is easily recognizable by the way he dresses, as his royal attire will give him away every time. He prefers dramatic combinations of color and clothing, always in good taste, but probably designed to attract attention. He will rarely appear in public without his royal robes. If he is in sloppy condition, no doubt his ego has been wounded. Rather than show up at a gathering in a depressed state, attired in less than glorious swathing, he'll probably stay at home. Since he may feel it is his job to entertain everyone around him, and be on stage at every occasion, he'd rather postpone the appearance if he is low in energy.

Leo is a fire sign. The person with this ascendant needs the warmth of the Sun, as he gets cold very easily. He seems to come alive in a new sort of way when the weather is pleasant. He may wear several sweaters at times when everyone else is quite comfortable. He is electric in energy and needs warmth to recharge his batteries. The Sun reinforces his natural enthusiasm and zest when his energy flags. Leo is a fixed sign, indicating determination. There is no stopping him once his mind is made up. He cannot be influenced or swayed from his course. He knows where he is going and knows just how to get there. Very little will stand in his way if he has made up his mind about a particular plan of action.

It is fascinating to watch one with Leo rising. Everything he does has a natural sense of heightened energy about it. The way he moves, the pauses he takes are not necessarily calculated for effect. It simply reflects his natural sense of the dramatic. Whatever he is doing can be tremendously interesting to observe even if he is only lighting a cigarette or talking to a friend. His sixth sense about prestige, dignity, and command are part of his overall effectiveness. He can seem to make a grand entrance, whether it is a business meeting or a social gathering. He wants to be noticed entering a restaurant or party, and usually is. If he really makes a bid for attention, no one can hold a candle to him. He doesn't seem to have to do anything special to attract recognition and have everyone's rapt attention.

Marilyn Monroe was born with Leo on the rise. She had a quality that attracted attention everywhere she went. Susan Strasberg, with Leo rising herself, wrote in her book *Bittersweet* that Marilyn could "turn on" like lighting up an electric bulb. Once when they were walking down Broadway unnoticed, Marilyn said, "Do you want to see me be *her?*" Instantly without seeming to do anything, she took on a new glow. People began to turn around and stare, where a few moments before, they had passed without a second glance. People respond to one with this ascendant automatically, as he can easily be the most interesting person around. This extra attention can actually put pressure on the individual with this ascendant, reinforcing his feeling that he must be "on" at all times.

The person with this regal rising sign will never forget a kindness. His devotion is boundless, his memory long. The story of the lion with a thorn in his paw is apropos of one with this ascendant. The lion never forgot the lad who removed that thorn and many years later was able to repay the kindness. The Leo rising will come to your aid when you need it most and expect it least. If, however, you have offended one with this ascendant, you'll see the chilly side of his personality. The gloom of the sky when the Sun has disappeared is nothing in comparison to the Leo personality when his ego has been hurt. He may never say anything about the situation, but will disappear to lick his wounds in private. He will restore his sense of self-worth in his own way and in his own time.

The Leo personality is loyal as well as devoted, if he is appreciated. There's nothing he won't do for a friend, as he loves to be helpful and kind. Since Leo rules the heart, his loving warmth and generosity are boundless. He will want some thanks periodically, and will find his own way to remind someone that he is due for strokes in return. He will be truly hurt if a friendship is soiled. He won't hold a grudge, he just won't be available and can be too cool for comfortable association. He will simply not acknowledge the presence of someone who has done him wrong, reducing that individual to an insignificant place in his life.

Nobility and pride are synonymous with the Leo personality. If this individual is at the bottom of the heap, and without resources, it will be sad indeed. He must be able to show his generosity, graciousness, and flair for good living, or he will suffer deeply. He can be extravagant, as he wants to have the best of everything. He also has royal taste. He can be tempted to run up bills if necessary to keep up appearances. He will be particularly lavish if his sense of luxury is shared and appreciated. He will want to provide comfort for those around him at all times. Fortunately, he is usually able to take care of his extravagant needs very well. His insult to himself is extreme if he fails in his own expectations.

The sense of drama, pomp, and ceremony is typified by the life and times of Lord Mountbatten of England. Throughout his entire career, he showed that strong leadership ability and nobility of heart. His concern for his troops, his sense of loyalty and dedication to the throne and to England, as well as his need to be of service continued all his life. After his retirement, he continued exhibiting those qualities to the townspeople in his small community, holding open house and sharing in their lives and concerns. His love of pomp and circumstance was revealed at parades and public appearances, but the true dramatic event that climaxed his life took place at his funeral. Every detail of that magnificent tribute was planned by "Dickie" Mountbatten himself, many years before his death. He was as splendid after his life ended as he had ever been before.

It might appear that with this kind of dynamic personality the Leo rising would never relinquish the spotlight to anyone else, but that is not true. He's ready, willing, and able to share the limelight. He will love to sponsor someone, especially if that person succeeds in his accomplishments. He will want to share in the reflected glory, however. If the Sun is well aspected in an individual chart, and his ego is healthy, a small acknowledgment will do. If, however, the Sun is badly aspected, indicating a lack of ego or self-esteem, the individual may do everything for the glory he receives in return. He will then appear unconcerned about anything anyone else is doing and be totally self-absorbed. Underneath what appears to be a vain, conceited personality, however, lies a heart of gold waiting to be recognized for his true worth. The Leo rising can be persuaded to perform for anyone who'll listen to him. Sometimes elevator operators and cab drivers will be the recipients of his best material. He may need to be encouraged to find a wider audience.

Since the rising sign indicates decisions about survival, the qualities of leadership become apparent early in life. The person with this ascendant evidently decides that he is on safe ground when he is in charge. It is probable that the child with this rising sign loses respect, to some degree, for the people around him, and feels he must take over as the strongest member of the family. He easily assumes the role of leader of the pack. He may do so without anyone being cognizant of what he is doing, and may, in fact, be unaware of it himself. It is so important to give a child with this rising sign the compliments he deserves, to encourage his natural leadership and executive tendencies. If his ego is well nourished, he channels that wonderful ability in healthy ways. If he is appreciated for his good values, good behavior, and noble actions, he will rise to his greatest height and continue on the positive path. If his ego is stamped out or neglected, he will get attention any way he can. He learns early on just how to get the recognition he craves. Negative strokes are better than no strokes at all. If he is rewarded for bad behavior or is ignored, he will be a sucker for flattery all his life.

Since drama is the key to his existence, he needs a positive opportunity to release that flair so he will avoid searching for drama strokes in everyday life. He begins performing as soon as he becomes aware of the sweet sound of applause. He can express his dramatic ability and leadership in innumerable ways, as long as he thinks well of himself and his abilities. Some of the outstanding personalities, leaders, and talents in our society were born with Leo rising. Actors Douglas Fairbanks, George Sanders, Yul Brynner, and Robert Mitchum were born with Leo rising. Actresses Susan Strasberg, Nina Foch, and Gina Lollobrigida have this ascendant, as did Marilyn Monroe and Mae West. Entertainers, singers Tom Jones, Gary Collins, Paul Simon, and Art Garfunkel also have Leo on the rise. Phineas T. Barnum, Muhammad Ali, and Jean-Claude Killy became well known apart from their chosen professions. Their colorful personalities won't remain hidden. Cecil B. De Mille was quite often more dramatic than the actors he hired.

The dramatic quality is also expressed through writing by other exceptional people. Eugene O'Neill, Ernest Hemingway, Honoré de Balzac, Alexandre Dumas, Christopher Marlowe, and Thomas Hardy share this ascendant. Henry Wadsworth Longfellow showed his particular sense of style through poetry. Publishers Horace Greeley and Paul Clancy, chess champion Bobby Fischer, coach Knute Rockne, and dancer Rudolph Nureyev were born with this sign ascending. The list of famous musicians and painters include Pablo Picasso, Paul Gauguin, Edouard Manet, Anthony Van Dyck, Henri Matisse, Franz Liszt, Erik Satie, Paul Hindemith, and Johann Sebastian Bach.

The list of people with Leo rising is exceptionally long. The natural ability to seek recognition can lead to the acclaim that is accorded them, no matter what their field. The person with a Leo ascendant is able to express his personality more easily than many other people. Some world leaders with this ascendant have been Otto von Bismarck, Marshal Tito, Nikita Khrushchev, and Lyndon Johnson. Mayor John Lindsay, Stephen A. Douglas, and Benjamin Harrison, as well as Leon Trotsky, have, or had, this dynamic personality along with the powerful Joseph P. Kennedy. These are men the world could not ignore.

When royalty has this royal sign on the ascendant, they seem especially natural for the role to which they were born, as if they chose on a soul level, that ascendant that would allow them the easy way to express leadership qualities. John I, James II, Charles I, Richard I, George III, and Charlemagne were the forerunners for the present-day royal Leo rising, Prince Charles of England, the Prince of Wales. Christopher Columbus, Kit Carson, Buffalo Bill Cody, Galileo, and Marcus Aurelius all had Leo rising. John Dillinger and Joseph Goebbels chose other ways to treat their ego needs.

Some Leo rising personalities chose service to their country as a way of expressing their true strength of character. Indira Gandhi and Jawaharlal Nehru, social worker Jane Addams, and Paramahansa Yogananda share this quality with Martin Luther. Present-day politicians Senator Thomas Eagleton and Senator Henry Jackson also have this ascendant. Perhaps the quality that endears people to one with Leo rising is expressed best by Bob Hope and Maurice Chevalier. The true quality of the actor with this personality and dynamic magnetism is typified by Richard Burton, with Leo rising, in his portrayal of King Arthur in *Camelot.*

The Sun in an astrological chart indicates the ego and the male, dominant part of the personality. In psychological terms, it represents the animus part of the personality. The placement of the Sun in the chart indicates where that ego is focused. It also indicates where recognition is likely to come from. It can tell what factor affects the sense of pride. The aspects indicate the health and strength of the ego and sense of pride. With the Sun as the ruler of the ascendant, the pride and ego have to do with self-expression, conditions of childhood, and the appearance of things. Recognition naturally follows the ease of expression. The natural release of this ego comes from the sector where the Sun is posited.

If the Sun is also in the first house of personality, these dramatic, dominant abilities are even increased. The Sun placed in the second house indicates that financial ability comes from self-expression and executive ability. Pride has to do with the earning capacity. Since the third house indicates communications in general, when the Sun is placed in this sector of the chart, the pride has to do with the ability to communicate, write, speak, negotiate. A fourth house position connects ego and pride with home, property, the parent of the opposite sex. It also indicates that the life comes full cycle with much of the early potential finally released later in life. The full force of personality is revealed around home base. Involvement with land, real estate, ecology is important.

Since the fifth house rules self-expression, and Leo is the fifth sign, with the Sun posited in that house, the acting ability, creative style is assured. Service is strongly indicated with a sixth house position. The individual has a great need to work in areas where recognition is assured. He may become a workaholic as well, needing to work in order to feel self-worth. Partnership is the matter of most concern with a seventh house Sun. The Leo rising will look for a mate or business partner to share the executive control with him. He wants his "soul mate," someone as strong as he is. He will attract someone who reflects his personality and sense of self.

An eighth house position of the Sun indicates an ability to get his needs met and a quality of strength that is his individual gift to humanity. This person with Leo rising may need to be recognized in order to fully release his influence for the betterment of others. He is truly able to deal in the world at large with a ninth house position. He is at home in other countries, with the advertising world, the publishing world, and can either represent others as an agent or get plenty of recognition for his own accomplishments. Legal matters, law, higher education are a natural focus for his ability.

Public life is indicated for the native with the Sun in the tenth house. He must be involved in career activity where his own personality will emerge. He shows his leadership ability in connection with career projects where he is in the spotlight. His career will be the most important focus in his life. With an eleventh house position, friendship and group activity are the natural outlets for ego needs. He selects friends that he is proud of, and who are able to stand tall, as well as being able to attract attention to their projects. He likes to be around people who are doing exceptional things with their lives. He enjoys people who command respect. He is drawn to people who reflect his own ego and sense of worth.

When the Sun is in the twelfth house, the individual has a tremendous need for solitude, periodically. He will recoup his strength, enthusiasm, and energy by spending time alone, even if only fifteen minutes in a day. He is able to delve deeply into hidden matters, can be especially perceptive and tuned in to psychic awareness, the occult, and the subconscious. He will show only the tip of the iceberg of his true personality. Depth of personality is apparent with this placement, but the individual may feel caged, restricted early in his life.

Since the person with Leo rising expresses the masculine part of the personality, dominance is characteristic of the personality no matter what sex. Both male and female portray these strong leadership, "masculine" qualities more easily than the feminine characteristics. In a relationship, there is no question as to who is the boss. It can sometimes be difficult for women with this ascendant to handle the dominant quality. If she has a well-aspected Sun in the chart, indicating a healthy and well-placed ego, she can handle her assertive qualities. She will be able to assume the stronger role. Peace of mind comes with the awareness of her need to have her own way, express her executive talent, and take charge. If her Sun is not well aspected, indicating a lack of ego recognition on her part, she may resist this strength and try to play the weaker role, making her life more difficult in the process. Sooner or later, these strong qualities will emerge. If she can channel these energies constructively, acknowledge the dominant survival issues, she will select a partner who is easy with the kind of role reversal that is probable.

The lady with this ascendant will never be a clinging vine, hard as she might try. She may or may not like having to make the decisions, but she will end up in that role even though outer circumstances appear to be quite different. It is possible that she will set up a situation, subconsciously, that will end in her having to take over. She may resent the position, without realizing it is her way of feeling safe. As soon as she accepts the fact that she was born to be a leader, she will find healthy, constructive ways of being just that.

If the Sun has strong aspects in the chart of a woman with this ascendant, she is always in touch with her strength and will be forthright about commanding respect. She has no sense of inferiority to men and will lose respect for any woman who plays the shrinking violet. She is not lacking in femininity, and may actually be the most feminine lady around because of her sense of nobility and proud bearing. Her sense of drama sends an electrically charged aura around her whole being. She lights up at will like a thousand incandescent candles, but no matter how strong she is, she responds to attention and recognition of her inner values like the cuddly kitten she can be inside. If she is willing to expose her vulnerability, the lioness in her can be tamed.

The planets aspecting the Sun in an individual chart will add other colors and hues to the personality of one with this ascendant. Modification of those natural qualities are indicated by the relationship of other planets to the placement of the Sun. If the Sun is conjunct, or next to, Mercury in the chart, the intelligence is linked with the strength of personality. He will be a master of words and ideas, and will express his thoughts dramatically and in an interesting way. His pride is connected to his intellect and ability to collect facts or analyze a situation.

When the Sun is aspected to Venus, a particularly charming manner is part of his ambience and attractiveness. He can be talented in artistic areas, have a bent for diplomacy, and be interested in social causes. With strong aspects to Mars, more drive, ambition, determination, and aggressive qualities will be appar-

ent. Sexuality is emphasized and his need to pioneer new projects or be involved with sports is obvious. Impatience compels
him to take action, start things moving, do battle with life. A
Jupiter conjunction reveals the true optimist of the zodiac. The
dramatic quality of the ego combined with the enthusiasm for
challenges gives an unbeatable leadership potential. Vitality,
humor, and abundance of philosophical energy sweep this individual to constant new heights of attainment.

You may not recognize the Leo ascendant if Saturn is also
affecting the personality. Even if Saturn is well aspected in the
chart, if it is conjunct the Sun, a natural subduing of the dramatic behavior is evident. Saturn is the cautious planet, exhibiting a conservative and careful manner. Some insecurity is probable as well. The color represented by this practical planet almost
completely reflects an opposite quality to the Leo brilliance. It is
like sweeping a wash of gray over a brilliant red. The red color
shows through, but subdued somewhat. Insecurity may compel
the Leo rising to be "on stage" even more. He may seek approval
through the use of his executive, leadership, and dramatic qualities rather than express them because it's what he *wants* to do.
This aspect indicates lack of self-esteem and self-confidence, obviously stemming from a childhood where his ego was not
stroked, or where he felt rejection. He may have developed a
pessimistic point of view if he was not encouraged to express his
natural exuberance. These insecurities can come not only from
childhood but from a dim memory of a past life condition, or
from both areas.

This neglect of the dominance is particularly interesting in the
chart of a female, indicating that fear of being strong. If it is in
evidence in a man's chart, it can compel him to blow his own
horn in case he isn't liked for himself. He resists assuming the
noble role. He appears to have an exaggerated sense of self-
worth rather than the deep insecurity that is really there. (One
lovely actress with this aspect gives a rundown of her accomplishments and credits in case she is unrecognized.) The individual with this aspect must, of course, learn to like himself. Others
will probably follow suit, but if an activity is performed because
of a desire, it won't matter whether the accolades come or not.

More than likely, they'll come eventually, perhaps when Leo rising least expects them.

When Uranus is affecting the personality of one with Leo rising, the individual is a free soul indeed. This person will be ahead of his time, or will be rebellious in the extreme. He will be attracted to avant-garde ideas, will assume leadership for anything that appears humanitarian, inventive, or metaphysical. He may be a healer, or a genius, or have a musical talent. He may just wish to run away. A Neptunian color to the personality compels the Leo rising to adopt a more naïve outlook on life. He can be a visionary or just unrealistic. In extreme cases, manic behavior is possible. The individual will be able to deal with life if he sees events through rose-colored glasses. He is happier living above the clouds of ordinary humdrum existence. He can be totally unrealistic about himself and others. Occasionally, he will carry others along with him on his dreams of grandeur. The positive outlet gives him the quality of vision, a talent for photography, film, or therapy. The glamour world can provide a perfect outlet for his ability to see life in vivid colors. In a negative sense, he can be a dreamer with nowhere to go.

When Pluto colors the Leo ascendant, true power and potential puts this individual in the royal seat with very little effort on his part. He exudes a magnetism that attracts the right people to his side. If that planet is well aspected, his natural sense of potential enables him to put together big deals, make contact with the "right" people, or people right for him, and gives him benevolent leadership. If that planet is not well aspected, the tendency to manipulate to get what he wants is possible. He is like a child who wants what he wants when he wants it, and will stop at nothing until he reaches his goal. He may not know his own strength and may actually push people away from him instead of toward him in his search for power. He has the potential to light up cities—or get the rug pulled out from under him if he uses unscrupulous methods. High motivation gets him where he wants to be.

No matter what planet is affecting the personality of one with Leo rising, it is a certainty that the king of the beasts will not fade into the background. The ease of achievement has much to do with his early conditioning. "As the twig is bent, so grows the tree" is particularly true for this individual. He senses his "royalty" and will thrive on the chance to show his true nobility of spirit if given half a chance.

FINANCE

Virgo is the sign that rules the second house of financial matters when Leo is ascending. Past the dramatic exterior, the true objectivity of the person with this leadership quality lies with his earning potential. Mercury is the planet that rules the sign of Virgo, and Mercury is the planet associated with the mind, the intellect, and the thought process in general. It is also connected to speech and ideas. The placement of Mercury in a chart indicates what a person thinks about, and with Leo rising, thoughts naturally go toward financial matters. The Leo personality earns income through his ability to think, speak, and analyze situations. He uses his *mind* to make money. What he says and how he thinks has much to do with his financial potential.

A writer earns income through his thoughts and ability to communicate ideas. An actor makes his living through speech and communications, but no matter what the chosen profession, the person with this ascendant utilizes his analytical quality to bring about his eventual financial reward. The Virgo ability to do research and be involved in painstaking, detailed work enables the individual to be discriminating about selection of the proper vehicle for his expression in the financial world. Phineas T. Barnum used this power of analysis in his work. Bob Hope and Horace Greeley expressed this in slightly different ways. Jawaharlal Nehru, Indira Gandhi, and social worker Jane Addams thought about money for others, using their energies in that direction.

David Cogan, an outstanding business manager in New York City, is a Leo with Leo rising. He handles financial affairs for a multitude of well-known and successful people. His mental prowess is exercised constantly in his efforts to increase financial stability and establish growth for his clients. He must be constantly aware of details in the financial arena, not only for his "family" but in the world market as well. His power of discrimination along with his dramatic sense comes into play in his capacity as a Broadway producer. He uses his profound perceptions and power of analysis in many ways. With quick awareness of a situation, he cuts to the heart of a matter instantly, especially when it comes to details about contracts and negotiations. He possesses not only an editorial capacity but a sixth sense about people. He knows how to help people on the road to success.

David expressed his dramatic ability as a child prodigy, playing the violin on stage at Carnegie Hall and starring in his own radio show in his teens. His mental capacity is such that in spite of the vast amount of data surrounding him, he is totally aware of what is going on with his clients. Absolutely nothing escapes his attention. He earns money through the cognizance of others' needs and through his willingness to deal with financial details.

The second house in a chart indicates not only how we earn funds but how we spend money as well. Leo rising will always be enticed by anything that appeals to the mind. He spends on books, newspapers, trade journals, or anything that will keep him informed about what's going on in the world or in his particular field of interest. Theater, literature, and material that present new developments cannot be ignored. He prefers mental stimulation to food, for that is the food that feeds his hunger. The placement of Mercury in an individual chart indicates the particular area of life that will appeal to him for financial focus. But it is the aspects to Mercury that tell how successful the person with this ascendant will be in the development of his ideas, and therefore financially.

When Mercury is posited in the first house, the income is derived from the personality and through self-expression. He will be at ease with his display of the leadership qualities, and will use his mind as his protection. Another color to his personality comes through his analytical qualities. He will show a marked ability to collect facts and can easily express his ideas. His ability and desire to write and speak intensify the dra-

matic quality. A second house placement for Mercury only intensifies the need to earn funds through intellectual pursuits.

Since the third house in a chart is related to communications
in general, a placement of Mercury in that house indicates the
inclination to seek avenues for the expression of those talents,
as well as a natural ability to earn funds through those abilities.
This is the sign for the writer, speaker, actor, negotiator. The
need for communication of any kind is strong. Since the third
house rules community, neighbors, and siblings, community
affairs can hold special interest in a financial way. If Mercury
is placed in the fourth house, the thoughts are also directed
toward land, home, real estate. Financial considerations are connected to information imparted by the parent of the opposite
sex, whether overtly or subconsciously. There will be strong
identification, financially, with that parent. If that parent was
financially successful, the potential for the individual with Leo
rising is intensified. Financial power is increased as the individual grows older. The latter part of life is more closely concerned
with successful fulfillment of ideas and intellect. Not only will
money be earned through real estate and land, but the individual will spend funds on his home and lifestyle.

With Mercury posited in the fifth house, an expression of creative intelligence is the prime source of earning power. Gambles
of any kind can be a lure, whether through the stock market or
through "gambling" with life. The entertainment field is a natural source of earning power. Since the fifth house is connected to
creative ability and children, occupations concerning the welfare
of little ones or to their interests are a possible source of income.
The sixth house is the house of work and service. Health programs can stimulate a need to work in a service capacity. Ideas
about individual or national health can lead to financial progress. This Leo rising not only earns funds through those areas,
but must be mentally and financially stimulated in order to be
healthy. His thoughts or worries about financial matters will
affect his overall well-being.

When Mercury is placed in the seventh house, partnership is
connected to financial matters. Earning potential is increased
through joint effort. Cooperative ventures may be started with a

mate or a business partner. The individual with this placement is attracted to a partner who operates on a mental level. He will be interested in someone who shares his thoughts and ideas about money. He thinks a great deal about partnership and marriage. With an eighth house position, an individual is able to raise funds in order to make his own money, or to utilize venture capital or other resources as a base for his own financial operations. He can earn funds through residuals, dividends, or commissions. His gift to humanity can be through his ideas, words, speech, and financial instruction.

Advertising, promotion, public relations, publicity, publishing are good sources of income for one with Mercury placed in the ninth house. His thoughts are on distances, higher education, and other countries. Importing and exporting or legal affairs can be sources of good income. Ideas related to lecturing or matters that bring personal recognition will be lucrative as well. A tenth house placement connects income and career. The individual cannot be involved in financial matters unless he is given an opportunity to build a strong reputation in connection with his ideas, words. He will be known for what he says. His thoughts are generally focused on career matters or on public concerns.

The earning capacity is connected with group projects, friendship, or association with organizations when Mercury is placed in the eleventh house. The Metropolitan Opera is an eleventh house organization, for instance. The dramatic expression of a singer with Leo rising and a strong eleventh house Mercury would naturally find an opportunity for success in connection with such an organization. A Broadway singer would be attracted to musicals, rather than concentrating on a nightclub act or recordings, if Mercury was posited in this house. When the mental planet is placed in the twelfth house of "secret" or "hidden" affairs, the individual will work alone in order to earn funds, or will need to work behind the scenes in some capacity. Writers with this placement are able to seal themselves off in order to earn money through their ideas. An individual with this placement can be inspired subconsciously through his mentality or intellect. Any psychic awareness comes through a knowing, rather than through flashes or electrical impulses. The aspects from other planets to Mercury in an individual chart tell how fluid ideas will be or how easy it is for an individual to express those thoughts and intellectual decisions.

COMMUNICATIONS

Libra rules the third house of communications when Leo is ascending. Libra is the sign of diplomacy, charm, refinement, grace, and beauty. Libra, with Venus as its ruler, is the sign of the artist and the diplomat. The ability to communicate with charm and diplomacy is coupled with an exceptional ability to negotiate. The artistic sense and charming way of speaking leads many natives with Leo rising into artistic pursuits, whether in the theater, the literary world, or through art. The native with this ascendant no doubt has many avenues of creative expression, but painting can be an exceptionally satisfying form of communication, even as a hobby.

Since Venus rules many things associated with pleasure and beauty, the list of activities possible for one with this ascendant is long. Primarily, communications of any sort hold pleasure for the individual, but Venus is primarily associated with the artistic expression. Painters with this ascendant include Leroy Neiman, Jan Vermeer, Henri Matisse, Anthony Van Dyck, Edouard Manet, Albrecht Dürer, and Paul Gauguin. A strong diplomatic ability enables one with this ascendant to successfully deal with politics. Mayor John Lindsay attracted a great deal of personal attention because of his dramatic, as well as his political, ability. Stephen A. Douglas was never a man to remain in the background of life. The Marquis de Lafayette expressed his artistic ability through architecture, but perhaps Pablo Picasso expresses this combination of drama and talent to its ultimate.

Venus rules color, design, texture, textiles, decorating, designing. Jane Everett is a successful young designer in the garment industry, while Harvey Rosenberg, also with this ascendant, started a fabric library as a service for New York designers. He later became involved in the music field and became well known, appearing on the cover of *Fortune* magazine for inventing a line of dolls intended to break down barriers between people of all social dispositions. Venus is connected not only with society but with social reform. The individual with this dynamic personality has no trouble in becoming a champion for humanity, as his natural diplomatic, gracious manner of speaking can cut through to the core of concern more quickly than arguments and strife. Leon Trotsky, Indira Gandhi, Jawaharlal Nehru, Martin Luther, and Jane Addams expressed their concern for the welfare of their particular groups in their own idealistic way. Drama was certainly a part of getting the point across.

Venus indicates the bargaining ability. Artistic personalities either use this Venusian trait to make deals, cement contracts and agreements, or they can take the easy way out in areas of negotiations. People involved in art, theater, and dance are notorious for working in order to express their talent while neglecting their own best interests, yet many Leo personalities are especially good at striking a good financial deal. Angela DiPene, with Leo rising is one of the top TV commercial agents, heading the William Cunningham office in New York. She is especially good at negotiating contracts for her clients. The aspects to Venus in the individual chart give a strong indication as to the way a person comes to agreement. Good aspects to that planet indicate an exceptional ability to charm people into agreement, while difficult aspects show a tendency to keep peace at any price and a hesitancy to make waves. There is always a need for one with this ascendant to have harmonious interpersonal dealings. The aspects to Venus indicate how that individual goes about getting that civility and rapport he craves. He either creates harmony and beauty, using Venus in a positive manner, or keeps peace by inaction, still attaining his goal of harmony but in a passive, less-than-productive way.

HOME LIFE

Leo rising really shows his sense of style in connection with his home life and lifestyle. He wants royal splendor around him and usually manages to create a symphony of lavish living. He needs a king's castle to really feel on top of the world. Somehow he will find his own Taj Mahal, or a similarly opulent base from which to go forth into the world. His castle is his home rather than the other way around. Some individuals can operate within a small space, but the Leo rising needs a surrounding fitting for his expansive nature. He may express his personal power or effectiveness in connection with land or real estate. Paul Horton, a Dallas attorney, is involved in negotiation of bond issues for new roads and construction in Texas. He acts as a potent force for progress in his state. His own beautiful home reflects the excellent taste and comfort associated with this royal rising sign. Paul has been recognized for his work in "Who's Who in America."

With Pluto, ruler of Scorpio, describing the fourth house of home, the biggest change in the life of one with Leo rising comes with the attainment of the kind of home he really wants. Even if his surroundings early in life are less than fitting to his royal nature, he manages to acquire his own mansion later in life. How easily this is accomplished depends on the photographs he has made of the parent of the opposite sex. Since he is capable of fulfilling the unrealized potential of that parent as he grows older, it can be essential to examine the qualities in that parent that he truly admires. He may have to look closely at any feelings he may have about getting even with or proving something to that parent, which could be causes of rebellion sooner or later. He may wind up jumping out of the frying pan into the fire.

Pluto is the power planet. It relates to the child ego state, as described by Transactional Analysis. Pluto can best be characterized as a powerful body of water, turbulent in its dynamics. If a body of water of that power is left to flood the riverbanks, it can bring destruction in its wake, yet can be especially dynamic if it is dammed up and controlled. The parent of the opposite sex is always a powerful force in the life of the person with Leo on the ascendant. He either sees that parent as powerful, charismatic, magnetic, and childlike in a positive way, or as someone who manipulated or used negative game playing to get what he wanted from life or from his Leo rising child. He may have felt the rug pulled out from under him by that parent. The parent is never someone to be ignored.

The aspects to Pluto in an individual chart indicate just how that parent used his forceful, charismatic, magnetic nature and how the Leo rising assimilated the lessons from that parent. If Pluto is well aspected, the individual inherits a sense of universality, resulting in the same high motivation that characterized the parent. If, however, Pluto is not well aspected, it may be that the parent neglected to utilize his personal magnetism for a high purpose, resorting instead to game playing, manipulation, and a refusal to grow into his potential. The strongest message conveyed from that parent is: "I want what I want when I want it and I'll get it any way I can."

The positive image of Pluto indicates that the Leo rising is aware of the enormous effect that parent has on the people around him, uplifting them by some seemingly magnetic force. This is certainly true in the case of Susan Strasberg, whose father, Lee Strasberg, has trained many outstanding actors of our time. Susan writes of her relationship with her powerful father in her book *Bittersweet,* and also talks of her own rebellion. But she has inherited the same quality of power, and has started to express her concern for people around her, encouraging them to transmute their lives through the message of her book. She reaches masses of people to say, "You can do it, too." Nancy Hughes, now involved with real estate, had especially close ties with her father, former Clerk of the Supreme Court. Nancy's homes reflect her dramatic quality and need for opulence in her surroundings.

Each person with this ascendant has the potential of reaching the most fulfilling time of his or her life with the passage of time. All the seemingly unattainable things or situations desired early in life come easily later on, although perhaps in unexpected ways. The Leo rising begins to develop group consciousness and to become aware of his true potency, perhaps heading his own organization, but certainly reaching out to masses of people in whatever way he chooses. The more he becomes in tune with the universal flow, the more dynamic he becomes. With the highest motivation, he flies like the eagle to show mankind the right road to take. Inadvertently, he may end up with his own castle or mansion, especially if he needs it as a base of operation for the good of all. Jens Jerndal, formerly in the Swedish diplomatic corps with a background in International Law, and now an astrologer, is in the process of building a holistic healing center on land he owns on the Canary Island of Lanzarote. His motivation is the well-being and health of all, and the conditions of his personal life have changed dramatically as a result of that high motivation.

ROMANCE • CREATIVE EXPRESSION

The fifth house in a chart indicates many things. Primarily it describes the creative outlet for an individual. However, it also indicates a natural progression from a creative desire fulfilled through romantic expression and brought to life in children. It is each person's choice as to how he expresses the creativity, whether through self-expression of talent or bearing of children who "inherit" his talent, or through both avenues. The planet that rules this house delineates the type of creative outlet that appeals to a person, as well as the type of children he will produce and the quality of their relationship.

When Leo is on the rise, the planet Jupiter rules this house. Jupiter is the planet of luck, abundance, philosophy, nature, humor. It is sometimes called the "great benefic." Since Jupiter is the "luckiest" planet in the zodiac, the person with this dynamic personality is most fortunate in all creative ventures. He is also fortunate in producing philosophical, outgoing, happy-go-lucky children. He will be attracted to a love who expresses the exuberant, outgoing personality, is philosophical, and wants a challenge.

The fifth house also rules the gambling instincts. Whether one gambles with creative expression, romance, children, or with the stock market, the results can be indicated by the aspects to the fifth house. For the most part, anyone with this ascendant is blessed with a desire to express this creative part of himself and to grow through his talent. Whatever he tackles in this area is coupled with high expectation, optimism, and a need to touch universal wisdom. The Leo personality can welcome the stimulation and challenge of something just out of reach to keep him from being bored or satiated with events around him that may become routine with repetition. With an eye on the horizon, his creative juices begin to flow. He is stimulated by the thought of a challenge.

If Jupiter is primarily well aspected in the natal chart, the individual with this ascendant can look forward to a life of good fortune through his ability to take a chance on self-expression in some form or other. Jupiter also rules salesmanship. Not only is he especially productive, but his contagious enthusiasm attracts others to his side. In all areas of entertainment he will be lavish, extravagant, and expansive. The more the merrier can well be his keynote.

The actor with this ascendant will enjoy the challenge of a stretch in the selection of roles to portray. He may choose the kind of creative outlet that presents a certain philosophy. He will certainly not be content with run-of-the-mill vehicles. Humorous roles can be an appropriate vehicle for him. Marilyn Monroe achieved her greatest success when she discovered her flair for comedy in such hits as *Some Like It Hot*. Susan Strasberg is still remembered for her brilliant portrayal of Anne in *The Diary of Anne Frank*, a play with a social and philosophical message. Artists with this ascendant can be especially prolific. Leroy Neiman is noted for high productivity, as well as his preoccupation with art that concentrates on sports, another Jupiterian interest.

The relationship between parent and child is one of natural good humor and philosophy. The Leo rising produces wise offspring. They can be quite naturally philosophical and outgoing, perhaps with a love of nature. The Leo personality is able to allow his children to experience life, perhaps unconsciously encouraging a bent for investigation. His children may never be content to stop their learning process. The dramatic quality expressed by one with this ascendant can be passed on quite easily to his children. Universal truths can be combined with a curiosity about the workings of the universe and expressed through creativity, teaching, or other forms of artistic expression.

If Jupiter is badly aspected, there is a possibility of some overexpectation with creative projects, romance, or children. Overoptimism about results ends in disappointment. Many times the individual is reluctant to be expectant for fear of the paralyzing effect of a letdown. If the native with this ascendant is aware of the tendency to build things up in this area, a counterbalancing attitude can be brought into play. If he sets goals, and allows for a percentage of positive results, he can neutralize the fear of disappointment. If ten projects are set in motion, the realization that perhaps seven will work out can keep the Leo rising optimistic in a realistic manner.

WORK • SERVICE • HEALTH

Saturn rules the sixth house of work, health, and sense of service when Leo is rising. Without the stabilizing influence of this planet, we would have difficulty in completing tasks, staying "grounded," or attending to duty. Many times, Leo rising will work diligently in areas where he takes on less than truly satisfying responsibility. He may pick work that is limiting and unfulfilling. When he works, he works long, hard hours. Just the opposite can be true too; he may avoid work altogether because he knows his tendency to put himself under incredible pressure, or for fear that he will never be perfect enough, or will never get out from under deadlines and pressures. When Saturn rules the sixth house, however, one can learn to assume the kind of responsibility that is ultimately on the right track.

In the most positive sense, and when Saturn is well aspected in the chart, a native with this ascendant is a dedicated worker, loving routine and stabilizing discipline. He will be able to work those long, hard hours happily, put himself under deadline pressures, really sink his teeth into exciting projects that require his assuming higher responsibility in line with his Leo rising executive ability. He is capable of tackling matters requiring detail or research. Certainly, responsibility is his forte. Technical matters appeal to his sense of perfection. He will not enjoy things that are too easy. Cynthia Adler, a Gemini with Leo rising, is one of the top "voice-over" performers in New York. Although Cynthia is a multitalented actress, she has achieved great success working in an extremely tough but technical area of the business. She is under pressure not only to express her variety of voices but to be aware of split-second timing under enormous pressure.

If Saturn is badly aspected in the natal chart, the problem lies in the overexaggerated need to be needed on the job. He will work too long, too hard, and with too little recognition, until he is so overburdened that he may have to get sick to get out from under that pressure. He can be pulled in by negative strokes, working all the harder to please someone who may never be pleased. If the native can learn to recognize that his sense of dedication will enable him to assume responsibility on the highest level, perhaps working successfully for himself, he will never work at anything he doesn't enjoy or that is not a first step toward an ultimate goal. Learning a technique will give this individual assurance of his value in any work situation. He needs to be on safe ground to be self-confident in his work.

With Saturn ruling the house of health, there is almost always a need to be disciplined about health matters and maintaining a regimen that is strict. He needs to live a disciplined life in order to have energy for his work. He needs a certain amount of sleep, but most important of all, needs to learn when to say no. He may discover an allergy to certain foods, or a need to be careful about overindulgence with food or drink. He may have a lack of calcium in the body with a tendency to stiffness of muscles or spine. Lowered resistance and vitality can compel him to look for stimulants instead of to the proper diet and vitamin supply. Since Venus is the natural antidote for Saturn, affection and "touching" can improve health. Routine massage will have a definite therapeutic effect. A careful examination of any judgmental messages from childhood about hard work and duty will enable the individual to release himself psychologically from the need to overwork and be overburdened.

MARRIAGE • PARTNERSHIP

Leo rising needs a great deal of freedom in marriage. He is attracted to someone who appears to be a free soul, avant-garde, spontaneous, and humanitarian. He really wants a genius as a mate. Unconventional behavior or a rebellious outlook can frequently be mistaken for freedom. The individual with this ascendant may need to examine his own rebellious nature in the process of selecting someone with whom to spend his life, or he may ensure more freedom than he expects by selecting the wrong person.

Since the Leo rising has much determination and fixity in his personality, he must call the shots and be the boss. He wants to be able to do what he wants, when he wants. He must have a partnership with someone who not only understands that need but can be spontaneous enough to adapt to his desires. In order to grow together, assuring the quality of spontaneity he wants, Leo rising must look for someone who is inventive and free-thinking rather than the person who is unpredictable, unstable, and unreliable. The Leo personality will be even more stimulated by someone who attains a share of the limelight and attracts recognition on his own. He wants a person who will justify his good taste and do him proud in the bargain.

The planet Uranus rules the seventh house of marriage or business partnership when Leo is ascending. That planet signifies freedom *or* the tendency to want to run away. It is inventiveness or anarchism. It is the planet that rules electricity, electronics, astrology, metaphysics, fame, science, recordings, radio, and healing. If that planet is well aspected in the natal chart, the person with Leo rising is in touch with his own genius and need for freedom, thereby selecting the person who uses the freedom urges in a healthy, creative way. But if that planet is not well aspected, the Leo personality may marry out of a sense of rebellion. He may attract someone not in touch with his or her own need for freedom, or look for someone who represents freedom in a particular fashion. That person may exhibit behavior characteristics that only appear to be free. He will always be attracted to someone who appears somehow different. If Leo rising resists his own genius, inventive impulses, he will attract a mate who is resistant to utilizing those same natural electrical impulses. That mate may try to calm down the energy by using drugs, drink, or hiding behind a conservative front. The resultant chaos will give Leo rising plenty of room to run away. When each partner is in touch with his need for spontaneity, their exciting interaction provides the healthy kind of stimulation that is necessary for a successful union. The Leo loyalty makes it difficult to break up an unsuccessful relationship. It's essential to look before leaping into a restrictive partnership situation, or the Leo ascendant may live to regret his impulse.

Stephen A. Douglas in his marriage to Cathy, many years younger, found great happiness, even though the marriage was unconventional. Joseph P. Kennedy was not married to someone content to remain in his shadow. Richard Burton found a free soul in Elizabeth Taylor, and Mayor John Lindsay, in his marriage to his marvelous Mary, attracted a unique individual to his side. Marilyn Monroe attempted a marriage to her "genius" when she found Arthur Miller. He may have actually been too conservative in the long run. Pablo Picasso tried many times to find the right person, and Leroy Neiman, in his marriage to Janet, bound a musician and a humanitarian to his side. Paul Horton is married to Susan, an astrologer and board member of the American Federation of Astrologers. Paul knows enough about astrology to read his own transits. Sally Nevius, chairman of the board of Mount Vernon College in Washington, D.C., with Leo rising, found the ideal partner in Jack, a dynamic Washington attorney who gave up a lucrative law practice to head the D.C. Council for a while, expressing his humanitarian (Uranian-Aquarian) concern.

NEEDS

The eighth house in a chart indicates how one gets needs met, whether those needs are physical, monetary, or otherwise. Since Neptune rules this house when Leo is ascending, the native with this royal outlook just naturally assumes that with his vision and willingness to work hard, he will get what he needs and wants from life. His idealism creates an aura around him that usually brings fantastic benefits and conditions. He really wants to save the world, and his dreams can come true. However, it is important for this individual to be totally aware of just what he is asking for from people or from life, since he is so good at getting what he wants. High motivation, vision, and goals are important for success.

The planet Neptune is the planet of vision, idealism, inspiration. It rules film, therapy, and the glamour world in general. It describes the essence of mind that enables us to visualize, thereby creating the conditions around us. Think of planting a seed in a flower pot. With the proper care, the plant will grow. But if one plants a zinnia, that is what one gets. If an individual plants that zinnia seed, but expects to grow orchids, he can be very disillusioned. The conditions one with Leo rising expects to get in life are exactly what he gets. He must be aware of the messages he is sending out to life and to those around him. He can change conditions for better or for worse by visualizing other results.

Human nature is such that the quality of energy that enables us to get our needs met is also the quality of energy we can send out to humanity. We seem to let ourselves have more of what we really need and want in life if we think we are doing good for those around us. This is especially true for one with this dynamic ascendant. When he is dealing with a vision for humanity, he just naturally allows himself to have whatever conditions are necessary for the task. He can raise funds, use venture capital, or have better financial conditions by being involved in situations where residual funds or dividends play a part in his income. The Leo rising has a particular talent for seeing the overall concept, visualizing the total picture, and expressing his idealistic nature for the good of all. He can dream of Utopia. If Neptune is well aspected in the chart, the results are fantastic. If Neptune is badly aspected, the native may adopt a Don Quixote outlook, leaving himself wide open for a letdown. It is then essential to take off the rose-colored glasses and become fully aware of the reality of any situation. Wishful thinking may have to go.

Actors use film as a medium for reaching the world. Artists use inspiration as their contribution to humanity. Visionaries such as Martin Luther, Gandhi, Nehru contribute their dreams for a better world. Edgar Cayce helped humanity through his psychic, dreamlike trances. Leo rising earns money through his *analytical*, practical mind, yet has extra income through his vision. The combination of practicality and concept is unbeatable. When he can see the forest and tend to the trees as well, his crop of timber is unparalleled, his contribution to others is of great value.

RECOGNITION

The ninth house in a chart indicates the impulse to reach out beyond perimeters, tuning in to the higher mind and inadvertently achieving recognition. On a practical level, it indicates advertising, public relations, promotional effort, legal affairs, higher education, travel, importing, dealing with countries at a distance. It indicates the state of philosophy, the willingness to expand, the publishing world.

When Leo is rising the ninth house is ruled by Mars. That planet is indicative of drive, ambition, determination, the fighting instincts. It also rules sexuality, metals, warfare. No matter what field is chosen, recognition is attained by aggressive action. Extra drive and ambition enable the native to deal in competitive areas. He will be known for whatever he pioneers. The more he harnesses aggressive energies, the more success he attains. He may discover he has a sixth sense about promotion, publicity, publishing.

Sally Nevius, is a champion and a fighter for a new system in education, pioneering studies for young women that will help them cope with a changing world. Her untiring, unflagging energy for woman's cause brought about positive changes at Mount Vernon College. She is a pioneer in her own dynamic way. Dickie Mountbatten utilized the military as his vehicle for change and progress. Marilyn Monroe was publicized for her sexuality, Muhammad Ali for his pugnacity, Paul Revere for his courage, daring, and bravery, and Rudolph Nureyev for the dance but also for his daring and courageous defection from Russia. All of these outstanding people have utilized the Mars energy in a different way. The Leo rising can be stimulated by new fields to conquer. He may become more energetic and well known in countries other than that of his birth.

If Mars is well aspected in the individual chart, the energy is well directed. If Mars is not well aspected, there can be some frustration in connection with publicity or promotional effort. In some instances, any publicity is better than none, and in many cases, headlines bear news of fights, sexual escapades, flaring tempers. Jackie Robinson, Guy Lombardo, Robert Mitchum, and Richard Burton have received less than flattering publicity, not to mention Joseph Goebbels, whose atrocities made world headlines. It is up to every individual to utilize his energy in the manner he chooses, but Leo rising, in particular, can channel pioneering, aggressive drive in a way that will bring positive benefits for everyone, or be recognized for doing just the opposite.

In any area connected to legal affairs, Leo rising can pioneer new trends, fighting for others or experiencing great frustration with his legal battles. Travel can bring reward and challenge, or frustration with delays and conditions of flight. Higher education and publishing bring opportunity to pave the way for others, or conditions full of strife, chaos, and opposition. Exceptional leadership qualities can bring opportunity to Leo rising to fight for change and pioneer new trends.

CAREER

Taurus rules the tenth house of career when Leo is on the ascendant. Venus is the planet that rules Taurus, and Venus is the planet of love, beauty, sociability, diplomacy. It rules the artistic world in general, whether that is art, theater, or dance and it indicates social life or social concepts. The person with this ascendant is naturally attracted to all artistic activities in his social life or in his career. He can also be interested in matters that bring pleasure to the public, or anything that brings beauty to people in general.

The tenth house not only describes natural attraction to a particular public endeavor, it describes the way the public reacts to an individual. With Venus ruling this position, the reaction of the public to one with this ascendant is especially favorable and full of love. Social matters are easy for one with this rising sign. He will always show the gracious part of his personality to the public or in his social life.

This house also describes the parent of the same sex. It indicates the relationship between that parent and the Leo rising child. It would appear that love is the strongest bond between them, unless Venus is badly aspected. The child photographs that parent as beautiful, charming, and gracious, but perhaps also stubborn and determined. He inherits a natural ease in social situations from that parent. Taurean expression frequently indicates a natural ability to entertain. This parent more than likely had a special ability to make people feel relaxed, at ease, and welcome. If Venus is not well aspected in the individual chart, however, there is a strong possibility that in the eyes of the individual with this ascendant, the parent of the same sex took the easy way out. There is then a natural tendency to avoid the artistic expression that is such a lure for one with this dramatic ascendant. It may also be more difficult since there was no natural example from that parent to follow.

Richard Burton was given tremendous encouragement by his adopted father, Phillip Burton. He was trained by Phillip early in his life. Marilyn Monroe adored her mother, but was abandoned by her. Marilyn had the adoration of the public, but always feared losing that love. Susan Strasberg was surrounded by people in the theater that her mother encouraged and cooked for. She had a natural drama coach in her mother. Paula Strasberg represents a perfect example of Taurus in the chart, as she was tremendously adept at entertaining. She was not only a great beauty in her time, but a fine actress. Dickie Mountbatten had deep affection for his father, living up to his father's image by becoming Lord of the Fleet. His social graces and charming manner enabled him to take over many functions for Her Majesty Queen Elizabeth. He continued to love occasions when he could "perform" in public. He was truly loved by not only the British people but by those around the world who knew him.

FRIENDSHIP

Leo rising looks for mental stimulation among his friends and acquaintances. He is naturally attracted to people who are intelligent, witty, and verbal. He enjoys situations where interesting conversation is paramount and exchange of ideas most important. He will never allow himself to be around people who are boring or shallow. He is rarely without companionship, as he needs the stimulation of the words and thoughts of others and will seek out people who share his views.

Gemini rules the eleventh house of group activity and friendship when Leo is rising. The sign Gemini is ruled by Mercury and is considered a dual sign. One Gemini characteristic is a tendency to get close, then pull away in order to gain perspective. One with a Leo ascendant may have a tremendous variety of friendships, spending a great deal of time with a particular group or person, then seeking stimulation from other sources. He never loses track of good friends, but is not likely to have only one good friend at a time. He needs to have feedback from many sources and gains knowledge through his curiosity about people, the way they think and new ideas they generate.

His loyalty is extreme, so it is never "out of sight, out of mind" for one with this ascendant. He maintains communication with friends however he can. He will value friendship even more with some perspective. Variety is the spice of life, but he will always steadfastly return to people who are fun and exciting to be around. Marilyn Monroe had a standing date on Friday afternoons with Warren Fischer, a former artists' manager, who was simply a friend, but someone fun to be with. Their weekly meetings lasted until her marriage to Arthur Miller.

The eleventh house indicates group associations as well as individual friendships. The Leo rising will identify with group projects where words and ideas are the theme. Actors work in association with other actors where communications are paramount. Politicians share views with other politicians who are aware of what is going on in the immediate environment as well as in the world. Writers are involved with other people who express thoughts and ideas. The person with this ascendant will always be excited by activity through which his adult ego state is activated.

If Mercury is well aspected in the individual chart, mental stimulation is always interesting and productive. When that planet is not well aspected, misunderstandings can occur, spoiling occasions that should be pleasurable and interesting. If the person with this ascendant learns how to say what he means and mean what he says, clarity of communication on his part leads to better association with people around him.

HIDDEN MATTERS • SUBCONSCIOUS PROCESS

The twelfth house indicates the facet of the personality that is most difficult to reveal. It indicates what is going on subconsciously or behind the scenes. With Cancer ruling this house when Leo is rising, the emotional nature can be the problem area. The Moon, ruler of Cancer, indicates feelings, emotions, sensitivities, moods, and the anima part of the personality. It is easy for Leo rising to be dominant, not so easy to be vulnerable. The lion tries not to let himself be seen when he is wounded. If Leo rising stays out of sight for a while, you can be sure he is dealing with a heavy emotional situation. If his pride is hurt, he will have to go off by himself to lick his wounds; he simply has to work it out in his own way. Leo rising feels a sense of responsibility to his public always to be seen at his best. Survival has to do with expression of regality. Marilyn Monroe was famous for her "no show" at times. Part of that had to do with an inability to reveal herself unless she felt totally in control of her emotions and in top form in her own eyes.

You may have to be very close to the Leo rising to enable this prideful person to confide the source of his troubles. He may not even let his family know when something is wrong. As he grows older, however, he can be more in touch with his feelings and may be better able to express that vulnerable part of himself. He may have to learn how to deal with his emotions, working through his own pain, to feel free to express overtly his nurturing capacity. He will eventually be on very safe ground in expressing his feelings if he is willing to go through that painful process of exposure. He can frequently appear unconcerned with someone else's problems and will rarely indulge in the sharing of woes. He may feel deeply for your problem, but will overtly encourage you to pull yourself together and carry on. He won't tolerate too much self-pity. His own survival issues have to do with showing strength of personality, not neediness.

When the Leo rising learns to integrate the sensitive, vulnerable, anima part of his personality with the dramatic, dominant exterior, he really is in a position to rule his particular world. He will then be kingly in his disposition, regal in his bearing, and royally aware of what his subjects need at any particular time. With his ego intact, he is the leader of his pack. No one can hold a candle to his majesty and regality.

VIRGO
RISING

THE RULER OF VIRGO IS MERCURY. This is also the planet ruling the sign of Gemini, but there is a vast difference in the way it is expressed in the personality of the two signs. These mental rising signs have a similar outlook on life in that they view the world through "adult" eyes, but Gemini is an air sign and Virgo an earth sign. The Gemini rising has a more restless, mercurial mind that may flit from one subject to another whereas Virgo rising is more practical in his intellectual activity and pursuits, enjoying research and the collection of data. He is the master of detail, objectivity, and analysis.

Virgo is a mutable sign, meaning adaptability, and is the sign of the workaholic. Virgo rising is a master at handling all the boring nit-picking matters others want to avoid. He is the epitome of neatness and order. The more he is absorbed in fact-finding missions, the happier he is. With a great deal of information stored away in his mind, he is like a squirrel storing away nuts for the winter in his quest for facts. He is perfectly content to analyze a situation many times. He may then reanalyze it just to make sure he hasn't missed anything.

It is easy to spot one with Virgo ascending by the way he takes in a situation around him. He will notice objects in a room that others may not know are there. He sizes up the immediate environment to get the feel of the lay of the land, and then may begin to feel comfortable. He needs to be aware of things, and though he may not be obvious about it, not much escapes his attention. When he begins to ask questions, it's a dead giveaway that he has Virgo on the rise.

Another giveaway trait is the Virgoan need for neatness and order in his environment. He can't function unless everything is in its place. He is a master at making lists, having everything he needs at hand, and perfunctorily taking care of any accumulated overflow of mail, phone calls, or errands. He loves catalogues! Periodically, he will reorganize his closets down to the last minute detail. Department stores conduct a booming business with

Virgo rising from garment bags and matching shoe bags down to sectioned containers and drawer dividers. He is a sucker for rotating shelves, appliance holders, and the like. He will buy anything that might do away with clutter and create more order. He will rearrange the counter top in his kitchen to make it just a bit more tidy and perfect. Felix Unger of the "Odd Couple" was surely someone with Virgo rising.

Joy Allen, a writer for the Long Island newspaper *Newsday*, expressed this Virgoan trait for detail in another way. She said, "I remember a time when I was six to nine months, being able to sit for hours looking at a blade of grass and a peony bush we had. I could focus on something tiny and see a whole world contained within it. I was aware of being a mind seeing the macrocosm within the microcosm."

The person with this ascendant is a fascinating conversationalist. He can hold the attention of those around him for hours with his endless store of knowledge and his interpretation of events, yet he may be so busy picking the brain of the person he most respects that it will be difficult to get him to share this information. He has a tendency to hide behind his inquiring mind. He is safe as long as he can put someone else on the witness stand. He may tend to quote other sources, rather than express his own opinion. If he is really feeling insecure, he has a tendency to criticize.

Mercury is the planet ruling intellect, speech, and communications as well as thoughts and ideas. Mercury was the messenger of the gods. His swift and speedy delivery of information was his chief function. Virgo rising adds another quality to this exchange of ideas in his ability to analyze, categorize, and delete unnecessary information. The Virgo rising is the one who "forges" ideas. He loves to pin himself down to long, hard hours of research. He is a fantastic editor because of his awareness of structure and detail. He can easily get to the essential fact of any matter. He is a natural critic. His biggest handicap is the tendency to overanalyze and become so immersed in detail that he forgets to see the overall picture. He can focus on what is in the immediate present, but may neglect his vision of the future. If he is able to see the trees and also be aware of the forest, he is a master at working out the details of a plan. He may sometimes go around in circles with his constant analysis and criticism, and may have to be helped in getting on with the larger picture. He can be overly much the perfectionist. He feels safe with facts but may be insecure when dealing with concepts. It can be important for him to learn the difference between intellect and wisdom.

Karen Zurawski, a speech therapist with Virgo rising, described this tendency by saying, "I find it very difficult to step out of a situation to look at the whole picture. I can only see what is right in front of me. I can get so involved with details I don't get past that to focus in on the overall message. I'm trying to change that, but I'm aware of a tendency to revert to old habits." The patience and willingness to handle details in connection with a broader concept can lead Virgo rising away from too much attention to unimportant matters.

Since opposite signs can reflect each other, it is interesting to see how Pisces and Virgo can teach each other some needed lessons. One with the Piscean personality is able to see the overall picture, but may overlook essential details. Virgo rising can be nit-picking with details and not so good with concepts. In a constructive synthesis of the two sides of a coin, an individual with Virgo on the rise must be on constant lookout for the grand design in his life. It is then that he can put his fine mind to work in the best way. He may neglect the intuitive mind in the constant use of his practical intelligence in order to avoid a letdown. He may have to be convinced of the validity of that higher intuition. His greatest fear seems to be that of having a pie-in-the-sky outlook. He won't chance being led down the garden path. He questions everything to avoid the danger of disillusionment. He keeps himself on the level of concrete fact in order to avoid the possibility of disappointment connected to idealism, for he would be devastated if his dreams crashed. He may use his left brain to the exclusion of right-brain activity. He may not realize that he tends to limit his perceptions as a safety device.

The individual with Virgo rising has evidently made early survival decisions about using his mind. It appears that he trusts his own ability only when dealing with facts. He arms himself with intellectual awareness against the onslaught of insecurity. The less safe he feels, the more he talks and analyzes. It may be difficult to look behind the words he says to discover what he really means. If Virgo rising really delivers an onslaught of opinion against the imperfections of those around him, it is difficult to avoid a negative reaction—but that may be the very time he needs reassurance most. If he can keep people away by his verbal attacks, he will never have to deal with that dangerous letdown. He may be crying out to be convinced of another point of view, but it takes a brave soul to break down his defense mechanism of skepticism. When the skeptic does fall, however, he falls hard. It may be necessary to present him with facts that are irrefutable, give him plenty of time to research the situation himself, and leave it at that. If he is asked to back down on an issue his security is threatened all over again. He can then hide behind new information, keeping the real issue at arm's length. His intellectual gymnastic ability is tops, but he will always respect someone more agile than he is.

Using the terms of Transactional Analysis, Mercury relates to the adult ego state. Virgo rising was born expressing his intellectual awareness. In a regression session, an individual with this ascendant is aware of himself as a "mind" even at the moment of birth. In even the early stages of his life, he sees things in an intellectual way. If he is encouraged to express his ideas from the beginning, he develops a clear way of communicating. He will then always be able to say what he means and mean what he says. If Mercury is well aspected in the individual chart, it appears that the circumstances or people around him as a child were conducive to his mental growth. His thoughts and ideas were acknowledged and validated and he was given permission to express himself verbally. If Mercury is not well aspected in the chart, it is difficult for Virgo rising to say what he thinks. He evidently was not given permission early on to think for himself or he was not heard. He may have felt it necessary to put extra sting or force into his words in order to get attention or to be heard. He continues the kind of communication he learned as a child.

If, for instance, he was encouraged to investigate for himself and accumulate knowledge, he easily continues in his quest for new information. He assimilates what he learns into what he already knows. His healthy skepticism becomes his most valuable trait. He can be an invaluable researcher. He enriches his life by finding balance on the integration of all levels of his mind. Each fact becomes another piece placed properly into the jig-saw puzzle of life. He tunes in to the enormous power of his mind. If Mercury is not well aspected in the natal chart, it is indicative that he was not given encouragement in the develop-ment of his own mind. One young lady remembers being told that she should be seen and not heard. A child with this negative Mercury may also have been reprimanded with the injunction "You don't know what you're talking about" or words to that effect. It is especially essential to encourage one with this ascend-ant to get in tune with his fine mind and to pursue his fact-find-ing missions. It is only insecurity and avoidance that keeps him stuck in an overly analytical process that keeps him going around in circles.

With a difficult Mercury in the natal chart, the individual with this ascendant can unwittingly antagonize people around him by his seemingly negative approach. He may develop an overly sharp manner of expressing himself. He can appear suspicious, overly cautious, and particularly skeptical. He may seem to be lacking in tact and consideration. His negative attacks and criti-cal approach keep him on safe ground until he is sure of where he stands. He is evidently in need of reassurance at that particu-lar moment. With some encouragement, he will investigate in-stead of negate.

Virgo rising loves to be able to quote sources of information. He reads voraciously and is well aware of what others are saying about myriads of subjects. He wants to be well informed but he may tend to accept as authority anything he reads in print, whether books or magazines. He respects anyone he considers an authority on a subject. He can quote what others are saying, but may resist or avoid expressing originality of thought. He is very aware of the newest trends, even though he may be cautious about accepting an idea or attitude as his own until others give their stamp of approval. He can be label-conscious, feeling that something is of value if its name is known. He will always be up on the latest fashion in clothes, food, and lifestyles, for he wants to be in the mainstream of life. He will feel uneasy about being out of step with the times. He needs to be encouraged to express his own thoughts and ideas and to take some chances occasionally, even if it is scary or risky.

This individual is attracted to occupations that require his brilliant ability to analyze. He is a marvelous teacher, editor, critic, actor, or writer. Nan Grubbs, a Gemini with Virgo rising, is an editor, yet theater provides an outlet for her restless mind. The Virgo rising needs to be involved with communications in general, as he can put others' ideas into crisp, clear form. Technique becomes his security. His creative expression may lean more toward the technical than toward the intuitive. He has fantastic ability to sort through all sorts of information to discover what is truly valuable. An ability to express a logic and order about his own life and world can be tremendously reassuring to those around him. He is a sound decision maker. He feels truly good about himself when he is on top of any situation at hand. He can handle detailed work better than anyone else. If you want something accomplished, look for the person with Virgo on the rise.

The symbol of Virgo is the virgin. In its highest sense there is an innocence and a purity about one with this ascendant. It shows most easily in the high-minded approach to anything sordid. He seems to emerge untouched even when he becomes involved in less than savory matters. Richard Nixon, with Virgo rising, emerged from the Watergate scandal *relatively* unscathed. Patty Hearst has emerged from her trying ordeal to live a quiet married life. Authors Jane Austen, Louisa May Alcott, Emily Dickinson, and Charlotte Brontë expressed that quality in their books. Doris Day was most successful as the innocent girl next door. Shirley MacLaine's role as a prostitute revealed her heart of gold. Deborah Kerr exemplified this purity in her role as Hannah in *The Night of the Iguana*, suggesting something dark in the past of that lady that had been reconciled, leaving her virginal outlook untouched. Rona Barrett could report the most scandalous gossip with honeyed tones, somehow suggesting wild pranks that should be laughed at. Frédéric Chopin's beautiful romantic music performed correctly is classically pure, rather than passionate. Perhaps only Andy Warhol could make underground movies that are considered art.

Virgo rising is rarely mean or ugly. Even the tendency to criticize is, more than anything, a bad habit developed early in life as a defense mechanism. He can be totally unaware of his ability to hurt or wound. He may not realize just how blunt or sharp he can be. He is the one most surprised when someone's sensitive reaction to his words is a cause for upset. He never seems to realize that his cool approach can come across like ice at times. He may appear totally unsympathetic toward another's problems, but more than likely his mind is already at work on the right solution. He may not be given to much pampering or coddling. Unless he can help with a problem, he may feel inadequate and unable to meet others' needs.

In the progression of the signs, Virgo is the sixth sign of the zodiac. The number six is associated with service, work, health. Many Virgo personalities are health addicts. The purity comes into play in their selection of pure foods and lifestyle. Howard Hughes, Capricorn with Virgo rising, became a fanatic about food and cleanliness later in his life. His reclusive qualities came from a skepticism and a mistrust about people. Alan Pressman has become one of the top nutritionists in this country, finding cause and solution to health problems in a no-nonsense, practical Virgo way. Among his patients is Leonard Bernstein, seeking the healthy way to increased energy and expressing his Virgo rising need for pure nutrition. Steve Vaccaro and Woodie Schwartz teach hundreds of people specific health techniques they can perform for themselves in order to lead healthier lives. A strong service capacity enables one with this ascendant to work with hospitals, service organizations, and in capacities others might find distasteful. Mitzi Applebaum and Charlene Huddleston supervise colonics as a part of an overall health regime, using strong Virgo rising qualities of service and purity so that others may lead a healthier, longer life. Their straightforward approach enables them to say, "Someone has to do it."

This strong service capacity may not always be on mundane levels. Franklin Delano Roosevelt, an Aquarian with Virgo rising, gave his life in the service of his country, even though his own health was an obstacle in many ways. Charles Evans Hughes, an Aries with Virgo rising, served as Chief Justice of the Supreme Court in the highest service capacity, using his brilliant and analytical mind to see that justice was done through the highest court in the land. Dwight D. Eisenhower also devoted his life to the service of his country. Florence Nightingale exemplifies the capacity for service that has been a beacon for nurses all over the world. Prince Albert stood behind Queen Victoria, perhaps in the most difficult position of all, to support her in her performance as Queen of England, shunning the limelight himself in his duty to her and to his country.

The positive use of Mercury in the chart gives the native with this ascendant an extraordinary power of discrimination. The way this quality is expressed is determined not only in the aspects to Mercury but in its placement in the individual chart. Mercury's placement indicates what the individual thinks about and talks about. If that planet is placed in the first house, the native with Virgo rising is doubly prone to intellectual observation. He thinks about himself, his life, and his identity. With a second house Mercury, financial matters occupy his attention. He earns money through his personality, intellect, ideas, and self-expression. A third house position puts additional emphasis on communications, writing, speech, and learning. With a fourth house position, the emphasis is on home, lifestyle, property, real estate. The full force of self-expression comes in the latter part of life. Early potential comes full cycle as the individual grows older. There is a strong identification with both parents, yet photographs of the parent of the opposite sex give an ability to fulfill the unrealized potential of that parent in particular in later years.

When Mercury is in the fifth house he is able to express true creative ability. He is a natural dramatist, entertainer, writer, and may have more of a gambling spirit than usual with this practical rising sign. The native is particularly service-oriented when Mercury is in the sixth house. He needs to work in areas where his objectivity and intellectual observation are key. He can be an "idea" person. Mental stimulation is essential, as boredom with work is connected with any health problems. His thoughts and conversation center on work projects. With a seventh house Mercury, one with Virgo rising needs partnership in order to feel truly fulfilled. Even in business situations, partnership is more satisfying than working alone. He looks for someone to share his ideas in any partnership relationship and may truly

desire a soul mate on an intellectual level. Good communication
is essential in that relationship.

When the ruling planet is posited in the eighth house, the native has an ability to have his needs fulfilled by simply asking
for what he wants. His words and thoughts are his gift to humanity, therefore what he says is of paramount importance in
his life. His ideas can benefit humanity in some way. The turning point in his life comes when he actualizes a desire to help
others through his words and ideas. Ninth house matters pertain
to advertising, promotional effort, travel, and legal affairs. When
Mercury is placed in this house, recognition comes through
ideas, intellectual matters, speaking, singing, teaching, or publishing. This individual may act as an agent for others. His
flair for promotional matters is high. He may be extremely effective teaching in a university or in dealing with other countries.

Mercury placed in the tenth house brings special importance
to career matters. Public image is connected with words, ideas,
and intellectual pursuits. Strong identification with the parent of
the same sex indicates the area in which career or public leanings may be manifested, and the individual may fulfill any
unrealized potential of the parent of the same sex in that area.
He thinks and speaks about career or social matters. His dedication to career and public life makes his ideas of value, and he
can have great impact on the public through the use of his
mind.

An eleventh house Mercury puts strong emphasis on friendship, group activity, and associations with people in general.
This individual will be attracted to people who are intellectually
oriented. He respects friends for their minds and thought
processes. When Mercury is positioned in the twelfth house, privacy is paramount to this Virgo rising. He is able to remain in
seclusion, happy in keeping his own company. He can do his
best thinking when he is by himself, and can write or work most
effectively in isolated places. He may show only the tip of the
iceberg of his true personality, for he will be a person of great
depth. Many of his thoughts come to him on a subconscious
level, and he may be more psychic than most individuals with
Virgo on the rise. He may not be able to easily express his true
thoughts until he learns how to release the intellectual part of

himself. He will need some time alone to gather his thoughts and research ideas for the most productive way of expressing himself.

Through the aspects to Mercury from other planets, it is easy to see some of the colors and characteristics that modify the pure Virgoan traits. These aspects indicate how the person expresses his intellect and thoughts, the quality of his ideas and speech, and how fluid his thought processes can be. It indicates other facets to his personality, and how his natural ability can be modified by his childhood decisions and experiences. Any conjunctions or positive aspects give added color, whereas the negative or hard aspects modify or nullify the natural ability.

When Mercury is in negative aspect to the Moon, the individual with this ascendant may overreact at times. He can find it difficult to say what he means with clarity, needing an upsetting situation or an emotional matter to release the dam of words. He has a more sensitive nature than is typically Virgo rising. He has a sentimental side and a mothering disposition. He can lose some of the Virgo objectivity with this additional color to the personality.

When Mercury and Venus are in negative aspect, the individual may soften his critique with more diplomacy. He may go too far toward that tendency and lose his effectiveness by being overly gentle. His speaking voice may be soft and mellifluous, but can lack authority and impact. He may be too charming, neglecting to say what he really thinks about a situation.

Sarcasm is the outstanding trait when Mercury and Mars are in difficult aspect to each other. This individual can develop the habit of speaking in a caustic manner to get the attention he may have missed as a child. There may have been competition from the parent of the same sex, creating frustration and annoyance in the child. The need to use shock effect to get extra attention may have started at an early age. Anger unexpressed can become habitual, so that the caustic manner is adopted even when it is unnecessary. He may need a strong competitive situation or a jolt to challenge the utilization of his perceptions in a less harmful manner. When putting his finger on the precise spot he may forget it has a sharp point. He can channel this energy by becoming a fighter with his words instead of wounding with his cutting remarks.

In a Mercury-Jupiter conjunction or difficult aspect, tremendous optimism may turn into a Pollyanna approach. He is tremendously fluent, yet may oversell. He tends to promise more than he can deliver, set too many goals for himself, scatter his mental energy. A philosophical nature is pronounced with this aspect, yet he can set himself up for many disappointments by overestimating situations and overshooting the mark. He comes into his own when he learns to temper his enthusiasm with matching action. He may find his true medium of expression later in life.

Limitation is keenly felt in childhood when Mercury and Saturn are in difficult aspect. This Virgo personality may tend toward a negative approach to life. Pessimism, overcaution, and an overly fearful outlook may be his way of staying safe. He may come into the world with a sense of a mission, yet a fear of failure. He may doubt his intelligence, being overly critical and judgmental to avoid his "ultimate" responsibility. He may be especially fearful of taking responsibility for his ideas and his life. He is the worrier of the zodiac and may blame the conditions of his childhood for his outlook until he learns how to break his negative patterns and programming.

Negative aspects from Uranus to Mercury indicate an unusual way of speaking. Many times the sentences are never finished, as the individual goes from one subject to the other. He may have such a rapid thought process that it is as if too much electricity rushes through his brain. He may not know how to stop this erratic thought process. He may talk in rapid-fire manner, become bored with ordinary communication, and be two steps ahead of everyone else in the development of ideas. He may have genius potential, yet have difficulty in focusing his attention for any length of time. He may try to resist his unusual mental ability, trying to conform early in his life. He may have to learn how to turn his mind off occasionally and may worry about "blowing a mental fuse" or having a mental breakdown. Meditation can be extremely important in learning to bring peace and tranquillity into his thought processes at times.

Neptune and Mercury in combination can create difficulty in dealing with concepts. The individual with this aspect may not be able to visualize easily and he finds it hard to deal with fantasy and dreams. When he does have a strong dose of inspiration he may overanalyze it and consequently pick it to bits. He can have difficulty in relating one subject to another. He worries about how concepts can be worked out on a concrete level, negating things before they have a chance to develop. He has a hard time with trust. He may have to learn how to separate his conceptual mind and his analytical process, no easy task for one with this aspect. He may have to learn how to take some matters strictly on faith. In a positive sense, a synthesis between left- and right-brain activity enable him to see the overall picture and also work with details.

One of the most interesting aspects occurs when Pluto and Mercury are affecting each other adversely. Since Pluto is the power planet, this individual is especially effective with words, yet he may not know it. He tends to be a compulsive talker and may manipulate with words. In his early life, he may have overtalked in order to receive any attention, and felt he had to play games with words to be understood. This individual has difficulty in putting his cards on the table and himself on the line. He may set people up with statements he makes, checking out their reaction before he pursues his line of communication. He has evidently felt it necessary to manipulate in his manner of speaking in order to get what he wants from people and life. He may say what he thinks someone wants to hear. He may eventually outsmart himself if he thinks he is outsmarting others. A rebellion against the parent of the same sex may keep him from playing it straight. He may want to "get even" through his words and ideas. His words may overwhelm others and overload them. His ultimate power comes with the realization of his true effectiveness and with the clarification of his motives. When he realizes that he is infinitely more effective when saying less rather than more, he learns how to come to the point in a concise way. His simple statement may be so powerful that he can transform situations by saying very little.

FINANCE

Venus rules the second house of finance when Virgo is on the ascendant. Venus rules beauty, pleasure, art, social matters. One with Virgo rising earns money through these Venusian avenues, but also loves to spend money on pleasurable things. He may be quite self-indulgent in his expenditures, but he also likes to provide beauty to others through his gifts. He may not be able to resist jewelry, art, clothing, and fragrances. He loves to buy flowers and ornamental items. He easily spends money on social matters, food, and entertainment. He may just love to spend money any way at all. Of all examples of Virgo rising, five men in history are particularly known for their extravagance, especially focused on love of spending to create opulent beauty: Tsar Nicholas II, Louis XVI, Henry VIII, Aristotle Onassis, and Cesare Borgia. Indulgence in the pleasures of the senses seems of prime importance in the lives of some people with Virgo rising, yet just the opposite is true with Florence Nightingale, Pope Paul VI, and missionary Junípero Serra.

Virgo rising can earn money through theater, music, art, or diplomacy. He can have income from social contacts, social services, or a strong sense of social justice. Tony Andrews, with Virgo rising, earns money through his own company, supplying food to other countries, combining the strong Virgoan trend to service with income that is connected to social consciousness. One with Virgo rising must love his occupation in order to be financially successful. Coco Chanel, with Virgo rising, earned a fabulous income through her couturier clothing, bringing pleasure and beauty to women. Sophia Loren earns income through talent and in the entertainment world, spending money on beautiful jewelry and a beautiful home. Marlene Dietrich earns money through her beauty and voice. Joan Sutherland, Frédéric Chopin, Igor Stravinsky, Pablo Casals, Mozart, Rachmaninoff, and Johann Strauss earned money through music while bringing pleasure and beauty to others.

Legal affairs and diplomacy are Venusian matters. Presidents

Franklin Delano Roosevelt, John Adams, Calvin Coolidge, and Dwight D. Eisenhower utilized their statesmanship and diplomatic ability in earning money, as did William Penn and Benjamin Franklin. Artists Modigliani and Georges Seurat supported themselves through their talent. Since Virgo rising is particularly mental, there are a preponderance of artists who used words as a source of income. Baudelaire, Ibsen, Emerson, Thomas Mann, Nathaniel Hawthorne, Anne Morrow Lindbergh, Maupassant, Elizabeth Barrett Browning, Albert Camus, Oscar Wilde, and Kahlil Gibran are prime examples of those using beautiful language to earn income.

Many spending and earning habits are indicated by the aspects to Venus in the individual chart. If Venus is well aspected, funds are easily earned and well spent, yet a badly aspected Venus can indicate indulgence or laziness (or both) in financial areas.

COMMUNICATIONS

Scorpio is the ruler of the third house of communications with this ascendant. Pluto, the ruler of Scorpio, is the power planet. Virgo rising has a particularly powerful ability to influence people with what he says. His intensity is so high that he may not realize he can knock people over with his words.

He may unintentionally antagonize those around him by putting too much force into his conversations. Pluto energy is dynamic and powerful. It can be destructive, but if it is channeled, it can be enormously effective. When the individual with Virgo rising becomes aware of his power, he will carefully release that energy on the highest level.

Pluto rules mass media, communications fields, television. Reaching masses of people is a way of transforming the intensity of the Virgo ability to communicate. Actors with this ascendant have particular charisma with the public. Peter Sellers, Doris Day, Shirley MacLaine, Sophia Loren, Roddy McDowell, Julie Andrews, Montgomery Clift, Helen Hayes, Deborah Kerr, Katharine Hepburn, Rock Hudson, Pat O'Brien, Lillian Russell,

Marlene Dietrich, Tallulah Bankhead, Clark Gable, Zsa Zsa Gabor, and Ralph Bellamy all have Virgo rising.

Since Virgo is a service sign, communications and the ability to negotiate and moderate can propel individuals with this ascendant into powerful positions. Larry Keith, an actor with this ascendant, became the president of the Screen Actors Guild, fulfilling his sense of service to his fellow actors. His powerful ability to moderate in the negotiation of contracts for performers in the television industry is a fine example of the Plutonian energy. Pluto energy is not only powerful but transforming. When the individual with this ascendant purifies his motivation toward the well-being of all, he rises like the phoenix from the ashes to reach mankind.

The third house rules early schooling as well. It may be through education that the Virgo rising gets in touch with his effectiveness. He not only transforms others but can transform himself, when he uses his powerful ability to communicate on a highly motivated level. If Pluto is well aspected in the natal chart, the individual is in touch with his natural ability to affect people through words. He will utilize thoughts and ideas in an effective way, knowing that he may not have to say much in order to get the message across. He will work through any media that reaches people on a mass level. If Pluto is not well aspected in the chart, the individual may be tempted to play games with words, manipulate with words, or be overly forceful.

Since short-distance travel can be indicated by the third house, the individual with Virgo rising will be attracted to powerful automobiles, motorcycles, or powerboats. Larry Keith commutes between two homes by way of his own airplane. Tony Andrews spends leisure time "playing" on motorcycles and racing cars. He drives an especially powerful automobile, channeling tremendous energy into winning races that require not only daring and courage but tremendous skill. Perhaps Walt Disney topped everyone in finding the kind of vehicles that are fun. Millions of people each year go to Disneyland and Disney World to ride on the fabulous fun machines.

Since Pluto is also the planet of play, one with this ascendant can release a great deal of pent-up energy through vehicles that challenge his skill and release his power. He may gain a greater sense of power when he drives, flies, or speeds across the water. He may need to play, through energy described by the third house, to avoid antagonizing everyone around him. Since this house also describes relatives and neighbors, the individual with Virgo on the rise may live around particularly influential people. His relatives and siblings may be especially magnetic. If Pluto is badly aspected, these same siblings, relatives, or neighbors may occasionally pull the rug out from under him, sending out the message: "Do as I say and ask no questions." He may need to avoid being motivated by a desire to get even with those people who have forced or manipulated him.

HOME LIFE

The fourth house in a chart indicates the kind of home life the individual will naturally be attracted to. He seems to pick a home and lifestyle that reflects his philosophical, expansive needs. This is the house that describes the parent of the opposite sex, and the conditions around the individual in the latter part of his life. Jupiter is the ruler of this sector of the chart when Virgo is ascending. Jupiter is the planet of luck, abundance, optimism, extravagance, and growth. The Virgo personality can express his greatest optimism and philosophy within the confines of his own home, gaining in intensity toward the third portion of his life. He becomes wealthier as he grows older, both in material ways and in spiritual ways.

This individual may be most extravagant in his home life, needing an opulent environment in which to thrive. Being challenged by the desire to constantly find a bigger and better place to live, he may end up owning several homes. Much of his enthusiasm is derived from the parent of the opposite sex. He has mentally photographed that parent as the philosophical, happy-go-lucky member of the family. If Jupiter is well aspected, that parent may be wealthy of purse and spirit. If Jupiter is not well aspected, it is likely that the parent has disappointed the one with a Virgo ascendant. The parent may have promised more than could be delivered or overestimated his own abilities, disappointing himself in the process. It may be necessary for this individual to look at his mental pictures of that parent in order to release and rechannel some of his desire for challenge and growth.

He may inadvertently set up situations connected to land or home that end up as disappointments. He may overestimate his ability to expand in areas of property and overspend. He may not give himself permission to have the kind of home he really wants for fear of disappointment. In a positive sense, he can challenge himself by aiming toward the kind of lifestyle he really wants, and by tuning in to "luck" connected to land, property, or real estate.

Certainly Louis XVI overestimated his ability and financial budget, causing his house of cards to fall with a resounding crash. His extravagance was the downfall of his society. Aristotle Onassis provided an opulent lifestyle on his private island as well as on his powerful yacht. Henry VIII, Cesare Borgia, Sophia Loren, Tsar Nicholas II, Charles II of England, James I of England, Prince Albert of England, Howard Hughes, and Franklin D. Roosevelt were not conservative in their selection of a lifestyle or home.

The expansive nature of one with Virgo rising will come full cycle when he is older. Wisdom replaces much of an insecure need for fact, his philosophy may be fully developed through his life and experiences. He is more willing to expand, grow, and take chances as he grows older. He may fulfill the potential of the parent of the opposite sex if that parent was not able to live up to all of his expectations. He will certainly develop his humor to the fullest and will more than likely have a luxurious life full of interesting experiences as he comes into his most mature years.

ROMANCE • CREATIVE EXPRESSION

Saturn rules the fifth house of romance with this ascendant. Saturn is the planet that indicates the primary karmic "focus" in life. It may be the area where the individual finds security. It can also be indicative of where limitation, restriction, and fear enter in. The fifth house rules not only romance but children, the gambling instincts, creative ability and focus, and ability to entertain.

Saturn is described as "the playpen Mother Earth puts her children in." Just as a playpen represents security, it can also indicate limitation. A baby must assume responsibility for himself before he is allowed out of his protective pen. In life, Saturn indicates areas where we need to assume responsibility and really take care of ourselves. It can indicate karmic lessons to be learned. Some individuals with Virgo rising may neglect their creative ability, either fearing the responsibility involved or worrying about being perfect. Many times the creative ability is connected to a "technique" or technical approach. Learning a technique can break down the barriers of fear and restriction.

Romance may be necessary for one with this ascendant to feel secure. He may pick someone who needs him. If the aspects to Saturn are good ones, the individual will find someone conservative, supportive, and "parental" in a romantic situation. He may attract a karmic situation. The Virgo rising may "go steady" in his youth, finding one person to be involved with. If Saturn is badly aspected, romance may be elusive, or restrictive. He may be pulled in by someone with tremendous insecurities, who appeals to the Virgo's need to be needed. He can feel unduly responsible to the one he loves.

Children born to the Virgo rising may have a serious nature. They will be particularly reliable, "old souls," and may feel a responsibility toward the Virgo rising parent. If Saturn is well aspected, there are strong ties, deep bonds between parent and child, but if Saturn is not well aspected, the parent may feel burdened or trapped by children. The children may be born with deep insecurities. In any case the children may have to be encouraged not to be perfectionists who are too hard on themselves.

Any feelings of rejection in the relationship with his children should be examined whether the Virgo parent or his children do the rejecting. The Virgo rising can be controlled by guilts about his children. Many times, a mother with this ascendant may use her offspring as an excuse not to tap her own creative ability. They can act as her "playpen." She may also have times of resentment toward her children. Love is the antidote for the relationship between parent and child. The child may have to be encouraged not to worry about or take on too much responsibility for the parent with Virgo rising, yet one with this ascendant can be motivated by a desire to provide security for his children.

In areas of entertainment, Virgo rising likes to be a perfectionist. He may be insecure early in his life about giving a party or entertaining his friends, yet as he grows older or refines his technique, his ability to entertain becomes a security. He will always want the details to be precise and may have to trust more of his spontaneity in areas of entertainment.

The Virgo rising may have difficulty in expressing any of his creative or gambling instincts, being especially conservative. If Saturn is well aspected, however, investments, the stock market, or other means of expressing his talent can bring security into his life. It is in these areas that the Virgo rising must take care about his judgments. He may be overly conservative, cautious, or hard on himself, assuming too much responsibility as an avoidance of assuming the "ultimate" responsibility with his creative ability.

As he grows older many situations become easier. He is not so hard on himself and finds true security in these fifth house matters. He can upgrade his level of reliability, building a strong platform of security through tapping his "gambling" instincts.

WORK • SERVICE • HEALTH

The planet Uranus rules the sixth house of service, work, and health when Virgo is on the horizon. This planet is called "the great awakener." It describes high energy that is almost electrical in its quality. It can also indicate sudden and unexpected changes in cycles of life. In its positive sense, Uranus rules genius potential, unusual qualities, and an inventive approach. In its negative connotation, it indicates disruption, unexpected change, the desire to run away.

The native with Virgo on the ascendant needs to be involved in work projects where he can not only show his genius but find his own unique, original approach. That may include being able to set his own time schedule. He may be a nonconformist in the type of work he chooses, and perhaps with the way in which he works, discovering a talent for accomplishing tasks rapidly. He will want the latest electronic equipment or computers to help him. Since Uranus rules anything connected to electricity, electronics, radio, unusual or "new age" health methods, astrology, inventions, music, and recordings, this native can find satisfaction in any of these areas. He may develop his own original concepts in connection with his job. Marilyn Ankeney, with Virgo rising, devotes herself to spreading information about Reye's Syndrome, a lethal disease that is counted among the ten major causes of death in children.

If the native with Virgo rising has a well-aspected Uranus in the natal chart, he will be willing to do free-lance work and express his true inventive genius. His nervous energy is channeled constructively, therefore his health is excellent. If that planet is badly aspected in the natal chart, he may resist doing free-lance or unique kinds of work, allowing his nervous energy to back up, creating problems with health. In childhood this individual can be prone to nervous reactions, rashes, allergies, or unusual health problems. He may have asthma, eczema, or be accident-prone. He will be less susceptible to these reactions if he uses these energies overtly and creatively.

Uranus rules anything that is ahead of its time. It also indicates humanitarian traits. In a positive sense, it indicates spontaneity; in a negative way, it shows unreliability and rebellion. Alan Pressman shows this quality in his work with nutrition, finding healing methods ahead of their time. Larry Keith works with recordings, doing voice-overs for commercials. Musicians use this energy constantly. Astrologers Cyril Fagan and Vivian Robson channeled their inventive, unusual qualities through their work. This planet also rules fame, high recognition, and inspiration. As long as the Virgo rising allows himself to be in areas where he is inspired and in the limelight, he releases energy that otherwise could cause nerves.

He may find his true work by rebelling against ordinary tasks. He can have ups and downs and face unexpected conditions connected with work. He may find great change in work-related areas in mid-life, going through strong seven-year cycles. He can find that the consumption of alcohol can be particularly injurious to health. He may try to calm his nerves through drink or drugs, such as tranquilizers. It can be more constructive to find unusual work, build a name for himself, and get in touch with his healing potential.

MARRIAGE • PARTNERSHIP

With Neptune ruling the seventh house of partnership, the Virgo rising with his practical outlook may be attracted to someone with an opposite view on life. He can find a visionary for a mate. He can expect and may be fortunate enough to find an ideal partner. The opposite can be true and he can let himself in for disillusionment in connection with partnership matters. Virgo rising may be totally unrealistic about marriage early in his life. He may feel that with a partnership situation all his problems will be solved. He may think that marriage will mean walking hand in hand with his love into the sunset of life. If he has donned rose-colored glasses in this respect, he may be very let down.

It is most essential to look at the aspects to Neptune in an individual chart to see the potential for happiness in marriage or success in a business partnership. When Neptune is well aspected, marital life can be ideal. He will find the combination of his practical views and the partner's conceptual ability a fabulous complement. He will be aware of any imperfections or faults on the part of the mate, be totally realistic about his own expectations, and can create a fantastic partnership situation with good communication as the basis.

When Neptune is badly aspected, this individual will be totally unrealistic about his expectations. He can be attracted to someone with a naïve approach to life and with stars in the eyes. He tends to put a loved one on a pedestal and can glamorize the whole idea of marriage or partnership. He may be unwilling to deal with everyday problems and may not notice signs of decay in a relationship along the way. He can expect a goddess, she a knight in white shining armor. He expects magic and can project his own dreams onto the mate, never allowing for the truth of a situation. He can make unreasonable demands on the partner and be tremendously shocked if the partner doesn't fulfill his dreams.

Virgo rising may have a rude awakening about his practical nature when he can be so impractical in selecting a mate. It is the one area where he allows himself to be unaware of fact. If his dreams are shattered, his love object has fallen from the pedestal, and the rose petals are scattered on the ground, it may be enormously difficult for him to recover. He would find it hard to trust his own perceptions again. If he can be totally realistic about his needs in a partnership situation and express those needs clearly, he can attract someone who will fit into his scheme of an ideal partnership. He may never be satisfied unless he has an almost perfect marriage or relationship.

Many times the individual fears a strong partnership situation before the fact. Fearing a letdown, he will never find anyone who could live up to his ideal. A mere hint of imperfection negates a possibility of strong commitment. He can keep himself safe by picking the very person who could never live up to his standards, thereby keeping at bay his fear of disillusion.

Henry VIII is a classic example of the Virgo tendency to overexpectation. With each wife, he was sure the situation was perfect. He went to all lengths to capture the princess of his choice and when the relationship was less than ideal, he quickly disposed of the person to again seek his dream. Tsar Nicholas was married to Alexandra, whose overly idealistic trust in Rasputin was a factor in the dreadful fate of the family. Clark Gable married an older woman who was much less than his ideal mate, but found his true love in Carole Lombard. Shirley MacLaine's dream of an ideal marriage ended in a separation across the world. Franklin D. Roosevelt was married to a true visionary, yet her dreams were not enough to make the marriage ideal.

NEEDS

In traditional astrological interpretation, the eighth house is commonly referred to as the house of "other people's money" or as the house of inheritance. In psychological terms, it indicates the way we get our needs met, and eventually, the quality of energy that an individual can send out to humanity. Aries is the sign on the cusp of the eighth house when Virgo is on the rise. Mars, the ruler of Aries, indicates focused energy, drive, ambition, fight, aggressive tendency, and resourcefulness. If Mars is well aspected in the natal chart, this individual can be quite resourceful and aggressive in getting his needs met. His gift to humanity has to do with pioneering new trends and fighting for people on a broad scale. In its negative sense, frustration and aggravation can be connected with getting what is necessary from life and people.

Mars rules the sexual energy as well as the highest creative drive. Mars also rules the fighting instincts, and metals. Howard Hughes reaped tremendous financial reward through working with metals used in airplanes. His needs were more than adequately met. He channeled his aggressive energies to pioneer new trends in world air travel. Stars Clark Gable, Zsa Zsa Gabor, Rock Hudson, and Montgomery Clift capitalized on their enormous sex appeal to get their needs met. Charles Evans Hughes was a fighter for humanity through the channeling of his Aries pioneering energy in the highest court in the land. Fighting for right, paving the way for the rest of humanity, is a gift to mankind from a Virgo rising.

The person with this ascendant can be challenged by a good fight. He may have developed a tendency to argue to get his needs met early in life. He can be bored by things that come too easily. If Mars is well aspected in the chart, he can easily be involved in competitive fields that bring in extra funds in a residual, dividend area. If he is involved in the stock market, he may reap his best benefit from companies dealing in metals, mining, or pioneering efforts. In the communications fields, he may have to fight for contracts that will bring in a percentage of the gross. He may deal in areas where competitive bids are necessary for success. If he has a pet project in mind where the eventual benefit will be for mankind's growth, he can become quite aggressive about raising funds and venture capital.

With a badly aspected Mars, the individual may experience a great deal of frustration in getting his needs met early in life and may resist taking up the challenge of fighting for those around him who are less capable than he. He may have a tendency to be impatient and argumentative where diplomacy would serve him better. He may want everything yesterday, becoming impatient when he doesn't get exactly what he wants at the time he wants it. He may discover that he can release and channel much of his excess aggressive energy in causes that pave the way for progress.

RECOGNITION

When Virgo is on the ascendant, Taurus rules the ninth house of recognition, travel, promotion, and legal affairs. Venus, the ruler of Taurus, indicates what one loves, where pleasure is derived, and areas of charm and sociability. The Virgo personality may be his most charming, diplomatic self when he is away from his natural habitat. He loves travel, and may have best ease of living in countries away from his birth where he finds it easy to attract recognition.

It is the artistic qualities that may bring the greatest recognition to one with this ascendant. This is certainly true in the case of all actors, artists, musicians, and writers with this ascendant. This aspect also indicates a special diplomatic ability that can bring opportunity for statesmanship. Benjamin Franklin was a wonderful representative of this country in his travels abroad. Publishing can also bring great prominence to one with this ascendant. For the most part, this native receives favorable publicity. It may be extremely easy for one with this ascendant to attract public recognition.

When Venus is well aspected in the chart, the individual with this intellectual approach to life will be especially sensitive to the love of his public. He enjoys the pleasure and ease of life when he is traveling and can be quite indulgent in satisfying the taste he easily develops. He may only travel in the most pleasurable way, with luxurious accommodations all the way. He develops the sensual side of his personality through the benefits of recognition from his fans.

If Venus is badly aspected, the native with this ascendant may not allow himself the pleasures he really desires and may avoid making waves with publicity or promotional effort, especially when he is away from his native soil. He may avoid expressing a positive, diplomatic approach. His philosophy may be based on the pleasure principle, and he may overindulge his tastes for high living when he is away from home. Publicity may be connected with the sensual side of his nature. Since Venus is the planet most associated with graciousness and sociability, the Virgo rising can find his greatest happiness when he is willing to express this loving side of his nature in constructive ways that will bring him recognition.

CAREER

The tenth house in a chart indicates the kind of career one is attracted to, how one behaves in public, and the public's reaction to the individual. Gemini rules this house when Virgo is on the rise. Gemini is also ruled by Mercury, so the Virgo personality needs mental stimulation in connection with his career. He can channel and release many of his thoughts, ideas, and mental energies in the public arena. Since Gemini is the "airy" expression of Mercury, he must be fascinated by his job or he will become bored and restless. Any career activity must be fast moving, and have variety. He seeks mental stimulation in connection with social life as well. He enjoys interesting conversation, mental games that challenge him, theater, and anything that appeals to his intellect. Gemini is a dual sign or the sign of twins. The duality really has to do with objectivity as opposed to closeness. If the person is too close in the public arena, he may have to pull away at times to gain perspective. In order to be truly stimulated and challenged mentally this individual may need to have two occupations at once, if one is not interesting enough.

The tenth house also indicates the relationship to the parent of the same sex. He identifies with that parent for good or otherwise. He may copy the behavior of the parent even though he may not like some of the qualities expressed by that parent. He may share many of the parent's opinions or judgments and may develop a tendency to criticize as a result of that programming. It can be most important to examine his mental photographs in order to break those patterns. He sees the parent as someone restless, full of mental energy, easily bored but stimulating. He will choose a career as a result of his pictures of that parent. He may hear dual messages from the parent.

One young lady was shocked when she examined her mother's messages and recognized their duality. She remembered her mother saying, "Do what you want to do. I'll support you in anything, but know your place and stay in it." She was aware that her life was less than fulfilling as she had followed her mother's example, remaining at home, running her domestic situation to perfection, but feeling frustrated at the lack of a career. She found it extremely difficult to break that early conditioning.

Many times, Virgo rising develops his skepticism as a result of early communications with the parent of the same sex. If Mercury is well aspected in the natal chart, the patterns set forth by that parent were encouraging and stimulating. The parent evidently was able to give permission to the Virgo rising child to express his thoughts and ideas, stimulating him on an intellectual level. If Mercury is not well aspected, communication with his parent is difficult. The parent may not have fulfilled his or her true intellectual potential, inadvertently frustrating the Virgo child in his career fulfillment. With awareness of the programming, the Virgo personality can express the unfulfilled potential of that parent, going beyond the parent's accomplishments and finding his true place in the sun.

FRIENDSHIP

The eleventh house in a chart indicates the quality of friendship and the kind of associates to which an individual is attracted. It can also indicate how a person reacts in group situations. When Virgo is on the rise, Cancer rules this house, with the Moon describing the relationship with friends. The Moon indicates emotion, sensitivity, feelings, and a maternal quality.

Virgo rising is most sensitive to his friends, caring about their welfare and extending sympathy and understanding to their problems. He may be quite mothering to those around him and can sometimes get hurt in the process.

Since he is attuned so closely to his friends' needs and feelings, he may have to exercise great care in the selection of associates. He may take on the color of those associations. He will be especially vulnerable in group situations and may be more easily hurt by friends and associates than in any other way. Since he will give the shirt off his back to those he cares for, he can expose himself unnecessarily to hurt. He can be surprised at jealousies from those he considers his closest acquaintances. He may have to learn to be discriminating with group involvement.

A friendship is never taken lightly by one with this ascendant. Since he adopts a mothering protective feeling, he may tend to try to "rescue" his friends. He may discover he lets himself be used occasionally. Since the Moon is the fastest-moving body in the heavens, he may find that his moods have much to do with his need for people. He can be particularly tuned in to group needs. When he understands the meaning of transference—the tendency on the part of others to project their attitudes about themselves—he will never be hurt by people, but always in touch with the trends of the times. He then expresses his natural service desires and capacity and puts his magnificent, analytical mind to the solution of problems. He learns to help others help themselves.

If the Moon is well aspected in his natal chart, the individual selects people who are sensitive to his needs and fill the emotional need for associations. He may discover that female companionship can be an especially satisfying friendship. Male friends will express a sensitivity and an emotional quality. There is a possibility of oversensitivity from male friends. If the Moon is not well aspected, this individual is especially susceptible to jealousies and hurts from his acquaintances, and he in turn may be envious of his friends. In that case, he is liable to protect himself, veiling his feelings and vulnerabilities by hiding behind his analytical mind. Underlying all is his care for the welfare of people who are close to him.

HIDDEN MATTERS • SUBCONSCIOUS PROCESS

The characteristics expressed by the ascendant are those most easy to deal with, whereas those qualities described by the twelfth house are the most difficult. Leo, symbolized by the Sun, rules the twelfth house of hidden matters when Virgo is ascending. The Sun rules the dominant, animus part of the personality, and so it may be difficult for one with this ascendant to show his true ego and dominance early on. Twelfth house matters can be more comfortably expressed in solitude or on a subconscious level.

The Sun indicates the dramatic part of the personality. It also describes the executive, leadership potential and the vitality or animation. With the Sun ruling this house, the individual may not easily express his dominant qualities. He may find it easier to express his sense of drama when he is alone or working on "closed sets." An actor with this personality may be more in tune with film and television than with stage work, or he may find rehearsal time alone essential for his developing a sense of himself and his potential. A writer or artist needs to work alone in order to tap his dominant energies. Anyone with this mental rising sign may feel the need to go off alone for a few minutes in a busy day to restore his vitality.

Many people with the Sun in the twelfth house spend long periods of time alone. Richard Speck spent his life in jail as a result of his crimes. Naturalist Anton van Leeuwenhoek necessarily spent a great deal of time alone with nature. Dick Cavett works on closed sets, interviewing famous and interesting people, rather than expressing his dramatic quality on stage.

The individual with this ascendant may have a natural curiosity about occult matters or metaphysical concepts, yet his practical mind may prevent him from exploring these matters overtly. He may have a natural sense of attunement with universal energy, but only use his knowledge to bolster his activity in the busy mundane world. Occasionally one with this ascendant may have to experience some hard knocks to his ego in order to propel him into a higher realization of self, in the true sense.

Eventually it is important for one with this practical outlook to get in touch with his core, and therefore the need for a deeper meaning of life. He will then be more easily able to vitalize himself and his existence. He can deal with practical matters on a different level when he finds ways to express his real ego and sense of self-worth.

With stronger, inner attunement and soul contact, the individual with Virgo ascending becomes aware of how he can be of true service to humanity. He identifies cosmically with mankind, and puts his fine mind to work to discover information, perhaps through research, that will bring forth needed facts. His voice, mind, and intellect become magical channels of expression that can provide important tools for awareness for all of mankind.

LIBRA
RISING

THE SYMBOL OF LIBRA IS THE SCALE of justice. This is the rising sign that seeks balance. Perhaps the primary quality associated with Libra ascendant is his sense of fair play. The primary need of one with this rising sign is harmony. He cannot stand injustice, dissension, or strife. He may spend his life attempting to create the peaceful and beautiful existence he so desperately needs. He is constantly readjusting to align himself to the forces around him to achieve an inner sense of balance.

The ruler of Libra is Venus. Venus is the planet ruling the arts, and describes anything connected to beauty. Graciousness, diplomacy, and sociability are obvious personality traits. Venus is also the ruler of Taurus, yet the difference between the two expressions of Venusian qualities is quite distinct. Libra is an air sign, while Taurus is an earth sign. Venusian traits expressed by Taurus rising are more earthy, while the Libran expression is more intellectual. Libra is a cardinal sign, indicating sensitivity and receptivity. Sometimes this sensitive nature can be troublesome to the individual, if he finds himself in a situation of disharmony and strife from which he cannot escape.

The beauty associated with this ascendant is apparent immediately. Refined features, delicate countenance, and perhaps a dimple or two are dead giveaways. The texture of the skin is velvety smooth and the disposition is usually as pleasant as the appearance is lovely. Men with this ascendant are particularly handsome and charming. The manner of dress is always neat and clean. You will rarely find a Libra rising whose appearance is sloppy, even when he is totally relaxed and off guard. Good taste seems to be an inborn trait. Subtle scent, a love of jewelry, and tasteful combinations of color can also be characteristic of this ascendant. The graciousness and sense of diplomacy are as much a part of his beauty as is his appearance. A sense of harmony surrounds this person that never quite disappears. He rarely loses his charm. Social graces come naturally to him. No matter what the circumstances of his birth, he possesses a quality of refinement, an appearance of culture, and a gentleness of manner.

Libra is the seventh sign of the zodiac. Libra rules the natural house of partnership. This individual has a distinct need for companionship and is rarely a loner. The desire for association brings him into contact with many people, but it is particularly important for him to find the right intimate relationship so that he can have the love and harmony he so desperately needs. Once he has satisfied his personal balance in a love relationship, he can begin to look further to his sense of social justice. He may have to take care of his partnership needs before he can go beyond to the broader scope. Without love in his life, he is one end of a seesaw, up in the air and rootless. He cannot adjust unless he has someone to adjust to. Sometimes this person will compromise his own desires just to have companionship rather than remain alone.

Anndee Larsen, with Libra rising, expressed these Libran characteristics in this way. She said, "I will overlook a lot to keep peace in a relationship. I will sometimes sacrifice what is good for me, in order to have someone to share things with, even if it is only a few dinners a week. I will do anything to avoid breaking off a relationship until I have someone else around. I seem to meld from one relationship to another. In a work situation, I cannot deal with tension or jealousies. I just cannot perform under that kind of tension. I can put myself under that tension, but I can't take it from someone else. If there's a problem I cannot solve, I'll leave."

Venus is the planet that rules anything artistic. Color, design, architecture, fabrics, clothing, and decorating are considered Venusian. Perfumes, makeup, beauty products, jewelry, gourmet foods, flowers, needlework, and crafts are ruled by Venus. Theater, music, dance, and art are also described by this planet. Many people with this ascendant find a natural attraction to occupations connected with these matters. Someone with Libra rising may prefer bubble baths and perfume to food. Other preferences include art or beautiful literature. The world of diplomacy and government is another form of Venusian expression. Legal matters and the courts of the land are Venusian in their concept because that broader sense of social justice is the highest expression of the need for peace and harmony for everyone.

The list of people with this ascendant who have shown an affinity for politics is outstanding. It has long been observed that the line between politicians and actors is quite thin. Sometimes the lines are crossed with tremendous ease. Early expression of talent and artistry can lead to stronger commitment and eventual participation in legal, political, or diplomatic fields. Many times, one with this ascendant begins to express an artistic talent after he has accomplished great things in his life through politics and world affairs. Winston Churchill found an outlet for his artistry through painting landscapes, and was able to enjoy some moments of peace and serenity through expressing his talent. Harry Truman showed his artistic leanings through playing the piano. After an extraordinarily successful acting career, Cary Grant began promoting perfumes when he went to work for Fabergé. Frank Sinatra, with a Libra ascendant, became interested in politics as well as the welfare of the automotive industry. He went to work for Chrysler when matters were difficult for that industry. Elizabeth Taylor, with that beautiful Libra ascendant, began to take an active interest in politics when she married John Warner, senator from Virginia. Whether one with this ascendant confines his activities to serving tea from an heirloom silver service with the accompanying cucumber sandwiches, or deals in matters that can affect social issues for mankind on the whole, there is a need to show that strong sense of sociability in one way or another.

The aspects to Venus in an individual chart can not only indicate how this individual is likely to channel and express his good taste and need for sociability, but will indicate just how far the person will go to achieve the harmony he desires. Compromise can be part of his characteristic ability to achieve his goals, yet in a negative sense, duplicity and deceit can underlie his charming manner. He can be particularly devious in such a subtle way that he is rarely found out. He can hide behind such a gracious façade that one would never suspect the dangerous personality behind the mask. In spite of his apparently nonchalant manner and charm, this individual is rarely an intellectual lightweight. He may not be able to clearly say just what he is thinking, or he may not want to put all his cards on the table and show his hand, but he is rarely as simple and uncomplicated as he appears on the surface. When Venus is badly aspected in an individual chart, he may go to all lengths to avoid making waves; peace is too important to him. The aspects to Venus will describe how various "colors" modify the pure Venusian personality.

The most dreadful example of this duplicity, deceit, and desire for beauty was shown by Adolf Hitler, who had Libra rising. His love of music was an obvious expression of the Venus personality, but the cold, inhumane lack of concern for anyone less than perfect—according to his Aryan concepts—led to a grim era the world will never forget. With both Mars and Saturn coloring his personality, his sadistic outlook overwhelmed any sense of social consciousness and turned it toward a terribly negative expression. Napoleon Bonaparte was born with this ascendant, as were Julius Caesar, Emperor Franz Joseph of Austria, Charles de Gaulle, ex-President Jimmy Carter, and Barry Goldwater. The Libran intellect and sociability were strongly expressed in the personality of Adlai Stevenson, winning him love and adoration from his numerous admirers. Obviously, the aspects to Venus are most important in considering how the individual will express his quality of graciousness and live his life.

Without a doubt, John Fitzgerald Kennedy, a Gemini with Libra rising, occupies a special place in history and in the hearts of mankind. His soft-spoken manner, charm, and good taste, as well as his political acumen, endeared him not only to the American public but to the world as well. His diplomatic ability was profound, his intellectual awareness extraordinarily keen, and his command of the language exceptional. He never alienated people by his intellect and language, but rather bound them to him in an unusual way. His broad sense of justice for all impelled him to seek a position where he felt he could do the most good for humanity. He certainly could have spent a comfortable life as a wealthy Venusian playboy, if he so chose. He was never found lacking in concern for those with less material comfort than he. His tastefulness was expressed in the cultural events scheduled at the White House while he was in office, and in his need to be surrounded by especially talented people. His entourage never lacked beautiful actresses and talented writers and artists.

When Venus is well aspected in an individual chart, the inclination is to express this diplomatic, gracious manner in a positive way. He will find an outlet for his abilities, rather than opting for self-indulgence and avoidance of anything difficult. Presidents with this ascendant are James A. Garfield, Chester Alan Arthur, John Quincy Adams, Andrew Johnson, Woodrow Wilson, Harry S Truman, John F. Kennedy, and James Earl Carter. General Robert E. Lee, Napoleon Bonaparte, and Emperor Franz Joseph, as well as statesmen Winston Churchill, Henry Clay, Charles de Gaulle, and Adlai Stevenson, share this rising sign. George VI of England, Julius Caesar, and Edward II of England were born with Libra rising. Nelson Rockefeller used his social position to better humanity's lot through endowment. Sir Isaac Newton, Louis Pasteur, Robert Fulton, and explorer Roald Amundsen shared their discoveries with humanity to better conditions for everyone.

Thomas à Becket, Archbishop of Canterbury, evangelist John Wesley, Theosophist Henry Steel Olcott, and Mahara Ji express the peace-loving personality in religious ways, while Carl Sandburg and Desiderius Erasmus express their artistry in a philosophical way. George Eliot, Stephen Crane, André Gide, and J. B. Priestley, as well as Booth Tarkington and Walter Scott, chose writing as an artistic outlet, while music became the expression for Felix Mendelssohn, Ignace Paderewski, Gustav Mahler, and Stephen Foster. Benvenuto Cellini chose sculpture as his vehicle of expression while Bing Crosby and Frank Sinatra utilized the golden sounds of their voices as their form of artistic expression, thrilling listeners in the process.

The list of actors with this ascendant is long. The men include William Holden, Robert Taylor, Sidney Poitier, James Dean, Cary Grant, Alain Delon, and Charlton Heston. All of these actors were blessed with gorgeous looks as well as acting ability. The women who chose acting as a mode of expression include some of the great beauties of the world: Rita Hayworth, Lana Turner, Jean Harlow, and Elizabeth Taylor. Sally Field, Diane Ladd, Debbie Reynolds, Sally Struthers, and Ethel Barrymore complete the list of beautiful and talented actresses. Princess

Anne of England and Josephine, Empress of France are also credited with the Libran beauty. John Lennon shared this ascendant. It is obvious that many avenues of expression are open to one with Libra rising.

It is when Venus is badly aspected in an individual chart that the person with this ascendant avoids self-expression. He wants to be pampered and prefers to lead an easy life, perhaps one of total self-indulgence. There may be good reason for this lack of active expression. Early childhood conditions have tremendous effect on the positive use of Venusian traits. It appears that one with this rising sign feels safe when he is quiet, *good,* and perfect. His very survival depends on his not disrupting the status quo. Jim Gaynor, a talented writer with this ascendant, became aware of this predisposition to avoid strife and learned how it worked against him as an adult, rather than to his advantage. His work in therapy opened up new avenues of possibility. He found a perfect expression for the outlet of Venusian energy in dance as well as in the writing that was so natural to him. He became aware that it is up to him to express his talent in whatever way he desires. When Venus is not well aspected in the chart, positive expression of talent is not as easy for the individual as it would appear.

Since the ascendant is indicative of early survival decisions, an understanding of the Libra rising's first moments in life will clarify his desperate need to avoid strife and to create harmony. In regression sessions, the pronounced similarity of the experiences of a number of individuals leads clearly toward a sense of responsibility to keep the peace in the family. The individual with Libra rising somehow decides that if he is *good* enough any upsetting conditions will disappear from the family scene. He becomes overly sensitive to the family environment and decides, unfairly, that it is his fault that things are the way they are. He thinks his goodness will affect the conditions around him. He adopts a pacifistic attitude quite early in life. Later on, in the social milieu or in a tense situation, he falls back on his charm rather than expressing a more positive diplomatic talent.

In childhood, he can overload himself in assuming responsibility and can feel extremely pressured, although maintaining an appearance of outward calm. He decides the only way he will survive is to give up, to be especially quiet so he won't stir up anything more that could be upsetting. He may unwittingly develop a lifetime habit of taking the easy way out for the sake of harmony. The problem is intensified as he is always rewarded by those around him for being *good*. He learns to get the attention he needs by his show of charm and niceness. He may never feel safe or secure in showing feelings of anger, jealousy, or competition.

One young lady with this ascendant was born a twin. Her sibling was frequently sick, while she was extremely healthy. During a regression session, she discovered that she felt it was all her fault somehow. She felt guilty as a little one for being healthy while her twin suffered and felt she had robbed that twin of vitality before birth. Her twin's sickness upset and worried the whole family, and would happen quite unexpectedly. She described her feelings at that time by saying, "I felt that somehow I was not nice enough. I decided that if I was a better person, somehow my twin would be all right. I decided to 'fast' on fun. It was my penance. If I didn't have any fun and I didn't let myself do anything that was not nice, my twin would be okay. I just didn't feel right about enjoying myself. I bottled up my love nature. I wish I could just love freely, but I've never felt clear about it. I could never ask for anything for myself and sometimes I felt I was acting in a counterfeit way. Sometimes I just didn't care [about my twin's welfare]. Naturally I felt guilty about that. It has been hard for me to do exactly what I want to do. I'm always behaving as I think I'm supposed to. It can paralyze me sometimes."

Many times, the Libran personality has difficulty in realizing his true identity. He may never have to learn how to stick up for himself. He may have had his needs met easily because of his nice disposition and his peacefulness. At times, he may have felt lost in the shuffle. It can be difficult to learn how to fight back. He may give up on things that don't come without a struggle. His ability to adapt can become a bad habit, hiding his real desires. He may not know how to say what he really means, trying instead to say what will please someone else. He can be sadly disillusioned when in the "real" world; his charming, easy manner just means he can be ignored. He may have to learn a whole new set of rules.

Sometimes the early decisions come through photographs of conflict between parents. The child can feel overly protective toward one parent and can feel rejection from the other. He may be overly obedient in hopes of getting the attention and love he craves from that rejecting parent. This was clearly illustrated in the chart of a beautiful young singer whose passive nature was obvious even though she had a thriving career. Her mother had taken care of everything in her career, acting as her manager until the lovely, talented singer was married. She seemed unable to fend for herself, so her husband took over for the mother, handling any difficulties that arose. Periodically, her husband noticed quite a strong character emerge when something was wrong musically. He was mystified, but still worried that if anything happened to him, she would be unable to care for herself. The singer ultimately realized that her passive behavior was her way of including her divorced mother in her life, as she felt protective toward her. It seemed easier to let her mother and her husband do things for her, as it seemed to make them happy; it was easier in the long run. With awareness, she began to take a stronger position in the management of her own career and was pleased to notice the positive changes that resulted.

Libra rising may not like to be around too many people. He can feel more comfortable in small groups and prefers intimate social situations to masses of people at any one time. He can easily blend with and adjust to two or three people, but when there are too many personalities, he feels pulled and scattered. His scale-of-justice personality becomes like a whirling dervish and his sense of tranquillity is thrown completely off balance. In a positive sense, this individual can create such an aura of peace and tranquillity that it is worth his while to learn how to express these traits with some self-assurance. An awareness of his artistic ability can start him on the road to self-expression.

Kari Copier channeled her artistic ability into fabric designs, consequently opting for work in advertising with Simplicity Patterns. She eventually discovered an additional talent in creating designs of her own. Peggy March Harris, known in her teens as

"Little Peggy March," was so well known in Germany that her fans followed her down the street. Her blond beauty and fabulous voice had already made her a major recording star when she began writing her own music. By combining her vocal ability with this new avenue of self-expression, she was able to bring her talent full cycle. Creative outlet through any art form will enable the person with Libra rising to tap and release a stronger manifestation of his love nature. It can lead to a more dynamic, less static expression of life.

FINANCE

When Libra is on the ascendant, the sign of Scorpio is the ruler of the second house of finance. Pluto, the ruler of Scorpio, is the power planet. It is obvious that the individual with this rising sign has fantastic financial potential. Pluto can indicate areas of life where the most drastic changes occur, for this planet indicates complete swings from one extreme to another. This individual earns money in large sums that come in periodically, rather than from a steady, consistent flow of funds. Therefore, careful budgeting is necessary to avoid riding up and down with the crest and waves of income. The natural spending habits, however, seem to coincide with these swings. One with Libra rising tends to save on small expenses in order to make major purchases. He can scrimp on carfare in order to buy a Rolls-Royce.

This planet can indicate fabulous potential for income. Whenever the person with this ascendant is involved in projects that reach masses of people, his income takes a tremendous leap forward. The motivation behind his earning power can indicate the greatest change in the life of Libra rising, as his magnetic ability to earn money seems to increase when he is concerned about the welfare of all. Many times, a product that is manufactured can be the source of income. Since Pluto rules television or major organizations, income can be derived in this manner. Usually the individual with this placement is willing to take risks on large sums rather than limit himself to routine sources of income.

The planet Pluto is related to the child ego state in terms of Transactional Analysis. The child in a family is magnetic, adorable, and the most "powerful" member. He is the center of his universe, and if he is in a loving family, gets his needs met easily. This child never worries about his effectiveness. He assumes things will continue to come his way. He exercises an unforced power. An individual with a well-aspected Pluto in the natal chart has a magnetism and self-assurance that enables him to put together deals that are for the most part tremendously effective. He may not have to expend much energy for his projects to fall into place easily. Pluto can also be described as a powerful body of water. If that turbulent water is left to flood the riverbanks, it is destructive. Yet when that same body of water is dammed up, it can produce enough electricity to light up cities. When Pluto is well aspected, the individual can light up cities, reach masses of people, and be involved in projects that uplift mankind. Louis Pasteur, Adlai Stevenson, Andrew Carnegie, Robert Fulton, and Winston Churchill were motivated by a concern for mankind and earned funds accordingly. Actors, bringing joy and entertainment to people, "playing" in the process, earn money in lump sums but may go through periods of no income. Writers earn funds through mass production of books, newspapers, and magazines, recording stars earn through distribution of records, and composers through wide use of their music.

The negative manifestation of Pluto is not only the damaging tidal wave which brings destruction in its wake, but the tendency to manipulate. Adolf Hitler lived a luxurious life made possible by the use of negative destructive power. Negative manipulation, by law of nature, always backfires. In financial matters Libra rising must always deal on scrupulously high levels or he can have the rug pulled out from under him. Any tendency to manipulate funds, gamble in a negative way, or make compulsive investments can backfire. He may go through periodic cycles of financial highs and lows. Funds can be earned through group projects, or in ways that will benefit humanity on a large scale. Frank Sinatra's public service campaign for the automotive industry may well inadvertently bring him better income than is expected.

COMMUNICATIONS

Sagittarius is the ruler of the third house of communications when Libra is on the rise. This house also rules early education, the learning aptitude and inclinations, and relationship with siblings, relatives, and neighbors. A cheerful outlook on life, natural exuberance and optimism, and an ability to enjoy humor and laughter are characteristic of one with this ascendant. His philosophical bent is as contagious as his charm.

Jupiter, ruler of Sagittarius, indicates happiness, philosophy, expansion, goals, selling, and areas of particular good fortune. Actors and actresses have a special ingredient in their makeup which enables them to sell themselves. Politicians, statesmen, and writers share this natural ability to communicate. Bing Crosby's golden voice, Frank Sinatra's special gift, and John Lennon's extraordinary talent are perfect examples of this blessing. Challenges in these areas keep this person high on life. Truth telling is part of his nature, even to the point of bluntness. With high enthusiasm, he may promise more than he can easily deliver, but his gestures are well meant.

Comedy can be a good vehicle for actors with this ascendant. Diane Ladd received an Academy Award in London for her creation of the humorous role of Flo in the film *Alice Doesn't Live Here Anymore*. Debbie Reynolds, Sally Struthers, and Sally Field have this comedic ability. Jean Harlow combined beauty with humor, and Cary Grant his extraordinary good looks with that quality. Philosophy is the opposite side of the coin. Many of Ingrid Bergman's roles expressed this quality, as did Diane Ladd's brilliant portrayal on Broadway of a southern girl's life in *Texas Trilogy*. Stretching toward new kinds of roles can be especially important for an actor with this ascendant.

The process of learning is of great importance to one with Libra rising. He needs constant challenges in areas of the mind. He may establish longe-range goals so that he is constantly stimulated. Philosophy, religious concepts, and the underlying patterns of life can especially interest him. His education continues long after his school years. He loves to read and is challenged toward new awarenesses as he is presented with more experiences. He has a natural curiosity about other cultures, other lifestyles, and loves to peer into other "neighborhoods." Everyday challenges can stimulate him and he enjoys running around, taking care of errands. He is a happy commuter, especially enjoying drives in the country, as he is a true nature lover. He naturally wants the most luxurious vehicle in his particular price range to complement and facilitate his missions.

Relationships with siblings are usually quite good. He is encouraging and generous with relatives and neighbors and attracts a similar response from them. If Jupiter is well aspected in the natal chart, he is especially fortunate in these areas. If it is not, there is a tendency to expect more of himself and of others than is always possible. He may overestimate his time and energy, "oversell," and let himself in for disappointment. He should take the promises of others with a grain of salt. He may have to schedule more tasks than he can accomplish in order to challenge himself (this can be both good and bad), and have many irons in the fire so that at least one of them will come through, preventing a letdown. He has a natural *"c'est la vie"* attitude. His humor will carry him through almost any situation he encounters in life.

HOME LIFE

With Saturn ruling the fourth house, security with a home can be of paramount importance. Land or property may be representative of the security, or compensate for the lack of it, in the relationship with the parent of the opposite sex. This house describes the "photographs" he has taken of that parent and can indicate the heaviest karmic lesson to be learned in life. The fourth house of home also indicates the conditions in the latter part of life. The individual with Libra rising comes into his strongest time of responsibility as he grows older. This was certainly true in the case of Winston Churchill, Nelson Rockefeller, and Adlai Stevenson.

Saturn has been described by the Kabbalists as the "playpen" Mother Earth puts her children into. A playpen represents both

security and limitation for a child. He is released from that playpen when he is able to assume responsibility for himself and can
take care of himself. Saturn is also related to the parent ego
state in terms of Transactional Analysis. The parent part of ourselves is developed by listening to the real parent's messages. A
parent may tell a child, "Be careful, you're too little. You can't do
that." An individual may continue giving himself limiting messages long after they are valid. The aspects to Saturn in the
natal chart indicate the kind of permission he was given from
the parent of the opposite sex. If the aspects to Saturn are extremely heavy, his parent messages could have ranged into the
destructive area.

With a well-aspected Saturn in the natal chart, the Libra rising has photographed this parent as the conservative, responsible, solid citizen who teaches him duty, discipline, and a sense
of high responsibility to himself and to others. As this individual
grows older, he assumes the same position of responsibility
carried by that parent, perhaps taking it a step further to express
any unrealized potential of that parent. He has been given supportive messages from his parent and may focus on establishing
a strong home base from which he can go forth into the world.
The care of family land and property may fall on his shoulders.
His roots and family tree are essential to his sense of well-being.
He feels great stability from his parent and knows support will
always be there. Any punishment or discipline from that parent
is just and to teach value. Good old-fashioned principles, a strict
code of ethics, and encouragement toward achievement in life
are inherited from this supportive, nonjudgmental parent.

More often than not, Saturn has at least a few difficult aspects
in a chart. When this is true, the Libra rising may feel rejected
by that parent, and may have felt an excess of coolness, reserve,
and caution in his relationship with that parent. Sometimes this
can indicate the lack of presence of that parent, whether physical or emotional. The parent may not have been around. Separation by death or by distance is possible as well as a detached attitude. Libra rising can photograph that parent with deep
insecurities. He may have "stayed in his own playpen" for
safety's sake and transmitted those same safety messages to the
child with Libra rising. In the extreme, the parent's deep in-

securities convey a "you're no good" message to this child. The examination of the aspects to Saturn in a natal chart are extremely important in enabling the individual with this ascendant to fulfill his highest potential and purpose later in life. The Libra personality can tell how far out of his playpen he has climbed by the kind of environment he chooses. If he lives in dark, small places, he may feel a safety ensured by having little elbow room, but still be plagued by the inherited insecurities. Many times, even if the individual lives in a large, spacious, airy home, he may have some small corner that he can call his own. That niche represents his safety and security in some way, almost like going back into the womb.

Liv Ullmann, with Libra rising, described her terror in being alone in an enormous castle by saying, "I, who as a child slept in the bathtub because that was the only place small enough to make me feel safe, now had a bedroom the size of a whole house. The fears that room evoked were beyond description." Many of these fears are directly related to the overly cautious, overly judgmental messages transmitted by the parent of the opposite sex. A turning point in that relationship can come when the Libra rising is able to encourage the parent to steadily climb out of the limiting circumstances. When he can overlook the negativity and see the insecurity or heavy programming or conditioning in the parent's childhood, the Libra rising may even motivate himself by a sense of responsibility to that parent, thereby fulfilling his ultimate potential in the long run. The healing of the karmic relationship comes through love. It is possible that the controlling, limiting messages from that parent were motivated by a fear that the Libra rising child would forget his filial duty, going out into the world never to come home again.

Many times, fearing his own imperfection, one with this ascendant can use his home situation as an excuse for avoidance of his highest sense of duty. He will tend to his home base stoically, keeping everything spotless, but eventually will feel trapped and limited. If he can knock down the walls of his playpen and convert it to a trampoline, he will always have the security of his home base to return to after his ventures out into the world around him.

ROMANCE • CREATIVE EXPRESSION

The person with this artistic personality can find his genius in artistic and creative expression. He may also use creative outlets as a means of rebellion, or to obtain freedom. The fifth house describes one's romantic inclinations and the types of people he will be attracted to, creative expression, children, and the gambling urge. One with this ascendant may channel his creativity into his offspring and produce exceptionally brilliant children. He may also produce freethinking, avant-garde children. His children may express his own rebellious nature, as they are likely to be free souls who are particularly opposed to discipline. He will no doubt encourage his children to express their individuality. If the aspects to the planet Uranus in the natal chart are positive, the relationship with his children will be spontaneous, electric, and exciting.

The planet Uranus, ruler of Aquarius, is on the cusp of the fifth house of creativity when Libra is ascending. This planet rules music, inventions or inventiveness, electricity, electronics, astrology, healing, and genius potential. The creative quality of one with this ascendant is usually special and unique. The person may achieve fame through an unusual approach. Bing Crosby and Frank Sinatra exhibit this special quality, as do Elizabeth Taylor, Liv Ullmann, and Ethel Barrymore. James Dean was perhaps the epitome of the genius, creative, electrical talent that can be easily expressed by one with this ascendant. It is not the kind of talent that can be pigeonholed easily. The individual with this quality must find his rhythm and style, and "create" to the beat of a different drummer.

Usually the romantic inclinations are toward someone unique and somehow "different." Love encounters can be unexpected and out of the blue. Sometimes the romantic situation can break with tradition in some way. It may also bring notoriety. Ingrid Bergman's romance with Roberto Rossellini made headlines and was considered extremely daring and unconventional at the time. Princess Grace found a fairy-tale situation in her romance with her prince. Princess Caroline expressed a need for freedom, perhaps rebellion, in an unconventional approach to her own marriage. Rita Hayworth found and married her prince. Frank Sinatra and Bing Crosby both had May-December love affairs. Mia Farrow is a most unique and talented individual and is certainly a free soul. Kathy Crosby gave up her own career to be with Bing. Both singers had children with talent and a sense of individuality. Diane Ladd's daughter, Laura, has already begun her acting career at an early age. If Uranus is well aspected in the natal chart, it is easy for one with this ascendant to tap and express his talent. If it is not, the individual may blow things up just before they are about to happen. Impatience, nerves, and high-strung energy may be too much to handle. Creative situations can be scary and full of uncertainty. Opportunity may always come totally out of the blue. Nervous energy can become hard to handle unless some creative outlet is found as a release for that rebellious nature, manifesting itself as nervous energy.

WORK • SERVICE • HEALTH

Neptune rules the sixth house of work, service, and health when Libra is on the rise. Neptune is the planet of dreams, idealism, and vision. It also rules therapy, or psychology, and the glamour world. Libra rising needs a vision and a concept. He needs to work in ideal surroundings. He may have to find a dream to keep him going. If he becomes disillusioned with his work, he may suffer health problems as well.

The artistic world holds a special lure and attraction to one with Libra rising. He can express his ideals and dreams through film, photography, and fashion. His special talent lies in conceptualizing the master plan. He can create work through the process of visualization, seeing the end results rather than the situation at hand. If Neptune is well aspected in the individual chart, the Libran personality is successful in his efforts to create ideal situations in connection with work. If Neptune is not well aspected, a naïve approach may lead to ultimate disillusion.

Therapy is the vehicle of work and service chosen by Roseanne Lawson and Dick Blasband, both with Libra rising. Roseanne uses imaginative methods in helping her clients to understand their problems. She uses fantasy imagery and metaphysical concepts as well as traditional therapeutic methods. Her idealistic approach combined with realistic training makes her a highly skilled therapist. Dick, a physician, chose Reichian therapy as his approach to healing. A scientific approach led first to medicine, yet now his visionary needs are satisfied through the constant incorporation of his own inspiration into the Reichian approach. His awareness of new methods in all fields provides a constantly fresh perspective on his work.

Patty McLain, a vibrant redhead with Libra rising, is a psychic. Her work is so exceptional that she has attracted many well-known clients, both in the film industry and in the political world. Patty is an exceptionally talented writer, choosing metaphysical themes for her plays and books. Her first play was published when she was quite young and is still performed in schools around the country. The degree of accuracy in her readings is especially high, even though her approach is idealistic. She has many projects in mind, including a film that presents metaphysical concepts in a humorous form.

Many beautiful actresses begin their career in front of still cameras. Film, whether still or moving, is a Neptunian-ruled occupation. Sharon Andrews combined both fashion photography with television work when she was a young teenager, finally portraying an innocent, naïve girl in her first film. Her interests gradually developed along more idealistic lines concerning social issues on a broader scale. Her interest in therapy and her perceptions give her added insight into any work she chooses to do.

If Neptune is badly aspected in a natal chart, the individual may never find any work idealistic enough to meet his needs. He is attracted to projects that appear high in concept and motivation, but may often feel led down the garden path when all is not up to his standards. In this instance, a realistic outlook comes with the removal of any rose-colored glasses. An ability to visualize and create ideal work circumstances is natural to one with this ascendant. He must remember to bring his concepts into reality through practical application.

MARRIAGE • PARTNERSHIP

In areas of partnership, the person with this easygoing ascendant is attracted to someone energetic, aggressive, sexy, innovative, and pioneering. The combination works well when each
partner is in tune with his own personality. They can complement each other and have a harmonious relationship as long as
an acknowledgment of individual needs is recognized. If Mars is
well aspected in the natal chart, the individual finds a mate who
reflects his own aggressive, sexual urges and who is in touch
with an ambitious, competitive nature. If Mars is not well
aspected, frustrations on the part of one with Libra rising find
reflection in a mate or partner who is impatient, angry, or unable
to release his aggressive urges. Strife in partnership areas can be
the result.

Aries rules the partnership house when Libra is ascending.
Aries is the first sign of the zodiac, indicating a natural pioneer,
or one who wants to be first. The symbol of Aries is the ram,
butting through any obstacles in his way. In a positive sense,
Libra rising is fortunate in finding a mate who is not deterred by
obstacles. If one with Libra ascendant is aware that he may unconsciously attract one who stirs things up in order to be able to
create harmony out of that strife, the relationship is one of balance. Ambitious goals on the part of the mate will channel much
of that dynamic energy, and life will be exciting for the peacemaking Libran personality. The charm and gracious quality of
Libra rising brings harmony into the life of the innovative partner.

The problems occur when the Libran personality looks for
someone to do his fighting for him and is not able to express his
own aggressive energies. He could then find an explosive situation with a mate who is actually inhibited, secretly angry, and
ready to release his frustrations on that peace-loving Libra rising. Hidden rage could be the most damaging part of a partnership situation. To be truly happy, he must be with someone who
constantly releases the fighting spirit in creative ways, or in

fighting for right. Jimmy Carter's Rosalynn maintained her right to be active and pioneering in spite of his public activity.

Elizabeth Taylor found frustration with Michael Wilding and Eddie Fisher, yet the ambitious, aggressive, innovative Mike Todd brought her happiness. Richard Burton spent much of his frustrated energy in drinking, a negative Mars activity. Their well-publicized fights eventually brought a parting of the ways. John Warner utilizes his aggressive spirit in political fighting for progress and the rights of others, tuning in to the Libra rising's sense of social justice.

NEEDS

When Libra is rising, the sign of Taurus rules the eighth house of needs. This is the house that indicates how an individual gets his needs met and, conversely, the gift he has to offer to humanity. With Venus the ruler of Taurus, his graciousness, charm, and diplomacy again describe a quality that works well in his behalf. His choice in the way he uses this energy is indicated by the aspects to the planet Venus in his natal chart.

If Venus is well aspected in the chart, he gets what he needs from life, and people, easily. His charming manner naturally attracts an abundant share of life's bounty. His sincerity, diplomacy, and love of harmony attracts the same qualities from people around him. If he really needs something, he will ask in a loving, gracious manner. He is an excellent fund raiser, as it is not easy to say no to one so nice. The Taurean Venus can be quite stubborn, so when this individual puts his mind to getting what he wants or enlisting cooperation, he will not give up. He will be especially determined if his efforts are for those he loves. He can be particularly happy to bring beauty, harmony, or better conditions to people who have less than he. His gift to humanity is his love nature, or his artistic contribution. Musicians bring beauty to people through their compositions or recordings. Artists contribute lasting beauty through sculpture, paintings; designers bring beauty through their designs. Actors contribute to entertainment, bringing pleasure and joy to many people.

If Venus is not well aspected in the individual chart, the person with this ascendant may be lazy about asking for what he needs or fearful of disrupting the status quo. It may be that he uses his charm to indulge his whims and need for luxury, without a thought to any contributions he can make. He may feel it is his due to be pampered and surrounded with luxury. Lack of sincerity is indicated by particular aspects to Venus and in this instance, he will say whatever he feels will work in getting what he wants from life or people.

Politicians must use diplomacy and tact in putting forth their ideas, so it can be interesting to note the quality of sincerity indicated in an individual chart. Aspects to Venus also indicate funds coming in on a residual, dividend basis. With investments, if Venus is well aspected in the chart, funds can come through projects connected with art or beauty. A Venus-Neptune combination can indicate an ability to raise funds for idealistic projects as well as funds from investments in film, art, or cosmetics, jewelry, and perfume. Actors with good aspects to Venus can have income from percentages of films they make, musicians from residuals, and politicians from campaign funds. With motives for the good of all, funds seem to come in more easily. Frank Sinatra is known for his generosity toward people in need, with no publicity or public acknowledgment involved.

RECOGNITION

Gemini is the sign on the cusp of the ninth house when Libra is rising. Mercury, the ruler of Gemini, has an airy quality, whereas the Virgo Mercury is more pedantic, analytical, practical. Gemini is a dual sign, indicating an ability to see both sides of the coin. It indicates areas where there is a need for excitement and mental stimulation. It can show restlessness or interesting mental activity. The ninth house rules promotional effort, legal matters, publicity, travel, dealings with distance, and higher education. It can also describe the ability to distribute, import, or export. The native with this ascendant must be stimulated mentally by some ninth house-related activity or he becomes quickly bored. Mercury indicates the things he thinks about. New horizons stimulate mental activity.

Since the sign of Libra is the sign of justice, it can indicate a legal talent as well. A lawyer with this ascendant is particularly adept at thinking on his feet. He is never at a loss for words or ideas, and can cleverly turn a situation to his advantage through his mental agility. An actor with this rising sign is able to think of promotional schemes, and has good instincts about how to attract the necessary attention to his work. Designers and artists with Libra rising can be especially successful at arranging shows, or finding galleries and agents who will promote them properly.

In many cases, the individual with this ascendant is more stimulated in countries away from his place of birth. Gale Gladstone, a dynamic actress with flaming red hair, found England to be her natural home. She returned to London, after years on the Broadway stage, marriage, and children, to star as Blanche in *A Streetcar Named Desire.* Sky Aubrey established homes in nine countries during the first six months of her first pregnancy. She went from Mexico to Los Angeles, then to Panama, Jamaica, New York, London, Paris, Budapest, and Rome—finally arriving in Geneva to have her daughter. She cut down on traveling with the second pregnancy, starting in New York, then moving on to Los Angeles, Canada, Nice, Paris, Zurich, and London before she went back to Los Angeles to have her son.

Kari Stuve married Jacques Copier, a successful French photographer who commutes between New York and Paris for work. Sharon Andrews began her extensive travels with her meeting and marriage to Tony Andrews. She has visited Guatemala, Iran, the Ivory Coast, Senegal, Argentina, Brazil, London, Paris, Rome, Geneva, Zurich, Lucerne, Nice, Cannes, St. Tropez, and Monaco. She has established homes in Manhattan, the East Hampton area, Paris, and Hong Kong, commuting between other places periodically. With the birth of her first child, Sharon transferred attention from travel to focusing on studies at a university. She has also continued perfecting her French with weekly sessions at home. Many people with this rising sign have a natural aptitude for languages. The mental energy seems stimulated by foreign cultures. This individual may feel he simply "knows" about life away from his place of birth. He will read about distant places, think about travel, and perhaps talk about his experiences away from home. If Mercury is not well aspected in the individual chart, he will have difficulty in expressing himself in other countries, at a university, or with promotional effort. Even with a well-aspected Mercury in the natal chart, there may be times when he is saturated with travel, publicity, and promotional effort. He will then need time alone in order to restore his perspective. He can actually do his best thinking alone, behind the scenes. He may need this solitude, periodically, to rest his active mind.

The individual with Libra ascending is able to be published, can lecture, teach, and express his ideas on his soapbox. His natural diplomatic ability extends to the understanding of other cultures. Explorer Roald Amundsen developed his best ideas while investigating distant shores. President Jimmy Carter seemed to have an understanding of the Middle East crisis, persuading Egypt and Israel to resume diplomatic relations. His effectiveness at home has been questioned, yet abroad he was held in esteem. Winston Churchill expressed his greatest concern for humanity during World War II, assuming a major role in peace talks. Richard Chamberlain may have played his finest role in *Shogun*, depicting a Japanese samurai, while Frank Sinatra has a notoriously bad time with the press on foreign shores.

CAREER

The Moon rules the tenth house of career, social life, and public life with Libra rising. The tenth house also describes the relationship with the parent of the same sex. Since the Moon rules the feminine sex, sensitivity, feelings, and emotions, the Libra personality photographs that parent as being especially sensitive, emotional, and vulnerable. He may see that parent as having been orphaned or abandoned in his or her early life. The parent-child relationship has deep emotional implications and can be extremely difficult for Libra rising to handle. The person with this ascendant feels as though he or she has to mother and protect that parent whether it is father or mother. He may feel he has to put his own emotional reaction aside in order to protect that parent. He hesitates to do anything that might stir up an upsetting situation. He comes to an early decision that he must keep peace in order to keep the status quo. He may not want to deal with emotional encounters, since they are painful to him. While he feels tremendously protective and mothering, he may resent having to be understanding all the time. He feels he gets the short end of the stick in the realm of being nurtured and understood.

My daughter Sharon, with Libra rising, was just a year old during one particularly difficult Christmas season. One day, when everything went wrong, the pressure cooker exploded potatoes all over the ceiling. It must have been the straw that broke the camel's back because instead of laughing, evidently I cried. Sharon came up to me, reached a tiny hand up to mine and said, "Poor Mommy." Her sensitivity and the perception of my pain astonished and shocked me. I was aware that I must control my own emotional reaction to protect her. The feelings are so deep between Libra rising and that parent that the "child" sometimes feels helpless to make situations better for the parent. He may appear unfeeling at times when in reality the feelings are just too hard to deal with. During a therapy workshop, one young lady with Libra rising became aware for the first time of a deeper relationship with her mother than she had previously acknowledged. She said she realized that she had compromised her whole life to please her mother. She felt she had never cut the umbilical cord, even though she was grown and now married.

In areas of career, the native with this ascendant may be especially vulnerable. If the relationship with the parent of the same sex was basically a good one, the Libra rising has a good relationship with his public. In a positive sense, this person understands the trends of the times and the needs of people perhaps more than almost anyone else. The Moon rules the collective unconscious. It indicates areas that we share as far as hunger needs and emotional needs. The Moon is the planet strongest in the charts of writers, for instance. If the native with Libra rising is able to work through his own emotional pain and any difficulty in the relationship with the parent of the same sex, he is especially gifted in writing about matters with which people will readily identify. He writes from his feelings, not his intellect.

If he is in the art world, he responds to the sufferings of people through his art, showing his concern through a desire to bring beauty and pleasure to mankind. If in fashion, he is able to sense what people will want in furnishings or clothing, and will cater to their needs. In the theater, he will portray especially sensitive roles. He can also appeal to women in particular. Omar Sharif, with this ascendant, certainly appeals to the feminine sex. Poet Carl Sandburg wrote poetry to appeal to the emotions of mankind. Albert Schweitzer devoted his life to the problems suffered by those unable to help themselves, adopting a nurturing role in his public life.

Libra rising can have great appeal to the public, seeming to touch people on a cosmic level. Mahara Ji appeals to people's need for nurturing. Arthur Godfrey and Frank Sinatra have tremendous emotional rapport with their fans. John Lennon and James Dean reached people on a deep, gut level almost beyond comprehension. Adolf Hitler was able to control the emotions of the German people to the point where they were capable of terrible destruction. Murderer Donald Kinman, with homicidal rage aspects, strangled women while making love to them, suffering great remorse and shame later on. Yet even with his violence, he appealed to women on an emotional level.

The Moon is the fastest-moving body in the heavens. Its many aspects daily can indicate changeableness or moodiness in public ventures. With good aspects, the compassion and sensitivity are high, but with difficult aspects, the individual can be vulnerable and take things too personally. He may have difficulty in career ventures at times, yet it is this very disturbing quality that can become his greatest asset in public life. Learning to work through his own emotional pain seems to enable this person to have a greater identity to, and therefore response from, the public in general.

FRIENDSHIP

Libra rising takes great pride in his friendships. He is able to attract people who are accomplished or have a great sense of pride and self-esteem. If the native with this ascendant has a healthy ego, he enjoys the companionship of other people who are strong and dominant. If his own ego is weak, he may have friendships or associations with people whose egos need bolstering, or who eventually hurt his pride.

The Sun is the ruler of Leo, the sign on the cusp of the eleventh house of friends, groups, and associates. The Sun indicates vitality, strength, leadership ability, and executive know-how, as well as the ego and sense of self-worth. It is also representative of the masculine sex or the animus part of the personality. The Libra ascendant picks people who show their strength and can assume a dominant role in group activity. He is particularly proud of the accomplishments of his friends and will support them, unless his own ego and pride are hurt. If his toes are stepped on, he will simply withdraw his friendship with no explanation at all.

The aspects to the Sun indicate the exact personality types that this individual prefers as companions. If the Sun is well aspected to Venus, he attracts beautiful, charming, sociable people. With Mercury aspects, he enjoys intellectual companionship, while Mars aspects indicate a possibility of competitive activities with friends. He may enjoy sports or activities where physical activity is part of the fun. When Jupiter is aspected to the Sun, philosophical projects or humorous associations are possible. He may attract friends who are wealthy of purse or wealthy of spirit. If Saturn is affecting the Sun in the individual chart, there may be periodic problems with friends. The friendship relationships may come into focus later in life, whereas the feelings of restriction come early on in childhood. He may have lifelong friends or associates who are of a serious nature. He may occasionally pick friends who are negative or who criticize him. He can feel especially responsible for his friends.

Uranian aspects to the Sun indicate a need for unusual companionship. The individual is hooked by genius. He enjoys group projects that deal with metaphysics, music, or humanitarian concerns. He may work off some of his own nervous energy by joining rebellious friends. With Neptune aspects, the idealistic type of person appeals to Libra rising. He is magnetized by those who are dealing with the glamour world, therapy, or who have great vision. Pluto aspects indicate powerful associations. This Libra rising can easily deal with major organizations and people who are particularly powerful and effective. With difficult aspects to Pluto, he may feel manipulated by his friends, or enjoy getting into mischief or "gamey" situations. He may feel that friends pull the rug out from under him at times.

Patricia McLain, a psychic with Libra rising, has many well-known clients who become her friends as well. She attracts people who are dynamic and are working through strong egos themselves. She attracts many executives as well. One of her strongest supporters is Sheila Weidenfeld, former producer and press secretary to Betty Ford. Sheila has demonstrated her executive, leadership qualities and her strength in many ways. Patty has received publicity in Sheila's book as well as in Susan Strasberg's book. Susan is another strong friend with a dynamic personality and dramatic, leadership quality. With a well-aspected Sun, strong support from groups and friends is indicated, but with a negatively aspected Sun, egos can get in the way of friendship or accomplishment in group endeavor. Loyalty to friendships is a strong quality expressed by one with this charming ascendant.

HIDDEN MATTERS • SUBCONSCIOUS PROCESS

The twelfth house indicates areas that are difficult to release early on in life. The person with Libra rising may have to learn to express his analytical quality. He may never quite accomplish the ability to clearly and concisely say what he means without couching it in soothing diplomatic terms. If he is on safe ground, he will have no difficulty in being quite precise, to the point, and clear, but those who don't know him well may see only the charming side of his personality.

In no way is the Libra personality attempting to hide his mind; it is just that his early survival decisions have to do with diplomacy, not analysis. He does his best thinking all alone, sometimes feeling scattered when surrounded by too many people. If he is confused about a situation, he needs time alone to gather perspective. Although he can think on his feet in a lecture situation or with a promotional effort and legal affairs, you can bet he has spent much time ruminating off by himself. This is a positive quality for one who writes, must rehearse alone, or perfect the reorganization of projects. Without distractions, he is able to be quite sharp and clear, practical and objective. He may enjoy studying or intellectual processes, stimulation that he can think about when he is away from the prying eye of the public. Authors must write alone, designers must design alone, composers are inspired while alone.

Eventually, the individual with Libra ascendant is comfortable in expressing his intellectual observations. He will never be critical to the point of hurting someone, as Virgo rising might be, as his function in life is to smooth things over, express his love and sense of fair play. He may be able to write critically, whereas he talks about harmony and peace. His psychic awareness or perceptions can be quite acute, coming to him on a plane of "knowingness." He doesn't receive flashes of inspiration, he simply "knows." His subconscious mind is active on a completely intellectual level. Many Libra rising personalities have acute perceptions and strong intellectual capacities, for Libra is an air sign and intellectually polarized—yet you may know this person for quite a while before he exposes his conversant brilliance. For pleasurable companionship, beauty, enjoyment, and fun, you could never top the joy of having one with Libra rising as your friend.

SCORPIO RISING

THE MYTH THAT SYMBOLICALLY DE-scribes Scorpio is that of the phoenix rising from the ashes. When this powerful sign is on the ascendant, the personality of the individual is so intense, magnetic, and charismatic he can literally knock people over without realizing it. He may have to go through times of feeling misunderstood to become aware of the force of his personality. After the possibility of great pain, he is able to complete his own personal transformation and express the eagle-like side of his nature.

Each sign has a positive and a negative expression, yet the Scorpio swing is extreme. There are no grays in the life of one with this ascendant. He sees things as either black or white. He has two symbols, each one an extreme: his lower nature is exemplified by the serpent, whereas his high spiritual nature is like the eagle, soaring to great heights, inspiring others through his majesty. Perhaps the hardest task in the life of one with this dynamic energy is understanding the most effective utilization of that power. Eventually, he must integrate his lower and higher self, burn out all lower feelings of revenge, and become aware of his ability to transform not only himself but others.

He may have a brooding, intense look, or appear almost innocent. Yet, if you look behind the surface appearance, you will notice that this person takes nothing lightly. He may have such a penetrating stare it is hard to look him in the eye. Even if he masks his gaze most carefully, he sees to the very depths of a situation. He makes an instant diagnosis of a person or situation, and forever follows his first impressions. He likes you immediately, or you simply are not part of his life. His deep, intense, cat-like eyes can turn warm and loving in an instant. He may appear quite formidable, yet there is a sweetness that can emerge in the twinkling of an eye.

The Scorpio personality may be the most misunderstood in the zodiac. He can be accused of being oversexed, full of evil intent, with desires only for revenge. He can be considered difficult to be around, yet some of the most powerful world leaders have this ascendant. The ruler of Scorpio is Pluto, who was Lord of the Underworld in mythological terms. Underhanded activity, manipulation, and revenge are attributes assigned to Pluto. Indeed the negative side of this energy can be tremendously destructive. The era of gang warfare, the Mafia, bootlegging, and black market activities can all be descriptive of the negative Plutonian energy. The positive manifestation of this force is so uplifting that many exceptional people have transformed the lives of those around them by channeling their energy for the good of their "group." Mohandas Gandhi changed the lot of his countrymen by tremendous personal sacrifice, dedication, and commitment.

In terms of Transactional Analysis, Pluto is related to the child ego state, the most powerful of all the ego states. A child feels that he is the center of attention within his family and sees himself as the center of his personal universe. His pure child ego grows into a healthy adult one, unless there are severe traumas in his early life. His natural free child state is then thwarted and he "goes underground" in a sense. If a baby is fed when he is hungry, he assumes he will always be "fed" throughout his life. If he grows up in a loving, warm, understanding family who fulfill his needs and some of his wants, he never doubts that life will fulfill his needs and wants. If, however, that baby is not fed, even though he cries loudly, survival depends on his somehow attracting attention. He bangs on the wall, shakes his crib, screams louder, throws everything in reach on the floor, and eventually gets response to his pleas. He then says to himself, "Ah-ha, *that's* how it's done." He has learned how to manipulate, play games, and kick up a fuss to get what he needs and wants.

As he grows older, not being sure that he will be effective, he continues the manipulation. His strongest message is: "I want what I want when I want it, and I'll get it no matter what or how." He manipulates to get a new bicycle when he is really too young, and not only falls off that bicycle but discovers he would have had something much better by waiting. He is in double pain because he forced a situation. He then has no one to blame but himself and is very miserable.

In life, the Scorpio rising may have learned to manipulate as a young baby, and feels effective only if he kicks up a fuss and plays games. He may have no idea that he comes on too strong until he realizes he is pushing people away from him, instead of bringing them closer. He feels particularly confused at times. He may have the rug pulled out from under him over and over before he realizes what he is doing wrong. He may not care that he is hurting himself more than anyone else. Scorpio rising can cut off his nose to spite his face. He may want things his way no matter what the outcome. He is willing to take his medicine if his manipulation backfires, but his internal suffering is very deep. It is said that the Scorpio will sting himself in defeat, and indeed the scorpion will sting himself before being devoured by a larger animal. After incredible pain, the individual with this ascendant rises to his greatest majesty and becomes the eagle soaring above, showing the way by his personal example.

The aspects to Pluto in an individual chart indicate the conditions of childhood and the survival issues adopted early in life. With a well-aspected Pluto, there is an indication that the individual has been the center of a warm, loving family and was well cared for. He grows up willing to let go of any situation that is not for the good of all. He never forces a situation or a person, and has learned that he is most effective when he is "laidback." He magnetizes the right situations and people into his life. He is tremendously effective in putting together projects, finding the right people to be involved, and is alert to any games or anything that is not squeaky clean.

If Pluto is not well aspected in the natal chart, the individual with this ascendant may not know his own power. He can be compulsive, so determined to get what he wants that he may run over everyone who stands in his way. He feels the ends justify the means. He may be motivated by a desire to prove something, get even, and have a thumbed-nose attitude toward life. He can play lots of games, be very mischievous, a gang leader, and use force as a way to get what he wants. He can be especially willful and is very determined and intense. Sometimes his games backfire and his house of cards falls down. He needs to "play," but his games can be destructive—and he may not care until it's too late. His revenge toward conditions in his early life may be stronger than he knows. He may also suppress his power until it erupts with a mighty roar. He may have no idea he is destructive in the use of his energy. He may notice that people tend to back away from him and may feel very hurt. He finally learns to pull back that magnetic force and channel his drive to a mass level where he can truly affect many people. He then gets what he wanted in the first place, only in the proper manner as a result of the proper motivation.

Consider two children entering a party. One is sure of himself, says hello politely, and sits in a corner eating his ice cream and cake. The other child yanks on skirts and says, "Notice me, notice me." Naturally, the adorable, magnetic child in the corner receives the positive attention. The other one gets the response: "Don't bother me just now." The Scorpio rising may have to learn that he is more effective sitting in a corner, letting people and situations come to him, but he is afraid to "do nothing" for fear nothing will happen. Once he is willing to transform his "little" will to the higher will, he is a force so potent that he transforms the lives of those around him by seeming to do nothing at all. He is a natural producer, and particularly effective if he loves what he is doing. Gandhi performed miracles by his passive resistance and strength.

Scorpio is a water sign. It is the most turbulent of all the water signs where depth of emotion is involved. It can be likened to a powerful body of water. If such a body of water floods the riverbanks, the end result is destruction, yet when that same body of water is dammed up, it produces enough electricity to light up cities. Motivation seems to be the key to the transformation of the Scorpio energy and personality. Scorpio rising can be more potent when dealing with large groups of people than on a one-to-one basis. He may be too much for one individual to understand and deal with unless he spreads some of that potency into mass expression. He blows himself up if he sits on his energy. He must have an outlet that will allow him to mass-produce or reach people on a mass level. If his desire and motivation is for the good of all, rather than just to satisfy his momentary desires, he will achieve true greatness. That may be extremely difficult early in life.

Oliver Wendell Holmes was born with Scorpio ascending, as was John Foster Dulles, Luther Burbank, Rudolf Steiner, and

Judge Hugo Black. Andrew Carnegie, Thomas Alva Edison, Rutherford B. Hayes, and Sigmund Freud shared this ascendant. Mass murderer Albert Dyer, Joseph Stalin, Hermann Göring, Benito Mussolini, Fidel Castro, and Ivan the Terrible also have this sign on the ascendant. Lenin, also born with Scorpio rising, was motivated by a desire to better the lot of his people. His downfall came when he bargained with the Russian secret police and compromised his power. Thus was born the police state of Russia. Religious founder Guy Ballard, Bertrand Russell, Mohandas Gandhi, and Joan of Arc shared Scorpio on the rise. Hero Eddie Rickenbacker, Lowell Thomas, and Henry Ford have the same ascendant as Louis XIV, Frank Lloyd Wright, Benjamin Disraeli, William Howard Taft, murdered Italian Premier Aldo Moro, and Richard III.

Some of the most dynamic entertainers in the world have this ascendant. Many have left a mark that will remain unequaled in history. Among them are Charlie Chaplin and John Barrymore. Red Skelton, Clint Eastwood, Tyrone Power, Dean Martin, Johnny Carson, Dennis Weaver, and Glen Campbell have this ascendant. Elvis Presley was also a Scorpio rising. The most publicized woman in the world is Jacqueline Onassis, born with Scorpio on the rise. Her exotic appearance is mystifying and enigmatic. She never seeks publicity, yet she cannot help but attract attention wherever she goes. Gloria Swanson, Bette Davis, and Joan Crawford have the same exotic, glamorous beauty. Joan Crawford received publicity for her compulsive, forceful, dangerous behavior. Ethel Merman has Scorpio on the rise, as did Maria Callas, Mata Hari, and Simone de Beauvoir. Such fair beauties as Janet Leigh, Joanne Woodward, and Mary Astor show the quiet dignity also associated with this rising sign. Helen Keller affected the lives of those born blind through the suffering in her own life. The hard-wrested change of her compulsive, almost primitive early behavior to the greatness and dignity of her later life is an example of the Scorpio personality in all its majestic transformation. She soared to the heights of personal greatness, showing others the way by example. Her message is: "If I can do it, so can you."

The native with this rising sign is never one to take things lightly. Intensity and purpose can be part of the overall package.

It is wise never to tamper with the explosive charge that can be set off by trying to outmaneuver or outmanipulate one with this rising sign. This native will never forget an injustice, just as he will never forget a kindness. He may forgive, but he will never forget. He can have some difficulty with personal relationships because of this intensity, yet he will carry on in spite of all personal obstacles. Group results are most important. He will overlook small tantrums on the part of his team members in order to achieve the projects at hand, but if someone attempts to outsmart him or play games, Scorpio rising is a master at finding the most effective way of getting even.

One with this ascendant is a natural Svengali. His attempts to transform others may be his way of avoiding his own personal transformation. He may be hurt at ingratitude when his suggestions are ignored and his advice turned down. He may have to learn how to give help only when he is asked for it. He is a natural detective. He knows secrets no one else knows, but he will never reveal confidences if he is asked not to. He seems to have radar equipment that picks up bits and pieces of information that eventually fit together like a giant jigsaw puzzle. He is a walking file cabinet of information and private classified data. He can sense a person's vulnerable spot in an instant. His secrets may be his own way of having fun with himself. You can be sure you'll never know everything about one with this deep personality. Even if he appears light and gay, he shows a mere tip of the iceberg of his personality.

He can be like Charlie Brown and the baseball team. He may need to learn rules to new games. Debra Smith, with Scorpio on the rise, said, "Everything is such a life-or-death issue with me. I get too intense and I need to learn how to play." If the planet Pluto is well aspected in the chart, it may be easier for this native to learn to take things easier. He can appear more mellow and relaxed. He enjoys solving life's problems and is especially effective in coordinating group activity. He works on levels where results count. Bill Dowling, handsome, personable, and dynamic, became vice-president of a major hotel chain at a very young age, after owning and operating his own unique hotel in the Bahamas, where he gained much valuable experience. He became involved with the expensive, luxurious Palace Hotel when it opened its doors in New York. His jobs combine work and play, since he travels to interesting places and exotic countries for his work. He is married to an equally dynamic lady, Lyanne Carl Dowling, also with Scorpio on the rise. Lyanne helped produce the powerful Picasso exhibit at the Museum of Modern Art in New York.

Linda Beatson Lloyd and Kathy Gallagher, both exceptionally beautiful blond actresses, established strong reputations in the advertising world in New York. Each one continued a successful career in other areas, achieving great success while still in their early twenties. Kathy opened her own restaurant in Beverly Hills, while Linda, after a marriage and a move to California, designed and manufactured her own line of hand-knitted fashions. Both Linda and Kathy could trade on their gorgeous appearance if they chose to do so, but both of them are blessed with a depth that augments their surface charm and beauty.

Aude Bronson-Howard was a mere eighteen when she left her Parisian home to find her way in the fashion industry in New York. She became a designer of men's shirts for Yves Saint Laurent while in her very early twenties, traveling all over the world to design, manufacture, and select fabrics to adorn the bodies of men who chose to wear her chic shirts. She also became the head of Saint Laurent's women's sportswear division until she resigned to begin a career in television.

Lynne Forbes became a producer at Paramount Pictures in her early twenties after training under Bill Cosby. She owned and operated a television production house with her husband in New York before going to Hollywood. Her natural preference in areas of self-expression is in connection with the film industry, an industry that can reach out to large numbers of people. Her magnetic, charismatic personality attracts interesting people and opportunities to her side.

When the individual with this ascendant is willing to release his energy on a level that will reach masses of people and motivate himself by a desire to affect other people, rather than by a desire to do what he wants, he seems to intensify his effectiveness. The bread he casts on the waters comes back in full dimension, bringing him all the things he thought he wanted in the first place. To convince someone with this ascendant that events will happen if he learns to let go, may be difficult. He is so conditioned to making things happen he may not know *how* to deal with life in any other way.

At an astrological convention, while trying to explain this principle, a fellow astrologer volunteered her feelings about coping with Scorpio rising. She said that even though she is well aware that a situation might backfire, she wants things *her* way, and is willing to pay the price if things don't work out to her satisfaction. Since the ascendant indicates survival issues, it is possible that, subconsciously, an individual with this ascendant will set up situations to backfire in order to avoid the high destiny and effectiveness he can attain. His fears keep him on a level of manipulation in order to survive. Having matters backfire can be a habit that is hard to overcome. It may be through long, hard hours of painful introspection that the Scorpio rising eventually realizes the eagle within.

FINANCE

An individual with Scorpio rising is not only especially effective in accomplishing whatever he sets out to do, he can be quite fortunate in financial areas. When Scorpio is on the rise, the sign of Sagittarius is on the cusp of the second house of money and financial ability. The ruler of Sagittarius is Jupiter, the planet of luck and abundance. The position of Jupiter in the chart indicates where a person has natural good fortune.

This personality attracts financial success easily as a result of his natural enthusiasm about financial matters. With his ability to set goals, think ahead, and take up challenges, he tends to think big in areas of finance. He can also be quite extravagant. High optimism can lead this person to take chances others would find too risky. A flow of funds can come in and go out just as easily, however. Because he is in touch with his drive and ability, he feels he should be compensated accordingly. He has no doubts about his ability to get the job done, and done well, so he expects to be paid on a grand scale. His self-assured manner convinces others he is indeed worth every penny he asks for.

With the profound ability to reach people on a mass level, he thinks in terms of abundance, can sell anyone anything, and earns money through his natural exuberance and optimism. He needs challenges in the financial arena, however, becoming dissatisfied unless he continues to make financial gains. No matter how big his salary, or how well he is compensated for his time and energy, he will take on more, just to beat his own system. His incredible luck seems to come from a natural sixth sense about financial opportunity. He knows the best way of getting what he wants.

Generosity is also part of the desire for good income. He loves to spread the wealth. He wants luxury not only for himself but for the people around him. Excellent taste and a desire for opulence challenge him to set higher and higher goals with income. The more he earns, the more he shares. If he cannot be a big spender, he is paralyzed to a degree. Financial abundance and high humor go hand in hand for his personality.

It is important to look at the aspects to Jupiter for an indication of the overall financial picture when this sign is on the ascendant. If Jupiter is well aspected, financial ease is assured, but if that planet is not well aspected, extravagance and overoptimism can keep him overextended and overexpectant. He may then constantly be disappointed in the financial arena, yet when he learns to set new goals and make an inner compensation for the natural overdoing, he comes out ahead in the long run.

The location of Jupiter in the chart indicates the best areas for financial success. If that planet is posited in the first house, he earns money through his personality. Good fortune can be intensified with a second house position. If that "benefic" is located in the third house, he earns funds through contracts, sales, communications, or negotiations. Real estate, property, or land can be quite fortunate for one with Jupiter in the fourth house. The desire for opulence in lifestyle leads to high goals with land, or matters connected with the land, such as food, mining, or gold. If Jupiter is in the fifth house, a gambling instinct is quite pronounced. He may be involved with the stock market or with investments. Creative projects, entertainment, or children may be areas of special good fortune in his life. Optimism with work is indicated by a sixth house position of Jupiter. Challenges with sales, expansion, and new growth motivate him to greater and greater success.

If Jupiter is posited in the seventh house of marriage or business partnership, money comes through a mate or business partner. He may look for a wealthy marriage or be attracted to someone especially optimistic and expansive. In business or in marriage, he may need to look for someone who has wealth of spirit as well. Since Jupiter can indicate areas of disappointment, he may be let down in the amount of wealth from the mate or partner unless his motivation is on a high level. A flow of funds is especially underlined if Jupiter is in the eighth house in the natal chart. This Scorpio personality may have funds coming from an inheritance or have income from residuals or dividends. He may raise money in order to make his own money. His greatest danger is that of constant overextension. His gift to humanity has to do with his ability to give permission and encouragement. He may become quite philanthropic with financial success.

Philosophy, higher education, travel, and promotional effort bring financial results for one with Jupiter placed in the ninth house. Constant travel can also bring financial abundance. Any matters such as import-export dealings, teaching, lecturing, or legal affairs can spell financial success. When Jupiter is in the tenth house of career, the individual with this ascendant is especially fortunate and protected in all public dealings. His contagious optimism in public areas brings chance for growth and respect. He can be involved in philosophical areas, sales, or public ventures that require enthusiastic response from people. His social life is expansive, his career abundant in opportunity.

With an eleventh house position, opportunities come from friends, associates, and groups. This person is quite lucky in associations with others who share wealth of spirit, philosophical outlook, and good humor. He looks for laughter and humor with friendships. He can attract wealthy people or optimistic individuals to his side. He earns money through situations that include interaction among people, strong growth potential, or constant opportunity for expansion and challenge.

The twelfth house indicates subconscious processes, energy

that is hard to release, and "behind the scenes" activity. It indicates how a person feels and reacts when he is all by himself. It also describes what goes on in the deepest recesses of the mind. When Jupiter is posited in this house, the person has a deep sense of religion, strong moral values, and philosophical insight. He may not show humor on the surface, but he has an inner sense of the ridiculous. He can laugh at himself while retaining a sense of awe at the workings of the universe. His inner growth carries him through tough times. He earns income by tapping his spiritual springs and by working alone or behind the scenes.

COMMUNICATIONS

The third house in the chart describes communications in general, early schooling, learning habits, telephones, commuting, and community affairs, neighbors and relatives. With Saturn ruling this house, communications become a focal point in life. Saturn indicates one's heaviest karmic situation to be resolved, and the eventual security and stability found in life. It always indicates areas where the person feels great responsibility, but can describe overkill with perfectionist tendencies, a burdensome sense of responsibility, guilt, and fears.

The person with Scorpio rising can be meticulous about details, yet can procrastinate in areas concerning communications. In school, he may worry about his work being perfect. He avoids tackling the job in enough time to complete it properly, and can then hide behind the excuse that it would have been better if he had had more time. He will redo a paper many times to be sure of its perfection, or decide it will never be right and avoid it altogether. School days may be boring or tedious for one with this ascendant because he puts himself under such pressure.

The aspects to the planet Saturn indicate the natural tendencies in his learning and study habits. If Saturn is well aspected in the chart, he develops strong, responsible study habits that form a base of security in later years. He appreciates an opportunity to sink his teeth into projects with learning or research and enjoys the details involved. He can pore over details in contractual matters, reading the fine print until he has everything in order. He has a strong respect for the written and spoken word. Sandra Accas, born with Scorpio rising, has a passion for words. She carries a thesaurus and dictionary around with her, and takes great care to use the precise words to convey her ideas. She is particularly articulate and deliberate in expressing thoughts and concepts. She cannot be rushed into an improper use of language.

With Saturn strong in the natal chart, there is a profound ability for research and technology. The person will leave no stone unturned in his quest for truth and clarity. He may overdo his research projects, but the facts will always emerge. He may get bogged down in too much technicality as an avoidance tactic, but he builds a platform of security with each new bit of information. Before he tackles new projects, study is necessary to give him a sense of being on solid ground. He may be slow to commit himself to new ideas before his own investigation.

If Saturn is not well aspected in the natal chart, insecurity about his ability to communicate can be quite pronounced. He can dislike the telephone, avoid running errands, and be insecure about his learning abilities because he puts himself under too much pressure. He could become bored or judgmental about school and go into strong procrastination procedures. Since Saturn is related to the parent ego state in Transactional Analysis terms, he may have had judgmental messages that negatively conditioned his ability to learn. In the resolution of satisfying that judgmental inner voice, he eventually learns to assume greater responsibility in the communications fields. Communications then become a stabilizing force rather than a fear. Mignon Dunn, a famous opera singer, born with this powerful sign on the ascendant, must learn not only music but many roles in many languages. She is pinned down to the constant perfection of vocal technique as well. Much practice is essential in her chosen field in order to achieve the brilliant kind of success she has attracted. Her dedication and determination to perfect her talent have paid off.

Since the third house also describes the relationship with brothers and sisters, or relatives in general, many feelings of estrangement may be associated with family relationships. A person may not have brothers and sisters and feel that lack, or attract strong parental judgmental messages from his family or siblings. If Saturn is well aspected, the family and siblings represent great security for the individual. He may understand that insecurities in the personality of brothers and sisters prevent the expression of warmth and encouragement. If Saturn is well aspected, the individual looks to his family for loving support and guidance.

Deep concentration and diligent application can be a positive trait in the makeup of one with this ascendant. The individual may discover that writing is a talent that emerges later in life. With the freeing of any insecurities, he may learn to express more than a technical approach to communications and writing, although the talent may always tend toward detailed work. Aude Bronson-Howard must spend many hours drawing tiny details to express her creative concepts about design on paper. Bill Dowling expressed strong creative concepts in the advertising world, but his talent lends itself to art as well. He also perfected a fine Spencerian handwriting. Sandra Accas spends much of her time in composing music. She necessarily takes much time dealing with the details of expressing on paper the intricate harmonies she hears.

HOME LIFE

The fourth house in a chart indicates the relationship with the parent of the opposite sex, as well as the kind of home life a person desires. It also describes the conditions and personality that emerge in later life. We tend to mentally photograph a particular facet of our parents' personalities, and the fourth house in a chart indicates the kind of influence the parent of the opposite sex exerts, and the quality of interaction. The person with Scorpio rising sees his opposite-sex parent as being unusual and unique, or unreliable and unpredictable. The relationship with that parent may be spontaneous, or upsetting and nerve-racking, as indicated by the aspects to the planet Uranus. There is the possibility of an unexpected or accidental death of that parent, or rebellious behavior that may go unreleased. Uranus, in some instances, can describe a tendency toward alcoholism or suicide.

Uranus describes inventiveness, genius, musical ability, spontaneity, humanitarian concerns, and high electrical energy. When that planet is well aspected, the Scorpio rising sees his parent as a free soul, having genius potential, and an avant-garde quality. The influence on the child is associated with his own freedom and permission to take chances. That parent may be in the limelight or spotlight in some way or another. The native with Scorpio rising has a natural ability to follow in the footsteps of that parent and has the potential to express his own inventive, unique qualities. He may reach the full potential of his particular genius later in his life, fulfilling the unfulfilled dreams of that parent. He will certainly be aware of his need for freedom and will never settle for an ordinary existence. He will desire excitement and unusual activity in his home life. He will not be content to follow a conservative approach or settle into routine in his later years.

As the native with this ascendant begins to let up on himself and allows more freedom and spontaneity in his life, he translates his intensity into greater effectiveness. He discovers his potential for genius, and allows himself to channel energy into humanitarian concerns and anything unusual, such as astrology, metaphysics, or healing. He acts like a catalyst for people around him and enjoys having the kind of home life where exciting introductions can occur and where he can combine interesting and unusual people. He may inadvertently attract fame into his life as a result of his walking to the beat of a different drummer. True inventiveness and unique qualities may seem to separate him from the crowd, yet the ultimate reward is worth taking the chance necessary for success in a unique way.

Many well-known artists, writers, and composers achieved their greatest fame as they advanced in years. Mark Twain, Horatio Nelson, Washington Irving, Sir William Crookes, William Wordsworth, Jean-Paul Sartre, Edith Piaf, Dr. Tom Dooley, John C. Calhoun, Upton Sinclair, Goethe, Henry David Thoreau, Clifford Odets, and Frank Lloyd Wright continued their brilliant achievements in their individual fields into their later years. Edgar Allan Poe, Vincent Lopez, Molière, Noël Coward, Dostoevski, and astrologer Marc Edmund Jones commanded the respect, love, and admiration of the public all their lives. Elvis

Presley achieved posthumous adoration even beyond the acclaim he commanded during his productive lifetime. Charlie Chaplin was adored even though his public appearances were limited for years. Time has not diminished the public recognition he receives.

If the planet Uranus is badly aspected in the natal chart, the parental influences can severely damage the person's willingness to take chances and achieve fame and recognition. He may not be easily able to deal with tension, unpredictable experiences, and chaos in his home life. He may become rebellious as he grows older or unpredictable in his habits. He could have photographed the parent of the opposite sex as unable to deal with the tensions, high electrical energy, or inventiveness that may be part of the personality. He may also feel unable to rely on that parent. Many times, in an attempt to calm down the electricity in the system, that parent may have turned to excess drinking. Or he may have indulged in unpredictable behavior to attract the limelight, instead of taking the risks that could also bring him attention. Most often that parent exhibits a high-strung disposition and a nervous quality. If that nervous energy was channeled properly, the child with Scorpio rising learns how to channel his own nervous energy into productive activity.

The habits connected with home life may include a need to run in and out of the house frequently. As the person grows older, he may not be able to keep to tight routines, preferring to act according to impulse. His nervous energy may keep him out of sync with his natural timing. He may tend to blow things up prematurely, run away just as events are about to propel him into the spotlight. He may want everything to stay in its place in his home, wanting nothing disturbed in case he can't put his finger on what he needs. Home base may be a stopping-off place in between travels. He is attracted to an unusual lifestyle, or an unusual home, in any case.

The excitement and sometimes nerve-racking situations at the base of his life keep him from being bored, although he may find a need for periodic peace and quiet just to restore his nervous balance. Music can become an important part of the serenity he desires. He is certainly not lacking in excitement at the base of his existence. He may have to learn how to upgrade that level of excitement, keeping some semblance of peace and quiet. He will rarely have to worry about life being dull. He can easily become the water-bearer to humanity as he grows older in years. The freedom he experiences in his choice of lifestyle helps him achieve a greater sense of identity with mankind's needs. He can then encourage and heal, and help lift restrictions from the lives of others.

Since the planet Uranus rules music, it is interesting to note how many musicians come into the fullest expression of their gifts as they grow older. Fame is assured for such talented musical figures as Maurice Ravel, Mario Lanza, Ethel Merman, Maria Callas, Ludwig van Beethoven, Georges Bizet, Niccolò Paganini, James McCracken, and conductor Herbert von Karajan.

ROMANCE • CREATIVE EXPRESSION

Pisces is the ruler of the fifth house of creativity when Scorpio is on the rise. Neptune, the ruler of Pisces, indicates vision, inspiration, an ability to see the overall concept, and a rich fantasy or dream life. Neptune can rule film, therapy, and the glamour or entertainment world. The Scorpio rising has a rich, creative life if he is able to tap his fantasies and highly inspired conceptual nature. Whereas Mercury indicates concrete intelligence, Neptune indicates a higher octave of intellect, or the intuitive process.

If the planet Neptune is well aspected in the natal chart, the individual has a natural idealistic, creative ability. He is easily able to create the circumstances for the outlet of his talents by tuning in to his vision, high inspiration, and perhaps almost naïve expectancy. Neptune indicates areas where the individual is high on life, and particularly intuitive. Since the fifth house first rules the creative, but romantic nature, this person looks for the knight in shining armor or the princess of his dreams. He is most idealistic when it comes to his romantic impulses, tending to put a loved one on a pedestal. He can worship and adore his children and be particularly adept in dealing with the film world, or areas where vision and high inspiration are a plus. The fashion world and the stock market are natural avenues for his gambling, creative impulses. Imagination leads to success in dealing with the conceptual process.

If Neptune is not well aspected, a naïve, unrealistic outlook leads to tremendous disappointment in areas of creativity, children, romance, gambles. He may expect those he loves to be perfect, ignoring their faults and forcing them to live up to his preconceived notions of perfection. He can be so blinded to the reality of the creative world that he escapes into his dreams and fantasies rather than expressing his vision in a practical way. He puts on rose-colored glasses when he is in love or adopts a Don Quixote attitude. The reverse can also be true. He may never find anyone to live up to his unrealistic expectations. He can almost force deception in relationships or with children due to his inability to confront real issues.

If one with this powerful ascendant is able to utilize the technique of visualization, the creative process, romance, and children have a better chance of living up to his expectations. As long as he confronts the reality of a situation, while retaining an idealistic outlook, he has a natural pipeline to the creative process. Many artists, using this high ability for vision, express their idealism and concepts on canvas. Raphael was born with Scorpio on the ascendant, as was Paul Cézanne, Toulouse-Lautrec, Rubens, and Rembrandt. Poet Paul Verlaine and writer Emily Brontë express this quality in their creative work. Giovanni Casanova epitomizes the romantic nature described by Neptune, while Melina Mercouri, Rip Torn, and Mistinguett join the ranks of creative performers.

WORK • SERVICE • HEALTH

Activity is essential in order for one with this dynamic personality to remain healthy and serene. Since Aries rules the sixth house of health and work when Scorpio is rising, a pioneering quality can enable this person to channel his energy in a positive way. Mars, the planet assigned to Aries, is the planet of sexual energy, creative drive, fight, ambition, aggressive action, pioneering tendencies, and determination. If that energy is backed up, dammed up, it turns into frustration, aggravation, impatience, and temper. In order to release an excess of Mars energy, a person needs an opportunity in his work to release the drive and ambition connected with this kind of energy. If he is involved in competitive fields, or where he uses a great deal of physical energy, the Martian quality is channeled in a healthy way. Since Mars also rules metals, work done with a typewriter, metal sculpture, or metal tools helps release any buildup of frustration or impatience. Musical instruments with metal strings can also provide a channel for the release of pent-up energy.

Athletes Vida Blue and Jack Nicklaus, with Scorpio rising, utilize their strong Mars energy in the field of sports. Johnny Weissmuller, with Scorpio rising, combined film work with lots of physical activity. His early years were spent in body building. Jockey Steve Cauthen keeps fit for races by constant exercise and conditioning of the physical body. Opera singers naturally expend tremendous physical energy in singing. Film stars utilize their drive in competition in their work as well as the energy that is expended in the work.

If Mars is well aspected in the chart, opportunities for much activity in job areas are indicated. The individual can deal with strife or arguments and can act as a troubleshooter. He is easily able to fight for the rights of his co-workers. Labor leader John L. Lewis was born with Scorpio on the rise. If Mars is not well aspected, an indication of frustration, aggravation, and strife is possible. Anarchist Auguste Boillant uses the Mars energy in his work, yet for the purpose of destruction rather than renovation. Pacifist Daniel Berrigan channels the Mars energy for positive purposes.

Mars also describes innovation. Nan Beecher Moore, with Scorpio on the rise, showed this innovative, pioneering Aries quality in her work by starting a stocking collection as a hobby. After a great deal of time, energy, and research, Nan now has the largest private collection of stockings in the world, with pairs dating back to the 1800s. She even has a set of Prince Albert's childhood stockings, along with a pair from almost every member of Victoria and Albert's family. Nan exhibits her collection in museums around the world.

In areas of health, dynamic and abundant energy is inherent, or frustration or lack of opportunity to use up the Aries energy creates nerves, temper, or a tendency to attract accidents. He can cut himself, burn himself, trip over things in an effort to release this Mars force. There is a possibility of high blood pressure or blood disorders, since Mars also rules blood. Surgeons and doctors with this ascendant use knives and instruments made of metal in their work, and deal with blood and accidents all the time. Doctors must necessarily have an abundance of physical vitality in order to work long, hard hours. Many doctors prefer a great deal of physical activity to fill up leisure hours. Tennis, running, skiing, and swimming are excellent ways to channel an excess of the aggressive energy that goes along with this dynamic rising sign.

MARRIAGE • PARTNERSHIP

Taurus rules the seventh house of partnership when Scorpio appears on the horizon. The planet Venus, ruler of Taurus, indicates pleasure, affection, artistry, charm, and graciousness. The Taurean Venus is easygoing to a point, but also stubborn, fixed, and determined. In matters of partnership, the Scorpio personality attracts someone who is sociable, gracious, charming, and sensuous, but who will periodically plant his or her feet and refuse to be budged. The Taurean type of personality is a strong counterpart to the compulsive, forceful, determined Scorpio personality, as the Taurean can express love and sensuality but cannot be pushed around.

This dynamic, charismatic Scorpio rising will only marry for one purpose: love. He is naturally attracted to someone with social graces, a gift of diplomacy and graciousness. He can also be attracted to someone with artistic talent. Venus also rules beauty of face and figure, so he prefers someone who is pleasant to look at as well. His strongest desire is to "play," so he needs a pleasure-loving person to share his life. Since he can be overly forceful at times, his mate must have a natural ability to smooth over rough situations, pouring oil on troubled waters and keeping things peaceful.

Scorpio rising tends to be a steamroller when he builds up energy. He needs someone who has a diplomatic nature but who will put his foot down when Scorpio overdoes it. If Venus is well aspected in the natal chart, the Plutonian personality is most fortunate in attracting the loving mate he truly desires. If Venus is not well aspected natally, the individual may find someone who is too easygoing, too amenable, and tends to cop out for the sake of peace. This mate may also be overly self-indulgent, leaving the Scorpio rising without the sensual pleasures and love he really wants. A self-centered attitude on the part of the mate ignites the Scorpio survival decisions about manipulation in order to get his own needs met. He may feel he has to compensate for the Taurean stubbornness in order to satisfy his own compulsive desires. Since his survival is connected to doing what he wants, when he wants it, no matter what the outcome, he is liable to overrun the partner or mate or go underground in secrecy and then feel guilt over his own compulsiveness. If the partner is too self-indulgent, he may feel justified in doing just what he wants to pay him back.

Jacqueline Onassis chose John F. Kennedy as her first love. John F. Kennedy, with Libra rising, felt a strong sense of responsibility to mankind, expressing his sense of social justice and diplomacy in a very high way. He was truly adored by the public. Aristotle Onassis fit into the pleasure-loving, indulgent Venusian pattern. John F. Kennedy was blessed with an abundance of social graces, charm, and graciousness, but Onassis filled a need for fun and pleasure in partnership for Jacqueline, born with Scorpio on the rise. Onassis' other love was Maria Callas, also born with a Scorpio ascendant. Charlie Chaplin had a long, happy marriage with Oona O'Neill Chaplin, a gracious, charming, easygoing lady. Joanne Woodward, married to Paul Newman—handsome, talented, and sensual—has had a long and fruitful partnership. Paul Newman is certainly no pushover, but just as certainly he is charming, gracious, and artistic.

Linda Beatson Lloyd, married to David Lloyd, one of Philadelphia's most eligible, sociable men, has a happy and tremendously harmonious partnership. Rip Torn, married for many years to Geraldine Page, chose someone who expresses an exceptional talent and artistic ability. In business partnership, the Scorpio personality may act as the "producer," while the partner is diplomatic, artistic, sociable, and genial. The ideal relationship is one where the partners accept and understand the epistemology of the situation. Each partner has his own personality and way of expressing himself, yet they arrive at the same conclusions—perhaps from a totally opposite point of view. Each partner can learn from the other: the Venusian sociability rubbing off on the Scorpio, enabling him to enjoy life and let go of his intensity, while the Scorpio power energizes and stimulates the Venusian partner.

NEEDS

With Gemini ruling the eighth house in the chart, the way Scorpio rising gets his needs met is through words, voice, and his ability to ask for what he wants. Since the eighth house also indicates the quality of energy one has to send out to humanity at large, it is the idea, intellect, fact-oriented part of the personality that is most important for this person. If Mercury is well aspected in the natal chart, he has no problem in asking for what he wants, and conversely has no hesitation in speaking his mind and utilizing mental energy on behalf of others.

When the individual with this powerful personality becomes aware of his effectiveness, he begins to speak out for what he believes in. Actors first use words in order to get jobs and pay the rent. After enough confirmation that he will indeed be able to get his needs met, the Scorpio rising actor can then get on his soapbox and speak out for the betterment of humanity. (Joanne Woodward is an excellent example.) Authors use words to make money, but the words they select give information to the public at large; words and thought are an author's gift to humanity. Kathy Gallagher, as an augmentation to the opening of her restaurant, has written a book called *Kathy Gallagher's 500 Club*. In this collection of recipes, Kathy shares information about interesting ways to cut down calories. Kathy's beautiful, slender figure can be a part of her ability to convince others that they too can look their best, but her words present facts and information, and spread her gift to many people who may never meet her.

Sigmund Freud's gift to humanity has to do with his ideas

about mankind's sexual programming. Glen Campbell uses his words and ideas in writing music that brings pleasure into the lives of others. Melina Mercouri, Faith Baldwin, Emily Brontë, Upton Sinclair, Edgar Allan Poe, Edith Piaf, Noël Coward use words in their own way to express their talent and gift. Joan of Arc, Mohandas Gandhi, and Helen Keller used their lives as well as their words and intellect as a way of reaching humanity.

If Mercury is not well aspected in the chart, there can be difficulty in expression of ideas, thoughts, and intellect. If Mercury and the Moon are in negative aspect, the individual may speak with emotional overtones, and become emotionally upset when he tries to say what he is thinking. With difficult aspects to Venus, too much diplomacy can prevent clarity of thought and speech. When Mercury and Mars are badly aspected, sarcasm and a caustic way of speaking becomes a habit. A perceptive mind can enable the individual to put his finger on any problem, yet he may forget the harm he can cause with his words and speech when he presents a solution. If there are difficult aspects to Uranus, too much "electricity" comes into the brain, causing erratic thought and rapid, disjointed speech. The person may worry about having a mental breakdown since he finds it difficult to turn off his mind. Jupiter and Mercury in difficult aspect give a tendency to oversell, overtalk, and overestimate ideas. When Saturn affects Mercury in a negative way, insecurity about the intellect keeps the person from his most effective thought and speech. He tends to think negatively, doubting his own and others' intellectual ability.

When Mercury and Neptune are in difficult aspect, the person sees the trees, not the forest. His overattention to detail may obfuscate the total picture. He overanalyzes his dreams and intuition, and in doing so blocks a flow of inspiration. The most difficult aspect to Mercury can be with Pluto. Early patterning causes the person to talk compulsively. He learned when very young to talk fast to get the attention he needed. He can manipulate with words, setting up situations that seem innocent enough in order to gain information. He may not be able to be direct in asking for the fulfillment of his needs. He may periodically trap himself in his own manipulative processes. If, when young, he was given what he needed, encouraged to ask questions, speak his mind, and share information, he was able to learn healthy habits in order to get what he needs from others. If he was not effective early in life, he may have to learn how to ask in a more honest and clear fashion for what he needs and wants from people and from life.

RECOGNITION

With Cancer ruling the ninth house of publicity and promotion, as well as recognition for the individual, the emotional nature has much to do with reactions concerning these matters. Since the Moon is the fastest-moving body in the heavens, each day can bring a different feeling about promotional effort. If an individual has a high emotional level to begin with, indicated by a well-aspected Moon in the natal chart, he has extreme sensitivity about the trends of the times. Aude Bronson-Howard, dealing with the fashion world, has special talent in choosing color and design that will appeal to people each season. Performers, entertainers, and artists seem to sense what the public will "buy." Scorpio rising can be particularly vulnerable to adverse publicity, yet the public can also respond to him on a deep and emotional level.

Elvis Presley evoked response from his public on a deep level that continues after his lifetime. That emotional reaction defies logical explanation. The thrilling voice of Maria Callas hit people on a deeply emotional, sensitive level. Mohandas Gandhi appealed strongly to the feelings of the English to transform the lot of his people. Charles Dickens wrote about painful situations that reached the hearts of mankind. In writing about cruelty, social injustice, and neglect, he told stories about man's inhumanity to man in the hard times in which he lived. His writing worked past emotional barriers or walls and penetrated deeply into the sympathetic nature of his readers.

The Moon indicates the hunger needs and feelings shared by mankind. It describes the collective unconscious, and women in particular. If the Moon is well aspected in the individual chart, the person with this rising sign has an innate instinct about and gut reaction to the needs of his fellow man. He easily expresses his mothering, nurturing instincts. He shows a protective nature through involvement in publishing, higher education, or by getting on his soapbox in some fashion. Betts Collett Ente, a dynamic Leo with Scorpio rising, expresses a particular ability to reach mankind on a mass level, satisfying deeper needs in several ways. She was a member of the original planning group responsible for the formation of a new college. After the foundation of the State University of New York, College at Old Westbury, she chose to create a student health service. The free clinic was part of an overall free health movement. The college itself was created to provide a school community to meet the needs of traditionally bypassed people. After the school was well on its way, the health program in full swing, Betts, a psychologist, became involved in Transactional Analysis, incorporating that system into her private practice. With such a strong ninth house in her chart, the need to express her nurturing nature on a broader scale found an outlet in publishing. She is now the founding editor of the feminist quarterly *Women in Therapy*, directing her Moon energy toward women's needs. Statistically, the Moon is the strongest planet found in the charts of writers. Betts is not only fulfilling her own emotional needs but expressing her strong instincts about the needs of women in common.

If the Moon is not well aspected, feelings and emotional reactions may get in the way of chance-taking. This Scorpio rising would be too easily hurt by adverse publicity, too vulnerable and sensitive to any negative reaction from people around him. If he can work through his own emotional pain and tune in to what others are projecting, he begins to expose his own vulnerability and neediness, and can then react to the needs of the public.

The ninth house also indicates feelings about travel and expanding the horizons in general. With a well-aspected Moon, the native with Scorpio rising can reach people at distances from his own home, and may travel to satisfy emotional hunger. If the Moon is not well aspected in the natal chart, an overly emotional reaction to other countries or to the routine of travel can keep him upset, overly sensitive, and vulnerable.

CAREER

Leo rules the tenth house of career with Scorpio on the rise. The Sun, ruler of Leo, indicates the ego, leadership ability, executive ability, and general vitality and strength. The person with this rising sign must find career opportunities where he can show true strength and leadership potential. If he has a good sense of his own worth, a good healthy ego, he is easily able to assume the mantle of leadership. He must be in a position where he will eventually receive public recognition. He must have a chance at reaching the top position in his field.

He is easily able to get the attention and recognition he needs as a result of his natural dominance in public life. A strong sense of pride enables him to work his way to the top of the ladder. With a well-aspected Sun, he becomes involved in career projects because he enjoys what he is doing. If his Sun is not well aspected, he has an ego need for recognition that drives him in a negative way. Much of his overall sense of ego depends on the photographs he has taken of the parent of the same sex.

When the Sun is well aspected, the individual has a high regard and respect for that parent. He sees the parent as a dominant force in the family structure, with a well-placed sense of self-worth and a strong leadership quality. In the case of females with Scorpio rising, the mother assumed the dominant role, so the woman with this ascendant has a natural sense of dominance and need for public life or a career. She has no sense of obligation about staying in a "woman's role." Because of a healthy ego, she naturally attracts the respect she assumes she will have in her career or public life. The individual with Scorpio on the rise can then fulfill some of the unfulfilled potential of the parent of the same sex. A male sees his father as the strong, dominant force in the family and follows in his footsteps. If that parent has achieved recognition in his or her lifetime, the native with Scorpio on the ascendant has no preconceived blocks to his own success in career or public life. He can also be the leader in social situations. He enjoys deciding the game plan for his group.

If the Sun is not well aspected, a lack of ego keeps him constantly stimulated and challenged toward the goal of recognition. If he is recognized in his field, or in social life, he feels good about himself, but if he does not get the attention he craves, he feels he must try harder or do something different. He may not feel secure about assuming the dominant role, denying himself the right to reach for the top of the ladder. He did not receive the ego recognition he needed from the parent of the same sex. His role model may not have had a healthy sense of self-worth and was consequently unable to pass on a certain vitality and strength. The feeling of inadequacy on the part of that parent is transmitted inadvertently to the child with this powerful ascendant, preventing him from easy attainment of career goals.

Since Leo is the sign of the king of the beasts, the potential in career is unlimited as long as the individual with Scorpio rising assumes a "kingly" role. Leo is the dramatic sign of the zodiac. Theater or public life feels natural to one with this sign ruling the career. The role of royalty seemed an easy gown to slip into for a regal Leo with Scorpio rising. Jackie Onassis became a public figure in her own right after ruling as the first lady of the land. Her marriage to Aristotle Onassis only fostered her legendary magic. The need for a career and public life led to the publishing world, where her royal image continued under another hat. Such top entertainers and actors as Charlie Chaplin and John Barrymore assumed the kingly position in their field, while Elvis Presley was the "king" of rock 'n' roll.

FRIENDSHIP

With Virgo on the cusp of the eleventh house of friendship, one with this ascendant looks for intelligence in friendships and personal relationships. He enjoys the sharing of ideas and thoughts in group situations. He is naturally attracted to people who are interested in literature and world situations, and can express the intellectual part of their personality. He wants "adult" stimulation and exchanges among people.

Mercury indicates thought processes in general, but can indicate an analytical approach to the collection of information as well as a fact-oriented approach. If that planet is well aspected in the natal chart, the individual is fortunate in his associations, attracting very stimulating people to his side. Jackie Onassis is famous for her collection of stimulating, intellectual friends. Writers Simone de Beauvoir, Molière, Dickens, and Upton Sinclair naturally associated with other writers or people in the vanguard of the idea world. Betts Collett Ente enjoys associations with educators, therapists, and intelligent people who will present new information for her consideration in connection with her trade journal, *Women in Therapy*.

If Mercury is well aspected, the Scorpio rising may have an almost analytical relationship with friends, expressing his objective opinion in conversations. He can see problems in a clear, concise manner. People seek his advice because of his sound judgment. If he is asked his opinion about any particular subject, you can be sure he will speak his mind in a very practical way. He is a fact collector who enjoys the exchange of information, and who can speak intelligently about a broad spectrum of subjects.

If Mercury is not well aspected in the natal chart, he may become overly critical and analytical. He can also attract much criticism from friends. He may have trouble communicating his thoughts and ideas in group situations. If he was encouraged as a child to express his thoughts and ideas, he is at ease in group discussions, but if he was criticized for his ideas he continues to feel mental frustration as an adult. He may feel that others don't listen to him, or may hesitate to express his opinions for fear that he will be put down, scoffed at, or laughed at.

HIDDEN MATTERS • SUBCONSCIOUS PROCESS

The twelfth house in a chart indicates areas that are submerged, unseen, difficult to express. In some interpretations, it indicates restriction. It can also describe the subconscious mind and processes, and may be the quality that is most strongly and easily expressed when the individual is alone or in comfortable circumstances. When the barriers are down, twelfth house matters can be released.

Since Libra is on the cusp of the twelfth house when Scorpio is on the rise, Venus is the ruler of this house. Venus indicates love, peace, harmony, serenity, beauty, pleasure, and sensuality. If this planet is well aspected, the person with this dynamic, magnetic, charismatic Scorpio personality needs to go off by himself to restore his inner serenity. It is when he is far from the madding crowd that he feels the most peace and harmony. He may not easily show his diplomatic, serene side, or be able to express his love nature, but he will feel it strongly when he is relaxed and comfortable. He is so powerful and effective in other areas that the diplomatic, sensual, pleasure-loving part of him may be submerged. Intensity is the most visible personality trait, yet there is a deep-seated subconscious need for love and affection.

If Venus is well aspected, the Scorpio rising has an inner talent for artistry. He is able to get in touch with his creative, artistic expression when he is alone. Many artists are born with this rising sign. The need for solitude in creating art in any form is obvious, but it is interesting to note the quality of the personality of the artists born with Scorpio rising. The power of the personality belies the deep, sensitive nature that is revealed in their work. Cézanne, Raphael, Rembrandt, Rubens, and Toulouse-Lautrec expressed very forceful personalities. Composers Ravel, Beethoven, Georges Bizet, and Paganini express a passionate, sometimes sensual quality in their compositions. These men perhaps were better able to express the love nature through their art and compositions than through their relationships. Dostoevski, Goethe, Molière, Dickens, Poe, and Noël Coward may have found the serenity in their lives through their solitude. Many solitary hours were necessary to perfect the technique of dance expressed by Nijinsky. It is necessary to love the solitary time in order to produce great works of art.

If Venus is not well aspected in the chart, the individual may not be able to harness his artistic talent, express the love nature, or even show affection. The aspects to the planet Venus indicate the blocks or inhibitions to that expression. Since Venus rules the house of marriage and love, the person with this ascendant may find restriction in love matters. He may have to learn how to allow love, peace, and harmony into his life. His effectiveness is without question. His need to play is well established, but the inner peace of mind and harmony of spirit are very necessary for one with this powerful, charismatic personality. Love may be elusive, but the inner harmony that can help to bring tranquillity into his life can be developed. With more expression of diplomacy, tact, and graciousness, Scorpio rising can affect people and situations around him in a profound way. He can truly transform himself and others.

SAGITTARIUS
RISING

THE SYMBOL OF SAGITTARIUS IS THE Centaur, half man and half horse. The human half is shooting arrows into the sky, aiming for the stars. The symbology accurately describes the Sagittarian personality, for the native with this ascendant is a goal-seeking individual. He can have his feet planted firmly on the ground, but he must have constant challenges and goals to stimulate him. He exudes such a positive, enthusiastic, philosophical outlook that his strongest statement can be: "Oh, well, everything will turn out okay." This can appear to be somewhat of a Pollyanna attitude, but it is absolutely essential for the Sagittarian personality to adopt it in order to deal with life. He is comfortable with a positive and happy outlook, even if the facts are quite contrary.

Jupiter is the ruler of this sign. Jupiter is called the "great benefic." It is the luckiest planet in the zodiac, describing optimism, good humor, a happy-go-lucky manner. It manifests in a philosophical attitude and a strong religious nature. Sagittarius is a fire sign, indicating great enthusiasm, and is mutable, indicating adaptability. The Sagittarius rising most of all wants to experience life. He has great curiosity about the workings of the universe, and is terrified of being trapped in an existence where he is limited. He cannot stand shackles of any kind. He may hesitate to settle into a particular lifestyle, preferring to have freedom to peer into the way others choose to live.

The person with this ascendant can either look like the girl or guy next door, or have an elegant, almost "horsey" look with long, thin face and high forehead. He has a habit of tossing his head around as if he had a mane. The person usually gives the appearance of wealth and ease of living, since Jupiter is the planet that describes abundance, elegance, wealth, and extravagance. The circumstances of life may not always be what the appearance indicates. One with this optimistic outlook on life may have excellent taste, leaning toward the classic, yet simple. Casual elegance characterizes the look he adopts. He is a nature lover and can be awed by a beautiful sunset. His curiosity is insatiable . . . his appetites may follow suit.

Since the ascendant indicates the easiest personality trait to express and can be a façade or cover-up, this easygoing optimist may hide his troubles behind a mask of breezy humor. He will never let you know if something is a problem or that he has worries, as the last thing he needs is someone else expressing concern for his welfare. His survival has to do with the assumption that good things are just around the corner. He can't stand to worry about himself, so he can't stand to have worry expressed by others. If he lets down enough to reveal his troubles, he will do so with a chuckle and a humorous twist to his tale. He sees everything in a funny light, which enables him to handle difficulty. Laughter is his balm for burdens.

Nothing gets him down for long, although disappointment is very difficult to handle. He naturally encounters a lot of that due to his penchant for seeing the bright side. He may not appear to deal with what others call "reality," as that implies a negative view. He hates being around someone who is pessimistic or overly emotional, as that pulls him down to a level of inactivity, and paralysis can set in when he is disappointed or let down. Survival has to do with activity and enthusiasm. Any grim view spells doom and disaster. He simply cannot deal with a negative outlook at all. A philosophical outlook enables him to survive.

He may tend to promise more than he can deliver and sometimes appear superficially glib or uncaring. He tends to overschedule his time and energy, be unrealistically hopeful and expectant where he should be wary. He may elicit "implied" promises from others and become overly enthusiastic over matters destined to be disappointing. He is deeply sincere, always means well and tends to assume that others adopt the same attitude. He may expect others to behave according to his standards and expectations without seeing the real intentions. He may exaggerate unintentionally. He eventually must learn to set high goals and continue his optimistic course of action while incorporating realism and facts into the overall consideration of a matter.

Consider that symbol again. The Sagittarius rising may have his head in the clouds, but he must have all *four* feet on the ground. The greatest lesson for one with this ascendant is that of balance between his own inspiration and world of ideas, and the practical application of inspired goals. If he gets too far ahead of himself, he feels defeated, yet he always needs to see into the future. He must have a goal or plan off on the horizon while he is working on current projects. He may scatter his energies in so many directions that he never accomplishes anything, or may never hit a goal squarely on target because of constant overestimation of everything.

The relationship of Jupiter to other planets in the chart indicates the true picture of good fortune and good "luck." If he has an especially well-aspected Jupiter, it appears he has almost divine protection. He accomplishes everything with apparent ease. He easily steers around disappointments. He takes careful aim at a goal, never loses sight of it, and sets out with practical methods to attain that goal. When he is determined to accomplish something, his optimism is especially contagious. He naturally attracts fortunate circumstances enabling him to get whatever he sets out to get. He can sell anyone anything.

But if Jupiter is badly aspected, or retrograde at birth, he is let down all the time. He may be afraid to set goals for fear of disappointment. He will continue to be disenchanted until he learns the lesson of applied practicality. He tends to put all his eggs in one basket. If his project is bypassed or rejected, the disappointment can paralyze him. He may have to learn how to set many projects in motion, knowing that some of them will work out and some will not. He then has many challenges and goals and can diversify the enthusiasm. With a practical approach to his projects and high goals he learns that challenge is his primary motivation in life.

The Sagittarius rising is born with a sense of awe at the workings of the universe. He may be religious in the traditional sense or "tuned in" on a philosophical level. He is a lover of nature and the natural order of things. He may tune in to his basic spiritual nature by taking long walks in the woods instead of sitting in a church, but his feelings about a beautiful sunset over the water or falling stars over a beach can make his heart swell to the bursting point. His sense of the spiritual side of life is connected to the life force in a leaf or flower as well as the breathing life force of people and animals. He can encourage others to see things in the light of the spirit through his eternal optimism. His ability to superimpose his ideals onto practical everyday matters enables him to be truly free, noble, and unfettered.

He naturally loves people and animals. The magnanimous, generous part of him has a hard time saying no. He may not know any limitations. Holidays are wonderful times of celebration, as he loves to share his good fortune with anyone who responds to his invitation. He is thrilled by inviting people who may have no place to go to his holiday feast. He collects "strays" whether those strays are people or animals. He can always make room for one more; he can't stand the thought of anyone going hungry. He reacts strongly to people in need, but can sometimes devote himself to losing causes. His generosity may not have a discriminating quality, but he expresses great nobility of heart.

Honesty is something that is an inborn trait. He would never steal anything and is therefore extremely trusting of others. He is willing to give the shirt off his back if it is needed. Next to Cancer rising, he can be the biggest rescuer in the zodiac. In terms of Transactional Analysis, the rescue triangle describes the eternal triangle lived by one with this rising sign. The rescuer rescues the victim, who turns persecutor and persecutes the rescuer. After one with Sagittarius rising has been through this process over and over again, he finally learns to help people to help themselves by teaching them rather than rescuing them.

By channeling energy in a positive manner, he becomes a truly inspired teacher. A sense of optimism keeps him from seeing the ugliness in his search for a better and truer way of life. He accomplishes monumental tasks by seeing life in a philosophical, humorous way. He must continue his own learning process throughout his life, for he will become paralyzed without a challenge or goal. If he feels that his freedom to investigate and explore is threatened, he experiences terror. He is not motivated by competition, but a good race can be a wonderful motivation. He actually wants to constantly outdistance himself, getting bored with routine experiences. When he has thoroughly mastered something he must go on to new activity.

Bobby Vinton expresses many of these Sagittarian traits. He is not content to rest on his laurels as a singer, but has several pet projects that express the humanitarian, philosophical outlook associated with this rising sign. He writes about his philosophy in his music, "sells" it through his songs and recordings, and constantly reacts to the circumstances of life with humor. He has one project so close to his heart that he has approached not only former President Nixon but many politicians on state and local levels. He has so far been frustrated in obtaining support, but hasn't given up the challenge of finding someone who is in a position to implement his plan. He wants to promote the study of "humantics" in the school system so that children will learn not only their ABC's but how to deal with their peers. This is a psychological study which enables children to understand why other people do what they do. Comprehension of behavior fosters love, not war, and understanding and compassion, not fear and barriers. He is also interested in the universal language of Esperanto, which will break down more walls between men.

Eleanor Roosevelt is a prime example of the humanity shown by this rising sign. She felt deeply for people in unfortunate circumstances, acting as a champion for the underprivileged and the underdog. Her smiling face was seen all over the country, particularly in areas where there were needs to be filled. She showed constant sincerity and nobility of spirit. Hans Christian Andersen and Lewis Carroll captivate their audiences with a humor that covers their philosophies.

Fred Astaire is rarely seen without a twinkle in his eye and a smile on his face. Jackie Gleason, Steve Allen, Jerry Lewis, and Lenny Bruce were born with Sagittarius rising. Jackie Cooper, Mickey Rooney, and Robert Goulet share this ascendant. Robert Cummings was interested in natural health foods long before they became part of the culture. Burt Lancaster, Ingrid Bergman, Brigitte Bardot, and Shirley Temple also have Sagittarius rising. Shirley Temple was not content to trade on the fame of her childhood and went on to become active in politics, devoting special attention to Africa, where she could work for a less-developed nation.

It is difficult for one with this rising sign to understand man's inhumanity to man. He assumes that everyone will love each other. He can be exceptionally disappointed when his friends dislike each other. It can sadden him to see intolerance of any kind. He may become quite vehement in expressing his feelings about how people should feel. He cannot stand any mistreatment of children or animals. He is quite convincing when he expects someone to care as much as he. It is hard to show disinterest in the face of his enthusiasm. He may not be able to tolerate apathy on the part of others. He loses sight of ugliness in his search for a better and truer way of life. He simply overlooks any sordid part of existence.

The native with this ascendant may reach the pinnacle of several successful careers in his life. The minute he has thoroughly mastered something, it is no longer a challenge. He can be like the donkey with the carrot in front of his nose; he wants things that are just out of reach.

The exceptional need for a challenge can cause difficulty in personal relationships until he learns what to look for in another person. He is often attracted to the very worst kind of person for him, simply because he can't resist someone who is out of reach. If a person is about to get away, the lure may be too much to resist. He is only interested in someone who intrigues him. Although he looks for intelligence in another person, he can mistake a quick wit and a fast talker for the true intellectual companion he wants. Once he conquers that possibly flighty, insincere person, he can become quickly disenchanted. It takes a most stimulating, unusual person to hold his interest for a long period of time. It is particularly important for one with this ascendant to know what he needs in relationships before he is committed. He can be terribly unhappy with the wrong person, because he cannot tolerate a situation that is limiting. He'll give you the shirt off his back, but he'll never get over the hurt of being used. Naturally he can be taken advantage of by many unethical people because of his trusting, open personality. He loves to be generous and doesn't need many thanks—but he needs to find worthy recipients.

The only way to "capture" the person with this cheerful personality is to constantly tell him he's free to do anything he wants to do. If he thinks someone has plans that don't include him, his curiosity may get the best of him. He won't be able to resist checking out the situation to be sure he isn't missing anything terrific. He's intrigued by what makes people tick. He enjoys the study of human nature almost as much as nature it-self. He is a natural explorer, loving to go into uncharted terri-tory. Astronauts Walter Schirra, Roger Chaffee, and Richard Gordon follow in the footsteps of Charles A. Lindbergh, all with Sagittarius on the rise.

Truth-telling is such a part of his nature that he may overstep the bounds and be brutally frank. He can sometimes have "foot-in-mouth" disease. He may never realize he's wounded someone with the bluntness of his comments, so he may not try to rectify the mistake when he's said or done something less than tactful. He can infuriate others by never explaining his actions; he just expects that they should understand his motivation. He feels friendship means overlooking any action to understand that his good heart lies behind it. He expects philosophical behavior on the part of others as well. Without so much as a backward glance, he'll leave even a long-time friend or loved one if any limitations or restrictions are put on a relationship. But as long as he's given free rein, his loyalty to a friend is forever. He rarely loses anyone from his life. Somehow he is forgiven even unforgivable behavior at times. He loves to dance, yet sometimes stumbles over his own two feet. He does everything with wild abandon and can outlast almost everyone around.

Since the ascendant describes the early decisions about sur-vival, the person with Sagittarius rising needs new horizons to motivate him. He must find his own ways to be excited about the daily, humdrum tasks of living. He has a hard time fo-cusing on tasks at hand unless he can create some kind of unu-sual excitement in the process, which is the fuel he needs for en-ergy. He can appear scattered, undirected, and impractical, yet he accomplishes more than most in his own philosophical kind of way. He may want to go around in circles, staying in a bit of a rut for fear that if he does everything too soon, he will run out of exciting things to do. He wants to save many experiences for later; he wants to come up with new "firsts" all through his life.

The Sagittarius rising will be young and fresh all his life. He will never adopt a jaded outlook, unless he was born with a badly aspected Jupiter in the natal chart. (If that is the case, he will never react to the challenges that another person with this ascendant will take up as a natural course of events. His fear of disappointment is the paralyzing agent that prevents him from seeing his goals clearly.) The willingness to conquer any situation keeps him from static conditions. He will share everything positive in his own experience with anyone else in order to illustrate the invincible nature of man. He possesses the fiery wings of an angel and carries the bow of promise with him everywhere.

FINANCE

Even though this person seems unconcerned about limitation of any kind and may be generous to a fault, he may have secret worry about funds. With Saturn ruling the second house of financial matters when Sagittarius is on the rise, this person may have a "poor" complex. He could have millions of dollars and still feel he doesn't have enough. Depending on the aspects to Saturn in his chart, he may have to learn the meaning of practicality when it comes to money. He may not want to have to deal with anything so mundane as financial matters, preferring to keep his sights on the horizon. When bills come due, however, he comes down to earth with a thud. He may be overly concerned about money.

Saturn indicates the heaviest karmic lesson to be learned in life. It can indicate limitation, restriction, fears, guilts, insecurities. The Sagittarius personality may have heavy guilts about luxury or ease of living as a result of past life experiences. He may be concerned about money only to the point of financing the kind of lifestyle he wants. He will tend to look for bargains, spending just as much by buying things on sale as he might otherwise, yet he convinces himself he is being practical. He might keep himself in a limited situation, opting for a steady salary, for instance, even though he may have many opportunities to better his condition. If Saturn is badly aspected in the chart, it seems he can deal with limitation, whereas he may not be able to handle ease or luxury.

Saturn also indicates the parent ego state in terms of Transactional Analysis. Parent ego is developed by listening to real parents' messages. This individual has obviously been told that he must be practical with money. He may have photographed hunger and limitation in his early childhood, indelibly imprinting "cautious" pictures in his mind. He may have been cautioned to get a good steady job and look for financial security rather than take chances in financial areas. He may worry that he will never make enough money to support the kind of lifestyle he really wants. He tends to avoid taking an "ultimate" responsibility that can establish security on a big level. He tends to trap himself in routine work that keeps him under some kind of financial pressure.

Saturn indicates the "playpen" Mother Nature puts her children in for safekeeping. It shows areas where lack or limitation may be for the benefit of the growth of the individual. When the person with Sagittarius rising is willing to be really practical, he finds more security in financial areas than he dreamed possible. He may have to get out of his playpen by taking on responsibility for mankind in some way or another. When he convinces his higher self that he is ready to take care of his karmic guilt, he finds himself in the kind of secure financial position he desired early in his life.

The aspects to Saturn indicate how easy it is for the individual to deal with financial matters. If Saturn is well aspected, the person with Sagittarius on the rise has a natural sense of responsibility concerning financial matters. His parents' messages were supportive, not fearful. If Saturn has difficult aspects, he can be a worrier. He lets up on himself as he grows older, however, removing some of the pressure he has built up over the years. He begins to find easier ways to secure income. Examination of heavy programming or conditioning from early years can help him to understand the source of some of the worries.

COMMUNICATIONS

The third house in a chart indicates communications in general, early school years, and feelings about the learning process. It describes the methods adopted concerning communications, discussions, and relationships with siblings, relatives, and neigh-

bors. Uranus, ruler of Aquarius, describes the type of spontaneity the Sagittarius rising develops in areas of communications.
In its positive sense, Uranus describes genius qualities and high
inspiration; in its negative sense it indicates nerves, rebellion,
and erratic behavior.

Nervous energy may prompt someone with this ascendant to
say whatever is on his mind, supporting the image of one with
foot-in-mouth disease. He can be impulsive or erratic about keeping in touch, and his frequent use (or overuse) of the telephone
reflects this. He is nervous about school work or the learning
process in general. Yet he can be brilliant, a genius, ahead of
his time if he can channel his high mental energy. Either he becomes tremendously excited over stimulating ideas, or he can
appear almost unconcerned. His mood seems to change as far as
communications go. Erratic concentration may make it difficult
for him to regiment himself. Routines don't seem to fit with his
sudden bursts of inspiration.

The planet Uranus describes electricity, music, electronics,
healing, inventions, metaphysics, and humanitarian concerns. It
is the planet that rules astrology. If the person with this ascendant is able to channel this unusual energy into a proper outlet
connected with communications, he prevents a backup which
could cause mental strain, erratic thought processes, and rebellion. Thomas Blackmore conceived the idea of horoscopes-by-
telephone, thereby releasing the unusual, creative mental process
described by Uranus. Bobby Vinton, Henry Mancini, George
Gershwin, Jimi Hendrix, and Robert Goulet express their genius
in the musical field. Writers Engels, Katherine Mansfield, John
Milton, and Friedrich Nietzsche made their contributions to the
field of literature. Elizabeth Karaman writes about the field of
nutrition and is adept in the field of astrology. She uses much of
her psychic, intuitive sense in her interpretations of an individual horoscope and in her recommendations about nutrition.

Dane Rudyhar, one of the deans of astrology, has Sagittarius
on the ascendant. He lectures and writes about the humanistic
approach to the subject. His concepts were unique and ahead of
his time. Writers with this ascendant may find it difficult to keep
to schedules and routines. Inspiration hits at odd hours, and
nervous energy may be hard to channel or control. Sagittarius

rising seems to have a wavelength pitched too high for mundane conversations, so his discussions may seem disjointed and scattered. His thoughts may be far ahead of his tongue, so his ability to present ordered, sequential explanations is not his strong point; he can sometimes run on, rambling in conversations.

Water seems to be a good conductor for this kind of energy. One person with this ascendant says his inspiration always seems to come when he's taking a bath. Another writer has difficulty in pinning himself down to the typewriter. His thought processes seem to percolate best when he is moving about, running errands or preparing food. At an unexpected moment, inspiration can hit.

The person with Sagittarius rising is constantly stimulated, but sometimes distracted, by new and different concepts. He is naturally responsive to humanitarian needs, excitement in areas of discovery, and inventions or concepts that are ahead of the times. Lieutenant Colonel Larry Ankeney, recently earning his Ph.D. in electrical engineering, is involved in a project for the Air Force that projects at least ten years into the future. He must use his genius to anticipate incredible technological advances in defense weapons and computer systems.

Since Uranus describes learning ability, as well as the thought processes, children with this ascendant may be more stimulated by non-mainstream types of education. This child may be so far ahead of his class that he becomes bored and easily distracted. He may learn much faster if he has freedom in connection with education. A natural environment is helpful in restoring peace and tranquillity to his mind. Bobby Vinton's ideas about humantics fit in with this concept of unique expression in the field of education.

Relationships with family, siblings, and neighbors are also described by third house planets. Communications with family members can be spontaneous, exciting, or unpredictable. If the planet Uranus is well aspected in the chart, the person sees his relatives and siblings as free souls, ahead of their time and perhaps geniuses. He may also see them as rebellious or unpredictable if that planet is not well aspected. He may have an uncertain, unpredictable, unstable relationship with family, siblings, or neighbors. He may very well want to run away from family influence, rebelling in some fashion. Freedom comes through the communications field or through breaking away from traditional learning patterns. He can be stimulated to express the genius qualities he possesses by doing things that are unique. As long as he has freedom of expression he can release his need for rebellion in a healthy manner.

HOME LIFE

Neptune rules the fourth house when Sagittarius is on the rise, indicating how the person feels about his home life, the parent of the opposite sex, and the conditions during the third portion of his life. It describes the kind of environment he looks for as a base of operations. Neptune is the planet of dreams, idealism, and vision in the positive sense, but describes disillusion, naïveté, or lack of reality in a negative connotation.

Neptune describes a tendency to put someone or something on a pedestal. The parent of the opposite sex may have been a visionary or a dreamer, idealistic or unrealistic, intuitive or disenchanted. Whatever the case, the young Sagittarius rising probably glamorized that parent. He may be very unrealistic about the qualities of that parent, preferring to project his own dreams or colors onto that parent. Confrontation may not have been easy between the two, yet the decision to look at the reality of the relationship can be vital to progress later in life.

Sagittarius rising can be very sensitive to his environment. He must have ideal conditions surrounding him in order to function well. He may look for the kind of environment that will provide an escape from the harsh realities of life, that will be a haven in which he can dream his dreams. If Neptune is well aspected in the chart, he can be quite fortunate in attracting the kind of home that reflects his ideals and he can be a visionary when it comes to land or property. If Neptune is not well aspected, the individual may settle for less than his ideal, be unrealistic about real estate, or be disillusioned as far as home life is concerned.

Neptune indicates areas where one creates circumstances by visualizing what he wants. The person with this optimistic, happy-go-lucky outlook can find perfect solutions to living problems through his creative process. He may be inspired by living close to water, such as a lake or pond. A swimming pool may be another solution to the need for water close to the home. Since Neptune rules oil and gas, the luck of Sagittarius rising may have to do with land where oil or gas is found. If Neptune is not well aspected, the person may be disillusioned or defeated before he begins to create an ideal lifestyle. He lets other considerations prevent him from using his marvelous visionary ability.

As the individual with Sagittarius rising grows older, he follows in the footsteps of the parent of the opposite sex, perhaps taking the inherited potential one step further. He may fulfill the unrealized potential of that parent, or limit himself by the photographs he has taken of that parent. He either becomes more of a dreamer, visionary, and idealist—or settles for disillusionment. If the parent of the opposite sex lived up to his expectations, he is more likely to allow himself full range with his dreams. He brings illusion into reality. If the parent disappointed him or was disillusioned, unrealistic, or naïve, confrontation on some level is essential in order to better conditions in his own life. He may become quite disillusioned due to an impractical course of action. He may have to learn how to keep his goal or vision intact while he works out the practical steps toward achieving it. He may eventually become involved with concepts that will better the lot of humanity, for he secretly wants to save the world.

He may be worshipped and adored as he grows older. Certainly Dane Rudyhar is idolized by many of his fellow astrologers. Lenny Bruce expressed the opposite qualities of cynicism, disillusion, and drugs. Ingrid Bergman was first adored and idolized, then fell from her pedestal and was scorned because of her liaison with Rossellini, but was finally adored by her public once more as she matured. Conditions may enable this individual to express more of his dreams with the passing of years. He learns to be realistic about the situations that could come crashing down, becomes focused and selective about life. When the rose-colored glasses are finally removed, productivity is enhanced. With the desire to inspire others, he achieves many of the dreams of his early years.

ROMANCE • CREATIVE EXPRESSION

Sagittarius rising may be the most romantic person in the zodiac. He is attracted to romantic adventures like a moth to a flame—and he can get burned just as easily. The planet Mars rules the fifth house of romance, creativity, the gambling instincts, and children. Mars is also the planet that rules action. In its positive sense, it describes courage, daring, competition, adventure, aggressive action, pioneering spirit, and the sexual energy. If that dynamic drive is backed up unreleased, it becomes frustration, anger, temper, aggravation.

In order to find a healthy release for the most basic urges, whether sexually or simply for activity, a creative outlet is very important for one with this ascendant. Mars also describes physical activity, and the fighting instincts. This person is attracted to very energetic, sexy, dynamic members of the opposite sex. If Mars is well aspected in the chart, he will be quite aggressive about expressing his romantic needs, having fulfilling sexual encounters, romantic situations, and opportunities to express a creative urge in competitive areas. If Mars is not well aspected, he may encounter much strife in expressing the gambling urges. He may only want a conquest, attracting frustrated individuals and arguments in romantic encounters. He may be chivalrous and gallant, showering attention with flowers and poetry, or he may use antagonism in a relationship. Jackie Gleason, with Sagittarius rising, expressed this kind of antagonistic relationship in his hit series "The Honeymooners."

If the planet Mars is well aspected in an individual chart, the individual can also channel much creative drive through physical activity such as sports, dancing, or competitive creative activity. He can be most successful with romance when he funnels that dynamic energy into other areas, learning how to "stay out of his own way" so that he avoids blowing things up prematurely. His children will be aggressive, innovative, resourceful, and competitive in a healthy way. Mars also rules metals. Much impatience or frustration can be released through musical instruments with metal strings, or through sculpture or painting with a palette knife. Metal typewriters seem to serve the same function. Investments in mining or minerals are indicated by good Mars aspects.

If Mars is not well aspected, the Sagittarius rising's primary interest in a romantic situation is challenge. He enjoys difficult members of the opposite sex, perhaps desiring competition, perhaps attracting it. He may have much frustration with love, creative opportunity, investments, and gambles. He may want everything to happen yesterday, and be especially impatient with children, entertainment projects, and creative opportunities. When he learns to channel his own sexual, aggressive, creative drives into healthy areas, he is more likely to attract the positive situations he desires.

Gypsy Rose Lee used her sexual energy in performance. Kim Novak projects a strong sexual image. Ingrid Bergman played heavy romantic roles. Frustration with children was part of the picture of her life. Burt Lancaster and Robert Goulet combine sexual attraction with action in the kinds of roles they play. John Derek expressed the same energy through directing, after his own acting career. Shirley Temple danced her way through her films but was not able to make the transition to the sexy roles of her teenage years. Madame Du Barry's romantic escapades earned her a place in history. Erich Maria Remarque wrote about love in war-torn times. Jennifer Leak, a talented, charming, lovely actress with Sagittarius rising, played a sexy but bitchy lady in the soap opera "Another World."

WORK • SERVICE • HEALTH

The person with Sagittarius rising is especially sensitive to harmony in the work environment. He reacts to color, vibrations, and people, needing serenity and pleasant conditions most of all. He can be artistic or diplomatic in his work, but must love what he is doing for greatest success. Venus rules the sixth house of health and work when Sagittarius is on the rise. Dr. Gerald Ente, a neonatalogist, uses color as a therapeutic adjunct in his work with tiny babies.

Venus is the planet that describes beauty, harmony, graciousness, ease of living—and self-indulgence or laziness. Tact, charm, and social graces may be important in work areas for this individual. The aspects to Venus indicate whether the person utilizes his artistic nature in areas of work or instead tends to take the easy way out. If Venus is well aspected in the chart, artistic, creative occupations lead to pleasure in work. He may be involved in situations where a sense of social justice is especially important. He will be most charming and sociable with co-workers. If Venus is not well aspected, he may hesitate to make waves in a job situation or be undisciplined and self-indulgent in getting the job done.

The sixth house also indicates health conditions. Venus rules sweets and sugar. This native may tend to overindulge in food and drink, not knowing when to say no. The hips are ruled by Sagittarius. Overindulgence can cause overweight in that area particularly. The liver and kidneys are also part of the area governed by Sagittarius, as well as the pancreas. Lack of proper diet can unbalance those areas causing digestive and energy problems. If Venus is negative in the chart, a tendency to hypoglycemia is probable, indicating a need to avoid excess use of sugar. If the person overdoes the intake of sweets, he augments the sluggish, lazy feeling that prevents accelerated productivity with work.

With Taurus on the cusp of the sixth house, preparing beautiful food can be an ideal artistic outlet. He may be a gourmet cook, or take great care to make the setting beautiful. The sixth house indicates animals in the chart as well. Sagittarius rising is the animal lover of the zodiac, but may spoil his pets with lavish care. Venus describes love and affection. He may expend much of his love nature on pets that are pampered and groomed.

The creation of harmony and love is essential within any service capacity. He may take care of family members, animals, co-workers, or extend his range to humanity at large. As long as he has harmonious living, his health will be excellent. The desire for fine food, fine wines, and condiments may lead to lowered vitality, yet pleasure is essential for one with this ascendant. Finding creative artistic work projects can mitigate a desire for too much food and drink and keep this happy-go-lucky individual in fine shape. Overweight is still a distinct possibility when Sagittarius is on the ascendant, however. Directing energy into productive and pleasurable pursuits is important for vitality and good health.

MARRIAGE • PARTNERSHIP

Gemini rules the seventh house of partnership when Sagittarius is on the rise. The seventh house indicates the kind of person one is attracted to in partnership areas, whether business or personal. It describes the quality of the relationship and the inner dynamics of cooperative effort. The ruler of Gemini is Mercury, the planet ruling intellect, speech, thought, ideas, and "adult" programming. The individual with Sagittarius on the ascendant is primarily attracted to intelligence in partnership situations. Good mental rapport is essential.

Romance begins under fifth house aspects. With Mars ruling the fifth house, sexual energy may be the first link to the relationship, yet with marriage, the quality of the association takes on a different tone. Good communication is essential for a harmonious marriage. Since the Sagittarian ascendant needs constant challenges, he looks for someone so stimulating that he will never be bored. The Gemini personality is also in need of constant excitement, so the relationship will never be dull if there is mutual agreement and mutual understanding. When rapport exists, the two personalities seem to spark each other, yet the possibility exists that Sagittarius rising is attracted to individuals unattainable or not worth the effort in the long run.

Aspects to Mercury describe the kinds of marriage possibilities for Sagittarius rising. If Mercury is well aspected in the chart, he finds a partner who is intelligent, funny, and quick-witted. The Gemini quality is airy, sometimes skittish, but always lots of fun. The Geminian gets close to a situation, then pulls away to obtain more objectivity. Sagittarius rising can be seduced by this type of mentality, as he reacts to a challenge. He may never be able to pin this type of individual down completely and is therefore constantly on his toes. Since one with Sagittarius rising doesn't want anything that is too easy, as long as the relationship is full of fun and stimulation, he is filling his needs.

The problem may come when Sagittarius reacts to a challenge and discovers he has chased a losing cause. If Mercury is not well aspected in the chart, he can be attracted to someone who appears to be intelligent but may only have surface wit and verbal agility. The object of attraction may be critical, argumentative, or just a fast talker. He may actually have a "dual" personality. Mental frustrations would be hard to take if Sagittarius discovered lack of communication in a marriage or business partnership, or discovered unfaithfulness on the part of the mate, for the Gemini personality can be fickle as well. Sometimes the person with Sagittarius rising tends to be attracted to two people at the same time. Choice may be difficult if Mercury is not positive in the chart.

The Pollyanna, optimistic attitude of Sagittarius rising subconsciously avoids associations with anyone practical. He can't stand to be bogged down by analysis of a situation or too many discussions. He is motivated by enthusiasm and is paralyzed by squelchers. In business or personal situations, the Sagittarius personality must be the salesman or goal seeker, while the partner tends to details, facts, and an analysis of the situation at hand. If Mercury is positive in the chart, the ability to have healthy discussions and reach conclusions seems likely. If not, there can be difficulty in clarification and reaching agreements.

Mercury describes the adult ego state in Transactional Analysis terms. The adult ego state can analyze, collect data, and clearly state opinions. If children are given permission to speak their minds, the possibility of developing a strong ability to communicate is likely. With good Mercury aspects in the natal chart, Sagittarius rising is attracted to someone who has those abilities. If not, the resulting frustration in relationships is mentally wearing. Arguments can ensue, or misunderstanding in areas of communication or discussion.

When the optimistic, outgoing Sagittarius personality understands what he really needs in a relationship, he looks for the kind of active person who is full of ideas, and busy and productive enough in his own life so that he allows the Sagittarius person lots of room to grow and expand. Freedom to explore interesting new facets of life and people promotes survival for this person. Jennifer Leak, with Sagittarius rising, has a wonderful, happy marriage to James D'Auria, an architect by profession. Both James and Jennifer travel periodically for their work. Jennifer, an actress, must be on location at times. With some rearrangement of schedules, they travel together if possible. If not, the separation gives each some space. The harmony and understanding are such that the inner excitement in the relationship is automatic; it was a love-at-first-sight romance. The strength and continuation of that relationship are "givens" since mutual understanding, stimulation, and attraction are so strong. Berith and David Henesy also had that instantaneous, love-at-first-sight romance. Berith, with Sagittarius rising, never needs to worry about a static marriage or boring conditions since David travels a great deal. She may join him for a weekend in Paris or look forward to time spent in the Orient.

NEEDS

How a person asks for what he needs and wants, and the success of his requests, are described by the eighth house in a chart. When Sagittarius is on the ascendant, emotions color his ability to get his needs met. He may appeal on a very sensitive level, or use emotional blackmail or tears to get what he wants. Since he actually wants emotional reinforcement, his requests may disguise hunger needs from long ago that went unfilled. He equates gifts or aid of any kind with love. The Moon describes feelings, vulnerability, sensitivity, and the quality of needing. It may be hard for one with this ascendant to ask for anything, since he must risk exposure of feelings in the process. Consequently, a need or emotional desire may have to be very strong in order for him to subject himself to the inner trauma of getting it met.

The Moon is the fastest-moving body in the heavens, describing changeable moods and feelings. If the Moon is well aspected both natally and by transit, the Sagittarius rising will appeal to the sympathetic, nurturing or mothering instincts in another individual. He will enlist support for sensitive causes. If the Moon is not well aspected, he may threaten subtly to withdraw emotional support if his requests are refused. He may be unaware he is using emotional blackmail, however.

The eighth house also describes the quality of energy one can send to humanity on a broad scale. After Sagittarius rising has worked through his own emotional pain, the depth of his understanding is tremendous. He has a natural pipeline to the needs of mankind, is sensitive to the trends of the times, and can express nurturing as a result of whatever he may have suffered in his own life. The Moon is the planet strongest in the charts of writers. It also describes the collective unconscious. The Sagittarius rising has a natural attunement with people and an uncanny sense of response to them. When he is willing to expose his own feelings and vulnerability, he touches the core of common hunger needs. He then inadvertently gets whatever he needs to augment his position.

Eleanor Roosevelt suffered more than the public was aware during her time at the White House. She always had a ready smile, expressed great optimism and warmth, yet her private life was not fulfilling on an emotional level. She was available to people of all walks of life, however, even going into the mines of West Virginia to talk to miners and their families. She sensed more of suffering than her outward appearance would indicate. The compassion she felt for others was undoubtedly connected to her own emotional lack in some way. The "gifts" she received from the people she helped were deeply, emotionally rewarding, perhaps more than any personal situation could have brought.

No matter how successful he is in life, Sagittarius rising is rarely snobbish. He is aware of his own luck, and is more interested in experiences, starting new projects, or peering into lifestyles than he is in cultivating steps on the social ladder. He is most sympathetic to others' troubles and can be a rescuer par excellence. In fact, he is a walking reference library of services that he can perform. When his desire to help backfires, he can be deeply hurt, for he expects the same kind of help and understanding that he offers others. When his projects provide nurturing to people or satisfy needs of mankind on an emotional level, he is fortunate in attracting support. He can raise funds for anything that serves or satisfies a universal hunger. It would seem that when he takes care of others' needs, he inadvertently takes care of his own.

RECOGNITION

Recognition can be important for one with this ascendant. Ego gratification comes easily through promotional effort, or through activities that bear his personal stamp. Depending on his motivation, he may work in order to get extra attention for his projects or he may just naturally find the spotlight a comfortable place to be. Leo rules the ninth house of travel, higher mind, publicity, publishing, and recognition. Leo is the dramatic sign, ruled by the Sun. Since the Sun is the energy center of the universe, the placement of the Sun in the chart indicates the area of greatest vitality in life.

Aspects to the Sun describe the quality of inner strength, inner vitality, soul quality, and sense of self-esteem or ego. It is also related to the animus, or male, dominant part of the personality. If the Sun is well placed and aspected in the chart, there is indication that the individual has a healthy sense of self-worth. He may be aggressive if the Sun is aspected strongly to Mars, intellectual when aspects are formed to Mercury, especially charming, loving, and gracious when Venus makes aspect. With a Jupiter aspect, no matter what the sign, the individual is "Sagittarian" in quality, or happy-go-lucky and optimistic. Aspects to Saturn describe a serious quality, or insecurity and lack of ego if in conjunction, whereas Uranus aspects describe a rebel, genius, or unique personality. Sun-Pluto aspects describe a special kind of magnetism and power that is either effective or hard to handle.

If most of the aspects to the Sun are positive, the person is motivated to step out into the public arena because of a need for expression. He values time and energy, is in touch with his ability, and projects his self-assurance into projects that can eventually be connected with his name. If the aspects to the Sun are not positive, the individual may be motivated by a need for ego gratification. He may have a sense of self-worth in direct proportion to the publicity he receives. The quality of his vitality quite naturally leads to exploration of other countries. Travel energizes this person tremendously if the Sun is well aspected. His natural curiosity also leads to the taking of chances with public ventures, which result in success and recognition, or bad press.

Sagittarius rising is a natural teacher. Since the ninth house also rules higher education, he may focus on this area. Publishing, advertising, and lecturing follow along the same energy lines. Many actors and actresses who have achieved recognition through publicity are also published. Travel and promotion of their books bring them into the public arena in another fashion. Higher education can also translate into "higher mind," or philosophical concepts. Sagittarius rising can always be an ambassador of good will whether he acts in an official capacity or not. Berith Henesy, a beautiful Swede, lives in New York City and works for the Swedish consulate. She is an especially attractive, even though unofficial, ambassador for her country. Her frank, open manner, honesty, and graciousness, together with exceptional physical beauty make her a perfect representative for her country. She has the potential for a great deal of travel in her life, not only through her own efforts but through her marriage.

Sagittarius rising cares about sharing his insights and concepts of a life on a broad scale. His natural curiosity about the workings of the universe easily propel him into a position of authority. Wanderlust is probable, as the need for constant challenges continually takes him into new territory, both literally and figuratively. He is most alive when exploring lifestyles in other lands. Travel can become as much a necessity as food and drink. If the Sun is not well aspected, lack of ego may prevent him from the exploration of either other territories or his own potential. He may fear "bad notices" so much that he defeats himself before he begins. Self-exploration and healthy chance-taking can help him to discover a new sense of self-worth.

CAREER

Virgo rules the tenth house of career for one with this ascendant. The ruler of Virgo, Mercury, describes mental capabilities, intellectual activities, and ideas or speech. Sagittarius on the rise needs a career in which he can express his practical, concrete

observations and his thoughts and theories. He will be bored unless his career requires the exchange of ideas. Verbal acumen
leads to activities where he expresses his particular point of
view. Since the tenth house also describes the parent of the same
sex, the photographs he took of that parent precondition success
in that expression.

Mercury is the planet describing the adult ego state. The
adult part of ourselves learns to express thought in a clear, concise manner, collect data, and be aware of what's going on in the
world. If Mercury is well aspected, the intellectual capabilities
were no doubt encouraged by the parent of the same sex. The
Sagittarius personality may have enjoyed great rapport with that
parent, shared and exchanged ideas, and respected the mental
ability of that parent. He photographed that parent as one who
used his mind, was interested in education and the exchange of
data. The Virgo Mercury is analytical and objective, however, so
the parent may have encouraged research and attention to details. The Sagittarius rising personality can participate in anything from editing to acting to writing. Any activity that requires a focus of mental concentration will appeal to him. Words
are his vehicle.

If Mercury is not well aspected in the chart, the relationship
with the parent of the same sex may not have felt comfortable
and easy. Areas of communication could have been colored by
that parent's own intellectual insecurity. Misunderstandings may
have occurred, or lack of agreement and understanding may
have been constant. The parent may have been particularly critical, overly analytical, or picky. The Sagittarius rising may have
to overcome many mental blocks before he can easily express
himself. If a child is given free rein to express his own ideas or
share information, his growth develops along those lines. If he is
shot down or criticized for expressing himself, he learns not to
risk saying what he thinks. He may have to relearn how to communicate.

There are always positive and negative interpretations of the
energy described by various planets, and also various levels of
energy that can be tapped. If Mercury is well aspected in the
chart, the native reaches for the highest level of expression he
can find. He will want to be in a career position where com-

munications are involved, and where his ideas, information, or speech are important. He may be the decision maker. If Mercury is not well aspected, the individual may avoid the particular career activity that would bring the most fulfillment. Social activities are also described by the tenth house. The person with Sagittarius rising cares about how he spends time socially. He wants to be around people who share ideas, or to be in situations where he is stimulated mentally. He will enjoy lectures, theater, concerts, or just good conversation. If Mercury is not well aspected, the Sagittarius rising may avoid activities where he is stimulated intellectually. Self-criticism may be his worst trait, as he may become especially critical in social situations. He may take up the criticism where the parent of the same sex left off. Learning to express the objective, analytical part of himself may bring the person with this ascendant into tremendous fulfillment with work and career, however.

FRIENDSHIP

Venus rules the eleventh house of friendships, associations, and group activity. Venus is the planet that describes what one loves. Sagittarius rising loves his friends. Venus also indicates beauty, charm, sociability, graciousness, art, theater, dance, and music. (The Muses are Venusian in character.) Artistic pursuits bring this person into contact with people who share his tastes. He is exceptionally sociable, loves people, and derives much pleasure in association with his friends.

When Venus is well aspected in his chart, the Sagittarius rising easily combines people of all walks of life. He becomes actively involved with projects that bring beauty and pleasure to all. He may become a sponsor of the arts. He loves to gather together an interesting group, enjoying the sharing of friendship and companionship, especially if he stimulates friendship among his friends. Berith Henesy acts as hostess to many of her Swedish friends who visit New York. She loves to introduce them to her American friends. Betty Haniotis, a red-headed Scorpio psychic, loves to introduce her clients to each other. She acts like a diplomat in many situations, unbeknownst to those involved.

Her charming, gracious manner endears people to her, so that many of her clients become friends as well. Her Sagittarius ascendant enables her to combine a sense of humor with a serious approach to her work.

If Venus is not well aspected in the natal chart, there is a tendency to take the easy way out, be overly diplomatic or gracious, and perhaps too amenable. He may be unable to assert his personality in large groups, only feeling comfortable with one or two people. He may be intimidated or feel left out. He may simply not make the effort necessary to cement friendships. Association with people who are artistically talented may bring out feelings of inadequacy. He may have to learn to make more effort in group situations.

Since Venus also describes social consciousness, any activity connected with bringing better conditions to bad situations provides an outlet for one with this ascendant. With Libra on the cusp of the eleventh house, harmony is the attribute most sought in group projects. That may mean harmonizing on a purely social level or working for harmony on a broader scale. Eleanor Roosevelt was constantly trying to better the lives of less fortunate people, expressing her sense of social justice through her many activities. She spoke, lectured, and was on her soapbox about many issues, instead of settling for the easier social situation she could have had. Billy Graham is part of many organizations established for the betterment of human conditions. Queen Elizabeth I fought constantly for social reform.

HIDDEN MATTERS • SUBCONSCIOUS PROCESS

The true power of the Sagittarius rising lies on a subconscious, inner level. Motivations have much to do with the outer conditions of his life. If he lives up to his true potential, this rising sign, above all, seems able to act as an instrument for the awakening of mankind. He can transform and affect many people by saying and appearing to do little in an obvious way, yet the power of his thoughts is profound. The powerful planet Pluto rules the twelfth house when Sagittarius is on the rise. This planet describes the quality of energy that governs the secret thoughts of this person. Behind that cheerful façade lies intensity and dynamic energy.

Pluto can be described as a powerful, turbulent body of water that can be destructive if left uncontrolled. If that body of water floods the riverbanks, the damage can be severe. Yet if that same body of water is dammed up, it can produce enough electricity to light up cities. The energy of Pluto can be the most difficult to deal with because of its very power and intensity. Most often, with Pluto ruling this "behind the scenes" house, the individual is unaware of the power of his inner thoughts. If he realized he could hurt people by what he thinks, he would be more careful to channel his thoughts constructively.

It would appear that one with Sagittarius rising has achieved a level of evolution where he subconsciously knows many secrets of the universe. Since twelfth house matters are difficult to express overtly, he may have resistance to the expression of power. He relates that energy to evil or downfall and chooses to ignore it within himself. Yet he is powerful on a subconscious level, whether he knows it or not. Pluto describes the child ego state in terms of Transactional Analysis. The child's strongest message is: "I want what I want when I want it and I want it *my* way." Pluto can be related to will. The unevolved will is like the child's message, but the higher will is in tune with universal consciousness. Pluto is also the planet of transformation. Wherever it is located in the chart indicates the area of the greatest personal transformation in life. Many times that transformation may come as a result of having the rug pulled out from under, however.

"Motivation" may be the key word for the use of this powerful, transforming energy. In its negative state, indicated by difficult aspects to Pluto, the key word may be "revenge." The individual may have an inner motivation of "I'll get even, I'll show you" or "I'm going to get what I want even if I have to run right over someone to do it." The Sagittarius personality may or may not be consciously aware of this motivation. Like a child, he says, "I want that situation, that job, or that person" rather than "I want the right situation, person, or job." He is powerful enough to get what he wants, but may discover that a better situation awaited him just around the corner if he had let himself

be open to it. He finds himself trapped in his own games and
may live to regret outsmarting himself.

When Pluto is well aspected, or when the individual is willing
to change a negative motivation, he is able to tune in to higher
will, is willing to let go of any situation that is not squeaky
clean, and finds himself dealing on a much more effective level
than he might have dreamed possible. The willingness to let go
can be a Catch-22, however. He feels that unless he pushes and
forces on a subconscious level, manipulates and maneuvers inwardly, nothing will happen in his life. He has difficulty trusting
the universe to provide the right conditions for his growth. As
long as he wants things his way, like the child, he gets things his
way. Unfortunately, his vision is limited, as he is unable to see
the higher plan of his life. The willingness to hook up to the universal plan puts him in tune with not only his own inner rhythm
but a rhythm of much higher vibration. He is so effective by
doing almost nothing except "thinking" that he is amazed by the
results. When the inner motivation is for the good of all, for
mankind as a whole, and when he, by his own free will, decides
to act as an instrument for others, he is given all the conditions
he thought he wanted when working from his little will or child
ego. Goodies come in different ways, however. Whatever is
needed for his work seems to appear almost catalystically.

It is as if he pulls back all that power of thought, transmutes
it to a pure, innocent level, hooks up to his inner hydroelectric
plant (the universe) and proceeds to light up cities. Inadvertently, he creates a void on the mundane level that enables
him to pull in conditions that he needs and wants. Billy Graham,
in his work, does not lack for comfort and ease, interesting and
stimulating travel, dynamic associations with exciting people
throughout the world. Eleanor Roosevelt had material comforts
which enabled her to do her job well. Mary Baker Eddy lived
a comfortable life while spreading her word. George Washington
Carver rose to a cherished level of esteem by working for his
people.

The Sagittarius personality has such power of thought he can
actually trip people up when he is angry. His thoughts are like
silver bullets, hitting the mark with accuracy. Others can sense
his feelings even though unaware of his hidden anger. He may

do harm on a psychic level without knowing it, or he may be aware of an ability to "play with minds." His feelings of revenge are just like a boomerang, however, which ultimately backfire on him.

Meditation is extremely important for one with this ascendant, since he can become such a powerful force for good. He can uplift and energize others with his thoughts. When he transforms the lives of those around him, he immediately transforms his own. What he formerly tried to accomplish by force, he now accomplishes with ease. His own free will leads to the ultimate destiny and to the rapprochement with cosmic consciousness.

CAPRICORN
RISING

THE PERSONALITY OF SOMEONE WITH this rising sign can be the most intriguing of all personalities described by the signs of the zodiac because of its very depth and complexity. This individual may appear to be aloof, cool, or remote, yet an elegant quality may conceal an inherent shyness. He is the most responsible of all the rising signs. The ruler of Capricorn is Saturn, the planet that indicates solidarity, security, caution, and reliability. Capricorn is an earth sign, and is one of the cardinal signs, representing sensitivity. The symbol of Capricorn is the mountain goat, who takes one step at a time, finding sure footing on the steep slopes of his habitat. The Capricorn personality follows this cautious route, setting long-range goals, but reaching the top of the heap in his own sweet time. He must be on sure ground before he can progress.

Traditional astrology pictured Saturn as the planet to fear, teaching that Saturn brought nothing but hardship, burden, and drudgery. It was called the taskmaster. But Saturn has also been named the great teacher. It is true that it seems easier to learn from difficulties than from ease and pleasure. Modern psychology has brought new understanding to the meaning of this planet. Examining Saturn from all directions proves that Saturn is much more than an energy to be wary of. It indicates areas of stability, determination, and practicality. It is the planet of "gravity" that manifests spiritual qualities on the earth plane. If Saturn were not in the chart of an individual, he wouldn't be on earth, for Saturn indicates the karmic task he comes back to solve and dispense with.

A person with Capricorn on the ascendant can be quite serious and old before his time, for he is not able to take matters lightly. He may even have graying hair early in his life. As a child he appears most self-sufficient and mature, yet there is a lack of security inherent in the personality. He will carefully conceal any pain he feels so no one would know he is needy in any way. His proper behavior is a façade that protects him.

He has somehow steeled himself against the world with a stoic attitude. He secretly wishes he could let down his walls, but he simply doesn't know how. He may be dying for someone to look past the barriers he erects and show the warmth and reassurance he so badly needs. He may be judgmental, cool, and aloof just at the very time he craves affection most. His defensiveness protects him in a strange way. He can seem chilly when he is anything but that.

This ascendant describes someone who has assumed the burdens of all those around him early in life. It may be entirely subconscious, yet he has what is called an "Atlas complex." He desperately needs to be needed. Therefore it is better to be needed by someone than by no one at all. He can overload himself to the point where he is under tremendous pressure, yet he is motivated by assuming responsibility, perhaps to the breaking point. He tends to wear the "hair shirt" and is masochistic to some degree. The more he beats himself up, the more he can justify his existence. Deep insecurities stem from early childhood; he feels rejection on a very basic level. More than likely this rejection comes from before his birth, when he felt unwanted by one or both parents.

The interesting complexity of one with this ascendant comes with his decisions about survival. Since the ascendant describes the conditions of birth—the initiation into the earth plane—as well as the conclusions derived due to these circumstances, habits formed at the very first moment can precondition life behavior. Unfortunately, patterns are established before accurate analysis of a situation is possible. These patterns and decisions may be re-examined later on, but until that time, the photographs made early in life set the stage. The birth decisions are especially strong for one with Capricorn rising. The feeling of rejection can seriously inhibit him throughout his life. The birth process itself, for one with this ascendant, is particularly long and drawn out. It appears that one with Capricorn rising is reluctant to come into the world at all.

During regression sessions, the standard memory for one with Capricorn on the rise, or with Saturn in the first house, is that of dreading entry into the world. It is as if he sees the conditions that await him and decides to put off confronting them as long as possible. The resistance to birth is so strong that many individuals with this ascendant recall a feeling of digging in the heels until fatigue set in. The reality of having no way out and no choice in the matter forced him to give in and be born. This extreme dread of life seems primarily concerned with the feeling of not being wanted. Rejection spells lack of safety, with no one to depend on but oneself.

One of the earliest decisions about survival for one with this Saturnish color to the personality is that he is only safe when he is in control. He doesn't trust anyone but himself and feels he is all alone in the world. He starts out controlling his own birth as long as he can. In effect, he says, "Just a minute, I'm not ready . . . please don't make me do it . . . I may not be ready for this ordeal for a few thousand more centuries." To resist birth, he tenses his muscles, grips inwardly as hard as he can, and generally armors himself against the onslaught of life. Later on, he has muscles that go into spasm, and sleeps with tight jaws and teeth grinding. He feels tensions across the shoulders in particular, as that is where the Atlas complex bears down hardest. He can become tired quite easily, as he tends to constrict the breathing mechanism from habit. The general tension of his body wears him out. He may not realize that he is tight in attitude as well.

The Capricorn personality is born with a sense that he is destined for something important. He wants his life to count for something, yet he goes about delaying his "destiny" as long as possible. He procrastinates constantly, as he has a strong perfectionist quality. Perhaps if he is perfect in all ways, he will be loved and appreciated. His fear of failure is extremely strong. He sets up conditions around him that may border on hardship in order to build character, or so that he won't muck up his opportunity to do what he came into this life to do. He seems to give himself not quite enough elbow room for fear of straying from the straight and narrow.

Childhood is never easy for one with this rising sign. Luxury and ease of living don't seem to be in the cards for him early in his life. He seems to choose to pay back any karmic debt as soon as possible in order to get the worst over with early on. The burden he carries deep within his subconscious can make him sad and lonely, unhappy about his lot in life. He has deep guilts, whether from memories of a past life or from the situation he sees around him. Somehow he feels responsible for any difficulties in the lives of his parents or those around him. If he hadn't been born, all would be roses. Since he sees himself as the straw that broke the camel's back, he decides to be particularly good and *perfect*. If he is able to accomplish that, perhaps he will survive the worst. He shouts, "I won't take up much space, I won't eat very much, and I'll be so quiet and good that you'll hardly notice that I'm here." The shout is heard by nobody.

Capricorn ascendant comes into life feeling as though he is the parent. He feels he has to take care of his own parents, as he is the strong one, reliable, responsible, and stoic. He is able to bear burdens no one else is capable of handling. He may have a karmic relationship with his parents, feeling that he is responsible for them somehow or another; that their lives would have been easier without him. His insecurities come from an awareness that he is too little to properly deal with the total responsibility he feels he must undertake. His fear of letting someone down is connected to survival itself. He is handicapped right from the start with a sense of defeat. He cannot solve problems for everyone until he is grown. He worries that it may be too late then. He puts himself under such pressure to perform that his performance is hampered by his own concern. He will take whatever anyone dumps on him, as he feels it is his obligation. He will take it and take it, long after it is necessary. When he has finally finished being the doormat in a particular situation, with a particular person, his walls go up so solidly that there is never any question about his decision; he will never deal with that person or situation again. He may never give an indication that he is reaching his breaking point. Only he foresees the end in sight, and he cannot give any clues that it is coming.

The Kabbalists say that Saturn is the "playpen" that Mother Earth puts her children in. A playpen is designed primarily to keep a baby safe from harm. It is a restriction, yet a safety. A baby graduates from his playpen when he learns to take responsibility for his actions. He is allowed more freedom if he learns not to "play in traffic" or get into situations that will harm him. Life seems to provide a "playpen" for one with this ascendant through restrictive situations early in life. He may have very strict parents who curtail his activities or he may have losses early in life that put a natural damper on his personality and opportunities. He may have to assume special burdens in the family very early on, making him old before his time. Some sadness can be due to an actual loss of a parent in his childhood. Whatever the actual source of heaviness of heart appears to be, the inner feeling of loneliness, sadness, and rejection causes him to assume responsibility all his life. He will never get away from his need to be needed and relied on. He simply learns how to upgrade the level of responsibility and pressure he takes on. He learns how to be in control without being controlling.

Eventually, the Capricorn ascendant is able to be somewhat objective about his childhood. He can then re-evaluate some of those decisions he made, perhaps without even knowing he made them. His willingness to probe through painful memories lifts great burdens from his shoulders, as he can clearly see that his early decisions are no longer viable. Since his survival depends on his trusting no one but himself, however, he cannot easily give over the control to someone else. He finds it hard to consult another person in order to gain the objectivity he needs. If he continues to hide behind his fears, guilts, and insecurities, he may be avoiding his ultimate responsibility and destiny. A refusal to examine early issues may be his way of staying safely in his playpen. Finally, if he becomes tired enough of attracting or feeling continued rejection, loss, and hardship, his weariness enables him to give in to what he came into life to do. He begins to take better care of himself.

Transactional Analysis proposes the theory that we have three ego states that are all equally important to express. The use of one ego state to the exclusion of others results in blocked energy. Saturn is the planet associated with the parent ego state. We develop that ego state early in life by listening to our parents' messages or injunctions. The directives necessary for a two-year-old's safety can be very inappropriate later in life, yet we record those messages in our subconscious and act on them long after they are valid. A two-year-old is told such things as "You're too little, you can't, don't embarrass me, be perfect." In some cases, these messages become even more stringent and poisonous. If we continue telling ourselves the same things long after those directives are useful, we may be saying, "I can't, I'm too little, I'm not good enough," when we're old and gray. Parent messages can reinforce insecurities or contribute to their development in the first place. The aspects to Saturn in the natal chart indicate the severity of these early injunctions.

One with Capricorn rising was born expressing the parent ego state. It is the easiest ego state for this individual to deal with because it is developed in him extremely early in life. He seems to set up situations and conditions of life that reinforce a need to take charge, be in control. Past life memory may subconsciously bring in an especially strong sense of duty. He seems to choose to be born to the very parent or parents that will reinforce his feelings, memories. One young lady, during a regression session, experienced a prenatal feeling of not being wanted. Circumstances were not ideal for another baby in the family and the father was definitely upset over the situation. She remembered her defensive attitude and was aware that she rejected the father before he could further reject her. She assumed a strong parental role very early in her life, deciding that she could do a better job than her father. Later on she was motivated by a responsibility she felt for her family and for almost everyone around her. Tremendous guilt set in if she felt she wasn't doing everything for everyone and satisfying the expectations of all those around her.

Another lady with Capricorn rising sensed a mission and important destiny before she was born. She knew she had to come to the earth plane to play a decisive role in helping people. She had a very strong sensation that she literally "used" her mother to get to the earth. It seemed to explain many things in her childhood. She had no real connection with her mother during her growing years, yet often felt guilty for being unresponsive, without knowing why or being able to change. Many times one with this ascendant feels as though he simply doesn't belong to the family he was born to. He feels he is the outsider and somehow different from other family members. His sense of aloneness and isolation begins very early on.

The person with this Saturnish cast to the personality berates and bombards himself continuously with negative, overly judgmental injunctions. He may or may not be aware of the damage he is doing to himself. Authority figures, social mandates, religious influences (Thou shalt not!) can make a deep impression on one who is already convinced he is not good enough. He is afraid of causing trouble, avoids taking up too much space, and tries to be perfect. When he enters a room, he pulls in his aura rather than extending his energy. He may not stick up for himself and demand his rights. If he does, he will probably be defensive about it. He actually feels he doesn't have any rights, suspecting that a showdown will confirm his worst fears and proclaim that he is in reality an unworthy being. A lack of self-esteem prevents him from asking for much. When he has trouble getting the things he does need, it only reinforces his decision that he must get what he wants by himself, for himself.

The person with this rising sign can go through tremendous suffering. The fear that he will never be able to trust another living soul isolates him to the extent that he becomes particularly independent because of his very need to be dependent. He has already decided that no one can accomplish anything as well as he. When he is finally willing to take a chance, letting down some barriers, he is likely to pick the very people who won't appreciate him. And so he ends up doing everything himself, as usual, perhaps getting "dumped on" to some degree. He then feels that life has treated him particularly unfairly, but sees no way out of his predicament. He reinforces his decision to depend on no one but himself, but feels terribly alone, pressured, and begins to pull away. He isolates himself by putting up his protective walls. He can then feel noble, tired, overburdened, and under extreme pressure. Tension mounts and he is once again comfortable wearing his hair shirt. He hides behind his martyrdom, assumes total control, and feels safe once more.

The person with Saturn ruling the ascendant tends to project onto others through the same kind of judgment he imposes on himself. He can be extremely demanding, expecting perfection from everyone. Since he will never totally please himself, he may never find anyone else who can live up to his standards. It is sometimes difficult to be around him if he is not on safe ground. He makes it impossible to enjoy simple companionship when he builds his walls. He projects his insecurities and judgments onto others, becomes quite defensive, and may bite the hand that tries to feed him. If he is left alone, he has set up another self-fulfilling prophecy. When he begins to understand that his negativity and judgmental nature is only a safety device, he may be able to find better ways to feel safe. The simple awareness that he is seeing "danger" in a situation—which might normally trigger safety-device behavior—can sometimes be enough to prevent this non-productive behavior.

This is the person with a workaholic tendency. He expects other people to have the same ability and tendency. Since he is a perfectionist, he may procrastinate a great deal. If he gives himself not quite enough time to do a perfect job, he has a built-in excuse for some imperfections along the way. He works best under pressure anyway, and may have to overload himself to have a sense of accomplishment. The Capricorn personality can never be pushed or threatened. He is so hard on himself that he simply won't take pressure from someone else. He will respond to reason and a sense of duty, but pressure simply builds his walls higher. The best way to deal with him is to appeal to his need to be needed.

In matters of affection, the individual with this ascendant may appear to be totally unresponsive to overtures of love. It is hard to know just how to reach him. Because of a basic insecurity, he sets up constant tests. He wonders why anyone would love him for himself, so he looks for a reason. All of this behavior can be entirely subconscious, but when he indeed is able to push someone away, he feels justified in the tests he set up. He knew he'd be left sooner or later. He may deny himself true love and end up with someone whose primary quality is staying power. When he does let love into his life, the need for constant reassurance can be a bore. He seems to do little to encourage reassurance when he is feeling insecure and scared. He may seem especially cool and aloof just at the time he wants love and affection the most. Intimacy is something he craves, but the fear of rejection can be stronger. He can even pick the very people who will be most disloyal, again setting himself up for the ultimate rejection. If someone tells him of loving feelings, he may easily think they only want to use him. Low self-esteem can cause him to doubt true affection. Finally, some intense pain or loss makes him reexamine his choices and defense structures.

Capricorn rising may choose to live a lonely existence rather than go through that maddening cycle. Of course, his loneliness makes him feel more rejected than ever. His fear produces extreme caution. He can be accused of being selfish, but it is the fear of loss that makes him hang on to whatever he has. He is very proper, conservative, and sometimes timid or shy. His solemnity may hide a completely different personality. He may not know that he hides behind a façade of bitterness and distrust, withdrawing from society because of the fear of getting too close. He may be totally unaware that he holds people at arm's length.

The secret to the reversal of his negative traits lies in his willingness or ability to decide to take care of himself in a healthy way. Venus is the antidote for Saturn. The "wisdom of selfishness," learning to develop self-love, will finally enable him to learn when and how to say no. Depending on the aspects to Saturn in the natal chart, however, the individual may still overload himself in some form or another even when he becomes aware of his tendency to do so. He may trap himself in occupations where he is pinned down to details, heavy responsibility, and where he constantly has to prove himself. In relationships or marriage, he tends to attract situations where his masochistic tendencies can be played out. If he realizes he made a bad choice, he may continue to let himself be a doormat, rather than leaving, feeling he has made his bed and must lie in it. His need to be needed can attract the very person who won't appreciate his devotion and loyalty. Since he believes that his survival depends on being perfect, it is hard to admit he has made a mistake. He may punish himself unmercifully for having been wrong.

As an individual reaches the approximate age of twenty-eight, when Saturn has completed its turn around the chart and once again arrives at its natal position (it takes Saturn twenty-eight years to complete a revolution through all the signs), the person with a Saturnish personality begins to let up on himself. He takes the first major step out of the playpen. A new determination and confidence in his ability allows him to assume some sort of higher responsibility. The new decisions may be born out of pain, as that playpen gets tighter and tighter and the individual feels no choice but to go up to a higher level of activity, where the burdens will be of a higher quality. With each major turn of Saturn in the chart, he works out certain problems and learns to take care of himself in a healthier way. It may take years of hard work to finally understand that he has a right to say no. When he becomes a good parent to himself, he has won a major battle. He trusts himself more, and therefore his trust in others increases. He takes off the hair shirt, values himself, understands just how responsible he is. He learns not to overload himself quite as much as he has in the past.

When Saturn is well aspected in the natal chart, the individual comes into life with a deep sense of destiny and duty. Living is serious business. He may still have a less than easy childhood, yet some of the fears are lessened and much of the critical attitude is mitigated. He develops the supportive parent ego state as a result of the supportive messages he received from his mother and father. He still needs to be in charge and may have a somewhat grave disposition, but will find worthwhile projects to sink his teeth into. His support and encouragement to associates endear him to others. He is someone to be reckoned with and relied upon. He chooses to provide some kind of security for others and will seek an occupation of high service. His natural sense of responsibility and denial enables him to survive hardships others might find unendurable. Many Presidents of the United States have either Capricorn rising or a strong Saturn affecting the personality. Many statesmen are born with this ascendant. A need to break through restrictive walls can lead one with this rising sign to the theater.

Actors with this rising sign include Spencer Tracy, Dustin Hoffman, Sean Connery, Alan Alda, and Rex Harrison. Dedication to their craft is a trait all these fine actors share. Professionalism is part of the package. An emphasis on technique and technicality enables them to rise to the top of the luminous heap. Comedian Jack Benny's dour humor and jokes about his penurious nature fit the Capricorn description. Alan Alda also has this kind of sardonic humor. Harry Houdini worked constantly to "prove" himself. His dedication to perfection made him rehearse constantly, performing increasingly difficult feats as he perfected old routines. He constantly challenged himself to be perfect. Brilliant violinist Yehudi Menuhin reflects the perfectionist, technical qualities of Capricorn rising, swiftly ascending to the heights of virtuosity through constant practice. Conductors Arturo Toscanini and Michael Thomas must be consistently perfect. Mr. Thomas became a director of a major orchestra when he was only twenty-six years old. Tremendous dedication must join hands with talent to result in such accomplishments. Rudolph Bing, with Capricorn rising, was the former director of the Met. The responsibility was enormous.

Journalist Ernie Pyle and explorer Richard Byrd endured tremendous hardship to achieve results. Their sense of service and dedication was certainly high, but a stoic nature was essential to endure the kinds of conditions that their chosen tasks entailed. Poet John Greenleaf Whittier, short-story writer Bret Harte, and writer Jess Stearn all share this ascendant. Discipline is essential for a writer. Jess Stearn writes ten pages every day in order to produce the volume of work he has published since his days as a reporter for *Newsweek*. Jess may have tuned in to his destiny by writing about the metaphysical field in such a practical, reportorial manner that he reassured people, encouraging them to continue their own investigation. Psychologist Carl Jung made valuable contributions to the field through his constant research and dedication. His interest spilled over into the area of astrology, and only a lack of time prevented his delving more deeply into the field. (Jung had an added color to the personality, with Aquarius intercepted, making him more adventurous and avantgarde than his Capricorn ascendant alone would indicate.) Pianist Liberace, baseball player Willie Mays, musician Merle Haggard, and entertainer Jack Paar were born with this rising sign.

Both Jimmy Carter and his brother Billy Carter share a Saturnish caste to the personality. Billy Carter was born with Capricorn rising and the ruling planet Saturn in the third house of siblings. That describes his relationship with and the personality of his brother accurately. He may feel that Jimmy is the judgmental father rather than just a brother. Jimmy Carter has Saturn in the first house, even though Libra is on the ascendant. That placement of Saturn gives the additional characteristics de-

scribed by Saturn. The personality traits are the same whether
Capricorn is on the ascendant or Saturn is in the first house. Ted
Kennedy not only has Capricorn rising but has Saturn posited in
the first house as well. He chose a particularly heavy role in life,
it seems. Joseph Stalin, J. Edgar Hoover, and Mao Tse-tung were
born with the Sun in Capricorn and with that sign on the ascendant. The need to control and be in charge is evident in the
lives of all these men. Orator Daniel Webster and gangster Al
Capone had this double aspect of Capricorn, as did General
Joseph Joffre. In a biographical statement, it is revealed that this
Marshal of France, during World War I, was replaced because
he was considered too cautious. The Saturnish influence can
work both ways. Caution or control is indicated by the particular aspects to Saturn in the chart.

Many monarchs were born with this ascendant: Queen Elizabeth II, King Hussein of Jordan, Crown Prince (now Shah)
Aoorosh Ali Reza, Chiang Kai-shek, as was the Emperor Ti-
berius. President Zachary Taylor had Capricorn rising. General
Erwin Rommel and the Duke of Wellington share Capricorn rising. The Duke of Wellington was called "the Iron Duke." Chief
Justice Earl Warren, politician Wendell Willkie, consumer advocate Ralph Nader, and statesman Paul von Hindenburg share
the Capricorn ascendant with Machiavelli, whose name is associated with the most negative of the Capricorn characteristics.
He was also a statesman and student of politics, but felt the end
justified the means. The leader of the American Nazi party,
George Lincoln Rockwell, has Capricorn rising, as did international financier Ivar Kruegar, reported to use totally dishonest
and unscrupulous methods. Yet Pope John XXIII, and Leonardo
da Vinci have this same ascendant. Kirk O. Oakes was found
guilty of charges of practicing medicine without a license, taking
money under false pretenses, and practicing ministry with a
purchased minister's certificate. Jim Jones had Capricorn rising.
Naturalist Charles Darwin, herbalist Nicholas Culpepper, seis-
mologist Charles F. Richter, astronaut James Lovell, and pub-
lisher Hugh Hefner share this rising sign with composer Robert
Schumann, sculptor Auguste Rodin, poets Robert Burns and
George Santayana, and writer James Joyce. Grandma Moses is a
testimony that with practice and dedication to one's chosen

cause, it is never too late. That is a particularly Capricorn-like characteristic, for life seems to get better as one with this ascendant grows older.

The Capricorn personality is patient to the end. He sets long-range goals and takes one step at a time in order to safely reach his destination. He cannot be hurried. He may not reach his true destiny until later in life. This may be due to a gradual easing up on the restrictions he sets for himself. He may have used the restrictive influences of Saturn to hold him back until he is really ready to assume his ultimate responsibility and destiny. He can be the Rock of Gibraltar, or just be stuck in the mud. He is most often his own worst enemy.

Choices seem especially important for one with this personality. Letting go of judgments "rights and wrongs," and learning to live and let live will propel him to the top of the mountain. He is to be relied upon, depended upon, and respected.

FINANCE

Uranus, the planet of freedom, genius, and rebellion, rules the second house of financial matters when Capricorn is on the ascendant. The cautious personality of Capricorn takes flight when it comes to money. He works best when he is able to earn funds through free-lance methods. The need to be in control coupled with difficulty in taking directions pushes him toward occupations that will lead to more freedom with funds. He may express his rebellion in connection with financial matters rather than in other areas of his life. He earns money spontaneously and can spend impulsively and sometimes nervously.

The aspects to the planet Uranus indicate how he channels the freedom urges and describe not only the earning habits but the spending habits as well. Funds tend to come and go spontaneously no matter how that planet is aspected, as the person with this ascendant releases some need for freedom by taking lots of chances, financially. This native may look for opportunities that are most unusual, out of the ordinary, inventive, or where he can express his genius. If Uranus is well aspected, he may be involved in humanitarian projects, with recordings, electronics, music, healing, health foods, or where he can act as a catalyst for people. Since Uranus rules things like astrology, metaphysics, and matters that are ahead of their time, he may be one step ahead of everyone else. He may rebel against any authority where funds are concerned. Money may tend to run through his fingers, yet an unexpected flow of funds keeps him on his toes. He loves the excitement of the unexpected.

If that planet is not well aspected, difficulties with financial matters can be quite nerve-racking at times. He may run away from healthy financial activity, be an impulse shopper, or tend to blow up his financial opportunities by running away at just the wrong moment or being generally unpredictable. He may spend money when he is nervous and upset. Financial matters in general can make him quite agitated, but can also excite him. When the Capricorn personality has difficult aspects to Uranus, he may not be able to coordinate financial activity in a productive way. He tends to take unnecessary risks, walking out on the edge of a limb to avoid entrapment. He may reveal an unpredictable, even unstable part of his nature through his financial habits. Mail-order minister Kirk Oates earned money by running a religious scam. Jim Jones financed his church and took his flock to Guyana through violent rebellious action. The order and decency usually connected with freedom of worship in this country worked against his need to be totally autocratic and in control. Negative aspects to the planet Uranus also describe anarchistic tendencies.

Scientists earn money through discoveries, musicians earn funds through music (activities described by Uranus), artists earn money on a commission basis, and many writers earn money on a free-lance basis. Leonard Green, an investment banker with Capricorn on the rise, puts much of his energy into "healing" companies that are in trouble. With a well-aspected Uranus in his natal chart, Leonard trusts his fantastic instincts, but also relies on a sound technical background and conservative training. Risks are always inherent where the planet Uranus is involved. Chance-taking works for one with Capricorn rising when he values the intuitive process and looks for projects that demand his own special talent. Unique opportunities seem to be best for producing good income. Jess Stearn writes about psychics, astrology, yoga, past lives, and metaphysical subjects in particular. He earns money through reporting on unusual subjects, all Uranian in concept. He was, incidentally, light-years ahead of the trend toward awareness of these subjects that are apparent in the world now.

COMMUNICATIONS

The third house in a chart describes the ability to communicate, write, learn, and negotiate. It also describes the relationship an individual has with his siblings and relatives in general. It can indicate feelings about telephones, driving a car, and the conditions of early school years. It describes how an individual photographs his neighbors, brothers and sisters. Neptune rules this house when Capricorn is on the rise.

Each planet has a positive and negative connotation or identification. Neptune is a "tricky" planet because in its positive interpretation it indicates great vision and inspiration, but in a negative way it can describe delusion and lack of a sense of reality. With Neptune ruling this house of communications, one with Capricorn rising immediately grasps the overall picture on an intuitive level, or sets himself up for a big letdown due to an inability to confront or deal with details. Neptune is related to strong right-brain activity.

When Neptune is well aspected in the chart, the native has the gift of inspiration. His slightest conversation will inspire someone else to live up to ideals. His words give insight into problems and he immediately comprehends on an intuitive level what he studies or plans to communicate. He may idolize his brothers or sisters, and photograph them as visionaries. He may get his best ideas when he is driving a car. He learns easily, enjoying the exploration of concepts. He grasps the overall picture, and may or may not have problems with details, facts and figures. Since Neptune rules film, therapy, photography, and idealism, if he is able to communicate his thoughts along those lines, he will feel especially uplifted. Actors with Capricorn rising can be idolized for their work in the communications industry. Whenever this individual can express some of his dreams, he recharges his own batteries.

If Neptune is not well aspected, there is a tendency to be somewhat naïve, overly trusting, and even very unrealistic. There can a fine line between vision, dreams, and a con or scam. The practical Capricorn may mitigate some of his native sorrow by putting on rose-colored glasses to hide the ugliness of the harsh, cold reality he sees around him. He may be disappointed by relatives or siblings, expecting them to be their best selves and "perfect." He may tend to glamorize people and situations, leaving himself open for disillusionment. He may be unable to confront details and find that implied agreements have no basis in fact. He may stick his head in the sand like an ostrich when it comes to negotiations or confrontations.

When a child with Capricorn rising is taught how to see the broader scope, and is then encouraged to deal with details too, he may be able to learn more effectively. If he tries to focus on facts before he understands the concept, he can be bogged down, defeated before he starts. Learning how to visualize can help him study. When he is inspired, he can lift himself and those around him to great heights through expression of his ideals. He needs to learn practical application of ideals as well. Neptune is like photographing a beautiful sunset. If one remembers to focus the camera, the picture is awe inspiring. If the focus is forgotten, all that comes out is a blur of color. Arthur Miller wrote his own version of his life with Marilyn Monroe in *After the Fall*. Through that interpretation, perhaps he was able to put in perspective a sector of his own life. He was criticized severely for his interpretation, yet he could only see that episode through his own vision. Jacques Copier is a well-known French photographer who can glamorize products for the advertising world through his lens, yet his dream is to express his view of life on film, telling a story of man's individual perspective. Grandma Moses expressed her views on life through her art. It was her way of communicating her vision. Carl Jung wrote about psychology, seeing the underlying patterns of man's psychoses. Jim Jones conned his people through a convincing description of Utopia in Guyana. Jack Benny and Alan Alda express humorous cynicism as a way of conveying ideals.

HOME LIFE

Aries is the sign on the cusp of the fourth house when the ascendant is Capricorn. The fourth house describes the kind of home life one is attracted to and the kind of activity within the home. It also indicates the personality of the parent of the opposite sex, as seen through the eyes of the individual. It generally paints the portrait of the third portion of an individual's life, or the conditions of his personal environment as he grows older.

Life seems to become more active and dynamic as the Capricorn personality grows older. He becomes very courageous and daring, the antithesis of his behavior as a child. The planet Mars, ruler of Aries, indicates sexuality, drive, ambition, and the competitive spirit. In its negative sense, it describes frustration, temper, aggravation, and impatience. Perhaps when the individual with this cautious personality understands his relationship with the parent of the opposite sex, he can begin to work through some of his anger, and transform his energy into dynamic action. If Mars is well aspected in the natal chart, the person is easily in touch with sexual energy, drive, and ambition. He has photographed the parent as energetic, active, ambitious, courageous, and expressive of a healthy sexuality. He will then be resourceful in connection with land and his home, will be energetic within that home, and will become a pioneer as he grows older.

If Mars is not well aspected in the chart, the relationship with the parent of the opposite sex is full of frustration and rage. He may photograph that parent as frustrated, with much submerged or overt misdirected anger. The parent's inability to deal with sexual feelings can impair the Capricorn rising's future relationships with the opposite sex. A woman with this ascendant may see her father as an "impotent" male, frustrated in his own drives, and feel strong overt or sublimated anger toward him. She can be paralyzed in her own sexuality and drives—including ambition—as a result. She may have fights and arguments with her father that resolve nothing, and attract a mate as "impotent" as her father. A continuing rage toward her mate and home life is likely. She may feel guilt about that and suppress her own energy, sexuality, and rage. One young lady with this ascendant remembered many beatings that she received from her military father. Another lady with Capricorn rising was the target of sexual advances from her father. In both cases, the mother was protected from that knowledge. Both girls grew up with frustration in male-female relationships. One chose homosexuality, the other was trapped in an unfulfilling marriage.

These patterns can be broken if the individual becomes aware of them through therapy or some other means. The energy level becomes especially high after those patterns are broken. Much energy is then channeled into the home life, and activity becomes even more important as the individual grows older. Since Mars rules physical activity as well as sexual energy, any activity that provides a physical outlet within the home keeps the individual healthy and happy, free from temper tantrums. Mars also rules metals. Creative activity such as metal sculpture, typing on a metal typewriter, needlework, building, gardening with metal tools, or sewing will release frustrations felt within the living situation. If the patterns of negative relationship with the parent of the opposite sex are allowed to remain undiscovered, the likelihood of bitterness and frustration in later life is a distinct possibility.

In cases where Mars is well aspected, the individual may become more sports-minded later in life. Pioneering energy is developed, with tremendous resourcefulness coming to the surface. Since Mars has strong two-year cycles, the individual with Capricorn rising may feel an impetus to move or make changes in his environment every two years. Moving furniture, remodeling, or rebuilding can relieve the itch to make a drastic change.

ROMANCE • CREATIVE EXPRESSION

The fifth house is ruled by Taurus, with Venus ruling that sign, when Capricorn is on the ascendant. The fifth house indicates the creative ability, the gambling urges, romantic inclinations, and children. Venus means love and beauty, harmony, and graciousness. A natural artistic ability leads to self-expression in the arts. Since Venus is the natural antidote for Saturn, any creative activity, romantic involvement, or children can mitigate the hardship and pressure felt in his early life. Whether the Capricorn rising channels his love energy into creative expression, social activity, or children, he harmonizes his life through love and beauty.

We learn to express a creative part of ourselves early in life, but with maturity, the fifth house energy may turn to romance. When that romance becomes serious and marriage is considered, that romantic energy is then described by the seventh house of partnership. With marriage, a fifth house unexpressed energy can lead to desire for children, or increased creative activity. Entertaining or involvement in social situations can use up much of this energy as well. If Venus is well aspected in his chart, he easily expresses the creative energy, but if Venus is not well aspected, he can become lazy, overly pleasure loving, indulgent, or spoiled. He may take the easy way out in matters related to the expression of creative, artistic talent.

Venusian activity can include architecture, painting, designing, decorating, theater, or dance. Actors use this Venusian energy in their activity in the theater, but can also be heavily invested in romance. Artists release the Venusian energy onto canvas, designers into clothes, furniture, or interiors. Adrienne Landau, a Scorpio with Capricorn rising, is tremendously talented in many areas. She paints huge murals with acrylics, designs fabulous furs and accessories that are constantly photographed on fashion magazine covers, and gives terrific parties. The Venusian fifth house energy is well expressed in her romantic life as well; her love is Menasha Kadishman, a famous Israeli artist. Poets express the love nature through the beauty of their words, politicians express the Venus energy through social situations, entertainment, and diplomacy. Much business is conducted through entertainment and social situations.

Capricorn rising adores the children he bears. His children are beautiful, artistic, talented, and have social graces. If Venus is well aspected in the chart, his children are the love of his life. He will be fair, considerate, loving, and affectionate to his children and attract that from them in return. If Venus is not well aspected, he will dote on his offspring, spoil them, or give in to them for the sake of peace. Edward Kennedy has a strong parent image, with children who are charming, gracious, and pleasant to look at, yet his romantic life caused a notoriety that has cost him a great deal. Queen Elizabeth II has produced beautiful, refined, cultured children also known for their enjoyment of life's pleasures as well as duties. Hugh Hefner has built an empire on his romantic inclinations.

WORK • SERVICE • HEALTH

Capricorn rising must be stimulated intellectually in his work in order to be fulfilled. Intellectual challenge keeps him healthy, as the way he thinks has much to do with the condition of his body. Gemini rules the sixth house of work, service, and health. Mercury is the planet assigned to Gemini and indicates mentality, intellect, and the adult ego state. Gemini is an air sign and a dual sign. Capricorn rising can be more productive when he is working on two projects at once, or when his mind can flit from one idea to another. Mercury also rules the voice. If he can express his thoughts, voice his opinions, he remains happy and healthy.

Capricorn rising reacts in a positive way to mental challenges in his work. He cannot stand to be bored with his job, so he constantly needs new mental stimulation in work situations. The aspects to Mercury in the chart indicate how he functions on an "adult" level. If the planet is well aspected, he communicates ideas clearly, expresses opinions in a concise manner, disseminates information easily, and is curious about activity around him. He finds work situations that will be stimulating. If Mercury is not well aspected, he can scatter his mental energy, be unable to express himself with clarity, and could repress many of his ideas. He could find himself in a position where his advice is ignored, or where mental aggravations keep him in ill health. Disagreements occur with co-workers or gossip occupies his time and energy.

As he has such a strong sense of destiny, the Capricorn rising can make significant contributions to the world of ideas when he expresses his intellect on an important level. Living up to his karmic destiny makes it imperative to speak his mind and be the person to lead the way through to a decision. Statesmen with this house placement must be able to think on their feet, make swift appraisals of situations, and come to practical conclusions. Writers, orators, actors, and speakers are willing to commit their ideas to the public or on paper. Journalists, such as Ernie Pyle, must be able to disseminate newsworthy information to the public with rapidity. Ever alert to what is going on in the world, one with this position must be discriminating as well. Research projects excite the individual with Capricorn rising if the information he deals with is stimulating, exciting, and new. Charles Darwin, Commander Byrd, and astronaut James Lovell explored fascinating, out-of-the-ordinary situations. Carl Jung explored the mind, truly a Gemini type of activity.

MARRIAGE • PARTNERSHIP

Partnership and marriage may be the most emotionally charged area in the life of one with Capricorn rising, for the Moon rules the seventh house of partnership or marriage for one with this ascendant. Sensitivity, feelings, emotions, vulnerability, and nurturing instincts are qualities assigned to the Moon, but the Moon can also describe changes of feelings, moodiness, and extreme sensitivity. Since the Moon is the fastest-moving body in the heavens, making an aspect to another planet every two hours, the feelings about marriage can be extremely changeable. The Capricorn rising can be attracted to someone moody, and changeable, or the relationship may be an especially sensitive, nurturing one, exciting in its changing phases.

The Capricorn personality expresses a strong parental quality. Since the seventh house describes the opposite qualities looked for in partnership, the Saturnish personality seeks someone who is nurturing, sensitive, mothering, vulnerable, and "feminine," the qualities he may not easily express himself. He can be attracted to someone who is in need in some way, augmenting his own need to be needed. The aspects to the Moon in an individual chart paint the picture of marital happiness or unhappiness.

If the Moon is well aspected, the likelihood is that wonderful emotional bliss is possible in relationships. Deep ties on an unconscious level make for deep feelings. The Capricorn personality can find someone especially understanding and mothering as a partner. He, in turn, will learn to release more of his own neediness and vulnerability. The stoic, walled-in personality of Capricorn eventually wears down, so that the individual can truly take care of himself and therefore care for those he loves. If he continues to play the parent role in a negative sense, he sets himself up to be dumped on—but he certainly feels needed. He may buy into emotional games on the part of the partner, not know how to say no, or not even feel he has a right to say no occasionally.

In the case of a female born with Capricorn rising, the attraction to someone sensitive may describe role reversal in marriage. If each partner is aware of his individual needs and is in harmony with that role reversal, everything can be beautiful. The switch in roles is more common now than in former times. This lady attracts a man who is more the "mothering" type. She may attract a mate who works at home. Many times the mate assumes responsibility for their children on a daily basis, while Capricorn rising goes away from the home to work. Since the Moon is the strongest planet in the charts of writers, the husband may be a writer, or someone who is especially sensitive to the trends of the times. He may be a consultant, or work with women. She may handle the details and more routine responsibilities in the partnership. If the Moon is not well aspected in her own chart, she is liable to attract someone who cannot express the vulnerability that is, nevertheless, there. The mate may put up walls to protect his own feelings and may be easily hurt. She may have to avoid taking on the role of the parent during her courtship. She may not be able to ask to have her own needs taken care of. She will then end up feeling that she has been treated poorly or unfairly.

In the chart of a man with Capricorn rising, the attraction may be to someone who was wounded or abandoned in childhood. He may love the thought of protecting an emotional, vulnerable woman. As the Moon indicates his feelings toward and interaction with women in general, it is especially helpful if the women in his life were good role models. He will tend to play "father" very easily, but that role can become tedious later on. The examination of any rejection complex enables both sexes to reveal feelings, needs, and hungers. Putting the feelings into perspective through analysis allows for the attraction of a more satisfying relationship and partnership.

NEEDS

The eighth house describes how we get our needs met, the way we learned very early on to ask for what we want from individuals and from life. When Capricorn is on the rise, the Sun rules the eighth house. The Sun describes the dominant part of the personality, the animus, executive, leadership qualities. The sign of Leo, ruled by the Sun, is the dramatic sign as well. If the Sun is well aspected in the chart and the person has a good sense of self-worth, he can be quite successful in getting what he needs from life and from people. The eighth house also describes the quality of energy that can be sent out to humanity. For one with this rising sign, leadership and recognition can be essential gifts to give humanity at large. When the Capricorn rising discovers his inner identity, he takes charge of not only his own life but, in a healthy way, that of others.

If he has a strong ego and leadership quality, described by good aspects to the Sun, he projects assurance, and earns rewards, bonuses, encouragement, and aid when he needs it. His quality of leadership is a vital energy to use in the service of mankind. When his name is known, he is in a position to influence people in a positive way. The more he uses that energy in a dynamic, responsible way, the more he increases his own energy and flow of funds, and the better he feels about himself. Energy feeds more energy and vitality. Leaders such as Chiang Kai-shek, Chief Justice Earl Warren, Queen Elizabeth, and President Taylor must have, or have had, self-confidence and a well-placed ego to do their jobs. Actors, contrary to popular opinion, must first feel good about themselves in order to then receive the acclaim of the public. Self-confidence brings the opportunity to serve.

When the Sun is not well aspected, the ego demands constant feeding in the form of compliments, ego boosting, ego strokes. This person with Capricorn rising may always seem to be asking

"How am I doing?" rather than acting in ways that bring self-satisfaction. The turning point can come when a re-evaluation of his level of responsibility allows the Capricorn rising to become involved in projects that need his executive strength, or quality of energy. He needs to be in charge in some way. He then inadvertently gets the encouragement or financial backing he needs in order to fulfill the tasks he has set for himself. He will have a sense of self-worth in proportion to the ego strokes he received as a child. If his needs were met easily then, he never doubts they will be met again.

RECOGNITION

Ninth house matters include travel, recognition, promotional effort, publicity, and distances of any kind. The ninth house also describes countries away from the place of birth and legal affairs. With Virgo on the cusp of the ninth house when Capricorn is on the rise, the planet Mercury describes those ninth house matters. Mercury is related to the adult ego state and any intellectual activity, such as writing, speaking, or even thinking. Whatever Mercury rules in a chart indicates what an individual thinks about.

The intellectual activity of one with this ascendant can be stimulated by trips to far-off places. He is interested in foreign ideas, thoughts, speech. He can lecture, be published, or receive publicity for his ideas. He can find wonderful solutions for the promotion of products, in the advertising business, for instance, or for the promotion of people. The Mercury of Virgo is more analytical and practical than the Gemini Mercury. He can be stimulated by exciting intellectual work, but be quite analytical when it comes to the publication of such ideas. The adult ego state is concerned with the collection of facts and the ability to present thoughts and ideas with clarity. Capricorn rising has a particular ability to make decisions concerning foreign policy or the promotion of his own words.

When Mercury is well aspected in the chart, it would appear that the person with the Saturnish cast to the personality was given every opportunity to develop intellectually. If a child is given an opportunity to express his thoughts and observations, he grows up with an excellent ability to express himself. But if he was criticized or ridiculed for his opinions, it is difficult to express his intellectual observations as he grows older. He may have to become angry or emotional before he feels he is heard. If his adult ego is carefully nurtured along the way, however, his awareness of practical solutions becomes quite strong. He can be well known for his words. He may become involved in educational projects, use a lecture platform as a springboard to prominence, or travel a great deal for his work. There is a natural tie-in between work and promotion for one with this rising sign, as both the sixth house and the ninth are ruled by the same planet.

When Mercury is weak in the chart, or badly aspected, lack of confidence or clarity may prevent him from expressing himself through the exchange of words and ideas. The aspects to Mercury indicate how the person first learned to use words and can indicate hang-ups or traumas connected with verbalization. He may be fearful of publicity, overly antagonistic with the press, or use words in a manipulative way. Learning how to communicate can be a challenge as he learns to sharpen his analytic abilities. He may eventually enjoy collecting data concerning world events.

The ninth house also indicates travel and distances. Astronaut James Lovell, an Aries with Capricorn rising, takes his urge for travel all the way to outer space. Billy Carter's dealings with faraway countries backfired, bringing him bad publicity. Jim Jones's travel brought disaster to many innocent people. Journalist Ernie Pyle used the Virgo objectivity to report the progress of our troops in other countries. Jess Stearn uses a reporter's approach in analyzing, for his readers, the unusual subjects he finds of interest. He retains an objective viewpoint, drawing no conclusions for anyone else. Consumer advocate Ralph Nader analyzes the safety, value, and legality of a variety of products, collecting data that are of great benefit to the public. Explorer Richard Byrd combined his pioneering of the unknown with a practical analysis of facts in order to increase our knowledge of new territories. The combination of Scorpio with Capricorn rising enabled him to research in depth, enduring hardship, to bring great recognition to himself as well as to his projects. Both

Machiavelli and Al Capone managed to build a negative posthumous public image.

CAREER

The tenth house in a chart describes the type of career a person is best suited for, his social preferences, public image, and the photographs he has taken of the parent of the same sex. With a Capricorn ascendant, Libra rules the tenth house. Libra is the sign of balance, diplomacy, graciousness, charm, and art. It is an air sign, indicating intellect, so the Capricorn rising's social inclinations are stimulated by interesting people who have interesting ideas. Mary Ellen Mulholland, president of the Officers' Wives Club at Fort Eglin Air Force Base, makes choices of speakers for her group. She selects people who will present new or thought-provoking information. She must be especially diplomatic in her job. Venus, the ruler of Libra, describes anything of beauty, love, and harmony. In social life, one with this ascendant is gracious, charming, diplomatic, and the balance wheel. He is loved by his public, and whenever he is in the public arena, the loving, beautiful part of his nature emerges fully. He loves social life and activities connected with the arts, and has strong cultural inclinations. Helga Philippe, a Scorpio with Capricorn rising, is the personification of the master diplomat in social situations. She is the epitome of graciousness, charm, and femininity, yet she has assumed a responsibility few women would be ready or able to tackle. Helga continues a tradition started by her late husband, Claude Philippe, of elegant gourmet dinners attended by members of the Lucullus Circle. Helga acts as hostess for about fifty or sixty of the most internationally prominent men and their male guests at a dinner where perhaps seven courses of gourmet food are served with perhaps thirteen or so of the finest wines in the world. Helga is ultimately responsible for these exceptional dinners prepared by Chef André Rene and his staff at the Pierre Hotel in New York City. Helga not only makes and approves choices about the food and wine, but makes the all-important decisions about seating arrangements, which could cause international friction or harmony. Her years of acting as hostess for her friends on Claude's and her beautiful farm gave her a head start on the undertaking. Her almost shy, sweet countenance belies the inner strength and competence that enables her to undertake anything she chooses.

When the aspects to Venus are good in the natal chart, the parent of the same sex is exceptionally gracious, charming, and loving. The native with Capricorn rising loves that parent, feeling great affection and consideration. His photographs of that parent are positive and beautiful. Mutual adoration makes for a very harmonious relationship. The parent may be particularly artistic, sociable, beautiful, and diplomatic. He tends to copy that parent in choice of career, perhaps assuming the unfulfilled potential of that parent. Alan Alda followed in his actor father's footsteps, taking his father's career a few steps further. Edward Kennedy has certainly tried to fulfill his father's ambitions to be President.

If Venus is not well aspected, however, the Capricorn personality sees that parent as being overly diplomatic, too easygoing, or one who cops out for the sake of peace. The parent may have avoided taking action, hesitating to make waves, or may have been lazy, undisciplined, or self-indulgent. If that is the case, the Capricorn rising's tendency may be to avoid career activity that is pleasurable, or he may behave more "diplomatically" in career situations than is really natural. Self-indulgence is possible in social areas. The individual may associate with people in the theater world, artistic world, or social scene, yet have no real personal closenesses in his social life.

Both the fifth house of creativity and the tenth house of career are ruled by Venus when Capricorn is rising. The tie-in between talent and career is obvious. If one with this ascendant expresses his creative ability in connection with career, he enjoys great fulfillment, has pleasure with career activities, and truly loves what he is doing. He will then surely be successful. If, however, the early parent messages were such that he represses his creative energy and overburdens himself, he will lack pleasure in connection with career projects, and may continue his own self-fulfilling prophecy of no joy in his life. Any career activity can be a mitigating force in the hardship of his early life, since Venus is a natural antidote to Saturn. If he rewards himself through pleasurable social or career activity, he finds his tasks easier by far. His natural abilities to harmonize, create beauty, and work easily with people are tremendous assets in his life.

FRIENDSHIP

Pluto rules the house of friendship and group activity when Capricorn is ascending. Pluto is the "power" planet, and describes the charismatic friends this person attracts in his life. The combination of factors that make up his personality enables him to work well in group situations, or with projects that require group effort. The turning point in anyone's life is indicated by the planet Pluto. If Capricorn rising had few friends in his early life, he attracts masses and myriads of friendships later on. He finds himself surrounded by people who are powerful in whatever they tackle. He loves friends who enable him to "play." He can be especially effective when he acts as the coordinator or producer for his group. He may discover his true power and charisma when he is dealing in group situations.

If the planet Pluto is well aspected in the chart, he will attract powerful people, or people important to him and his interests, with particular ease. Rulers and statesmen with this house placement naturally deal with powerful leaders all the time.

Group effort is essential, and matters cannot be forced or manipulated. The planet Pluto is like a turbulent, powerful body of water that can either be destructive or productive. If one with Capricorn rising chooses to focus his powerful, charismatic energy into projects with the purpose of uplifting the lives of humanity, he is utilizing energy in a positive, productive way. If Pluto is well aspected in the chart, the natural inclination is to use the energy for the purposes of transformation, or to change conditions that are negative.

When Pluto is badly aspected, friendships or associations can go through changes and transformations that may be unpleasant at times. The tendency to force or manipulate situations may backfire with a tremendous blast. Friends may be unreliable, manipulative, or game-playing. Pluto rules television and powerful companies, or in its negative sense, the underworld. Al

Capone chose to pick his friends from the society of gangsters. These associations eventually backfired. Machiavelli manipulated in areas of companionship or association. His association with the Borgias was full of political intrigue and conflict.

Since planets and their aspects only *indicate* natural inclinations, the way to change energy patterns is through choice. When one with Capricorn rising is willing to let go of any associations that require game-playing of any sort, he will find himself in the clear, as far as friendships are concerned. The transformation of his own life is apparent through the willingness to let go of anyone or anything that is not aboveboard, open, and clean. Being aware of manipulation on the part of associates is important as well. One with Capricorn rising can get caught in the middle of messy situations with friendships unless he is very careful to walk a fine line of innocence. "Motivation" is the key word where Pluto is concerned. When the motivation of any friendship or any group participation is for high purposes or for the good of all, rather than for selfish purposes, the end result is fantastic. Otherwise, he may find the rug pulled out from under him periodically. Ralph Nader's group is able to point the finger at any consumer activity that is detrimental to people at large. George Lincoln Rockwell's group has a less than high motivation for all of mankind. Jim Jones manipulated many innocent people through his "charisma" and misuse of power.

HIDDEN MATTERS • SUBCONSCIOUS PROCESS

The cautious, cool, perhaps shy countenance of Capricorn can hide a deeply religious, philosophical nature. When one with this ascendant is on safe ground or alone, he becomes humorous, joyful, and enthusiastic. His inner happy-go-lucky nature pulls him through many difficult times. If he can let that optimistic personality emerge more often, he learns not to take himself or life quite so seriously. It is then that he begins the painful climb out of the playpen. Luck lies with his secret ability to see humor in all situations and to see the best in everyone. He may not reveal that part of his personality early in his life, and may in fact never be able to freely expose the humorous, philosophical side of himself. It is difficult for him to let down the guard that has protected him since childhood. His safety lies in the stoic acceptance he projects—yet joy lurks just behind every judgmental observation.

If Jupiter is well aspected, the deeply private religious nature shines through as he grows older. He needs time alone in meditation, or simply tuning in to nature. His inner curiosity compels him to seek new goals, new horizons. He keeps some things quiet until he's had a chance to implement his optimistic plans, and he can be motivated by new projects that are not completely worked out in his subconscious, while he is finishing old projects. When he is by himself, he can tune in to a wellspring of bubbling Pollyanna-ish optimism. He rejuvenates himself through his deeply religious, universal subconsciousness.

If Jupiter is not well aspected, the tendency to inner disappointment may paralyze him in a way that cannot be helped. He is not motivated to accept challenges in life, preferring to remain in a rut, reliving old rejection messages, avoiding his ultimate responsibility. Subconscious disappointment can keep him in limited circumstances all his life. Fear of disappointment may be the real inner motivation of his life. Many people with Capricorn rising discover a past lifetime spent in high religious pursuits. If those pursuits had endings of tragedy or imprisonment, however, the inner working of the mind continues to reinforce those conditions throughout his present life. The inner thread of hope has somehow been severed. It is up to the individual to retie those threads through conscious choice. Re-examination of past conditioning is more important to one with this ascendant than to almost anyone else.

Perhaps Commander Byrd was also motivated by a religious sense, or an awe of raw nature, or perhaps simply by a curiosity about the unexplored world. One would hope that powerful world leaders have a strong "religious" sense directing them from a subconscious level—or at least the motivation of concern for bettering conditions for humanity. Jupiter also describes the ability to give permission. Encouragement from inner levels is essential for anyone who has chosen a difficult task in life. If one with Capricorn rising were able to tap all of his subconscious powers, he would be able to transcend any feelings of limitation in his life. The choice is entirely up to him.

AQUARIUS RISING

AQUARIUS IS THE SIGN OF THE water-bearer to humanity. When this sign is on the ascendant, the individual has a unique approach to life that makes him somehow "different" from other people. He may have a most unusual personality, or be so far ahead of his time that he is accused of being eccentric. He can be especially inventive, spontaneous, original, and unique. If he is in touch with his individuality and special qualities, he can express strong humanitarian concern, have a strong sense of freedom for himself and for others, and be ahead of his time. He may be musical, and a genius. If he resists being unique and "different," trying to conform in order to be like everyone else, he may rebel at crucial times and be very high-strung, unpredictable, or even unreliable. He can brand himself as a maverick or an oddball. He screams to the world, "Don't fence me in." The universe is his playground.

The ruler of Aquarius is the planet Uranus. Aquarius is an air sign, denoting intellect, and is fixed and determined. Uranus rules electricity, among other things. The energy associated with this rising sign is "electrical" in quality. It can be difficult energy to channel or control, yet when the person with Aquarius rising finds the right outlet, he expresses a genius quality that puts him in the forefront of mankind. He becomes the water-bearer by walking to the beat of a different drummer. He may be the person to bring back information that has been lost to civilization for centuries.

The person with Aquarius on the rise can be very avant-garde. He is a forerunner in setting style, discovering new methods, and showing the rest of humanity the way. He may be especially enlightened, metaphysical, scientific, and inventive. He can be like a rolling stone, gathering no moss. He is a chance-taker. He is willing to let go of the trunk of the tree to walk out on the edge of a limb. He knows where the fruit grows and where the spotlight can hit. He is not one to hide his light under a bushel.

The need for constant variety and freedom can bring fascinating experiences into his life, yet he can be unpredictable in the extreme. His life will never be boring, as there are always exciting new experiences and discoveries for him to investigate.

Time becomes infinitely more pleasurable when this person begins to understand his internal rhythm. He must have the freedom to be spontaneous, or to do what he feels he must. He may have difficulty in keeping to schedules. He may have no idea what he will be doing next week or even the next day. Freedom is a survival issue for him. Restlessness may be a clue that nervous energy is backing up. He can break out in rashes, be high-strung and allergic to everything. He can become a rebel or even an anarchist, philosophically. If he channels this unique energy in a creative way, he can express a genius quality. He will never go unnoticed and may achieve a great deal of fame in his lifetime. He can become excited about everything, or be scared and hysterical. Nothing will ever be static, however, as he sets up the conditions around him that provide exciting variety. He may sometimes "zig" when he should "zag."

Uranus can be like having all the plaster fall down when it's time to remodel a room. In the midst of the remodeling job, it's hard to see the new conditions that will come as a result. The temptation to keep the old room as it is can be strong. Familiarity is at least comforting. In order to have a new room, it is necessary to let everything fall down. Running around, trying to pull the old debris down faster, or trying to put it up again, will only result in more chaos. When this unsettling energy describes the personality, survival may have to do with running away from change or upsets.

Since the rising sign describes the decisions about survival, as perhaps seen at the time of birth, it is probable that conditions were a bit scary or unsettling at that event. The individual about to be born may be undecided about whether to go through with the ordeal, or turn around and run back from whence he came. He may have felt he made a "wrong turn." He may be born prematurely or before his nervous system has a chance to be fully developed. In later life, he may keep one foot out of the door in order to run away if conditions become too scary, nerve-racking, or dangerous. He may be inclined to take premature action to pull down the "plaster" a bit faster.

The Aquarius personality may be misunderstood by society. In the days when conformity, stability, and "proper" conduct were the code of behavior, when conservatism was the vogue, the Aquarius personality had a difficult time fitting into society. He was too much of a maverick to conform to the dictates of others. Since we are coming into the Aquarian age, sociological conditions have changed rapidly, with individuality the highest goal to strive for. Enlightenment has become the new business, and awareness the keynote of the day. Change has come about in every area from family structure to morality, to manner of dress and lifestyle. During the process of change, however, drastic action was necessary to break up old conditions. The war between the "hippies" and the establishment has now settled into a reasonably comfortable balance of individuality and concern for the rights of humanity.

The planet Uranus is on the ascendant of the chart of the United States. Freedom of speech and opportunity was the cornerstone of the Constitution. Inventions flourished, humanitarian concerns made us friends to all. We became the water-bearer, broadcasting our message of human rights. The underlying motivation for the settling of this country was to provide freedom of expression, with equal opportunity for everyone, regardless of race, creed, or color. Abraham Lincoln, an Aquarian with Aquarius rising, was President at a time when those rights were severely challenged.

Aquarius is the sign of fame and genius, as well as individuality. Once that right becomes an established fact, the next step up is to produce something that manifests the spiritually unique reflection of the creative flow. Thomas Edison was able to tap that universal flow and discover electricity. Thomas Edison was an Aquarian, with Scorpio rising. Coincidentally, the planet Uranus was discovered at approximately the same time that electricity was brought into reality.

The Aquarian personality expresses the most humanitarian instincts of all the signs. He cares about people in a special way. He is the best friend one could hope to have. He is often accused of neglecting his family or those close around him to take care of matters that concern him on a broader scale. He is a person who shatters old traditions. He rebels against stagnation of any kind. He wants to change outmoded methods and improve on stodgy conditions. He is awakened on a different level. He wants his friends and loved ones to climb those lofty heights with him. He is a free soul, who dares to become charged with spiritual insights of a different quality. Since Uranus is one of the higher-octave or "spiritual" planets, it is associated with the higher mind. It can indicate genius. The thought processes are unusually intuitive. One with Aquarius on the rise can be a healer, have a profound interest in metaphysics (or things unseen), and have a universal approach to almost everything. He believes in the philosophy of live and let live.

Astrology itself is ruled by the planet Uranus. Carl Jung, a Leo with Capricorn rising, but Aquarius intercepted, did much research into the subject of astrology. He realized its value as a language of symbols, and as a key to the unique combination of qualities inherent in an individual. Jung said that if he were to do it all over again, he would spend more time in researching astrology, using it as a valuable tool in conjunction with psychology. Jung also read tarot cards, a pictorial presentation of universal truths, also rich in symbology and Aquarian concepts. (The planet Uranus describes psychic activities and awareness as well as astrology and metaphysics in general.) Jung is noted for his unique contribution to the field of psychology. He did not hesitate to investigate and use new methodology in order to come closer to the understanding of the human condition.

Queen Elizabeth II, with a Capricorn ascendant but Uranus intercepted (or co-ruler) in the first house, consults her astrologer regularly, following an age-old royal tradition. John Pierpont Morgan, an Aries with Aquarius rising, consulted Evangeline Adams in relation to his investments. He said, "Astrology is not for millionaires, but for billionaires." Jeddu Krishnamurti embodied the spiritual approach of the Theosophical movement. Krishnamurti, a Taurus with Aquarius rising, traveled far and wide to spread the concept of Theosophy. H. G. Wells, a Virgo with Aquarius ascendant, wrote of the future. His science fiction described events not yet dreamed of by the majority of mankind.

The person with Aquarius rising needs to understand himself almost more than anyone else, perhaps because he is most misunderstood by others. Because he sees things in a special or different way, he seems to be scattered or "spacey." Life is dull unless he can investigate and tune in to concepts on other planes. He seems to have an electrical energy coursing through his system and is charged with unusual, perhaps nervous vitality. It takes great balance to maintain a centered position and allow the energy to flow. He needs time alone in order to understand and rebalance that high vibratory charge. His nervous system is not like another's nervous system. He can be like an electrically charged unit, ready to blow at the slightest short circuit. He is so sensitive that a shift in atmospheric pressure can be disturbing to him. He eventually learns how to deal with this interesting kind of "wiring." He may find his own particular formula that enables him to survive. Working in sync with his own inner timing prevents his blowing a fuse.

When tensions and aggravations, or changes in the atmosphere around him, become too difficult for him to handle, he may need an outlet. Sometimes hysteria is the method of releasing the tension. Eruptions may occur if healthy release is not found. Rashes, eczema, pimples, fever blisters, sneezing, and tears may prevent damage to the total nervous system. Just as a proper electrical outlet must be found for an appliance or computer to prevent blowing a fuse, a "Uranian" activity can prevent one with this ascendant from blowing too many fuses. When his nervous system sends him a signal, he must react to his inner timing. Inventions, astrology, music, singing, recording, or any humanitarian activity helps to keep the energy fluid and flowing. When he learns how to channel this vital energy through his system, he is highly inspired toward unique productivity. He then shows his genius qualities.

Until one with this ascendant learns about his habits, he may try to control this energy instead of utilizing it creatively. He tries to pressure himself into schedules that seem to work for everyone else, but may find it difficult to work efficiently with routine hours or in a regimented style. He may need to do freelance work so that he can adjust to his inner schedules. He may work best at night, sleeping during the day. He can appear disorganized and non-productive at times, yet he is inspired at certain times with bursts of insight. One young lady with this ascendant was criticized in her acting class for having uninspired performances in class at times, yet showing tremendous talent at other times. She was described by her acting coach as sometimes performing as though she forgot to turn on the switch. The person with Aquarius rising responds to certain stimuli and is totally unresponsive to others.

He can be subject to involuntary twitches and nervous reactions that can be most annoying to him and to everyone else. It can be difficult to get his body to behave in the way he wants it to. It seems to have a life and a mind of its own. He may need special early medical attention to the nervous system. He may discover that acupuncture and work with the meridians of the body help establish a more even flow of energy. Massage therapy can also stimulate the nerves to perform, as well as vitamin therapy. He may literally have to learn how to rearrange his entire system to avoid bursts and spurts of uncontrollable shakes. Yoga exercise also stimulates the spinal column, helping to redistribute the vital flow.

He is recognizable not only by his unusual vitality but by the unusual clothes he wears. If he is interested in fashion, he may combine unusual colors and styles that start a trend. If he is typically Aquarian, he can be totally unconcerned and unaware of what he puts on his body. He will tend to wear whatever is handy at the moment. One gentleman in his middle years is known to walk around New York with a lady's hat perched on his bald head. He does not own a suit. His Aquarius ascendant sticks out in neon lights. Adrienne Landau, with a progressed Aquarian ascendant, has started a major fashion trend for men by copying her accessories for women in a larger size for her male friends. Gilded snakeskin belts and fur vests adorn her male friends as easily as her female friends. Feathers and dainty suede pouches go over jeans and cowboy boots or hats for both sexes. Any unisex trend is distinctly Aquarian in character.

A secret resistance to fame and prestige can be a birth decision when one has Aquarius on the ascendant. Since the ascendant is a mask or façade that hides inner realities, the unpredictable behavior of one with Aquarius on the rise may be his way of avoiding ultimate responsibility. He may have deep-seated fears that prevent his taking up the sword of duty. He may have heavy subconscious karmic fears and guilts. He may subconsciously plan failure, having a morbid fear of success. Nerves, tension, unique behavior, and rebellion may be his way of staying safely away from his ultimate destiny. Johannes Michael, a brilliant German psychiatrist, a Scorpio with Aquarius rising, admitted feeling that he had a shadow on his soul. He was aware that at certain times he lost "prizes" he knew he could have easily attained. On the one hand, he was disappointed at certain losses, yet was relieved on the other. He knew he could have reached out a bit more forcefully for certain things that were within his grasp, but something seemed to prevent him from doing so. During a regression session, it became clear to him that a karmic memory that was exceptionally important was still preconditioning the patterns of this life. The resistance may show up in bodily behavior and mannerisms.

Children with this ascendant need special consideration. They may be so sensitive, high-strung, and active that parents try to calm them down continuously. Hyperactivity may require special outlets to release nervous energy. If the child, in his attempt to please, puts himself under pressure to be perfect or to conform, his repressed energy can produce allergies, rashes, skin disorders, or unpredictable behavior. One young man, with a tendency toward nervous twitches, remembered embarrassing incidents in school when he was expected to use the bathroom at regular intervals. His kidneys seemed to fail him at the most inopportune times. Bed-wetting, asthma, and unpredictable shakes can indicate a need for a healthy outlet for energy. Autistic children, living in their own special world, describe a type of Aquarian energy, difficult to channel and control.

The child with this ascendant may need special education to encourage his creative brilliance. He may become bored if he is made to plow through an ordinary curriculum. He is already a nonconformist and should be encouraged to express genius and individuality in his own way. He must be free to learn at his own rate of speed. Worry about being somehow different, becoming bored with slowness of other students, having to learn by rote or in a routine way, or not making steady progress in

others' eyes can squelch his unique assets. He may be especially
musical. Electronics and computer toys can provide an outlet
for inventiveness. Erector sets can appeal to this child as well as
scientific toys. Singing can be a wonderful outlet for nervous
energy, bringing better health and calmer nerves just through
learning proper breathing. The lungs are stimulated, carrying
oxygen down the nervous and circulatory systems, energizing the
whole system. Upgrading the level of "rebellion" early in life
builds good habits for the child with this rising sign.

Aspects to the planet Uranus in the individual chart describe
the exact degree of erratic energy or genius potential. They are
especially important in determining the proper outlet for the
high-strung energy described by this planet. The placement of
Uranus in the chart describes areas of life affected by this elec-
trifying planet. If Uranus is well aspected in the chart, the individual easily adapts to change, and can be spontaneous and in
tune with universal energy and inspiration. Fame is a distinct
possibility, coming as a result of the free expression of talent,
musical ability, or genius. Sensitivity can easily be channeled
into healing, unique theories, and inventive ideas.

If Uranus is badly aspected in the natal chart, change and variety are frightening. Traumas come with unpredictable situations and nerves can be hard to control. The Aquarius rising
who has difficult aspects to the planet Uranus may constantly
run away at just the wrong moment. He tends to blow up a good
thing by becoming itchy and impatient to go on to new stimulation just as previous opportunities are about to be manifest. He
may not know how to channel his rebellion. Sudden, aggravating, upsetting situations keep him constantly off balance. He
may dislike the surprises life has in store. He can have difficulty
with mechanical or electrical things. His nervous system seems
to stop tape recorders, short-circuit radios or television sets. He
can spill things, lack dexterity, or tend toward hysteria. He can
be accident-prone. Evel Knievel, a Libran with Aquarius rising,
looks for consistently more daring stunts in which he risks his
life on a motorcycle. He was a high school dropout and hell-
raiser, spoiling for trouble. Uranus has many difficult aspects in
his chart, indicating this daredevil, rebellious quality.

One of the major changes in life is indicated by the transit of the planet Uranus as it reaches its opposite position. It happens somewhere around the age of forty, bringing in sweeping changes that may be totally unexpected. It indicates a major life crisis. A là the book, *Passages,* certain critical times come into life bringing opportunity for growth and change. Old patterns and static conditions are no longer viable, old formulas no longer work; new decisions are necessary for growth. Uranus opposing its own position indicates times of drastic change. This may be life's way of blasting us out of a comfortable rut we've established. New conditions may cause us to make completely new decisions or change our perspective. F. Scott Fitzgerald, a Libran with Aquarius intercepted, moved to Hollywood at approximately the time this opposition aspected his chart. He began drinking more heavily, a trait sometimes related to Uranus in the chart, and found less appreciation from the film world than he enjoyed before that time. His life was a panorama of typically Uranian activity. His travels included an entourage of friends, and the slightest impulse would prompt them to behavior considered outrageous by more staid members of society. Yet the brilliant work he produced catapulted him into the Hall of Fame. He may be one of the most brilliant writers of his time.

Upsetting conditions with his wife and financial pressures forced him into new situations that were no doubt very difficult to accept. He was given small dark rooms in which to work, forced to conform to time schedules set by Hollywood producers, and his work suffered. His health and personal life deteriorated, even though he found love that helped sustain him. Ultimately, death saved him from almost unbearable conditions. The drastic change from having the world at his feet to lack of appreciation by filmmakers must have been intolerable. Lack of freedom may have been the worst humiliation of all, however.

One hopes that growth can occur with change. The cleaning up of stagnating conditions allows for reformation and new opportunities. A sense of humor and a *"c'est la vie"* attitude may be helpful when these difficult, uncertain crises take place. The individual with Aquarius rising may really come into his own when he emerges from this period. Since Uranus has strong seven-year cycles, moving through each sign in just that amount of time, the "Seven-Year Itch" was aptly named. The universe seems to give us just that amount of time to explore conditions described by each sign of the zodiac. Uranus completes the turn around the wheel, transiting all twelve signs, in eighty-four years. Perhaps that's the natural time to complete the experience of life and go on to other planes of existence.

Since Uranus indicates impulse and the desire to run away, survival seems to depend on being able to get away from restriction, limitation, turn back or flee, at any given moment. In certain instances, a flirtation with suicide exists. Inner decisions may almost be: "Stop the world and let me off" or "There's always suicide as a way out." Whether one deliberately sets out to kill oneself, or tends to drink oneself to death or tempt fate by dangerous exploits, the underlying conscious or unconscious motivation may be the same. This conscious decision was borne out in the end of life for Harry Crosby, a Gemini with Aquarius rising. His death was a result of a double suicide pact with his mistress, another man's beautiful bride. There was no logical explanation for this death and no apparent reason could be discovered. The riddle remains unsolved to this day.

Harry Crosby seemed to have everything he could have wanted or desired in his life. He was the nephew of J. P. Morgan, wealthy beyond his needs, and successful in his own literary career. He was loved and adored by many women, including his own beautiful wife, Caresse. After a close call with a bullet in World War I, he returned to Boston and thereafter flirted with death, ultimately choosing to meet it on his own terms and in his own time. He became a rebel, scandalizing Boston society by provoking his beloved Caresse into divorcing her husband so that he himself might run off with her.

Harry and Caresse lived in great style in Paris and had friends among the very rich and very talented of the world, but chose to associate with princes and rogues alike. Harry and his friends gambled constantly, always setting higher and higher stakes in the name of sensation. At the same time, he was able to express his creative genius through writing. He started the Black Sun Press in Paris, which published not only his own works—which were steadily gaining in reputation—but that of some of the greatest literary figures of the time.

Finally, he elected to drive himself mad, believing that

madness and genius are one and the same. While visiting New York, he attempted to persuade Caresse to share the ultimate experience of jumping off the roof of the Plaza Hotel in a double suicide. She evidently refused. Undaunted by her refusal, he planned a rendezvous with his lovely young mistress, very newly married to someone else, at the apartment of a friend who lived at the Hotel Des Artistes on the West Side. He shot the lovely lady, seemingly with her consent, walked around New York for hours, even returning to the Plaza Hotel for a while, and then returned to the Des Artistes to kill himself, completing the terms of their pact. He once wrote, "Time is a tyranny to be abolished."

Descriptions of Harry Crosby by friends read like a rundown of Aquarian traits. Ernest Hemingway said, "He has a great, great gift. He has a wonderful gift of carelessness." Ezra Pound said, "Crosby's life was a religious manifestation. His death was, if you like . . . a death from excess vitality. A vote of confidence in the cosmos." "He looked like a god," said his stepdaughter Polly Peabody. "He didn't look like anybody on the street, or in restaurants, or anywhere. He was just different." Malcolm Cowley: "He had gifts that would have made him an explorer, a soldier of fortune, a revolutionist. They were qualities fatal to a poet." Edith Wharton described him thus: "Walter's young cousin turns out to be a sort of half-crazy cad."

But most descriptive of all was Stuart Gilbert's comment. "Harry Crosby could stroll that dizzy, aerial path as easily, as carefree, as if he were walking down a garden alley of his country home. . . . If ever he felt a qualm of vertigo, it was, I imagine, when he walked the plank laid out on terra firma, that safe and sensible promenade. . . . He feared the terre à terre, the normal, as most of us fear celestial heights." J. P. Morgan, Crosby's Uncle Jack, was charmed by the young man, but didn't know what to make of him. "He walked around town like a dancing master, without a hat, with lacquered fingernails, wearing a black cloth flower in his buttonhole."

Eccentricity is normality for one with Aquarius on the rise. He is gregarious, wants to do "crazy" things, and can't be confined. He will attract the limelight in one way or another. He will always do the unexpected, rather than the predictable. He may attract notoriety by simply being himself. He is the original stock-broker who refused to wear a suit and tie. His exploits often attract publicity, even though he may not necessarily seek it. He experiments where others dare not tread. He may refuse to ac-knowledge the pecking order of society, antagonizing people not secure enough to stand on their own inner merit. He can have an attraction for anything new or undiscovered. He enjoys things not easily pigeonholed. Fascination with unique people or proj-ects leads to greater and greater heights of attainment. He may be a natural political revolutionary, since change and reform are urgent to his nature.

The Aquarius personality may need to have many projects going on at once. He cannot stick to one activity for too long a time, as he becomes impatient. Switching from one thing to an-other will suit his quick mind much better. He may have to use unique methods to get his motor running. He may not appear to be working, yet while he is performing seemingly meaningless tasks, his flashes of genius have a chance to emerge. His time clock may not synchronize with standard working hours, so it may be useless to try to pin him down to a schedule or routine.

This unique person may give others a nervous breakdown if they try to figure out his behavior patterns. He does what he can, when he can, and may not understand why others are upset about his need for flexibility. He may be late for the most impor-tant engagement of his life. As far as he is concerned, the event doesn't start until he gets there. He has a strange time clock that tells him when to arrive and when to leave. If he has a deadline, he may work all night to meet it, or stop work altogether to go to the gym, ignoring the fact that time doesn't stand still. An art-ist friend, Vasili Lambrinos, an Aquarian at birth, amazes every-one by painting at odd hours. He can dress for an evening with friends, apply a few brushstrokes to the canvas he is working on, have cocktails with clients, run back home to apply a few more brushstrokes, and then go elsewhere for dinner and dancing. He may return home to paint a bit more before retiring for the eve-ning. He has a prodigious level of productivity.

Thomas Jefferson, an Aries with Aquarius rising, left a store-house of treasures in his home at Monticello as a testimony to his inventiveness. Mary Pickford ended her life, after the greatest fame imaginable, a cripple as a result of alcoholism. Rollo May, Immanuel Kant, Carl Jung, and Benjamin Spock express the unique Aquarian quality through work that is inspired and ahead of the times. The Japanese emperor on the throne in 1852 expressed a universality in allowing foreigners to see him in person. His Aquarian ascendant found satisfaction in making more contact with his people than any former ruler.

The Duke of Windsor—who gave up his throne for a commoner—and Mary I of England shared an Aquarius ascendant. Warren G. Harding, Thomas Jefferson, Abraham Lincoln, James Monroe, and William McKinley are Presidents who expressed the strong humanitarian concern indicated by Aquarius rising. Literary figures such as Sir Francis Bacon, Havelock Ellis, Robert Louis Stevenson, André Maurois, George Sand, William Butler Yeats, Alfred de Musset, John Ruskin, Ernest Renan, and journalists Bill Moyers and Ross McWhirter have Aquarius on the ascendant. Karl Marx developed the theory of socialism, helped found the Social Democratic Labor Party, and initiated communism, all rebellious, reforming Aquarius personality traits exhibited in action.

Actors Jimmy Stewart, Henry Winkler, Vincent Price, Walter Slezak, Charles Boyer, and actresses Mary Pickford, Carole Lombard, and Leslie Caron share this unusual ascendant. Their work in film expresses a unique quality never touched by anyone else. There is no mistaking their individual stamp. Composers Ferde Grofé, Jules Massenet, Leonard Bernstein, George Fredderick Handel, singers Leontyne Price, Desi Arnaz, Jr., and Ritchie Valens chose music as an outlet for the Aquarius energy. Roy Rogers, singer and actor, falls into a category by himself, as his Aquarius rising would indicate.

Explorer Daniel Boone, a Scorpio with Aquarius rising, football hero Joe Namath, a Gemini with Aquarius rising, labor leader James Hoffa (who disappeared unexpectedly from his home, never to be seen again), an Aquarius with Aquarius rising, and scientist Tycho Brahe, a Capricorn with Aquarius ascendant, carved special niches for themselves through their own special talents. John Dean and Heinrich Himmler share a Libra Sun sign with Aquarius rising. They managed to attract infamy instead of fame. Joachim von Ribbentrop, top diplomatic agent for Hitler, was tried for war crimes and hanged after the Allied victory. His Taurus Sun and Aquarius ascendant led to anarchy rather than humanitarian expression. Revolutionist Maximilien de Robespierre, also Taurus Sun and Aquarius rising sign, chose the negative expression of Uranus energy, whereas Meher Baba, a Pisces with Aquarius ascendant, chose the mystical path. Alcide De Gasperi, Italian premier, saved Italy from falling under the control of communism. He was imprisoned by Mussolini yet later emerged to become leader of the Christian Democratic Party. His Aries Sun coupled with Aquarian ascendant enabled him to fight for humanitarian rights.

Artists Edgar Degas, Piet Mondrian, and Pierre Renoir expressed unique talent and style in their painting. Renoir became crippled with arthritis, yet continued to paint with brushes tied to his hands. Degas, a Cancer Sun sign with Aquarius rising, was the son of a wealthy family. Without the need to please critics, he developed a unique style, but broke with the Impressionists later on and became a virtual recluse. Both Mondrian and Renoir shared a Pisces Sun with the Aquarian ascendant. Humanitarian qualities, inventiveness, genius, and uniqueness make the person with Aquarius personality one of a kind, special and gifted in his own right. He may express the highest spiritual qualities manifest on earth or choose to blow things up around him. But one thing is certain—he will never be overlooked or lost in a crowd.

FINANCE

Pisces rules the second house of finance when Aquarius is on the rise. Involvement in idealistic causes, visionary pursuits, film, photography, or the glamour world brings income to one with this ascendant. Humanitarian instincts can lead to financial activity where projects that are uplifting can be connected to income. The planet Neptune, ruler of Pisces, describes therapy as well as film, with the underlying theme one of inspiration. Gas and oil are other areas ascribed to this planet.

Neptune describes the process of seeing an overall concept rather than dealing with nitty-gritty fact. In a positive sense,

Neptune indicates a wonderful ability to earn income by being idealistic and inspired, but in the negative, a blindness to reality and lack of attention to detail can keep financial success in the realm of wishful thinking. If aspects to the planet Neptune are good in the individual chart, the probability is that the person can be successful in bringing dreams into practical focus. Difficult aspects to Neptune indicate a special need to pin matters down, get firm agreements in financial negotiations, and adopt realistic measures with material matters in general.

Neptune indicates the ability to visualize needs easily. When the chart indicates success in financial areas, the individual can almost put himself on a "mental salary," sending out thoughts of what his financial needs are and bringing in funds to match his expectations. He seems to guide himself to the source of financial activity by focusing on the ideal sum he thinks necessary for his own satisfaction. It is therefore important to have good, clear concepts about principles of financial success. When the individual senses that money is only another form of energy, he can raise the level of energy he puts into earning income. He earns funds more easily by focusing on ideas that will uplift humanity in some way. Carl Jung said that unrealized energy or potential exteriorizes in the form of fate. The external financial conditions in Aquarius rising's life may reflect his inner conditioning. When he changes that program, he can attract money like iron filings to a magnet.

Jung earned money through the field of psychology, a Neptunian activity. Actors Charles Boyer, Mary Pickford, Carole Lombard, and Henry Winkler earn money through activity in film. Renoir was able to earn funds through his inspired painting, and John Pierpont Morgan was a visionary when it came to financial matters. F. Scott Fitzgerald went up and down the financial ladder, dissipating much energy when he was lacking in inspiration. When he wrote for the film world, there was less glamour and idealism than he required and his writing suffered, yet he earned money in spite of the results.

Negative aspects to Neptune indicate an unrealistic approach to financial activity. The individual may have wonderful dreams but be unable to bring them into focus. His dreams of riches can be dashed to the ground if his projects are too high-flown for practical assimilation. He may fear that he would lead himself down the garden path if he tried for ideal circumstances, or if he deluded himself into thinking his projects were salable. Clear conceptualization, with idealistic goals in mind, must be carefully combined with a practical approach to money matters. Vision and inspiration lead to ultimate success in the financial arena if the dream is important enough. A sense of timing and intuition about directions to take may be the most important financial asset with this house placement.

COMMUNICATIONS

An Aquarian personality channels much drive and ambition into areas of communications. The third house in a chart indicates not only contracts, negotiations, commuting, early education, but telephones, neighbors, and siblings. The sign of Aries rules this house, with Mars the ruler of Aries. This person must be on the go all the time, running around town, fighting traffic, finding challenges in areas of communications.

The aspects to Mars in the chart indicate his basic relationship with brothers and sisters, perhaps preconditioning his later relationship to school and communications. If Mars is well aspected, he photographs his brothers or sisters (and relatives in general) as active, pioneering, innovative, and competitive. He learns how to deal with competition in a healthy manner and is willing to fight for what he wants in negotiating agreements or conditions. Since Mars is the planet ruling sexual activity as well as high creative ability, he may well channel much of the sexual, competitive energy into matters dealing with communications. In considering the chart of an actor with Aquarius rising, it is easy to see how the competitive urge serves him well. After much aggressive and innovative activity, he will find an outlet for challenging creativity in areas of communications. Mars also rules metals. Inventors, if this energy is fully utilized, may work with metal or metal pens all the time. Musicians work with metal strings on instruments.

In any area where Mars colors the energy, it is vitally important to release that energy creatively, rather than in aggression and anger, allowing that drive to do internal damage. Impatience, temper, and aggravation can be sidestepped through creative activity. If Mars is badly aspected, the tendency is to allow frustration to back up until it reaches the boiling point. Accidents and outbursts of anger may then be the only way to release this backed-up energy. If a little old lady in the grocery-store line is slowly trying your patience, you may feel like kicking her out of the way—and then suffer terrible guilt at even having such a thought. Focused creative Mars activity will help keep you patient. If you've been running five miles, releasing your energy in a physical way, the likelihood of objections over delays is diminished considerably.

Needlework, math, building things with hammer and nails, dance, or any physical activity helps to channel the aggressive energy into smoothly flowing action. Since writing is a third house activity, working with a typewriter or metal pen rather than with a pencil releases more of this frustrated energy. A person with this rising sign may find it hard to wait for people. If there are delays with appointments, he will be more amenable, after a wait, if he can find an outlet for his energy. One young actress takes her needlepoint with her to auditions, in case delays try her patience and upset her careful mental preparation.

Since the third house also rules commutation, it is important for one with this ascendant to work out any frustrated energy before tackling traffic jams. A long line of cars caught by some unseen snarl is enough to bring out the worst in disposition. Telephones may also try patience, especially if Mars has difficult aspects in the chart. If aggravations begin to build, the healthiest release is to exercise in order to keep the drives fluid. Impatience may present a daily challenge for an individual with Aquarius rising.

HOME LIFE

The fourth house in a chart describes the relationship with the parent of the opposite sex. It also indicates the kind of home life the person is attracted to, the lifestyle he chooses, and the conditions toward the latter part of life. When Aquarius is on the rise,

Taurus rules this house. Venus, the planet that rules this sign, indicates pleasure, beauty, harmony, art, serenity, and graciousness. It also describes affection, love, and sensuality. If Venus is well aspected in the natal chart, a beautiful exchange of love and affection between the individual and the parent of the opposite sex is indicated. The Aquarian personality photographs that parent as sociable, charming, gracious, and handsome or beautiful. If Venus is not well aspected, the parent may have been lazy, self-indulgent, or inclined to take the easy way out in life.

In the positive sense, an Aquarian personality enjoys greater peace and harmony in his later years. He needs a home that provides solace and beautiful surroundings. He may have a wonderful art collection. He will certainly be sensitive to the right color and decor in his home. Since Taurus is the sign most associated with gourmet food, land that provides food, or an "estate" designed for entertainment and enjoyment, becomes a strong desire for this native. Mary Pickford had one of the most beautiful homes in Hollywood in her lovely estate, Pickfair. Thomas Jefferson filled his beautiful home, Monticello, with inventions that made for more gracious, pleasurable living in his day. The Duke of Windsor gave up his throne, but always managed to have an exceptionally beautiful place to live.

If Venus is not well aspected, the individual with this innovative rising sign may have felt a lack of support from the parent of the opposite sex. Affection may have been withheld or the parent may have backed away from conflict. The possibility of following in the footsteps of that parent in areas of assertion can be strong. The individual may tend to take the easy way out at home, wanting only a haven or refuge from the storms of the world. In the most extreme form, the individual may hide out at home in order to avoid outside conditions. Structuring time, especially with artistic projects, enables the person to find an antidote or missing ingredient in life. If he can sink his teeth into projects, he finds a way out of a morass. Venus, one of the "benefics," is never all bad. Enjoyment of social life, friendship, affection, and pleasure are important for someone with this rising sign. At its worst, self-indulgence, laziness, or overinterest in pleasure to the exclusion of anything else is ascribed to Venus.

The possibility of avoidance of anything remotely distasteful or ugly in connection with home or lifestyle is a Venusian trait. Gracious living seems to come naturally to one with this rising sign.

ROMANCE • CREATIVE EXPRESSION

When Aquarius is on the ascendant, the individual must have strong mental stimulation in connection with romance or creative activity. Gemini rules the fifth house of "gambles," whether those gambles take the form of romance, the stock market, children, or creative expression. Mercury is the planet ruling Gemini, and Mercury describes the adult ego function of analysis, mental activity, and the collection of data. Gemini is the sign accused of duality, yet the duality of the Gemini is the need to be close and objective at the same time. When boredom is removed, the need for duality is also.

John Pierpont Morgan chose to channel this exciting mental energy into the stock market. George Sand, Havelock Ellis, and André Maurois chose writing as an expression of the mental, creative energy. Leontyne Price sings, whereas James Stewart, Henry Winkler, and Leslie Caron chose to act, using their mental energy to learn scripts and make the most fascinating acting choices. F. Scott Fitzgerald, Capricorn rising with additional Aquarian energy affecting his personality, wrote exciting novels.

In romantic areas, the native with Aquarius rising will choose someone who appeals to him on an intellectual level. If the object of love is witty and fun, intellectual and stimulating, an exciting romance is born. If the love object is just swift enough to stay out of reach, the excitement is intensified. Since the Aquarius rising is such a free soul, he needs to share love with someone challenging and interesting. Good communication may be the strongest bond in love areas.

Children are described by the fifth house as well. Whether an individual chooses to release his creative energy through children or through "brain children" is a matter of choice, but in the former situation, his offspring inherit his love of intellectual stimulation. Benjamin Spock chose children as a subject of importance in his life. His thoughts and observations about children have made the task easier for several generations of new parents.

WORK • SERVICE • HEALTH

Cancer rules the sixth house of work and service when Aquarius is on the ascendant. The Moon, ruler of Cancer, is the planet that indicates sensitivity, vulnerability, nurturing, and emotion. The Moon is the fastest-moving body in the heavens, indicating changeability or moodiness, but in the positive sense is related to the collective unconscious. It describes the feelings and emotions we all share in common.

When the Moon is well aspected in the natal chart, an individual with Aquarius on the rise is naturally attracted to work where he can be tuned in to the needs of people. Strong service capacity can mean anything from working in a hospital or serving food in a restaurant to providing a service organization. The Moon has been proven statistically by Gauguelin to be the strongest heavenly body in charts of writers. It seems that when the Aquarian personality is willing to work through his own emotional pain and expose his vulnerability, he can become quite nurturing to people, sensing their needs on a deeply profound level. He will be most vulnerable and sensitive about his work, but also the most understanding person on the job.

If the Moon is not well aspected, however, he can be overly sensitive, upset about work all the time, and suffer terrible indigestion in connection with upsetting work situations. Since Uranus describes the nervous system in general, and the Moon, the digestive system, the biggest health problem may come with overly sensitive reactions, stomach problems, and a delicate nervous system. If he can work in a capacity where his genius and sensitivity are rewarded, his energy is working creatively to keep him in tune and healthy. Psychologists Rollo May, Carl Jung (Capricorn rising with Aquarius intercepted), and Havelock Ellis chose work where their sensitive understanding and nurturing instincts would serve the public on a profound level. Writers Robert Louis Stevenson, Sir Francis Bacon, F. Scott

Fitzgerald (another Capricorn rising with Aquarius intercepted), André Maurois, and William Butler Yeats were obviously extremely sensitive to the feelings and situations mankind shares in common. Abraham Lincoln adopted a greatly nurturing role as President at a time when our country required sensitive leadership. The Duke of Windsor was known to be an especially sensitive man, perhaps too much so for the job to which he was born.

Whenever a particular energy threatens to become a problem, the working out of that particular energy in a constructive, creative manner enables the release of steam. Otherwise, that negative energy backs up and eats up the individual from the inside. The person born with Aquarius on the rise can keep himself healthy by dealing with his emotional nature through releasing nurturing instincts. It seems that when he understands how others project their thoughts and feelings about themselves into statements and accusations, he is less easily hurt and learns not to take things personally. He then depersonalizes what might otherwise threaten to debilitate him, transmutes this understanding into a more profound look at mankind's patterns as a whole.

MARRIAGE • PARTNERSHIP

Partnership in a chart indicates both personal partnership, such as marriage, or business partnership. The Aquarian personality looks for someone dynamic, dramatic, strong, and vital in a partnership situation. Leo rules the seventh house of partnership when Aquarius is on the ascendant. The Sun, ruler of Leo, indicates the personable, dynamic, executive qualities that are connected with a Leo type of person. The Sun also describes one's inner sense of self-worth, ego, and self-esteem—vital characteristics for strong leadership. The Sun naturally rules the dominant or animus part of the personality.

In partnership areas, the Aquarian personality seeks the exact reflection in a mate or partner of what he feels about himself. If he has a strong sense of ego and self-esteem, he attracts a strong, self-assured mate or partner, perhaps one who is willing to run things while the Aquarian rising is free to be spontaneous and inventive. F. Scott Fitzgerald, with both the Capricorn and Aquarian cast to his personality, chose a very dramatic mate in Zelda, but someone very unstable. (The Moon and the Sun described partnership in his chart.) Abraham Lincoln chose Mary Todd Lincoln, renowned for her strength and dominance, sometimes unpleasantly so. The Duke of Windsor was taken by storm by a very strong lady from Baltimore; the Duchess of Windsor has never been known to be a shrinking violet. Carole Lombard was captivated by Clark Gable, the very personification of the masculine image. Pat Nixon, with Aquarius rising, chose Richard Nixon, bordering on egomania. Mary Pickford also chose a strong mate in Douglas Fairbanks, who exhibited a dominant, masculine personality.

It can be especially important for the individual with this rising sign to develop a strong sense of ego and self-worth in order to attract a person with that same ego quality. If insecurity is part of the package when Aquarius is on the ascendant, the possibility of looking for someone else to take care of matters for him is strong. The end result of such an alliance is a negative power struggle between two people, each hoping the other will control the reins. The opposite can also be true. When ego battles occur, it may be due to the determination to have one's way and call the shots completely with no compromise. Cooperation comes when the partner assumes the reins from a standpoint of healthy executive, leadership ability, leaving the Aquarian personality free to express his genius quality.

NEEDS

Since the eighth house describes the way in which a person gets his needs met, it can be important to know the survival behaviors developed in childhood. Sometimes these behaviors were effective early in life but became less so with maturity. In the case of Aquarius rising, the natural inclination is simply to ask for what is needed or wanted. Depending on the aspects to Mercury in the individual chart, the person with this rising sign is able to state his needs in a clear, concise form, presenting the facts of a particular situation.

Virgo is on the cusp of the eighth house, with Mercury the ruler of Virgo. Mercury relates to the adult ego state, describing the ability to gather information with precision, analyze, and speak or write factually. Since the early manner of getting one's needs met is also the quality of energy one can send out to humanity, the Aquarian rising is not only able to ask for what he needs and wants; his intellectual conclusions, analyses, and ability to collect facts are his gifts to share with others. Carl Jung made innovative and brilliant inroads in the field of psychology, doing research and collecting data which he later shared with the world at large through writing and teaching. His Aquarian ascendant most naturally led him to research in the field of astrology as well. Metaphysics, ruled by Uranus, became part of his analytical process. He attempted to bring the unknown into clearer focus.

Harry Crosby, for all of his rebellion and unorthodox lifestyle, edited a literary magazine to share with the public. F. Scott Fitzgerald negotiated terms most carefully and methodically after his original success as a writer. George Sand shared her intellectual discoveries through writing, speaking, analyzing. Scientist Tycho Brahe shared his research results and discoveries through writing and speaking. Since indepth research was an essential ingredient in his life, his gifts to humanity were the scientific, factual results of his experiments. Leontyne Price has shared the golden gift of her voice with the world, as Leonard Bernstein has shared the results of his choices in music.

RECOGNITION

The ninth house in the chart indicates the philosophical tendencies, travel inclinations, possibilities of recognition. This is also the house that describes promotion, public relations, publicity, publishing, and legal affairs. When Aquarius is on the ascendant, Libra, with Venus its ruler, is on the cusp of the ninth house. Venus describes beauty, pleasure, diplomacy, graciousness, charm, and art. Venus also indicates the situations a person loves. The Aquarian personality loves to travel, is gracious in areas of public recognition, and enjoys the publicity he receives.

Many Aquarian personalities have a natural inclination for the spotlight. If Venus is well aspected in the individual chart, he is associated with artistic projects, or is well known for his graciousness and charm as well as his diplomacy. If Venus is not well aspected, there is a tendency to take the easy way out as far as publicity and promotional effort is concerned. Libra is the legal sign. Cooperation and a sense of social justice are ascribed to Libra. In legal areas, the Aquarian personality can shine. The ability to harmonize and smooth over difficulties is profound if Venus is well aspected. John Dean chose to work through the positive side of Libra in his testimony about Watergate. He may have vacillated originally about the justice of the situation, but his cooperative manner on the witness stand, the fairness and sense of justice in his willing acknowledgment of his part in the scandal, exonerated him to a great degree in the public eye. The publicity he received was never as hard or harsh as other offenders'.

In the negative sense, Venus also indicates a tendency to show only the most favorable side of oneself in relation to publicity and promotion. There may be a tendency to compromise, if not actually cop out, for the sake of peace. Self-indulgence and vacillation are negative characteristics of Venus. Mary Pickford was absolutely loved and adored by her public. Although she continued to command that public adoration, the fact that she was an alcoholic leaked out. Many of her fans chose to ignore that fact in order to keep her on the pedestal of perfection.

CAREER

Scorpio rules the tenth house of career when Aquarius is on the ascendant. Pluto, the ruler of Scorpio, indicates tremendous power, charisma, intensity, forcefulness, and effectiveness, depending on its position in the chart and the aspects to other planets. If Pluto is well aspected, the individual with this inventive rising sign can attain powerful positions in the public arena or with his career, if he so chooses. Much of the preconditioning of his career potential depends on the photographs he took of the parent of the same sex.

Pluto is the planet perhaps least understood, possibly because its power is so intense. The Scorpio energy may not *appear* to be what is usually considered powerful, yet when this dynamic force is channeled to its highest level, effectiveness seems incredibly easy. In terms of Transactional Analysis, Pluto relates to the child ego state. The child can be totally innocent and therefore very magnetic, or manipulative and "powerful" in a more overt way. The innocent child will always be more effective than the manipulative one.

Consider two children at a party. One child, sure of himself and his ability to get his needs met, can sit in a corner, quietly eating ice cream and cake. He is so adorable and charismatic that the people in the room naturally gravitate to him, patting him on the head, telling him what a good child he is. The other child, not knowing that he is magnetic, feeling unable to easily get his needs met in the family environment, yanks on skirts, saying in effect, "Notice me, notice me." That child is eventually admonished or brushed away. Plutonian energy is like the child energy. If it is held back, it is infinitely more powerful and effective. It is somewhat like a powerful body of water. If that water is left to flood the riverbanks, it can be very destructive, yet if dammed up, can produce enough electricity to light up cities.

When Pluto describes the relationship with the parent of the same sex, the individual sees that parent as a "child," enormously charismatic, playful, and getting results all the while. If Pluto is well aspected, the parent has a power that is natural, easy, not forced. But if Pluto is not well aspected in the individual chart, the parent may have been overly aggressive and manipulative, unaware of the intensity of his energy. The parent may have unwittingly used force to overrun the Aquarius rising, and perhaps everyone else. His message may have been: "Do what I say and don't ask any questions."

In public life or in career matters, the native with Aquarius rising can be enormously effective. He acts like a "producer," reaching people on a mass level. He may manufacture things, be involved with major organizations, or deal with the television industry, a Plutonian occupation. The negative side of Pluto smacks of the underworld, or of manipulation that eventually backfires. In a more subtle sense, it describes whether the ends justify the means. Scorpio is the sign of transcendency or trans-mutation. The image of the Phoenix rising from the ashes describes the process of burning out the negative Scorpio energy of revenge, manipulation, or childlike determination to want what is wanted whether the end results are good or not. A child and the Plutonian energy have a similar message: "I want what I want, when I want it. I'll get it and no one will stop me." The child reaches maturity when he can let go of non-productive sit-uations. The Scorpio evolves in the same way.

In a metaphysical sense, Pluto describes the will. A child's will is strong and effective, but his concern is for his own pleasure or needs. The evolved will is related to Universal will, or the desire to do only what is for the good of the whole. Then the "inno-cence" of the child ego state emerges. When the individual with Aquarius on the rise is willing to use, as his motivation, the desire to transform energy to the highest level, working for the betterment of mankind, he taps the highest universal energy. He then becomes truly effective. Thomas Jefferson, Immanuel Kant, James Monroe, Abraham Lincoln, Warren G. Harding seemed to work on the highest level of the Plutonian energy, as did Carl Jung, who ultimately evolved to high spiritual concepts in his work. George Frederick Handel certainly influenced humanity through his music, Renoir through his painting, Tycho Brahe through his discoveries, Sir Francis Bacon through his writing.

Heinrich Himmler and von Ribbentrop chose the negative Plutonian energy in public life. Jeddu Krishnamurti transformed the lives of many people who came his way, as did Meher Baba, Ernest Renan, and Immanuel Kant. Suicide was the ultimate ex-perience for Harry Crosby. The disappearance of James Hoffa was no doubt the result of revenge from those working on the negative level of Pluto.

Many times a person with Aquarius rising feels caught by a desire to get even with the parent of the same sex. Rebellion against the standards advocated by that parent can result in a stymied career for the individual. He may be forced to trans-mute his thumbed-nose attitude in order to achieve his own goals. In most rebellion, the only person who is hurt may be the rebel—the individual with Aquarius on the rise. If he is truly able to march to the beat of a different drummer, rise to the highest motivation with career or public life, he may end up with all the overt symbols of success he may have wanted early in his life. The Duke of Windsor let go of a throne to have the woman he loved. Who is to say what inner motivation propelled him to his destiny?

FRIENDSHIP

Jupiter rules the eleventh house of friends when Aquarius is ascending. Jupiter's natural, contagious enthusiasm, sense of freedom, and humanitarian instincts seem to attract wonderful people to his side. He can be surrounded by philosophical, happy-go-lucky people, wealthy of purse or of spirit. He seems to attract outgoing, expansive people. He is said to be the best friend one could have, perhaps because he is so inclined to live and let live.

When Jupiter, the "great benefic," is well aspected in the natal chart, good fortune and "luck" seem to be connected with friendships or group association. Jupiter is the planet indicating not only philosophical trends and riches but the religious outlook. Universality is characteristic of the Aquarian energy, with curiosity about lifestyles and the workings of the universe quite naturally leading to associations with people in all walks of life.

If Jupiter is not well aspected, some disappointment in friendships or with groups and associations is likely. The individual tends to expect more than can be delivered and generally set himself up for a letdown. He will have an abundance of acquaintances, and may tend to promise more than he can live up to as well. Generosity and encouragement attract many friendships, some deep and sincere, others less than illuminating. The person with this rising sign may have to adopt a *"c'est la vie"* outlook in some situations.

If he is free to express the genius he possesses, he can be especially excited about sharing his goals and enthusiasm with companions. He may be like a lightning bolt, however, here today, there tomorrow. He loves to surround himself with associates who are challenged by life, outgoing, fun loving, and who live by an underlying philosophy about the workings of the universe. Those friends may be religious or simply have a sense of humor. Harry Crosby surrounded himself with the most fascinating people in Paris society. Some of them were from the literary world, others from society, and still others were less than savory characters. He loved to mix people from all walks of life with each other. F. Scott Fitzgerald and Zelda were surrounded by an entourage wherever they went. They picked up people in their travels who loved the extravagant lifestyle as well. John Dean may have been slightly disappointed in his associations. Sir Francis Bacon joined his friends almost daily in coffeehouses to discuss key issues. Carole Lombard was adored by her friends. Carl Jung chose friends to share new discoveries in the field of psychology. He was sometimes very disappointed in his friends, though, as they were in him. Georgia George, a television stylist with Aquarius rising, travels extensively for her work or with friends from all parts of the world, and her contagious good humor is the source of many enduring associations and friendships.

HIDDEN MATTERS • SUBCONSCIOUS PROCESS

The twelfth house in a chart has been described by traditional astrology as the house of imprisonment, jail, or hospitals. In psychological terms, the twelfth house describes the subconscious mind. It indicates qualities that are difficult to expose or deal with overtly. When Aquarius is on the ascendant, Capricorn rules this hidden house. The ruler of that sign is Saturn, the planet of responsibility, gravity, or, in the negative sense, restriction or limitation.

In the language of Transactional Analysis, Saturn relates to the parent ego state. That ego state is developed by listening to the real parents' messages early in life. The individual transcribes the same "be safe" messages onto a tape that runs inside his own head, until he learns to re-record those early injunctions. When Saturn rules the twelfth house, however, those restrictive or supportive parent messages seem to come from a past life or on a deeply subconscious level.

Johannes Michael described this aspect in a most profound

way. He said, "I feel like I've had a shadow on my soul. Sometimes I see situations that I know belong to me, yet I don't let myself get them. I am aware that I stop myself on some level. It is as if some subconscious fear prevents me from grasping rewards." Trissie Callan, Pisces with Aquarius rising, describes it in another manner. She said, "It feels like you're always swimming upstream, against the current. It seems, in a cosmic sense, as if you can't win. It's like missing a piece of the puzzle that you need and having it inaccessible . . . the country where it exists burned down. Imagine having an engine part missing and the part is no longer made."

The "fantasy" involved in this subconscious feeling of restriction or limitation can be uncovered through regression sessions. It seems as if a deep subconscious feeling of inadequacy, perhaps from a past incarnation, keeps the individual wearing the hair shirt. It can sometimes be connected with group or racial guilt, where the person feels responsible for the failure of a plan or situation. His inner decision is: "Never again." When he becomes aware of that subconscious self-punishment, he can begin to release energy and be aware of the inappropriate reason for stopping himself.

If Saturn is well aspected in the chart, however, much of that unnecessary punishment seems to be mitigated. A deep sense of responsibility enables the Aquarius rising to enter life determined to find his destiny, and allows him to value himself so that he can assume the highest responsibility of which he is capable. Abraham Lincoln obviously had a profound sense of responsibility for mankind, yet he was a man in inner torment in many ways. In working past his subconscious fears, the individual opens doors that he may have been afraid of before. If he fears a monster behind those doors, bringing him into daylight may reveal that monster to be only one inch tall. The full rein of genius connected with this enlightened rising sign can begin to manifest in surprising ways. He will find the true freedom of life and a profound spiritual connection to mankind.

PISCES
RISING

THE RULER OF PISCES IS THE PLANET Neptune. When this planet is on the rise, idealism, vision, and high inspiration are strongly in evidence. The person with this ascendant deals with life by seeing only the best in any situation. He adopts a viewpoint of high expectancy and survives by seeing concepts from an overall perspective that may be considered naïve by more factually oriented people. He may have a Don Quixote complex and tend to glamorize people and situations around him, yet he can walk through the most difficult times with a clear view of the road ahead. In spite of apparent circumstances, the dreams that parade before his vision have little to do with life as others see it. He puts on his rose-colored glasses, heightens the colors a bit, and carries on. No harsh glare of reality will enter his field of vision unless he chooses.

Pisces is a water sign and is mutable, or adaptable. The symbol of this sign is two fish, swimming in opposite directions. The most obvious interpretation of the symbology is the inability to take decisive action. The person with this ascendant can keep himself in a hopeless quandary by duality of direction, yet he accomplishes what he must in life by taking this indirect approach. Confrontation and clear-cut decisions are not his way of handling situations. Since he operates strongly from the right hemisphere of his brain, he may have to wait until his intuitive powers point to the right direction.

The appearance of someone with this idealistic outlook is a dead giveaway. He may be myopic with large dreamy eyes, and can almost look like he has a halo around his head. The angelic face completes the picture. That faraway gaze seems to reflect the rosy pictures that parade before his mind. He may appear to be wrapped in cotton batting or gauze and can sometimes appear to be too fragile to live in a world of struggle and difficulty. He seems to stay ten feet off the ground and be high on life all the time. He expects people to be perfect and to live up to his expectations. He may be totally unaware of any faults. He exudes a naïve charm that is exceptionally contagious. Since he is so gentle and kind, almost no one can resist the temptation to go along with his concept of life. He is worshipped and adored, put on a pedestal of adulation.

Neptune can be described in several ways. It is, first of all, the planet that rules film, therapy, and the glamour world. Photography provides a natural outlet for this kind of energy. But Neptune is the planet that describes the ability to create the circumstances around us. It is like planting a seed in a flower pot. If one plants a zinnia seed, a zinnia grows, if cared for properly, or if an orchid is planted that is the plant that emerges from the soil. Metaphysically speaking, whatever one can conceive is what emerges and is manifest in the outer circumstances. If conditions are not ideal, the fault lies in the seeds that are planted on a daily basis.

Janene Schneider describes this process as sending out "purchase orders" to the universe. If five "desks and chairs" are ordered, that is what is received, yet if imperfect orders are released, imperfect "merchandise" is returned. Neptune, in good aspect to other planets, describes a fantastic ability to order a good life through being idealistic and expectant. The refusal to see ugliness seems to prevent its existence in the life of one with this ascendant. The effectiveness of this talent is indicated by the aspects to the planet Neptune. The visionary quality is connected with a desire to save the world and to lift circumstances to the ideal level. The problems that can occur stem from an unwillingness to be realistic, however, or a tendency to overglamorize people and events.

Learning to utilize this ability in a practical manner can be like taking pictures of a beautiful sunset. Unless the camera is focused properly, the sunset comes out a blur. Since the person with Pisces rising is constantly "taking pictures" of events around him, he can manufacture fantastic results by simply combining intellect and practical application with the visionary trait. As long as he believes in his dreams while maintaining awareness of their realistic direction, he finds ideal circumstances. The trouble arises when he sees only the forest and not the trees. When his misty eyes become clear and bright and he faces certain unalterable facts that he may have overlooked, he can feel deceived, let down, and disillusioned. He may become aware of his own naïveté, the most devastating awareness of all. He can feel like an ostrich who has hidden his head in the sand for too long. The letdown is extreme and the dreams in a state of ruin.

If the person with this ascendant comes crashing down from the heights, the reverberating sound can be heard and felt for a long time. His original inability to confront may have been to avoid realistic facts that could be painful, yet the pain is more extreme after a long period of time spent in unrealistic realms. If he can confront, up front, he will avoid the later despair that sets in if circumstances are not what he conceived. The willingness to take a cold, hard look without losing the vision and sense of perspective brings sharper pictures into reality.

Neptune is like putting a valuable art object on a pedestal. If it comes toppling down and crashes to the ground, the pieces can never be glued together again. The cracks show and the object loses its value. It is no longer perfect. If, however, that object is bolted to the pedestal or enclosed in a glass case, it is still high enough to see, but protected from the possibility of ruin. Keeping the overall concepts in view while working out the details brings projects and situations into manifestation in a clear, concise manner. If one with a Pisces ascendant trains himself to look at life in a totally realistic manner, he can be more effective in every way. He can then inspire others while commanding the respect due him. If he glamorizes, in the Don Quixote manner, he may lose the following of those trained in facts and figures. He waters down his plan and becomes disenchanted.

Leigh Taylor Young, a beautiful actress with this rising sign, described this idealistic tendency by saying that she used to project her own vision of beauty and idealism on the outer world. "As long as I can remember, even as a child, I've taken my inner idealism and put it on the world outside to make it match. I finally became secure enough on the inside to let go of the rose-colored glasses. What *is*, is so much more beautiful. You finally know where you stand. Separation exists when you idolize. To the degree delusion is present, there is separation."

The person with this ascendant has a tendency to swing from the extremes of being high on life to the depths of despair. This tendency to vacillate is especially strong if Neptune is not well aspected. Rick Williams, with Pisces rising, describes this tendency by saying, "Inasmuch as there's one course of action one must take, there is always a part that says it could be some other way. There are an infinite number of variables. That's when problems occur. It's too cloudy with too much going on inside. That's when you have to step out for a while." Desperation is not long-lasting, however, as the Pisces rising will find some way to get back on top. Sometimes the means of finding the way back up the ladder to dreamland can be less than healthy. This is the planet that rules drugs and alcohol. In the extreme, this swing of the pendulum can indicate a manic-depressive state. If high hopes and dreams are shattered, the soothing cushion of an artificial high can bring wonderful mental scenes and beautiful colors back into his spectrum. The danger comes with a complete reliance on artificial means of realizing the dreams of an idealistic life.

When Neptune is well aspected in the chart, the individual may find that film, photography, poetry, or therapy can act as mediums tailor-made for self-expression. Nicholas DeVore is a photographer who travels all over the world photographing life as he sees it for *The National Geographic*. The Neptunian person can do enormous good for others by using his idealism for inspiration. His vision enables him to lead others out of miserable conditions by somehow bringing greater beauty into their lives. Whether he uses film to create images of idealism or greater vision to lift spirits out of the doldrums, his natural high is contagious. He may be able to sway people through a hypnotic ability. How could one dare disagree with his vision, even though the sight is obscured to others, when the Neptunian person is convinced of his dream? He may shun you completely if you try to bring him down from cloud nine. Be prepared to go to the castle with him, or remain scrubbing out the fireplace forever.

Some of the most adored and idolized actors of all time were born with a Pisces ascendant. Actor Ramon Novarro was a hero of the film world in the silent era. A present-day idol is Robert Redford, with a Pisces ascendant. Redford, in an attempt to deglamorize his image, has directed and produced a film of his own. His concern over being only a "pretty face" is now properly in perspective. David Carradine, a Sagittarian with Pisces rising, went through a trying time, and many drug trips, before finding a perfect Neptunian vehicle in *Kung Fu.*

Since the person with Neptune affecting the ascendant really wants to save the world, he can find an outlet for his vision and idealism through religion. John Calvin, religious reformer, was born with Pisces rising. Ernest Renan, Aquarius rising, but with Pisces intercepted, was a historian and religious scholar. He became famous for his *Life of Jesus.* He studied for the priesthood, but lost his belief in the Church—the opposite side of the Neptunian coin. Many psychotics with Pisces ascendant believe themselves to be Christ reincarnated, or have a Christ complex, feeling they must carry on where Christ left off. Manley Palmer Hall, with a Pisces Sun and ascendant, wrote metaphysical books that teach and inspire profound esoteric truths. Evangeline Adams, an astrologer with Pisces rising, won an important case in court for the cause of astrology by reading a chart for the judge's own son. Her analysis of the chart was so accurate the judge was astonished, for she described characteristics that only intimates of the young man would know. Her willingness to fight for a cause, another Neptunian characteristic, exonerated astrology from being only a fortune-telling device.

When one with this naïve and gentle rising sign gives in to despair and delusion, the results can be tragic indeed. The fall from grace leads from the Garden of Eden to the toil and sweat of daily labor. Many individuals cannot bear the letdown accompanying disillusion and lack of dreams or ideals. Playwright Tennessee Williams has written with brilliant perception about women and life in the South, yet his constant bouts of depression and drinking bring to a halt the productivity of his enormous creative vision. Algernon Swinburne, the English poet, undermined his health with dissipation after a life of writing "negative" Neptunian works. He shocked society with some of his acts and work. Bruno Hauptmann sank to the lower Neptunian depths by kidnapping and murdering the Lindbergh baby. (Neptune in his natal chart is badly aspected to almost every planet.)

It may be more important for one with this ascendant to find a healthy outlet for his vision than for almost any other rising sign. When this strong Buddhic energy is utilized on the highest level, the results are profound. English author and psychologist Havelock Ellis, an Aquarius rising with Pisces intercepted in his first house, paved the way for later work done by other psychologists. Immanuel Kant, a philosopher who wrote about aesthetics and ethics also had an Aquarius ascendant with Pisces intercepted in his first house.

Director Alfred Hitchcock was born with Pisces rising, as was German philosopher Hermann Keyserling. Dr. Alexis Carrel, a Nobel Prize winner with Pisces rising, was a visionary in the field of organ and tissue transplants. Warren G. Harding, Robert Louis Stevenson, Daniel Boone, Leopold Stokowski, Johannes Brahms, and Benjamin Spock were born with Pisces affecting their ascendant, either directly or by interception in the first house.

Comedian Carol Burnett, with Pisces rising, has gone to bat against drugs, a position she assumed after a drug-related tragedy hit her own family. Statesman Konrad Adenauer chose to express his vision through leadership, as did presidential aide Hamilton Jordan and Vice-President Walter Mondale. Actor Bela Lugosi had Pisces rising, as did singer Nelson Eddy. Writer Norman Mailer expressed all sides of Neptune through his writing. Acting in a film complemented his multifaceted expression in journalism, poetry, philosophy, earning him a Pulitzer Prize in 1969. (An additional Martian color also made him a pugilist, just to augment his Neptunian traits.)

Pierre Renoir had Pisces intercepted in his first house. Antony Armstrong-Jones, a photographer married to a princess, was born with a Pisces ascendant. Musicians Lawrence Welk, Mike Nesmith of the Monkees, Jack Teagarden, and conductor Zubin Mehta share this rising sign. Disc jockey Ben Hunter has Pisces rising. Desi Arnaz, Jr., and composers Ferde Grofé and Jules Massenet have both Aquarius and Pisces affecting the personality. Louis XV and the Duke of Windsor (another Aquarius rising with Pisces intercepted) shared this Neptunian view of life. Author William Buckley, skater Dorothy Hamill, actor James Arness, and actress Barbara Stanwyck express this uniquely idealistic quality in their work.

Life can be beautiful around a person with Pisces rising until it is necessary to make decisions. He may first ponder a situation, using his intuitive power to help him reach a conclusion, but after living with that decision for a few days he may take off on an exact opposite course of action. He can madden the people around him by indecisiveness, yet by his own peculiar circuitous route, he wins his own race.

If it is necessary to confront him on issues, trouble can occur, for one may never be able to win an argument with a person wearing a Pisces mask. He may not lose his temper, but the miserable, disillusioned look in his eyes can cause another person to feel like a heel. He may sulk and pout until a promise is elicited that the situation will never occur again. The other party may never know what he did wrong, or just what it was that upset the individual with Pisces rising, but the cloudy skies that will prevail over disagreements may simply not be worth the effort. The Pisces rising doesn't easily deal with the power of analysis.

When this trait of non-confrontation is studied in the light of survival, better understanding can emerge. When the individual with this idealistic ascendant is born, he decides he can handle life if he simply doesn't see the ugliness or tragedy around him. He may idolize family members or those he cares about, and adopt an overly idealistic point of view in order to deal with any potential pain. He'll fight to the death to defend his dreams and vision, as survival depends on his seeing things through rose-colored glasses. He can see himself in this same unrealistic, rosy light. He may never know the truth about himself unless he is forced to deal with reality. He seeks people who will confirm his point of view and continue to put him on a pedestal. He searches for associates and "prophets" who can live up to his own expectations. The alternative is despair, broken dreams, and dissipation. He cannot live without a vision of the ideal future. Utopia is home base for him.

Children with this ascendant need special care in the early years. Parents may encourage this dreamy tendency without being aware of the results. The child is so sweet and appealing, cooperative and gentle, that he never needs scolding or a reprimand. He appears to be "perfect." This little angel can get away with murder unless the parents are willing to do some confronting of their own. If small deceptions are not uncovered and he is continually allowed to "put one over" on his parents, he can go on to bigger and better deceptions. Eventually, the only one deceived is himself. Self-deception is the greatest danger of all. As he may never see himself as others see him, he can walk at odds with the world, living in his own fantasy, not accomplishing the goals he sets for himself due to the unrealistic approach he takes.

The child with Pisces ascendant can almost appear to wear a halo. The ethereal look can conceal facets of his personality that he is aware of but never reveals to others. Since people tend to expect him to be perfect, an unnecessary strain is heaped on the Pisces personality. He wants to be able to live up to others' expectations of him, yet he may feel secret guilt over the fact that he is very human indeed. When he is tired of bearing all these burdens and living up to expectations, he may fall from the lofty heights that others have escalated him to and indulge in the negative side of Neptune to find his balance. The seamy side of life can expose him to dangers of drugs in his attempt to climb back to the high side of existence. Finding a happy medium of balance can be a long, hard journey. Utopia seems better by far than reality and the ugliness of hard work and survival. Mental hospitals are filled with inmates living in their own private world of hallucination.

Since the tendency to delusion is strong with a difficult Neptune, there is an inclination to try to avoid letdown. Glamorizing is the instinctive way to get around seeing the cold, harsh facts, but glamorizing is a set-up for disillusionment. Thus the cycle is completed. Rick Williams continued his expression of this quality by describing it thus: "It saddens me, this overall human condition . . . ugliness. . . . Sometimes I feel frustrated because people can't see beyond their own noses. What I tend to see as obvious may not be apparent to others, but then, I may have missed the point entirely, because it was my way of seeing things. I make a picture out of everything. I can be aware of a negative situation, but instinctively know how to transform it to a positive one in my mind."

Pisces rising can be heavily invested in being right all the time, simply because if he is not, he might have to re-examine all of the concepts he has adopted throughout his life. He would never be sure what was real and what was not if he discovered he had been wrong. With deeper understanding of the survival issues involved, the person with Pisces on the rise can learn to confront situations up front, seeing the concept but examining the facts as well. He then has a profound ability to rise above potential obstacles, send his "purchase orders" out to the universe, and create ideal, but realistic, situations in his life.

FINANCE

Aries rules the second house of financial matters when Pisces is on the ascendant. The ruler of Aries is Mars, the planet describing action, activity, fight, drive, courage, and resourcefulness. In the positive sense, the Pisces personality can be quite aggressive and resourceful when it comes to money matters. He can work in areas where competition is involved, or where a great deal of physical energy is necessary. Mars describes the sexual energy as well as the highest creative drive. As long as the Pisces rising has an opportunity to release this energy in the financial arena, he remains calm and patient, but with delays or a lack of opportunity, he becomes frustrated, impatient, and aggravated. He may need to realize that frustration is connected with lack of challenge or activity in relation to earning money. He may be involved in projects that are most successful yet demand little of him in physical ways, and consequently feel tremendous dissatisfaction or lack of fulfillment inside.

Mars aspects in the individual chart indicate how easy it is for this person to channel energy into constructive financial areas. If Mars is well aspected, he will look for a way to focus his aggressive energy. He can work with metals or in areas where resourcefulness, ambition, and a pioneering spirit are necessary. Dorothy Hamill, a Leo with Pisces rising, skates on metal blades and is involved in constant competition, a Mars activity. Jack Teagarden played the trombone in order to earn money. Conductors Leopold Stokowski, Zubin Mehta, and Lawrence Welk use tremendous energy in their work and also are closely associated with musical instruments with lots of metal. Daniel Boone chose exploration as his "financial" avenue.

When Mars is not well aspected, the person may hesitate to become involved in competitive arenas. He may be especially impatient and frustrated over financial matters, wanting everything to happen immediately, spending money when aggravation is strongest. He may inadvertently set up aggravating situations in financial areas, continuing a pattern of resourcefulness due to necessity just to keep himself challenged. He loves a good fight when it comes to money matters.

COMMUNICATIONS

The third house describes not only the field of communications, telephones, agreements, and negotiations, but siblings, neighbors, and relatives in general. It also describes the quality associated with the learning process. When Pisces is on the ascendant, this house is ruled by Taurus. Venus, the planet ruling the sign of Taurus, is connected with peace and harmony, the arts, graciousness, and diplomacy. The speaking voice is most often melodious, the manner sociable and charming, and loving feelings about family and people nearby prevail.

If Venus is well aspected in the chart, it describes a love of communications, an artistic nature—whether channeled into painting, theater, or music—and an ability to negotiate diplomatically. This Pisces rising genuinely loves brothers and sisters, photographing them as charming, gracious, affectionate people. He loves school, or the learning process in general, especially if it is connected with the study of humanities or the arts. He can paint, dance, act, design, or compose works of art. He is particularly diplomatic on the telephone. Commutation or running errands is also ascribed to the third house. The person with Pisces rising enjoys running around, associating with people in his travels, expressing the sociable part of his nature.

If Venus is not well aspected, the individual may be lazy when it comes to errands, indulgent with family members or siblings, and inclined to keep peace at any price in discussions.

Venus describes the need for beauty and harmony. If Venus is less than positive in a chart, the individual may hesitate to do or say anything that will make waves, or upset the status quo. He may have to learn not to take the easy way out for the sake of peace. If he can become involved in artistic projects, he finds a release for this Venusian energy and learns how to be more direct in areas of discussion or communication. He can surpass the natural instinct to say what he thinks is expected of him rather than how he really feels about a subject. Evaluation of early relationships can pinpoint early patterns of excessive diplomacy. He will never be harsh or less than tactful. He can find balance through precision of thought and speech.

HOME LIFE

Home life, later life, and the parent of the opposite sex are described by the fourth house in a chart. With Gemini ruling the parent of the opposite sex, the Pisces rising photographs that parent as being especially witty, verbal, interesting, and exciting intellectually. Depending on the aspects to the planet Mercury in the individual chart, he will either have exceptionally good communication with that parent, respecting his or her ideas and thoughts, or have disagreements.

The planet Mercury, ruler of Gemini, is the planet associated with the adult ego state, in terms of Transactional Analysis. The adult part of oneself is the fact collector, with clear thoughts and ideas to be expressed. Strong opinions can be associated with the planet Mercury, as well as any intellectual activity such as writing, analyzing, researching, or studying. If that planet is well aspected in a natal chart, the association with the parent of the opposite sex is mentally stimulating, with shared ideas and witty discussions. The joy of the exchange of opinions and ideas leads to a later desire to have a home where ideas and thoughts are shared and examined.

If Mercury is not well aspected, the potential for disagreement with that parent is strong, and photographs of that parent are apt to focus on mental stress, flightiness, and criticism. If Mercury is badly aspected to Saturn, for instance, the parent may tend to think negatively, or be insecure about his or her intelligence. If Mercury and Mars are in difficult configuration, the parent may be sarcastic or caustic in discussions or with expressing views. When the Moon and Mercury are badly aspected, there is a tendency to speak and think emotionally or with lack of precision or clarity. Difficult combination between Mercury and Jupiter can bring about a tendency to say too much, oversell, or promise more than can be delivered.

When Mercury and the planet Uranus are not in good aspect, there is potential mental stress for the parent of the opposite sex. He or she may have an erratic way of speaking, with thoughts and ideas tumbling forth in jumbled profusion. In extreme cases, the parent may have feared a mental breakdown at some point in his or her life. Too much "electricity" coming into the brain may produce scattered ideas, rapid speech, and confusion in mental expression.

When Mercury and Pluto are in difficult aspect, there is a tendency to manipulate with words; the individual tends to say what he feels the weather will bear. The parent may have been a compulsive talker as well, fearing he would go unnoticed unless he poured forth a marathon of words. Mercury and Neptune in difficult aspect describe a tendency to overanalyze concepts and destroy dreams by nit-picking. The parent may have stressed practicality instead of encouraging the Pisces rising to follow his dreams. These aspects describe not only the personality of that parent but the quality of the relationship between parent and child.

Home life tends to be a place of activity with Mercury ruling this house. If Mercury is well aspected, the constant sharing of ideas will be stimulating and enjoyable, but if that planet is not well aspected, the Pisces personality may periodically have to get away from the overwhelming mental activity. Ideally, Pisces rising would like to have a salon where he could combine fascinating people from literary and artistic worlds, making his home a meeting place for the exchange of great thoughts. He will no doubt have a vast library or at least find a special place for books he collects. Since Gemini is a dual sign, he may need two homes in order to gain perspective and find occasional mental peace. One home may be more of a hideaway, the other a more public place. Each place may have a distinct personality of its own. The Pisces rising may find that his inclination to write and express concrete intellectual ideas increases as he grows older. He begins to bring many of his idealistic views into clearer focus, and learns how to clarify many of the vague ideas that formerly floated through his mind. He can become a brilliant speaker or writer, lecturer or teacher. Mental stimulation will certainly continue all his life.

ROMANCE • CREATIVE EXPRESSION

Romance and children bring out the mothering, protective urges. When Pisces is on the rise, the sign of Cancer rules the fifth house of creative expression, children, and "gambles." If the Moon, which rules Cancer, is well aspected in the chart, the Pisces rising's emotional security comes from the expression of his inner feelings, whether it be through writing, having children, or releasing *brain* children, or creative ideas, into the world. The Moon describes vulnerability, neediness, the feminine characteristics, or the anima part of the personality. Emotions can run high in areas connected with children or creative feelings. If the Moon is not well aspected, the individual may be especially sensitive in areas involving love or self-expression.

The Moon in a chart describes the collective unconscious. In a positive sense, the Moon enables a person to be tuned in to the trends of the times, aware of the needs of others, and able to express nurturing and understanding. In describing the fifth house with a well-placed Moon, the person can trust his gut reactions with gambles and the stock market, and may have great appeal to the public in connection with self-expression. He will produce sensitive, emotional children who may "mother" the Pisces rising, instead of the other way around. The child may feel especially protective, or, in a negative sense, overly emotional, abandoned, and vulnerable. In romantic situations, Pisces rising will either be willing to expose his deepest feelings or overreact to imagined slights. Love may be emotionally painful until he learns to deal with vulnerability and feelings in a positive way.

Since the Moon is the fastest-moving body in the heavens,

moods may change from moment to moment in connection with fifth house matters. The Pisces rising may feel emotionally fulfilled by his children at particular times and then suddenly feel upset and hurt by them. If he can learn to release his feelings in a creative way, working where he expresses this sensitivity overtly, he will find less emotional stress in his life. Writing is a particularly good way to gain some objectivity in connection with feelings. Learning the meaning of transference will also save some heartache. If he is hurt by someone, it is usually because he feels he doesn't deserve the offending treatment or comment. Looking beyond the words or accusation to understand the projection will enable him to tune in to feelings shared by humanity. He may derive some of his best creative ideas in this way. Observing feelings, hunger needs, and emotional reactions shared by mankind gives him a head start in working out his own emotional needs.

Carol Burnett exposed her heartache over losing a child to drug addiction, so that others could learn how to cope with this problem. Benjamin Spock has endeared himself to generations of mothers all over the world by writing about baby care. He reveals the mothering, nurturing instincts he feels through writing about children.

WORK • SERVICE • HEALTH

Pride in accomplishment is important for one with Pisces on the ascendant. Leo rules the sixth house of work, service, and health, with the Sun being the ruler of Leo. In a chart, the Sun describes vitality, ego, self-esteem, sense of self-worth. With good aspects to the Sun, the individual has a natural sense of dominance, executive ability, and leadership. He projects great vitality, drama, and a sense of self-worth, therefore attracting recognition and opportunity. The Sun also describes areas that are connected with pride in the chart. If the Sun is well aspected, the Pisces personality must work in areas where he will receive recognition and that brings a sense of pride in return. He must be in a position to express his inner ego and vitality, call the shots, and assume a leadership position.

If the Sun is not well aspected, the individual may not allow himself the right to work where his ego can be stroked. He may not receive recognition for what he does well, and may neglect to show his leadership quality. Since Pisces rising has a natural potential for the glamour world, actors with this rising sign must first recognize their own talent, then be "discovered" by someone else. Therapists must have confidence in their ability before others will come for aid. When the Sun is not well aspected, the Pisces rising may wait for someone else to give him "permission" to do what he wants to within work situations. He may work in order to receive recognition, putting the cart before the horse. His ego can suffer damage when he is bypassed or ignored.

Since the Sun describes the "name" one makes in life, if aspects indicate strong recognition, the Pisces personality may be motivated to work where his "name" is associated with a product or a talent. When he assumes the dominant role in his work, he will be healthy and vital. High energy enables him to work tirelessly. Yet if the Sun is not well aspected and he works in areas that are not ego-satisfying, he may frequently feel a lack of vitality. This individual may sense stronger energy at times when he is recognized and lowered vitality when he is not. The most important thing he can do for himself is to pat himself on the back, work in areas where he is fulfilled, and wait for his co-workers to give him strokes if they are able. Objective self-evaluation brings increased energy and vitality.

MARRIAGE • PARTNERSHIP

Opposites attract, or so they say. In astrology, opposite signs rule the ascendant and the house of partnership. This indicates a need for cooperation and the possibility of arriving at the same point of view from exactly opposite directions. If an individual knows what he is really looking for in a partnership, he has a better chance of finding the person to fulfill his needs. When Pisces is on the rise, the idealistic person is attracted to the intellectual who will balance him and help bring dreams into reality. In a cooperative way, the Pisces rising is the visionary, while the partner handles the details. Pisces rising is particularly adept in right-brain activity, while the partner focuses primarily in left-brain activity. If Mercury is well aspected in the natal chart, the Pisces personality is attracted to someone especially intelligent, analytical, and fact-oriented. If it is not, he is liable to find a mate who is critical, nit-picking, and too detail-oriented.

Virgo rules the seventh house of partnership with Pisces on the ascendant. Virgo is the sign of service, detail, and analysis. Intellectual pursuits are necessary for the Virgoan personality. He has the ability to work with great detail. Many editors have strong Virgo characteristics. The planet Mercury, ruler of Virgo, is related to the adult ego state. The adult part of the personality is the fact-oriented, detail-conscious, intellectual facet. In its positive sense, strong "adult" decisions are possible after research and analysis. In the negative sense, this facet describes an overly analytical quality that may make the resolution of problems difficult. When the Pisces ascendant with a well-aspected Mercury enters a partnership with a Virgo, the cooperative effort brings fantastic results. The Pisces rising will lift the Virgoan personality above the morass of fact, while the Virgo person helps to focus the Pisces. The balance of vision and intelligent application is unbeatable. In a negative sense, the Pisces person sets himself up for disillusionment by selecting a partner who can blow his dreams to bits. If he is more realistic up front, willing to deglamorize the mate, the partnership can work beautifully.

The Duke of Windsor, with Pisces intercepted, had an ideal marriage. Carol Burnett has a healthy marriage after many years in the glare of publicity. Actress Leigh Taylor Young is in happy liaison with her husband, Guy McElwaine, president and chief executive officer of Rastar Films.

NEEDS

The eighth house describes the ability to easily get one's needs met, and the way in which one learns to do just that. Naturally, the early life preconditions later requests. When Pisces is on the ascendant, the child gets what he needs and wants by being especially nice. Libra is on the cusp of this house, with Venus the ruler of Libra. Venus describes charm, graciousness, diplomacy, tact, beauty, and harmony. In its negative sense, Venus needs peace at any price and may hesitate to make waves. If the child's needs were met in early life, he seems to continue getting what he needs and wants in charming, gracious, harmonious, easy ways. He is able to stay on an even keel. He can simply smile sweetly and have a flow of goodness coming into his life. If, however, he was hesitant to ask for what he wanted early in life, he may not want to disturb the status quo by making any kind of demands later on.

Since the eighth house also describes the quality of the gift one can release to humanity, Venus indicates a great ability to love on a universal level. When Pisces is convinced of his ability to obtain what he wants, he begins to think about the outward flow of his energy. Venus can also describe a self-indulgent quality, however, so many times a negative Venus keeps the individual from emanating his love on a wider basis. Pisces ascendant leans toward idealistic occupations. If he is involved in the arts, his gift has to do with the artistic pleasure his talent brings to others. Theater is also a Venusian occupation. Tennessee Williams, Mary Pickford, with Pisces intercepted, Carol Burnett, Barbara Stanwyck, and Leigh Taylor Young, have given much pleasure through their work. They were also able to reap benefits financially through artistic endeavor.

RECOGNITION

The "power" planet, Pluto, rules the ninth house of higher mind, higher education, travel, promotion, legal affairs, and advertising. When this planet is well aspected, the Pisces personality has an incredible ability to reach masses of people through promotional effort, publishing, or by working with powerful organizations. Pluto describes areas of greatest effectiveness and potency. It also indicates the area which brings the greatest change in life. In terms of Transactional Analysis, it describes the child ego state.

The child's message is: "I want what I want, when I want it." Plutonian energy is very similar. It can indicate compulsion or manipulation. Pluto is also the planet of transformation or transmutation. The symbology of the phoenix rising from the ashes is related to the planet Pluto. Scorpio, ruled by Pluto, has two sides: it is either the serpent or the eagle. When this energy is transformed by motivation of the highest kind, it describes tremendous magnetic ability to transform others' lives. It is like a powerful body of water that is either destructive when at flood level or can light up cities when hooked up to an electrical plant.

With difficult aspects to Pluto, the Pisces personality may attract negative publicity or be tempted to gain publicity through manipulation or "childlike" rebellious antics. If Pluto is well aspected in the chart, an exceptionally magnetic presence naturally attracts recognition. This individual is most effective when he spreads the eagle-like wings to reach out to humanity. Through transmutation of his own higher mind, he transforms lives of mankind by seeming to do very little.

The ninth house describes travel, distances, and countries away from the homeland. Pisces rising may have a compulsion to jet around the world, playing with "the beautiful people" from many countries. He may want to live in the international social stream. Quite possibly he will not accomplish his goals, and may occasionally feel the rug pulled out from under him as a result of manipulation or exclusion. However, when his motivation is transformed from the child's will—"I want what I want, and I don't care how I get it"—to the higher will, motivated by the desire to do what is good for all concerned or humanity on a whole, he may indeed accomplish his goals. He may indeed jet around the world in association with "beautiful people" from all countries, accomplishing miracles through his powerful ability to influence. The subtle difference in motivation lifts him to the state of true power. He may have to be willing to let go of any negative or non-productive situation, no matter how comfortable or tempting.

He will rarely go unnoticed. He has a naturally wide sphere of influence. He can be published, be connected with his own institution of higher learning, manufacture, import, distribute. He can play Svengali, or inspire people on the highest level. Manley Palmer Hall chose the occult as his vehicle through life. His published works are profound in the level of teaching. He certainly has transformed the lives of many people without knowing them. Bruno Hauptmann received worldwide publicity through the kidnapping and murder of the Lindbergh baby. John Calvin chose to influence people through his concepts of religious reform.

CAREER

With the luckiest planet in the zodiac ruling the tenth house of career, the person with Pisces on the rise can have great good fortune in areas of public life. Jupiter is the planet that is associated with enthusiasm, humor, sales, wealth, wealth of spirit, and good luck. Sagittarius on the cusp of the tenth house (or the mid-heaven) describes optimism and the constant need for goals and challenges in career matters. There is a strong possibility that one with this rising sign will have several careers in one lifetime, as he becomes bored if a challenge is missing. If he can find an occupation that he *cannot* conquer completely, he will be successful.

When Jupiter is well aspected in an individual chart, the photographs he took of the parent of the same sex describe a happy-go-lucky parent, optimistic, perhaps religious, wealthy financially or wealthy of spirit. He sees that parent as one who is successful as a result of contagious enthusiasm and optimism. If Jupiter is not well aspected, the parent may have had severe disappointments in life that precondition the normal optimism of the Pisces personality. Since there is strong identification with the parent of the same sex in choice of career, it can be important to realize how devastatingly a parent's disappointment in the career arena can affect this person. In this event the Pisces rising may hesitate to be truly successful, in order to remain on the same level as that parent.

With a strongly aspected Jupiter, the parent encouraged the child to set goals and express enthusiasm in public life. If not, the parent may have inadvertently warned the Pisces personality about the danger of disappointment. In the positive sense, the relationship between parent and child was happy, optimistic, philosophical, and enjoyable. With a difficult Jupiter, the Pisces personality may have experienced great disappointment from that parent. Evangeline Adams had a proper Bostonian background and evidently had a healthy relationship with her mother since she apparently had no problems in setting and attaining high goals with her career. Her mother, in fact, encouraged her to do the original work in astrology. The Duke of Windsor was known to have disappointed his father because of a lack of understanding between the two. He may have worried about disappointing his public, as well as his father, when he chose to renounce the throne. He photographed his father as a most fortunate man, however, and continued to enjoy special social privileges after his marriage to the Duchess of Windsor.

A certain degree of spirituality, perspective, or vision and hopefulness is necessary for involvement in film or theater. Robert Redford retained a sense of vision and perspective early in his career, never losing sight of the goals that motivated him. Tennessee Williams presents a certain philosophy and a visionary, idealistic message through at least one of the characters in each play. Dorothy Hamill must have had strong goals and strong faith to help carry her through endless hours of practice in her early life. Leigh Taylor Young enjoyed great success in her career, choosing to retire for a period of time to work in spiritual areas. Her return to the screen heralds a new challenging period of her life. She "teaches" spiritual insights in addition to her film career. Manley Palmer Hall chose to devote his life to the teaching of metaphysical principles.

FRIENDSHIP

Capricorn rules the eleventh house of friendship when Pisces is ascending. The ruler of Capricorn is Saturn, the "heavy" planet of the zodiac. Saturn is described as the major karmic situation to be dealt with in life. It also indicates insecurity, fear, and restriction, or alternately, great responsibility, devotion, and support. Friendships in this case will be either totally supportive, long-lasting, and full of security and devotion, or restrictive and negative.

When Saturn rules friendship, the greatest task in life is to select friends with discrimination. In the positive sense, Saturn describes friends who will be eternally there. In the negative, there is a possibility of being attracted to people who are fearful, insecure, limited, and judgmental. In terms of Transactional Analysis, Saturn describes the parent ego state. The parent part learns to take care of ourselves and others. If we are truly caretaking, buying into negativity is a contradiction. Avoiding associates who express harsh judgment about activity or progress is essential if we are to give ourselves positive strokes and permission.

The six of swords tarot card describes a principle of allowing others to give us negative messages in order to keep ourselves safe. The six of swords pictures a red boat with a father, mother, and child going downstream. The father is piloting the vessel with a long pole. When he gets too close to the shoreline, he pushes away to find the clear channel. The mother and child are sitting down in the front of the boat, with swords or crosses obscuring their view, so it is up to the father to be the caretaker and pilot. The mother and child relate to conscious and subconscious mind. The father describes the godself, superconscious, soul or the higher self. If we operate through life from the highest perspective, or from the soul point of view, we never get stuck too close to the shoreline, as rocks and mud prevent smooth passage. Yet most of us operate from the conscious and subconscious levels. We say, as we hit a rock or a negative person, "It's a nice rock. I'll just smooth down the edges a bit." A rock is a rock is a rock. A rock that is stuck in the mud creates its own little whirlpool that pulls us close. The rock "hooks" our insecurities by saying, "You better tie up here where it's safe. The world is not round but flat, and you're liable to fall over the edge unless you stay with me. Danger lies ahead."

A rock is stuck in the mud, cannot be budged, and represents limitation, insecurity, judgmental attitudes. If we are willing to push past those negative, restrictive messages and continue downstream, the wake of our vessel may move the "rock" from its stuck place one millimeter. The rock is afraid to be left alone in its place in the mud, so it convinces us that we should be afraid too. In connection with friendships, Pisces rising may have to avoid the negative, jagged rocks that keep him from fulfilling his ultimate destiny. If he is willing to push away from those who are insecure and judgmental, he will find his way through life. If his own insecurities keep him clinging to negativity, it may be his way of staying safe.

Early in life, the Pisces personality may have few close friends or feel a lack of friendship, yet as he grows older, he attracts friends who share a strong karmic bond. He will enjoy the companionship of those who are older than he (though not necessarily in years) or who are serious, parental, and responsible. He may find group cooperation the strongest lesson to be learned. He would profit by finding a strong support group to encourage him in his endeavors. If he is willing to push away from anyone confining, judgmental, or restrictive, he will discover his true friends among those also rowing downstream in the mission of life.

HIDDEN MATTERS • SUBCONSCIOUS PROCESS

The twelfth house describes subconscious processes, particular characteristics that are difficult to expose, and matters relating to the occult or the psychic realms. When Pisces is on the ascendant, Aquarius rules this twelfth house of hidden matters. Uranus, ruler of Aquarius, is the planet of genius, humanitarianism, healing, and the unusual. In the negative sense, Uranus describes rebellion.

The dreamy tendency of Pisces rising is augmented by a tendency to easily leave the body. Astral traveling is a constant activity when the Pisces personality is afraid, or unwilling to deal with unpleasant facts in front of him. He may learn this technique early in life to avoid punishment, parents' displeasure, or the cold, harsh injustice of life. He can simply tune out and take off to realms of safety, traveling on the wings of fantasy.

This aspect can indicate a high degree of sensitivity or psychism. Uranus rules electricity. This individual seems to have a higher degree of electricity running through his subconscious, enabling him to tune in to other people or realms very easily. In the positive sense, and with good aspects to the planet Uranus, this indicates a healing quality on the subconscious level and a high degree of evolution. He is a "genius" on a hidden level. He may show the idealistic, visionary façade in order to conceal the fact that he is very different on an inner level. High humanitarian ideals put him ahead of his time in inner realms of awareness.

When Uranus is not well aspected, the individual may find this ability to leave the body or pick up the thoughts of others very unsettling. He may try to calm that energy down through drinking or drugs, yet that makes him even more unsettled on the subconscious level. Inner rebellion makes him run away from high awareness instead of utilizing that healing energy for the sake of humanity. Tremendous sensitivity keeps the inner mind in a state of constant change. Uranus is like the remodeling of a room. As the plaster falls, the dust and chaos make conditions most nerve-racking. The tendency to run away from the mess is strong, yet in so doing, the individual can get hit on the head by falling plaster. If, in the process, the person dons a hard hat, stands calmly in the center of the mess—knowing that soon he will have a new environment—changing those conditions can be easier. Uranus indicates "remodeling," or greater awareness, yet the breaking up of outmoded conditions can be difficult. Uranus rules music, high frequency, and radio. With a badly aspected Uranus, it is like having a radio station slightly off center with conflicting stations bringing in confusing sounds. If this inner, subconscious chaos is too difficult, and there are too many "voices," the individual may try anything to help drown out the sound. He can short circuit himself subconsciously.

If he learns how to tune the radio of his subconscious, he has true genius potential, psychic ability of an extraordinary level, and a healing, humanitarian quality that operates on a hidden level. By plugging that profound electrical current into the right outlet, he releases light and truth to mankind, sending out information that may have been lost to civilization for centuries. He will learn how to channel the current into a positive outlet to produce works that heal mankind. The acknowledgment that he operates on a higher frequency than most people may be a first step to the understanding of the genius potential. He will

explore spiritual realms that the more earthbound may never be
able to reach, and he can catapult others into greater awareness
as a result of his own willingness to work through the scare and
explore the higher realms of consciousness. Ultimately, his
greatest fulfillment comes from healing mankind through his
psychic, subconscious current. Idealism has an outlet and vision
has a practical application in his outer life.